ISRAEL ZANGWILL

Photography by Lewis, London S.W.1

ISRAEL ZANGWILL

ISRAEL ZANGWILL

by

JOSEPH LEFTWICH

New York · THOMAS YOSELOFF · London

© 1957 by Thomas Yoseloff, Inc.

Library of Congress Catalogue Card Number: 57-7644

Printed in the United States of America

CONTENTS

ILLUSTRATIONS

FOREWORD

IT had never occurred to me while Israel Zangwill lived that I would write his biography. I had not thought of myself as a Zangwillian, a term I have found increasingly attached to my name —"The staunch champion and faithful friend of Israel Zangwill," one admirer of Zangwill's described me in print.

I had known Israel Zangwill for the last ten years of his life. I did not know him in his brilliant youth. When I first met him he already looked an old man, though he was little more than fifty. I knew his brothers, Mark and Louis Zangwill. I knew Mrs. Zangwill, his widow, and I knew and know other members of his family, and many of his friends and associates. I come from his own milieu, from the same background of the East End of London; and I share much of his outlook on Jewish and English and human problems.

I do not follow him in everything. I do not suggest that I am wiser than Zangwill was. But although I started from similar beginnings and travelled by some of the same roads, I diverged at several points, and sometimes reached different conclusions. I am not that perfect disciple to whom the master's word is law and his judgment final.

Certainly, I hope I am not what Freud calls "fixated" on Zangwill as a hero, and devoted therefore "to a work of idealisation, instead of a man." I don't think I ever identified him with my "infantile conception of my father."

It happened that my own work involved a lot of writing about Jewish affairs and Jewish problems, and I gradually found that much of my thinking had been done before me by Israel Zangwill.

I was several times after Zangwill's death urged by his friends and by members of his family to write his biography. But Mrs. Zangwill made it clear to me that she did not want a biography written, at least not in her lifetime. "I cannot of course prevent anyone writing a biography," she said in one letter to me, "but in view of my husband's strong feeling on the subject I shall not authorise a biography nor give any help towards it, during my life-time." There were things she did not want written about while she lived, and while Zangwill's brothers and sisters lived. "As they are all older than I am," she wrote, "it is very unlikely that any of them will survive me."

Mrs. Zangwill did say to Dr. Jochelman and to other friends who spoke to her about a Zangwill biography that she had me in mind.

But "my husband did not want his life to be written," she kept repeating. "He had a feeling that biographies were never true—and so in spite of much pressure I have not allowed a biography to be produced." Some newspapers reported that Zangwill had in his will prohibited a biography, but there is no such prohibition. It is true, though, that he disliked biographies. In 1892, the year when his *Children of the Ghetto* appeared, he wrote: "Just as there are many persons of whose existence you are ignorant till you read their obituaries, so there are many of whose celebrity you are ignorant till you see the advertisement of their biographies."

"I am opposed to autobiography," Zangwill said shortly before his death. "If you tell the truth you hurt other people and still more yourself. So I have avoided it." "The difference between facts and truth is my real objection to biographies," Zangwill wrote in a letter to Holbrook Jackson. "This modern mania for picking ourselves to pieces," he called it.

Zangwill never wrote a biography of anyone, not even of Theodore Herzl, whom he admired immensely. "Watch that Man," he said once, pointing out Dr. Herzl to a famous actor-manager, "you will one day play him." "The noblest soul in Judah," he called him. He wrote a good deal about him. He wrote sketches about Heine, Spinoza, Disraeli, Nordau and others; he outlined their character and achievement, and he gave the few essential biographical details; but he wrote no biography. "Once and once only," he wrote, "did I strive to penetrate to the sources of history. It was the life of Spinoza, and I found to my amazement that the traditional detail of his doings and habits rested on little more solid than the mistranslated scribbling of a Lutheran pastor who had occupied his lodging a generation after his death."

He put his dislike of biography into verse:

> "It is the biographic Age.
> Every dolt who duly died
> In a book is glorified.
> All his unimportant letters
> Edited by writers gifted,
> Every scrap of MS. sifted,
> Till the man is—for their pains—
> Buried under his remains."

Yet Zangwill did not overlook the importance of biographical facts. When Holbrook Jackson was writing a long essay about his work, Zangwill sent him a letter: "Perhaps I ought to see the biographical paragraph in or before proof. (I shall hate to see the critical part in advance.)"

Authors have their own way of writing their biography, in their books. Shaw said: "The prefaces to my early novels contain as much autobiography as is worth writing." I believe that Zangwill has written in his books as much autobiography as he wanted, perhaps more than he wanted. Most of my story about Zangwill is drawn from his own published writings, and the material of the narrative is common public property. I had the advantage of knowing him, and of knowing members of his family, and of following his life and work with interest and with admiration, and I hope with understanding. And Zangwill did concede to the biographer that from "one point of view the post-mortem revelation of great men's friends perform a public good, even if at the expense of a private wrong." He was willing to agree that "however annoying and ridiculous the shapes it takes, interest in a genius springs at bottom from a sense of reverence and admiration."

*   *   *

"Why a writer of his quality should have ceased to find readers surpasses my understanding," St. John Ervine wrote to me about Zangwill. "*Children of the Ghetto, King of Schnorrers*, and all the rest of the books Zangwill wrote about his people, seemed to me to be overflowing with life. But it wasn't only about his own people that he could write. The last novel by him I read was entitled *Jinny the Carrier*, and it convinced me that his sense of the Gentile in East Anglia was as sound as his sense of the Jews in the East End."

Ludwig Lewisohn came to the conclusion that Zangwill's "books have sunk from sight partly because he shared certain attitudes and emotions with the minor Victorians." He was speaking in an American radio discussion about Zangwill. "Although an immigrant Jew and brought up in Whitechapel and all that," he said, "much of his writing is typically Victorian." Maurice Samuel, who took part in that broadcast, added, however, that Zangwill "should have written as finely as he did, in spite of his (Victorian) handicaps, is perhaps the measure of a certain type of greatness that we haven't yet acknowledged."

Zangwill was, of course, a Victorian. He was born in Queen Victoria's reign, and lived two-thirds of his life under her reign. He lived long enough into the 1920s, when it had become fashionable to sneer at the Victorians, to accept the fashion as the judgment of the new generation. In 1925, the year before he died, he spoke of his books as belonging "to the despised Victorian era," and contented himself with "the gratifying fact" that they had survived so long "the annual avalanche of myriads of new books and the distractions of an age increasingly oblivious of yesterday." But Zangwill was not unaware of the ideas that made Lewisohn and others dismiss him, and those of his generation. "I do resent Mr. Lewisohn's intolerant assumption," he wrote, "that I must share his sex view, and that I am sinning against the light because I am doubting the quality of his. The romantic circles Mr. Lewisohn admires I find heavy with heartbreak and egotism."

Nor was Zangwill ignorant of Freud, whom Lewisohn invoked. Before he wrote *Children of the Ghetto*, a young man in Fleet Street, editing his comic paper *Ariel*, he shared lodgings with his cousin, Dr. Eder, who was a disciple of Freud's. Freud said of Eder: "He was the first and for a time the only doctor to practise the new therapy in England. I was proud to count him among my pupils." Eder supplied Zangwill with the medical information in his work. Zangwill said so in his diaries: "Saw Eder about my medical facts." There was a novel published recently turning on a medical point, using an idea Zangwill had employed in a short story more than fifty years before. I mentioned this story once to Zangwill, because of its cleverness and oddity. Zangwill smiled and said: "Yes, that's the sort of thing I wrote when I was young."

Zangwill stopped writing that sort of clever plot story, with ingenious twists and turns, as he showed once in *The Big Bow Mystery* that he could write detective thrillers, and then stopped. He studied Freud, but he concluded that "Freud ruined a good case by obscene over-statement." He would have been delighted when his son, Professor Oliver Zangwill, a professional psychologist, who holds a chair at Cambridge, concluded in his book *Introduction to Modern Psychology* (1950), that while Freud's theories are not necessarily wrong, "the standard of evidence upon which the principal theories of psychoanalysis are based cannot, by any stretch of imagination, be held to fulfil the requirements of scientific precision. The reader would do well to bear in mind the shrewd verdict of the Scottish legal code—Not Proven."

Zangwill could not tolerate another "modern" method in Literature, of taking "any accepted proposition, inverting it and getting a New Truth." He went on to versify:

> "As a synonym for sin, Jezebel,
> I'll no longer drag you in, Jezebel.
> Now I know your glorious mission
> Was to spread the truths Phoenecian—
> Cultured Baalite, loyal wife, Jezebel.
> Protestant for light and sweetness
> Against the narrow incompleteness
> Of Elijah and Elisha's view of life."

"I have evolved," said Zangwill's Young Fogey. "Once I would not attach sanctity to ideas because they were old; now I attach no sanctity to ideas because they are new."

Yet Zangwill did not overlook the importance of modern psychology in literature. "We must go still deeper into Psychology," he wrote. He spoke of "our sub-consciousness" as "a tossing ocean of thoughts which feeds the narrow little fountain of consciousness. It holds," he said, "all our memories, the traces of vanished generations. In our sub-conscious are stored up all the voices and sounds we have ever perceived, and to all these reminiscences of our own are added the shadows of our ancestors' sensations—episodes that perchance we experience only in dreamland—so that part of the vivid vision of Genius may be inherited Memory." "All novels are written from the novelist's point of view," he said. "They are his vision of the world. Life, large, chaotic, inexpressible, not to be bound down by a formula, peeps at itself through the brain of each artist. All the novelists supplement one another, and relatively-true single impressions of life go to make up a picture of 'Life.' The artist selects, he studies tone and composition; he does not photograph real life. A good novel may be made of bad psychology; indeed, this is what most novels are made of." It is revealing of Zangwill's aims in literature that his "great novelists are Fielding, Cervantes, Flaubert, Thackeray."

Perhaps Sholem Asch got nearest to describing Zangwill when he called him in a talk with me, a folk-writer. Zangwill took his stories, indeed, from the folk; he repeated in his own way the tales he heard, which had come from the common stock of Jewish folk-literature. Zangwill is the genius who in his Jewish work has retold in English literature the stories that were handed down by generations of Jews in the old Jewish Pale of Russia and were brought to England by the immigrants. It is not only their lives that he re-created, their struggles to adjust themselves in their new home in England, but also their heritage of story and song and legend, of wit and humour and piety. He translated it and transmuted it, and made it part of English literature. "Have you heard the legend of the marriage of the Angel of Death with a mortal woman?" Zangwill asks in his collection of essays, *Without Prejudice*, and tells the story, which is a piece of familiar Yiddish folk-humour. He is full of it, in all his books, not only in his Jewish books. He tells his English readers the legend of the River Sambatyon, which rests on the Sabbath, tales of Elijah the Prophet and of the Messiah, the stories of the Pharaonic oppression and of the oppression in Russia, and the anecdotes which the Jews in Russia had made up about the Russian Czar and brought with them to England, and which, he said, "are not to be found in the official histories of Russia."

He recalled the "Purim Shpil," which has much in it of the Everyman moralities; he quoted lines from it in the original Yiddish, and made up verses of his own in similar "Badchan" (folk-rhymester) fashion. He repeats familiar Yiddish jokes, like that of some Jews waiting to be baptised and, tired of the delay, deciding to daven Mincha, to say the Jewish afternoon prayers. He tells his English readers about Meshumadim (apostates), and wages a battle against the conversionists who "set their baits for the helpless immigrants, offering bread in return for lip-conversion." He was the magic transformer through whom the Jewish immigrant masses in London told their story to the world and were listened to. He stated their case, not in statistics or "defence publications," but in literature, in his tales of the lives and the experiences of body and spirit of the Jews of London, of the Jews who have settled among and have become part of the peoples of the English-speaking countries.

"Self-expression," said Zangwill, "means pressing ourselves outside. All literature and art are our brains made visible; detachable and transmitable to our posterity." He had heard his father tell those stories, which come from the depths of Jewish folk legend and Jewish folk mythology, and had filtered through down the generations into his books, the stories which he put into the mouth of Moses Ansell telling stories to his children. He stored it up. It was he who as young Benjamin in *Children of the Ghetto* announced: "I'm going to write books—like Dickens."

Zangwill began writing at the same time as Shaw and Wells and Kipling. "There was a roaring of young lions," Gerald Gould, the poet and critic who married Mrs. Zangwill's sister, wrote of them, "Hardy and Wells, Shaw and Kipling and Zangwill."

It is thirty years since Zangwill died. In this time a number of new Anglo-Jewish writers have made their name. Zangwill would have rejoiced, as he wrote to Louis Golding at the beginning of his career, in 1918, "that so many young Jews are arising to uphold the torch of literature." One Anglo-Jewish novelist, Miss Hilda Lewis, writing recently on "The Jew in English Fiction," thought that Zangwill, "unknowingly perhaps, helped to pull the Jew down—his Jews were all nose"—and that "Golding, with his gallery of provincial lower-class Jews, beautifully rounded and fully human, has helped to lift the Jew to the full stature of humanity." Golding himself has confessed that his own feeling to Zangwill "is a reverence which I entertain towards few other men, dead or living." Alexander Baron, one of the most distinguished of the younger Anglo-Jewish writers, says: "In all the record of English literature there is only one writer who accords to the Jewish poor, the Jewish majority, their full human stature, as an artist does. This is Israel Zangwill." And Mr. Wolf Mankowitz, after criticising Zangwill's "limitations as an artist" goes on to admit that "of course, Zangwill is Anglo-Jewry's greatest writer." One should know how Zangwill's successors feel about him.

There is one other point Miss Lewis made that must be dealt with. Zangwill founded, she says, "a school of Jewish genre, and very profitable he found it." I think Louis Golding is the best man to answer that: "I should doubt that ever once in the wide compass of his relationships or endeavours, an infinitesimal idea of self-interest actuated him. I wonder how many men of letters, on the crest of a wave of success hardly paralleled so completely have deserted such golden waters to plunge into the snaggy and profitless shallows of public affairs. He gave up to Jewish politics and to all hopeless and dangerous causes the years that his genius might have made most profitable."

It would be wrong not to emphasise in this Foreword that Zangwill was not only a writer. To perhaps a greater extent than any other writer of his period Zangwill devoted years of his life to causes; most of all to the cause of the Jews. More than Shaw or Wells to Socialism he gave up years of his literary life to help his fellow-Jews. When Mrs. Zangwill wrote to Shaw about Zangwill, and suggested: "You probably feel that his earlier literary work was his best," she went on to say: "But the reason it is best is rather splendid. He felt that the prime purpose of his life was the helping of the underdog, and he quite consciously gave up his literary career to this end. He deliberately gave up his literary career at the height of his power in order to work for the suffering Jewish people, his own people." But she added: "He laboured not for Jews as Jews but as oppressed human beings. I remember his telling me more than once that had the Jews been as prosperous and powerful as the British" (he was thinking at that time of the millions of Jews living in poverty and oppression in the lands of the Russian Czar) "he would not have spent himself for them, but for others who stood more in need. He cared more for humanity as a whole and less for himself than anyone I ever met. This was the greatest thing in him. His work as a writer was only a small part of him, and his work for the Jewish people was only a small part of him. He felt that the prime purpose of his life was the helping of the underdog."

In 1908 Zangwill told the *Jewish Chronicle* that he was "no longer a writer." For he used to go every day to the London Office of the Jewish Territorial Organisation, of which he was President, and spend all day there, busy with Jewish emigration and Jewish relief work. "For seven years I dropped my literary work and went down to a city office like a businessman," he recalled afterwards. "I must have written or dictated at least ten thousand letters. The amount of work done was so great that when I looked at the documents it took me days and days merely to get them into any sort of order. One day," he said (it was three years before he died), "I contemplate writing the history of it, because it is enormously interesting, but I spent days merely throwing away, burning things up."

He gave, he said, "a businessman's day to the Ito, then find time for writing, as a Rabbi could in olden times be an artisan." He took up not only his own time; he annoyed other writers by worrying them to help him in his work. H. G. Wells grumbled to me that Zangwill pursued him with demands that he should interest himself in the Jewish question, which he said was "not on my doorstep." Wells wrote in *Homo Sapiens* that "Zangwill adopted the role of Champion to the Jewish race and brought his Championship to our deliberations." Holbrook Jackson told me that he remonstrated with Zangwill for not sticking to his writing, instead of fighting for all sorts of unpopular causes. "Why don't you stick to your own work?" he said. "But which is my work?" Zangwill retorted, and "of course," Holbrook Jackson added, "I could not say anything more after that. Because perhaps the other was really his work."

Zangwill found virtue in the fact that "the middle decade of my working life was monopolised" by Zionist and Territorialist work, or "I should possibly have succumbed to the current temptation to over-write."

Zangwill had shared the Victorian belief that man would "move upward, working out the beast, and let the ape and tiger die." But he came to see that "the ape and tiger are still terribly alive." "As a Jew," he wrote in 1908 to the Polish writer Sienkiewicz, "I cannot agree with you that the proposed outrage upon German Poles is 'the greatest iniquity and infamy in the history of the twentieth century'; that abominable title has already been earned by the massacres of the Jews in Russia." What would he have said of the massacres of the Jews of Europe by Hitler Germany in the Second World War? "Whence," he asked Sienkiewicz, "come your optimism, your generous belief in the power of 'the pillars of civilisation'? You and I should know that a people that has lost its power of military resistance is the doomed prey of the nations with teeth and claws." When the Russian Revolution came Zangwill said in May 1919: "I should be no honest advocate of liberty if I endorsed the Russian method of imposing Socialism by brute force. If Socialism encroaches too far upon individual liberty not all its loaves and fishes will save it from the soullessness attaching to all mechanical constructions. The question of the due boundaries between the State and the individual may be upon us sooner than any of us can foresee."

Then he said: "Not to make the world safe for democracy, but to make it safe for minorities is the true human ideal." The other way "leads to a hive, not to a human civilisation." This Victorian was very prescient.

In *The Nation* in 1918, while the First World War was drawing to its close, H. W. Massingham, the Editor, wrote: "Prophecy comes of the Jews, and Mr. Zangwill is something of a prophet; did he not foretell the coming of war?" A correspondent wrote to *The Nation* to suggest that his prophecy of the war had come very early—in *Children of the Ghetto*—"In a world of smouldering prejudice a scrap of paper may start the bonfire." I have sat in the garden of Zangwill's home, and heard Mrs. Zangwill tell me how in that same garden in 1911, before I had known him, Zangwill had foretold to a group of friends the war with Germany for the very year it started, 1914. "I foretold the war with Germany in 1911," he declared. He proclaimed himself an "obdurate anti-German." He spoke of "my uncomfortable prevision of the menace implicit in a race of Huns."

But though Zangwill liked to regard himself as a prophet, and once wrote a record of his own "prophecies as published in advance of the events," he was a prophet most of whose prophecies were not fulfilled. He believed that prophecy was the completion of a "curve on which two points, the past and the present, are already given." He rarely completed the curve so that it showed the future correctly. He confessed that there must be "risks of error in prophecy." History completed the curves differently than he anticipated.

Yet there was prophecy in him. He had left the Zionist movement. But he claimed the fulfilment of Zionism as one of his prophecies. He did not live to see the State of Israel. Yet he wrote: "My declaration that a Jewish State must and shall be, dates from 1904."

He claimed that he had foretold the coming of women's suffrage in *The Premier and the Painter*, published in 1888. Yet he had seen Christabel Pankhurst, whom he described before 1914 as having "the spiritual assurance and practical genius of a St. Catherine of Siena," become in the war a Jingo with whom "not one of the demagogues who whip up the beast in man could vie." When women's suffrage came, he found it "apparelled at all points like a man," not that victory of womanliness for which he had looked and worked.

In Territorialism too Zangwill did not reach his goal. It was not the "complete failure" Dr. Max Raisin calls it in his volume that brings up to date Graetz's *History of the Jews*, which Zangwill used to study, with what he called "its wonderful pages." But Zangwill refused to admit that the immigration work of his organisation did not succeed. He blamed "a perverted Zionism by its caricature of the Galveston work," for having kept back in the Ukraine thousands who might have escaped the coming massacre or the coming restriction of immigration into America. That restriction was one of his disappointments. America did not wait "centuries," as he had hoped she would, before she slammed her doors. Jerome K. Jerome said Zangwill had confessed to him "that he had wasted half his life on

B

Zionism." So he spoke of his Territorialist dream of a Jewish State, what he called at the end "the futile quest for a potential Jewish State." "I whose life has been half-wasted," he said, "in the attempt to bring about Jewish solidarity." He wondered long before why Mazzini had thrown away his life for Nationalism. "Moses, a greater than Mazzini," he said, "failed in his dream of a prophet people."

This is no hero who achieved gloriously what he set out to do. Indeed, Zangwill failed in almost everything except in literature, which he neglected and for a time abandoned for his causes, in all of which he was disappointed. He was a man whose reach was always beyond his grasp. But it is also true that he saw the prophet's task as "admonition and criticism rather than prediction." "The reward of battle is not victory," he said courageously, "but the beginning of new battle, and the cost of everything must be paid again and again. It is not liberty alone whose price is eternal vigilance."

I said that I do not follow Zangwill in everything, that I am not that perfect disciple to whom the master's word is law and his judgment final. He wobbled too much for me in his feeling about Judaism, though he did say that "the Jew cannot surrender even his right to criticise Christianity—indeed to criticise it is the sole *raison d'etre* of his separateness."

He shows a magnificent understanding of Judaism in his *Voice of Jerusalem*, yet even there he can speak of himself "as a Jew who has felt the ancient crime of his people," the crucifixion—"in vain I told myself that crucifixion was a Roman not a Jewish punishment; that the claim to be more than man was a blasphemy." "I do not like this commandeering for Christianity of that ideal of a brotherhood of nations which is common to all good men," he wrote. But he could write poems "To the Blessed Christ", in the very volume which he ends with his fine translation of the Synagogue hymn Adon Olam. And he who must have had a great religious feeling to be able to translate so much of the Synagogue service with passion and what must have been conviction could boast that he was so little a Jew that "I have not made my eldest-born a son of the covenant. I cannot with my vision and my knowledge of history carry on the nineteen-century old tradition of trying to sit between two stools."

I am sure he must have been a poet to translate the Synagogue hymns so marvellously, but his own poems seldom succeeded as poetry. I see the force of Shaw's remark to Zangwill's friend Alfred Sutro about Israel Zangwill's and Arnold Bennett's plays, that "these novelists will persist in inventing strings of fiction and calling them plays, instead of seizing a theme and developing it." I can agree with St. John Ervine when he writes of Zangwill's plays: "His *Cockpit* is no more convincing than his *Melting Pot*, partly because Mr. Zangwill has allowed rhetoric and melodrama to run away with

him. The intention is good and the purpose sound, but the play
leaves me longing for the Zangwill who wrote *The Children of
Ghetto* and *The King of Schnorrers*." Zangwill resented being told
that his plays were melodramatic. "The word was recently applied
to an old play of mine that had come straight out of the heart of my
work for Jewish emigrants," he wrote. He meant *The Melting Pot*,
of which he said that it sprang directly from his concrete experience
as President of the Jewish Territorial Organisation.

I would not have written this book if I were not sure, after all
my disagreements with some of Zangwill's attitudes, and my doubts
about some of his works, that he was a great writer, a great Jew and a
great man. I am not one of those of whom Louis Golding wrote in
an essay on Zangwill, that "they seek to show what brave wits they
are by a plentiful discharge of cheap arrows into the flaccid body at
their feet, the body which once by a mere projection of its chin
would have sent them scuttling."

But I am, like all of us, bound to my own personality; there may
be justification for Zangwill's feeling about biographies generally:
"How shall we abstract the personal equation from the reports?
How allow for individual prejudices?"

Chapter I

WHITECHAPEL

"IT was the bell of the great Ghetto school, summoning its pupils from the reeking courts and alleys, from the garrets and cellars, calling them to come and be Anglicised. And they came in a great straggling procession; bright-eyed children and hollow-eyed children; quaint, sallow, foreign-looking children and fresh-coloured English-looking children—spawn of all countries, all hastening at the inexorable clang of the big school-bell."

One of the children hastening at the clang of the big bell in this picture of Whitechapel, painted by Israel Zangwill in *The Children of the Ghetto*, might have been himself, unless, assuming as we may, that Moses Ansell's family in the book is his own father's, Moses Zangwill's family, he was himself, by the time the procession started, already in the school-playground, having gone there "an hour before to run about and get warm." For the Zangwill family was very poor. "Beyond saying that the family was poor, I don't think there should be details—e.g. income," Zangwill wrote to Holbrook Jackson in April 1914. But Mrs. Zangwill said in a letter to me, "My husband told me that his father never earned more than a pound a week." When his father died, Zangwill wrote a poem, which began "Rich as a Jew!" and went on: "A pound a week to him the wealth of Kings." There is something autobiographical in Zangwill's protest in his book *The Voice of Jerusalem* against the suggestion of the Webbs that "life on a pound a week" meant "a degradation of character, a spiritual demoralisation, a destruction of human personality itself." He had, he said, "known intimately many Jewish households in the slums on a pound a week or less, and in no instance seen personality destroyed or degraded, but in numberless instances accentuated and uplifted."

The home was cold and the children had had "a slice of bread each and the wish-wash of a thrice-brewed pennyworth of tea as their morning meal, and there was no prospect of dinner."

Israel Zangwill was a pupil of the Jews' Free School, and later a teacher there, before he threw up teaching to become a writer. He became a writer in fact, while he was a teacher at the School; even earlier, while still a schoolboy. His wife said, "He could never remember a time when he had not been certain that he was going to be a writer." His first book, he remembered, was a romance of school-life, written when he was ten in a couple of exercise-books, circulated in the class-room. An old school-fellow reminded him of an earlier novel written in an old account-book. "Of this," he said, "I have no recollection, but as he says he wrote it day by day at my dictation I suppose he ought to know." "The dignity of print," he proceeded, "I achieved not much later, contributing verses and virtuous essays to various juvenile organs." At sixteen he won first prize in a humorous short story competition in a paper called *Society*, where the story was printed in serial form, running through three numbers. It was a story he had written some time before, "an old work," he called it. He preserved it among his papers, where I read it.

At eighteen, while he was a pupil teacher at the Jews' Free School, he achieved the dignity of his first printed book. It was really a pamphlet, called *Motsa Kleis*, and it contained the description of "market day in Jewry," "the Sunday fair, so long associated with Petticoat Lane," of which the picture of the children hastening to school is part. He said afterwards that "it was really the nucleus of *The Children of the Ghetto*." He wrote it at the instance of another pupil teacher at the Jews' Free School, Meyer Breslar, whom I knew. Breslar wrote his own account of that adventure in publishing. The story was issued anonymously, for they both felt, correctly as the future showed, that the school authorities would not like it. Zangwill said that when it was discovered who the authors were, "the Committee of the School were horrified."

Breslar remembered that they printed 20,000 copies and, said Zangwill, "my first book (price one penny nett) went well. It was hawked about the streets and widely bought. There was great curiosity among Jews to know the name of the writer. Owing to my anonymity I was enabled to see those enjoying its perusal who were afterwards to explain to me their horror and disgust at its illiteracy and vulgarity. Still jealously keeping the authorship secret we published a long comic ballad, which I had written on the model of Bab. We had gorgeous advertisement posters printed in three colours which were to be stuck about London." The long comic ballad, *The Ballad of Moses*, did not sell well. So Breslar "decided without telling Zangwill of my resolution, to be my own Bellstriker. With pot and brush I rose at cock-crow determined to bill the City. I had managed to stick a good many bills on private and public walls before I was arrested."

The secret of authorship was out. "Our headmaster," Zangwill wrote, "walked into my room with a portentously solemn air." Zangwill was summoned before a number of the school committee, who told him that his novelette was "disgusting." Breslar was suspended, and was recommended to be expelled, but "was ultimately requested to resign, which I did." Zangwill was given the alternative of expulsion or of publishing nothing which had not passed the censorship of the school committee. "After considerable hesitation," Zangwill wrote later, "I chose the latter. This was a blessing in disguise, for as I have never been able to endure the slightest arbitrary interference with my work, I simply abstained from publishing."

According to another teacher at the school, L. G. Bowman, who later became its Headmaster, it was "the presentation of Jewish life in the East End, with its mixture of Yiddish and misspelt English that was bitterly resented and condemned by many of the more Anglicised members of the community. They criticised it as 'showing up the Jew', and holding him up to Gentile ridicule." Lord Rothschild, the President of the school committee ("the Lord I did not worship", said Zangwill), the Chief Rabbi, Dr. Herman Adler, and Moses Angell, who was Israel Zangwill's, Bowman's and Breslar's Headmaster, detested Yiddish, which they called gibberish, and waged a campaign to root it out. "A Jargon and slang like Yiddish," said Lord Rothschild. Zangwill commented that it was "as if English-speaking Scotsmen and Irishmen should object to 'dialect' novels reproducing the idiom of their 'uncultured' countrymen."

Zangwill's story of the immigrant Jews of Whitechapel pictured in *Children of the Ghetto*, and of their children called to be Anglicised, as he was himself "spawn of all countries"—is written against the background of his own life. It is a true book, because he put into it his own life, seen as the artist saw it, re-created. Many years afterwards Zangwill spoke at a Free School function, and recalled his first day at the school. It was mingled, he remembered, with the flavour of monkey-nuts. "There was brisk traffic in toffy and grey peas and monkey-nuts," he writes in *The Children of the Ghetto*, describing that procession of children hastening to school. I detect too a memory of his elder sister Leah, "a bright, earnest little girl who held her vagrant big brother by the hand."

L. G. Bowman recalled "Israel Zangwill as a dark, curly-haired school-fellow in the top-class of the Jews' Free School." He spoke of "a composite photograph of five or six selected pupils, including Zangwill, to determine the Jewish type of face, produced by a method suggested by Sir Francis Galton. The resultant picture," he said, "was markedly the Zangwill face." Zangwill told that story himself, when he recalled how Joseph Jacobs, who was a disciple of Galton, had come to the School with Galton, and had photographed not five or six but "ten boys to turn them into a composite portrait of the Jewish type. My brother Louis," he said, not himself, "was one of the boys, and like Aaron's rod he appears to have swallowed up all the others, for the final type was curiously like him."

The Journal of the Anthropological Institute of Great Britain and Ireland for 1885, which came to me with other books and papers from Louis Zangwill, contains a report of the meeting of the Society held that year, at which Joseph Jacobs read a paper, "On the Racial Characteristics of the Modern Jew," and Galton showed the composite photographs, which are reproduced in the *Journal*, and were later used by Joseph Jacobs to illustrate his article on "The Jewish Type" in the Jewish Encyclopedia.

As for the "Jewish type," said to be so "markedly the Zangwill face," Zangwill did not believe there was any such thing. In his *Dreamers of the Ghetto*, describing the First Zionist Congress, looking at the many different types of faces, he cried: "Who speaks of the Jewish type? One can only say negatively that these faces are not Christian."

When Zangwill, still a pupil teacher at Free School, collaborated with Louis Cowen in writing *The Premier and the Painter* ("for this time," said Zangwill, "my colleague was part-author"), they chose the pen-name J. Freeman Bell, evolved from Free School, Bell Lane. The idea of the book was Cowen's, but "owing to my collaborator's evenings being largely taken up by other work, seven-eighths of the book," Zangwill explained, "came to be written by me, though the leading ideas were threshed out and the whole revised in common, and thus it became a vent-hole for all the ferment of a youth of twenty-one, whose literary faculty had furthermore been pent up for years by the potential censorship of a committee." "There are odd people here and there," added Zangwill, "who know the secret of J. Freeman Bell, who declare that I. Zangwill will never do anything so good."

The book is nothing like so good as Zangwill's best work. The feeling that he had himself written seven-eighths of the book must have given Zangwill a sense of proprietorship of the joint name. I have *The Jewish Calendar* for 1888-89, three years after *The Premier and the Painter* was written, with a story called "Under Sentence of Marriage," credited to "J. Freeman Bell, Author of *The Premier and the Painter*." Mrs. Zangwill called it "my husband's story."

Later Zangwill dropped the name Freeman Bell even from *The Premier and the Painter*; it appeared among his collected works as by Israel Zangwill. When the *Jewish Chronicle* suggested that "Under Sentence of Marriage" by J. Freeman Bell was the work of two ex-masters of the Jews' Free School, working in literary partnership, "J. Freeman Bell" wrote to the paper contradicting the statement that he was dual. And when the *Jewish Chronicle* wrote later of a new popular edition of *The Premier and the Painter*, it explained that "Mr. J. Freeman Bell is a co-religionist," in the singular. Holbrook Jackson in his book *The Eighteen Nineties*, says that though *The*

Premier and the Painter was written in collaboration with Louis Cowen, it bears "what we now recognise as the Zangwill touch on every page."

A few years ago someone wrote to the London *Jewish Chronicle* to ask for an explanation of what he called a Zangwill mystery: he had come upon a book called *The Premier and the Painter* by J. Freeman Bell, which was so much like Zangwill's book of the same name that he wondered if it was plagiarism. Harry Ward, the Secretary of the Zangwill Fellowship, and I separately explained in the *Jewish Chronicle* that there was no mystery and no plagiarism, because it is the same book. But the suggestion that Zangwill might have plagiarised himself in *The Premier and the Painter* is interesting, because in 1905 Mr. Sinclair Lewis, writing in the *Critic*, suggested that Mrs. Thurston might have plagiarised Zangwill's *The Premier and the Painter* in her best-selling book of that year, *The Masquerader*. The Editor prefaced the article with a note saying that "we have not the slightest intention of accusing Mrs. Thurston of plagiarism. Coincidence is too common for one to be in a hurry to bring charges of plagiarism against a writer. It is quite possible that Mrs. Thurston never saw a copy of Mr. Zangwill's *The Premier and the Painter*, and it is this possibility that makes Mr. Lewis's discovery the more interesting." When Sinclair Lewis's article was brought to Zangwill's attention Mrs. Zangwill replied: "We had naturally noticed the resemblance in the books but my husband thought it was too close to be plagiarism—conscious at any rate."

Yet according to Sinclair Lewis "practically every situation, every character, every detail, together with the general plot, are doubled in *The Premier and the Painter*, written by Israel Zangwill under the pen-name of J. Freeman Bell in the early 'nineties. The resemblance is not simply the use of the time-worn plot of a prominent man's changing places with a man of low degree. But in following out the incidents of *The Masquerader* they are found to be identical with those of *The Premier and the Painter*." Sinclair Lewis proceeds to set out the resemblances in the two books. "Like the plot, the incidents, the characters," he concludes, "so do the 'atmosphere' and many little details correspond. It is popularisation which changes the vein of satire running through Zangwill's book, satire as delicate and puzzling as that of Anatole France, to the matter of fact style of Mrs. Thurston. *The Masquerader* has lost the most charming part of *The Premier and the Painter*, namely Floppington's character seen in adversity. This portrait is a very precious thing. *The Premier and the Painter* also contains all the interesting social and political experiences and struggles of *The Masquerader*, which is more popular than its double, just as *The Pit* is more popular than *The Cloister and the Hearth*. It may be that two books as similar as *The*

Masquerader and *The Premier and the Painter* are purely coincidental, but if so, it is surely one of the most remarkable coincidences in all literary history."

Mrs. Thurston's book in which Sinclair Lewis saw such similarities to *The Premier and the Painter* was a best-seller, but *The Premier and the Painter* was a failure. Though Sinclair Lewis thought highly of it, the book did not catch on with the public. It is not one of Zangwill's important books. The plot was Louis Cowen's, though Zangwill said he had completely transformed it. Cowen's idea, Zangwill explained, "was that a Radical Prime Minister and a Conservative working man should change into each other by supernatural means and the working man be confronted with the problem of governing, while the Prime Minister should be as comically out of place in the East End environment. He thought it would make a funny Arabian Nights sort of burlesque. And so," said Zangwill, "it would have done; but unfortunately I saw subtler possibilities of political satire in it. I insisted that the story must be real not supernatural, the Prime Minister must be a Tory, weary of office, and it must be an ultra-Radical atheist artisan bearing a marvellous resemblance to him who directs (and with complete success) the Conservative Administration."

Zangwill introduced a lot of realism. "I drew all the characters as seriously and complexly as if the fundamental conception were a matter of history. Numerous real personages were introduced under nominal disguises, and subsequent history were curiously anticipated in some of the Female Franchise and Home Rule episodes." The life in East End Bethnal Green (which adjoins Whitechapel), where the outgoing Prime Minister came to live, "was presented with photographic fulness and my old trick of realism."

Zangwill, as he often did, even in his best work, overloaded the book. "His cleverness verges on the prodigious," was Holbrook Jackson's complaint. "He has put enough wit in *The Premier and the Painter* to make three reputations, but too much to make one." He had the fault of other giants of literature of pouring all they have into their books. Mrs. Zangwill told me a friend of Zangwill's said to him of one of his plays: "Of course, it is a good play, a very good play. The trouble is that it is six good plays, and a sermon as well."

Zangwill was aware of his fault of over-brilliance. "The books which gain a reputation for brilliance," he said, "are those which are witty at wide intervals; the writer who scintillates steadily stands in his own light."

The failure of *The Premier and the Painter* with the public was such that Zangwill said: "It did not even help either of us one step up the ladder; never got us a letter of encouragement" (he wrote this in 1893, a few months after the publication of *Children of the Ghetto*, and twelve years before Sinclair Lewis was praising *The Premier and the Painter* in the *Critic*), "nor a stroke of work. I had to begin journalism at the very bottom, and entirely unassisted, narrowly escaping canvassing for advertisements, for I had by this time thrown up my scholastic position, and had gone into the world penniless and without even a 'character,' because I did not worship the Lord who presided over our Committee."

In 1888, at the distribution of Prizes at the Jews' Free School, Lord Rothschild "thought it of sufficient interest to allude to our departure from that institution," says a letter in the *Jewish Chronicle* by (in that order) Louis Cowen and Israel Zangwill. "As in doing so he used language which implied that we had been forced to resign or that we had been dismissed we trust that you will let us remove an impression so detrimental to our reputation and interest. So far from this step being compulsory, when in accordance with custom we handed the Headmaster our open letters of resignation addressed to the President and committee, he expressed himself greatly surprised. In the conversation which followed and which lasted nearly four hours he used every possible argument to persuade us to take back our letters. We should be loth to suspect Lord Rothschild of knowingly making an untrue and libellous assertion, and we have no doubt that his apology will be as public as his mis-statement."

No apology came from Lord Rothschild. Thirty-five years later, in 1923, Zangwill told the story in New York: "I could have gone to law, and probably recovered heavy damages, but I was a poor youth. I should be up against one of the richest men in the world, and therefore I simply wrote to a Jewish paper and asked him for an apology. I pointed out that he might have been misinformed, he probably was misinformed, but he had only to make inquiries to find out that I had resigned, and that I was not dismissed. Of course, he never apologised, and took no notice." This time the story is personal. It is no longer, as in the letter to the *Jewish Chronicle* in 1888, "Louis Cowen and Israel Zangwill."

The same Lord Rothschild, whom Zangwill did not worship and because of whom he threw up his job at the school over which Lord Rothschild presided, afterwards became Zangwill's colleague in the Jewish Territorial Organisation, which Zangwill founded and of which he was President. "Lord Rothschild actually worked under me," Zangwill said. "He became a member of a geographical commission which had the task of passing upon territories that should be submitted to them by scientific experts directed by me. I think it is fine of Lord Rothschild that he should have consented to work under me."

But Zangwill never forgot the conflict. Towards the end of his life, when he was sixty, he recalled the row he had with Lord

Rothschild when he was a penniless youth. "I after all was only the son of a Russian pedlar," he said.

Louis Cowen still appears in the British Museum Catalogue under the name J. Freeman Bell, given there as the pseudonym of Israel Zangwill and Louis Cowen. He is also described as "Joint Author of *The Premier and the Painter*" in the entry of a one-act farce *The Great Demonstration*, written in collaboration with "I. Zangwill," and played at the Royalty Theatre, London, on 17th September 1892, the very year and month when *Children of the Ghetto* was published. Yet in August 1893 Zangwill was writing to a friend, that he had "just done with the last proofs of 'Ghetto Tragedies' and the new edition of *The Premier and the Painter*," as though both were solely his.

Louis Zangwill wrote of Louis Cowen: "As he was collaborator with my brother in *The Premier and the Painter* I was brought into association with him in my boyhood in the 'eighties, both in his home and in ours. He was at the time near thirty. For the *Jewish Standard*" (an Anglo-Jewish weekly where Zangwill worked), "he wrote many of the leading articles, besides a humorous serial entitled 'The Schlemiel', based, I am afraid, on some of the absent-minded procedure of his friend Israel Zangwill. He came much into touch at our home with Israel Abrahams, Dr. and Mrs. Schechter and Dr. Eder, these forming the core of a vivid informal circle to whom my mother dispensed modest hospitality."

Louis Cowen's brother, Laurence Cowen, also had contacts with Zangwill, which were not always to the liking of Zangwill's family and friends. It was said that he gave Zangwill the idea of *The Mantle of Elijah*, as his brother had given him the idea of *The Premier and the Painter*. He was associated with Zangwill on *Ariel*, where he acted as a "lesser Labouchere," Zangwill explained, when he appeared as a witness for him in a libel action. He travelled about the country for the paper, he said, "and nearly got the editor (Zangwill) into several libel actions."

Later Laurence Cowen went into finance, and was known as the "Lesser Columbus." He built the Fortune Theatre, where Louis Zangwill and some of Israel Zangwill's friends believed he persuaded Zangwill to put on his disastrous series of plays in 1925, which resulted in his financial, physical and mental collapse. I have heard him described for that reason as Israel Zangwill's bad genius. But Israel Zangwill himself spoke of "the generous sympathy and support of my old friend Laurence Cowen, proprietor of the Fortune Theatre."

"Years of literary apathy succeeded the failure of *The Premier and the Painter*," Zangwill said. But those years were not unfruitful for him. He worked on the *Jewish Standard*, which became in *Children of the Ghetto*, *The Flag of Judah*, he edited the comic paper

Ariel, he published two pseudonymous short stories signed "The Baronness von S.," *The Diary of a Meshumad* and *Satan Mekatrig,* which are among his best work, he published an analysis of the Jewish Community in the *Jewish Quarterly Review,* which brought him the commission to write *Children of the Ghetto,* and he published "two funny books," as he calls them, *The Bachelors' Club* and *The Old Maids' Club,* which were afterwards issued together as *The Celibates' Club.* He said himself years after of his *Celibates' Club* that "there are pages in it which I myself find rather forced." His *Master,* of which he had a better opinion, does not differ from hundreds of similar novels. It does not stand out more than for instance John Masefield's book *The Street of To-Day,* of which Arnold Bennett, when it appeared in 1911, seventeen years after Zangwill's *Master,* wrote: "Cleverer small talk than this smothered and ruined a novel more dramatic than this—I mean Zangwill's *The Master*". "I am not likely to be suspected of under-rating Zangwill," I wrote in 1950, "but it does not do Zangwill any good to pretend that he is more than he is."

It was when Zangwill returned to his own familiar ground, the Whitechapel Ghetto, that he wrote the book that at twenty-eight took him into world literature. Alfred Sutro, the playwright, who belonged to the group around Bernard Shaw, felt that of all the writers of that period Zangwill was "the rarest spirit of them all." "Perhaps," he added, "as a Jew myself I may be inclined to exaggerate the quality of his work."

I have found the more usual reaction of "a Jew myself" when judging Zangwill is to dismiss him as unimportant compared with non-Jewish writers of his own stature. Zangwill suffered all his life and still suffers at the hands of Jews because he devoted himself so much to Jewish life and Jewish affairs. He became "one of ours," to be treated with familiar contempt. Zangwill was once stung to tell the story of a man who said there was nothing clever in a Jew writing about Jewish life because he knows all about it. "It is the fashion in some quarters," I wrote in 1929, "to decry Zangwill as having obtained his place in English literature by trading in Jewishness." I am not going to make the opposite mistake of denying that Zangwill, for all his insistence that "the bulk of my work has nothing to do with the Ghetto," and that he did indeed write good books about what he called "the general human life" leaped into world fame and will survive because in this field he found his true expression and did his best work. And though as Lucien Wolf related in his paper to the Jewish Historical Society of England when Zangwill died, he had felt the big world tugging at him, and it had therefore not been easy to get him to accept the commission to write the book which became *Children of the Ghetto,* he came himself to realise at the end that his Jewish books "represent my best work," and even to claim that "all my work is Jewish." I would agree with St. John Adcock when he says that *Jinny the Carrier* is a charming story of mid-Victorian life and character in rural Essex, but his finest, most memorable work has been done as the interpreter of his own people.

I was glad to find that Dr. Grayzel in his *History of the Jews*, seeing it from the American stance, feels that "Israel Zangwill's stories, though they dealt with conditions of immigrants in England applied almost as fully to conditions among the Jewish immigrants in America." Some such realisation must have been in the minds of the American Judge Sulzberger and his friends in America when they commissioned Israel Zangwill to write *Children of the Ghetto*. That is the greatness of Zangwill, that his work, though it deals with the life in one locality, in Whitechapel, in the East End of London, and with a family largely drawn from his own, and with the people living around that family, people he had himself known, at a particular period, at the end of the nineteenth century, is universal and timeless, because it applies almost as fully to the life and conditions in the East Side of New York and in many other places where Jewish immigrants settled and their children have grown up Anglicised or Americanised, and it applies almost as fully to-day as it did then, more than sixty years after it was written. Even in modern Jerusalem, Julian Meltzer, who was the correspondent of the London *Jewish Chronicle*, found "whole pages dragged from Zangwill's *Children of the Ghetto*." He has given us people who live and have meaning for us beyond his and their own time. Zangwill's *Children of the Ghetto* is the classic work of Jewish immigrant literature, of which so much has been written by so many writers, who have none of them achieved Zangwill's mastery. I found this feeling expressed in the Yiddish Encyclopedia's English volume *The Jewish People* (1952), where under "Jewish Literature in the United States and England" I read: "Israel Zangwill, a literary giant against whom few, if any American Jews can be matched."

Zangwill's work in fact succeeds in two fields. It is universal not only in its picture of the life of the Jewish immigrants and their Anglicised and Americanised children and grandchildren in the entire English-speaking world, but also as an authentic work of English regional writing. "He has his unique place," wrote Mr. St. John Adcock in his book *Gods of Modern Grub Street*, "as the novelist of Aldgate, Whitechapel, Hoxton, Dalston, all the roads and byways, mean lanes and squalid squares there and thereabouts." He is one of the great delineators of East London life. Ian Mackay, shortly before he died, wrote: "Considering how much history and romance has been packed into the East End it is strange that so

little has been written about it. Apart from Dickens and Walter
Besant, a few tales by Zangwill and Arthur Morrison, a grand book
by Robert Sinclair and a scene or two in Shaw's *Candida*, I can
think of nothing worth bothering about." The Sinclair book is *East
London*, published in 1951, largely a historical and topographical
survey. Mackay overlooked Barry Pain and Pett Ridge and W. W.
Jacobs, who wrote of the Riverside East London, across the road
from Whitechapel, St. George's and Shadwell and Wapping. Zangwill like them communicated the spirit of something that is London.
Writing of London Jews, and himself a London Jew, he is as true a
Cockney as any of them. It was his boast that he was born within
sound of Bow Bells, the mark of the Cockney, and he described
himself as and was described by others as "a Cockney Jew," even
when the term was not intended to be a compliment to him.

Holbrook Jackson placed Zangwill with Barrie for his studies of
Scottish life, and Jane Barlow in her books on Ireland, and suggested
that "the discovery by novelists of the value of local colour made
for the success of Zangwill's fine studies of Jewish life." Zangwill's
Yiddish-English seemed to him akin to "the Cockney dialect in
fiction, set to a tragic theme by realists like Arthur Morrison and
Somerset Maugham, but given a delightfully humorous turn by
Barry Pain, Pett Ridge and Edwin Pugh." Zangwill had made a
similar point when he compared his "vulgar English Yiddish"
books with the "dialect novels" of Scottish and Irish and English
regional writers.

In *The History of the English Novel*, published in 1938, twelve
years after Zangwill died, Dr. Ernest Barker called Zangwill one of
the slum novelists, for Whitechapel was indeed, like the whole East
End of London of which it is part, a slum area. "The most striking
and original supplement to the work of the native slum-writers," he
wrote, "came from a writer who was an Englishman, indeed, and a
Londoner born, but a Jew of the Jews, whose impressive studies of
his people are probably the greatest contribution of modern times
to the literature of Jewry. Zangwill knew his people as intimately as
his master Dickens knew his. His peculiar endowment was his
command of local colour in the broadest sense of the term; in this he
rivalled Kipling, who was making his debut about the same time."
Dr. Barker considers Zangwill a novelist of local colour also in *Jinny
the Carrier*, which he describes "as his best example of local colour
and human interest outside his special sphere."

Zangwill explained that "born in London in a Jewish milieu,
I had the advantage of intimate contact with both Gentile and Jewish
humanity." "Zangwill's stories of East End life were so authentic
in the truest sense," Barnett Litvinoff, one of the younger East End
writers, says "that they were lifted right out of their Jewish context."

Holbrook Jackson said: "Israel Zangwill, son of a Russian Jew, mastering English life and literature, and taking his place in English letters. . . ."

Yet there is something above and beyond that in Zangwill's work, which while it remains authentically part of English literature, belonging to the regional or local colour tradition, makes it also supremely, distinctively Jewish, part of the great stream of Jewish literature in all languages, Hebrew, Yiddish, English, German, French or Russian. The two can and do run together. The Yiddish novelist Sholem Asch, who has won his place through Yiddish literature in world literature, and who looks up to his master Peretz, the "father" of Yiddish literature, said to me that to his mind Zangwill is as authentically a Jewish writer as Peretz, though he did not write in Yiddish or Hebrew, the Jewish languages; he is not, he said, below Peretz or Shalom Aleichem; he called him "the classic of Jewish literature in English."

"Zangwill was not the only one who painted the Ghetto," Dr. Syrkin, who wrote as a Yiddishist, said, "but Zangwill was the first to lift up the Ghetto to greatness. In Mendele the Ghetto life is a life of foolishness, darkness, misery and fear, and being saved from this life is salvation. The children of the Ghetto were to leave no children in the Ghetto. Sholem Asch has no Ghetto, no children of the Ghetto, no Jewish street, only the Jewish township. Israel Zangwill is the poet of the Ghetto."

I know Zangwill himself at times (he was no more tied rigidly to consistency, when he found his opinions changing, or felt that "the other side of everything must be shown," than was Bernard Shaw, who told Zangwill, "I have never claimed to be consistent") took the view that Jewish books written in English or other languages than Hebrew or Yiddish were only "hybrid products, children of mixed marriages." Jewish opinion however has decided that though Israel Zangwill belongs to English literature he also belongs to Jewish literature. I have a German book, published in Berlin and Vienna in 1921, called *The Ghetto Book*, containing stories by Jewish writers in many languages, including Yiddish and Hebrew, including Peretz and Sholem Asch, and also Israel Zangwill; the editor in his Foreword begins with Zangwill and gives most of his space to Zangwill, as the most outstanding of the Ghetto writers.

From the London angle, it is a non-Jew, P. G. Wodehouse, who, including a story of Zangwill's of immigrant Jewish life in London in his anthology of "humour," calls *Children of the Ghetto* "a real contribution to social history, as well as a work of humour." Ashley Smith, an East End novelist, compiling an anthology of writings about the East End of London included Dickens writing of Ratcliff and Shadwell, and Zangwill of Whitechapel.

It is only if we see the two strands in Zangwill's creative work, the English, the general human life, and the Jewish life, that we can understand Zangwill. This is not having the best of both worlds, nor the worst of both worlds, but participating fully in both human activities that derive from the fact that one is both a human being and a Jew, in the same way as a Catholic writer is not only an English writer or an American writer, but also a Catholic writer. G. K. Chesterton devoted a good deal of space to pointing out the differences between English writers who are Protestants and English writers who are Catholics. The English writer who is a Jew also has his differences from the English writers who are not Jews. The human heart, Zangwill reminded us, has room for more than one loyalty. And the Jewish writer who lives in England, and participates in English life, who is numbered by his fellow-writers as an English writer, as Zangwill was, and who "practises his craft of English words," as Golding said of himself, belongs to English life as well as to Jewish.

Yet Holbrook Jackson, who numbered Zangwill with the English regional writers, with Arthur Morrison and Somerset Maugham, found in his work also "the highest and most convincing expression in English of modern Jewish life. From the point of view of art," he said, "his great achievement is the restatement of the seemingly endless tragedy of Israel in the light of modern experience and modern culture."

That is why Zangwill's work speaks to Jews everywhere, as well as to English readers. Of course, all great literature speaks to all human beings. But I mean something specific. During the Hitler occupation of France, and the Vichy Government, one of the young Resistance workers on a dangerous mission, waiting for the hour of his assignment, went into the public library, and got out Zangwill's *Dreamers of the Ghetto*. He was a Jew; he tells the story in one of the publications of the Centre of Jewish Documentation in Paris. It gave him courage for his task, he says, when he read "Uriel Acosta" and "Chad Gadya." "Perhaps there was indeed a mission of Israel."

It was that which infuriated Wells, what he called Zangwill's "Chosen People" idea, the idea that "we shall outlast you as we outlasted Pharaoh." But Wells came to see what Zangwill meant when the war against Hitler came. "It was something very different," he said, "from when Zangwill championed and threw out that glamour of racial romance and Maccabean heroism about the ancient ways. Those were tolerant days. Now the doors of escape were being closed from the outside. Some very sinister people indeed were saying: 'You insisted on being Jews. Jews you shall be.' "

Zangwill had always seen how hard it was to escape the Jewish fate. He had himself tried to escape, but had come back. His attitude

c

was perhaps that of his Meshumad, the apostate: "My poor brethren. Sore indeed has been your travail. Perhaps I could have helped a little if I hād been faithful. I long, I yearn, I burn to return."

Children of the Ghetto is the work of a young man; he would have written the book differently later. But Zangwill wrote it from intimate knowledge of his people, from recognisable models; he made it his aim to paint both light and shadow, and he was attacked because he was showing Jews in "a bad light." "He astonished Gentiles," said Holbrook Jackson, "by his fairness in recognising the evil as well as the good among the Jews."

Mrs. Zangwill tells a story of Zangwill saying to a vast audience in New York: "I don't care a pin what anyone thinks of me. I am going to tell the truth." They call this sort of thing tactlessness. But some people call it honesty. When Zangwill was asked to write the book which became *Children of the Ghetto* he wrote to Judge Mayer Sulzberger, who had made the offer: "I would not undertake for any amount of dollars to write a novel which would appeal exclusively to a section. Behind all the Jewish details must be the human interest which will raise it into that cosmopolitan thing, a work of art."

This young man from a poverty-stricken home in Whitechapel, whose family as he explained was "poor," who had only a short while before thrown up his scholastic position and gone into the world penniless, and was still struggling, told his American Maecenas, who was commissioning him to write the book that he would not "for any amount of dollars" write anything but what he wanted to write.

And when he wrote it American Jewry and all America were as interested as was English Jewry and England because, as Dr. Grayzel says, "Israel Zangwill's stories, though they dealt with conditions of immigrants in England, applied almost as fully to the conditions among the Jewish immigrants in America." Not only because the Jewish immigrants in England and in America shared a common experience, but because Zangwill in addition to the general human life shared and understood and expressed also the common Jewish experience, which is not exclusive to the English-speaking lands, though it is naturally influenced and modified by the English and American environment and tradition. Similar conditions brought the Jewish immigrants from the Pale in Russia to both England and America, and their early struggle for adjustment and their later development in both places were and are very similar. Most of the immigrants passed through England on their way to America, and for a time lived in England. Many stayed in England only because they hadn't enough money to continue the journey across the Atlantic, and often those who did go were, as Zangwill says in *Children of the Ghetto*, "assisted on to America." The Record of the

London Jewish Board of Guardians includes an account of this work: "It was thought expedient that the United States of America should be chosen as the new home to which to draft the trans-migrants." Professor Brodetsky, who became President of the Board of Deputies of British Jews, the organisation which represents Anglo-Jewry, said that his family stayed in England because his father had no money to go on to America. This was true of Zangwill's family, who went to Plymouth, from where the Pilgrim Fathers had set out, and to Bristol, from where Cabot had sailed, and then went back to London. If his parents had had more money Zangwill might have been an American Jew. He who was so proud of being an Englishman might have been a New Yorker or a Philadelphian. He visited America a number of times, and once when he was there he said that he had at one time thought of taking up residence in the States, but had changed his mind because his foreign birth would prevent him from becoming President.

Yet though the similarity between the East Side of New York and the East End of London is considerable, and they have their common problems and achievements, the East End of London, Zangwill's Whitechapel and mine and that of his generation and my generation that lives there now is a different place; it is a part of English and not of American life and tradition.

During the war the British Ministry of Information published a *Jewish Bulletin*. I had an article there in 1943, in which I wrote: "I am a Londoner. London is my home and the centre of my world. Most of my fifty years of life have been spent in London, and whenever I have come back to it from abroad I have wondered 'having left at home my heart, how I lived so long from it apart.' Its streets are to me full of memories, reaching back through early youth to schooldays and childhood. Here I grew to manhood and middle age, and whatever future I envisage for myself and mine inevitably has London as its centre and background. I have grown to be part of it. All that I am includes flesh and bone, mind and spirit, something that is London. In those far-off days when Queen Victoria still reigned, we Jewish children in Whitechapel grew up, as I did, as Esther Ansell in Zangwill's *Children in the Ghetto* did, with 'the knowledge that she was a Jewish girl, but far more vividly she realised that she was an English girl. Esther absorbed these ideas from the school reading books. The experience of a month will overlay the hereditary bequest of a century.' Esther Ansell is the prototype of us all. For in the land where we live are all our associations and what, apart from associations have we in life, what different people with different associations we would have been."

It was his childhood associations and memories that Zangwill poured into his Jewish books. He was criticised by the *Atheneum* when *Children of the Ghetto* appeared for having produced a good but carelessly constructed book—"it is good stuff, ill-digested, and shows signs of haste," it wrote. "The chief defect of the book is a want of care in putting the story together." In other words, Zangwill was still in a youthful whirl, as Chesterton says of Dickens in *Pickwick Papers*. "He tries to tell ten stories at once; he pours into the pot all the chaotic fancies and crude experiences of his boyhood; but from the first page to the last there is a nameless and elementary ecstasy—that of the man who is doing the kind of thing he can do."

Zangwill has the defects of his qualities. He had soaked up so much in his childhood and youth that it pours out of his work with an impetuosity, with a vehemence of speech, a torrent, swift and hurried. He is full of Whitechapel, of its sights and sounds among which he grew up, the people he knew, the lives that he saw being lived while he was growing and was most impressionable and the impress was deep and lasting. Whitechapel and the stories that his father told him, and the light that was shed on him by the dim candles in the little Synagogue where his father took him every morning, illuminated his life and his pages, even after he had revolted from his father's teachings and way of life, till the day he came back, perhaps not with his father's complete acceptance and pious observance, but with understanding and love and reverence. As with most great writers, Zangwill's work was determined by his remembrance of his childhood and of his childhood emotions. He could write *Jinny the Carrier*, an excellent, a living book, and show that he knew and loved rural Essex, but it is a later and acquired life. It is not, it could not be, as his Whitechapel books, as his Jewish books are, innermost, infelt.

Yet a man's failures are part of his work, of his development. They helped him to gain increasingly his mastery over words, and to treat them as instruments in the deeper purpose of analysing life, Jewish life and the general human life, and of trying to find and indicate a road to betterment for both. In that sense he was a social novelist, not only a novelist of the social scene. He who had at first "dazzled in flash and scintillation" became a master of literature. He had always been aware of something more than the surface comforts. In *The Master* he spoke of "The great lonely blackness roaring outside. We shut out the noise with our walls and hang them with pictures, but there it is the same. Don't you hear it in the darkness? The pain of the world." That pain of the world kept dragging him away from literature to his causes. "Personally I was saved by my daily business of plucking Jews out of the pale of Christian massacre from regarding life as altogether a huge good-natured comedy," he said.

He had lived among poverty and been brought up in it, and when he had escaped from it he had in the relief of the escape kicked up his heels and as Holbrook Jackson put it, "seemed, in these early books, to be doing nothing more serious than having a good time. He liked the tinkle of the jester's headgear." But there was a "higher seriousness behind the exuberant merriment." And when the novelty of the escape wore off, he went back or was called back to that old life of poverty and struggle in which he had grown up, to describe it with all the feeling he had, with tears and laughter. He had never really got the grimness and the tragedy out of his mind. "Don't fall into the trap of making me evolve from humour into tragedy," he wrote to Holbrook Jackson. "Half of my 'Ghetto Tragedies', though published after my comic books, appeared years before in an obscure Jewish diary annual" (*The Jewish Calendar*).

The History of the Novel in England by Lovett and Hughes, published by Harrap in 1933 speaks of "the new interest in the lower classes shown" in the 'eighties and 'nineties in "Mrs. Humphrey Ward's novels, in Sir Walter Besant's *All Sorts and Conditions of Men*, Israel Zangwill's *Children of the Ghetto* and Richard Whiteing's *Number 5 John Street*." Only Mrs. Humphrey Ward, Sir Walter Besant and Richard Whiteing came to "the lower classes" with the interest of philanthropists, from outside. Israel Zangwill had been part of them, had lived their life. He was in fact one of the first of the proletarian writers. It is strange: Zangwill, himself the child of immigrant parents painted recent immigrants as though at home in their alien streets, while the later writers of his kind, the children of native, Anglicised parents, paint their people, born in these streets and belonging there, like aliens, drifting on the surface of their life. These later, the "modern" Jewish writers in England and America, who have followed the fashion of "proletarian" writing, who are full of the jargon of Marxism and Freudism and of the tricks of expressionism, picture their people rootless, homeless, though they were born, are native in London or New York. Zangwill's people, though recent immigrants in London or the children of recent immigrants are at home there, have struck roots there, go about their business like people who are part of this life—they are not homeless. They get on with their life in the place where God put them, mould it to their character and their needs, make the streets of Whitechapel and of the East End of London part of the Jewish home, of the Jewish scene, of a rich, colourful Jewish life that fits in to English conditions and becomes part of English civilisation, a life that is poor but not squalid; Zangwill's people are not disillusioned and negative—they are filled with trust and belief, with faith and hope, with vitality and persistence, and with the humour which comes from the acceptance of life.

There is a little book on *The Jews in England*, by Mrs. Abrahams, who writes of the immigrants, whose life, she says, "is vividly portrayed in the *Children of the Ghetto* by Israel Zangwill"; "in that period there was a great deal of poverty in Britain among the general population. The poor lived wretchedly. The new immigrants began their lives in much the same way as their non-Jewish neighbours. Together with them they passed through that period of wretched poverty and played their part in bettering the conditions."

I lived and went to school and grew up in that Whitechapel, in the East End of London, under conditions very much like those which Zangwill had observed and described a generation earlier. I know my London, and I love it, a true Cockney. And I know that what Zangwill painted in his books is the portrait, the physical and spiritual portrait of English Jewry as it was in his day and as it largely continues to be in essence both in what remains of the East End after Hitler's bombing, and in those other places to which it has expanded, Hackney and Dalston, Golders Green and Crickle-wood, Manchester and Leeds and Glasgow, Johannesburg and New York.

Some later Anglo-Jewish writers complain that the colourful East End of Zangwill's day has disappeared, that there is nothing left for them to paint. Barnet Litvinoff, who paid me the compliment of describing me in an article published in 1950 as "happily a living and articulate link with Zangwill" and with the Whitechapel of his day though when *Children of the Ghetto* appeared I was just being born, finds Whitechapel to-day "drab and uninteresting." I am glad he suggests that "it probably always was." For indeed it was always, except to us who lived there, and spent our youth there, and remember it as the wonderful place in which our loveliest memories are centred. It depends on how you look at it. In Sholem Asch's *Salvation* Yechiel looks at his mother with love, and the poor harassed woman who stands haggling in the market place, screaming, scolding, telling lies becomes in his eyes an angel, with maternal love shining from her face.

The East End was not, Whitechapel was not, for all its rich Jewish life, ever exclusively Jewish territory. George Lansbury, writing in 1935, in his book *Looking Forwards and Backwards*, said: "If you were in Whitechapel sixty-five years ago" (that is in 1870, when Israel Zangwill was six), "I don't suppose you would recognise where you were. First of all you would have seen hardly any Jews. There was a small Jewish colony between Bishopsgate and Aldgate High Street, but it was not in the least obvious to the eye. There was an immense Irish population, which has now receded eastwards. The centre was Bucks Row. We were a large family, who lived in a large house in Bucks Row, in Whitechapel. It was not when I was very small, quite as ill-omened as the Jack the Ripper murders made it later, but it was pretty rough. There were no schools, and no evening institutes." (The Jews' Free School was a pioneer school, one of the first elementary schools, established long before the Compulsory Education Act, and maintained privately, largely by the Rothschild family.)

Lansbury's recollection is correct. Charles Booth, in his *Life and Labour in London*, recorded that "formerly in Whitechapel, Commercial Street roughly divided the Jewish haunts of Petticoat Lane and Goulston Street from the rougher English quarter lying to the East. Now (1889) the Jews have flowed across the line; Hanbury Street, Fashion Street, Pelham Street, Booth Street, Old Montague Street and many other streets and alleys have fallen before them; they have introduced new trades as well as habits."

The streets in which I lived were not entirely Jewish. My parents had many non-Jewish neighbours and friends. I played with their children. We shared our *Magnets* and *Gems*, *Marvels* and *Chums* and *Boys' Own Paper*. We played cricket and football together. We quarrelled and fought bare-fist fights in the streets, and were fast friends. It was as much a part of my upbringing as my Chedar (Jewish religious school), and my Yiddish-speaking background. Yet it was the London Ghetto. "Mr. Warner sneers at the Ghetto," Zangwill wrote, and he reminded Mr. Warner that "the Ghetto looked back to Sinai and forward to the Millennium."

To-day Whitechapel and the East End of London thereabouts are less Jewish territory. The tide has ceased to pour in. There has been an ebb. But a very considerable pool has remained, and I think will remain. The greater part of the Jewish population of East London has gone to live elsewhere; many have been pushed out by the lack of housing. Not only Jews have gone. Their non-Jewish neighbours, English and Irish, have also moved. Indians and Negroes occupy many of the derelict houses, coloured people, West Africans, British West Indians. You see turbans in the streets where once Jews carried their prayer shawls to Synagogue. Mr. A. B. Levy, in his book *East End Story*, says that the proportions of East End Jewry and London Jewry have been reversed. Nine-tenths of the Jews of London once lived in East London; now nine-tenths live outside it, in Clapton and Edgware.

Yet 25,000 Jews still live in the East End. They have not prospered enough to be able to move to better parts, or they are too much attached to their home or too indolent to change their abode— those who were not bombed out and so compelled to move. And people who live together become neighbours, and sometimes friends. I have seen Jews in the East End exchanging conversation with their dark-skinned neighbours. I have seen Jewish children playing in the streets with piccaninnies.

What is important is that there are still Jewish children and young people in the East End. I went through a stack of recent issues of the *Jewish Chronicle*, and noted what a large number of Jewish children who write to its Children's Page give their addresses in Stepney and Whitechapel. People tell me there is indeed a return to the East End, and that as housing goes up the return will increase. The Rev. M. Zeffertt, the Minister of the East London Synagogue, said in 1954: "A new East End is springing up. New families have taken up residence in the new fine modern dwellings." I stood recently outside the Stepney Jewish School and watched a crowd of children who looked very much like my own playmates, playing the same games we had played. There are still many houses there with mezuzas (small cases containing a text of Deuteronomy iv 4-9, 13-21) fixed to the posts of the door. And there are still kosher butchers' and small grocery shops and bakeries clearly catering for a Jewish population which, unlike those in the big market places, Petticoat Lane or Hessel Street, do not exist to serve Jewish shoppers coming from other parts of London, but the Jewish population of the streets round about. There are still, as in my time, Oxford and Cambridge undergraduates coming home to spend their vacations with their parents in the East End streets.

I have found the same spirit of eager Jewish youth that I knew in the East End as a boy in other parts of London where there are now large Jewish agglomerations; I have seen them walk up and down the Golders Green Road, arguing and discussing as we went up and down the Mile End Road and Whitechapel Road and Aldgate to the Bank of England or by way of the Minories to the Tower of London and the Thames. The spirit is the same. When Henry Cohen (Roland Camberton), writes about the Jews in North London, which the Mayor of Stoke Newington, a North London Borough, said has the largest Jewish population of any district in Europe, a discerning critic asks with justification: "A hint of Zangwill perhaps?" The critics said the same of Louis Golding's stories of Manchester Jews, and Zangwill himself recognised the kinship.

Zangwill was proud that he had through his books brought an understanding of the immigrant Jew to the English reading-public. Mrs. Zangwill sent me with other papers a copy of a letter Zangwill had written to Judge Sulzberger, who had commissioned *Children of the Ghetto*, written soon after the book was published, where he said that he had met the Editor of a leading Conservative daily who told him that influenced by *Children of the Ghetto* he had prevented the exclusion of the immigration alien being made a plank in the Conservative platform. The Aliens Act came into force some years later, but there are many Jews in England to-day who owe it to Zangwill's book, the *Children of the Ghetto* that their parents and grand-parents were meanwhile enabled to enter England and make their home and future there. Zangwill also brought understanding to the Anglicised Jews of the West End. "In the eye of the average Anglo-Hebrew of the epoch," his brother Louis Zangwill explained in an article in the *Menorah Journal* in 1927, "the entire foreign element in London was an uncivilised element." Zangwill's *Children of the Ghetto* showed them what these poorer Jews really were. There is a letter which Zangwill wrote to his friend Lucien Wolf, where he said: "Few of our Anglicised Jews will consent to understand the rich manysided life that pulses in the great Jargon-speaking communities." "So many Jews are ashamed of anything Jewish," he said.

The London County Council is busy with plans for the reconstruction of the East End of London. It seems certain that never again will the East End be as populous as it was in the days when its problem was overcrowding. The new plans err perhaps too much in the direction of dispersal and thinning out of population. I wonder as I consider the process whether it may not thin out the blood of the East End, and its vitality. I experienced overcrowding in my own life. In *Children of the Ghetto* Zangwill speaks of the homes in which his people lived, the Ansells and the others—for "the Ansells had numerous housemates; No. 1 Royal Street was a Jewish colony in itself. What with Sugarman the Shadchan on the first floor, Mrs Simons and Dutch Debby on the second, the Belcovitches on the third and the Ansells and Gabriel Hamburger, the great scholar, on the fourth."

But No. 1 Royal Street was also "close-packed with the stuff of human life." Zangwill knew and was always realising "afresh how much illogical happiness flourished amid penury, ugliness and pain." The name Royal Street, Louis Zangwill said, was suggested by Princess Street, in Whitechapel, "but the house described in the book was in another street. We lived in this street for some years after coming up from Bristol, and I only wish someone would present me with a freehold property there to-day. I believe the most interesting houses were pulled down many years ago." The memories of that great house crammed tight with human life, a house that Zangwill said "had been in its time one of the great mansions of the Ghetto, with spacious reception rooms," stayed obstinately in his brother Louis's mind (and no doubt in his own), as his idea of what a fine house should be. Repeatedly, when he was living in rooms in the Temple, with lovely furniture and fine pictures, a man of taste and culture, Louis told me that he would rather live in one of those grand old houses in Whitechapel than anywhere else in London. Thomas Burke expressed a similar feeling when he wrote: "There are on Stepney Green some Queen Anne mansions any one of which I would prefer to an entire floor of Dorchester

House." He said it too about the old houses (which no longer exist) in the streets of the Tenters, near where No. 1 Royal Street stood.

The blitzed Jews' Free School building, where Israel Zangwill was a schoolboy and a schoolteacher, and near which he was born and his family lived (his name appeared on the School Commemoration Board as the winner of the School Scholarships in 1877 and 1878, with just below, the names of his brothers Mark, winner in 1881 and 1882, and Louis 1883) has been bought by Mr. Halperin and Mr. Burston, of the Houndsditch Warehouse Company, near the School. Mr. Burston told me that they would like to bring into their rebuilding scheme the whole stretch from their Houndsditch Warehouse along Stoney Lane right up to the Free School site. Alfred Wolmark, the artist, who illustrated Zangwill's last collected edition, published in 1925, a year before his death, and whose portrait of Zangwill is in the National Portrait Gallery, has suggested that such a new housing estate if it comes into being would be aptly named Zangwill, as another East End area has been named Lansbury. For as Sir John de Villiers, himself an old Jews' Free School pupil, said, Zangwill was the most famous of all the pupils of the Jews' Free School and indeed "the most famous of all the English Ghetto children." Zangwill said of the Jews' Free School that "it was an institution to which he could not give greater praise than to say that it had produced himself."

Israel Zangwill was born a few steps from what is now the building of the Houndsditch Warehouse Company and one street away from the Free School building, in a court off Stoney Lane (which leads from the Houndsditch Warehouse Company to the Free School site), known at the time as Ebenezer Square, on whose site now stands a block of tenements, artisans' flats, called Artizan Dwellings, built in 1884, twenty years after Zangwill was born there. When Esther Ansell in *Children of the Ghetto*, who is not and yet is Israel Zangwill himself, came back as he did to the Ghetto, she found "the well-known street strangely broadened. Instead of the dirty picturesque houses rose an appalling series of artisans' dwellings, monotonous brick barracks, whose dead, dull prose weighed upon the spirits." They were new then, only about seven years after they were built; they have stood now for over seventy years, and are grimy and grim, but the description of the monotonous brick-barracklike Artisan Dwellings in Stoney Lane is accurate. Is it fanciful to suggest that Ebenezer Square—Sugarman, the Shadchan, one of the Ansell's neighbours in the big house at No. 1 Royal Street, named his son Ebenezer, and the boy grew up to work on *The Flag of Judah*—might be described in *Children of the Ghetto* as Zachariah Square, where Malka, Moses Ansell's deceased wife's wealthy cousin, lived?

"The houses in Zachariah Square were small, three-roomed,

without basements. Most of the doors were ajar, for the Zachariah
Squareites lived a good deal on the door step. Some of the doors
were blocked below with sliding barriers of wood, a sure sign of
small children, and there were swings nailed to the lintels of a few
doors, in which little tots were swaying." Moreover, "the Square
was an ideal playing-ground for children." Solomon Ansell loved
whipping his humming-top across the ample spaces. There was a
"little arched passage which led to the Square."

"What had she in common with all this mean wretchedness?"
Esther Ansell asked herself when she returned, like Israel Zangwill,
to the Ghetto, and wondered how she could "ever really have
walked these streets with a light heart, unconscious of the ugliness."
What had she in common with all this mean wretchedness? Why
everything. This it was with which her soul had intangible affinities.
That is Zangwill's whole attitude to the East End, to Whitechapel,
to the home of his *Children of the Ghetto*.

When Israel Zangwill died, the London *Jewish Chronicle* suggested
that a statue of Zangwill should be erected in Whitechapel, "which
owes so much to Zangwill." *The American Hebrew* of New York
backed the suggestion in an Editorial. "It is a suggestion which
should meet with favour among Jews the world over," it wrote.
"Now that he is gone it should be our affectionate task to erect for
him a suitable memorial. In this project Jews of all shades of belief
and disbelief will join. There is no doubt that many Christian
admirers of Zangwill's genius will welcome the opportunity to
perpetuate his memory. We on this side of the Atlantic will be glad to
do our bit when the project is started."

When *Children of the Ghetto* was first published in 1892, it roused
a good deal of criticism among a number of Jews, English and
American, who felt that the book showed Jews up in "a bad light
to the Gentiles." Mr. Cyrus Sulzberger in America wrote to the
American Hebrew: "If the Jews of England be as ignoble and detestable as Mr. Zangwill pictures—and being one of them he ought to
know—and if they are desirous of seeing themselves held up to the
scorn and contempt of their fellow-men . . ." It is the complaint
Zangwill anticipated in *Children of the Ghetto*—"It's a great pity he
had such detestable acquaintances. Why didn't he describe our
circle?" "I regret my lot was not cast among Mr. Cyrus Sulzberger's
friends instead of my own," Zangwill answered this complaint. "I
might have been painting nothing but saints."

There is still a lot of that feeling about. Barnett Litvinoff wrote
about it recently: "Suppose the Anglo-Jewish writer were to write
about Jews as Graham Greene writes about Catholics. Would
English Jewry accept the work tolerantly, or would it protest that
the writer was providing material for the antisemite?" I remember

an Anglo-Jewish clergyman writing to the *Jewish Chronicle* to ask what purpose was served by the publication of Sholem Asch's *The Calf of Paper*, and I. J. Singer's *The Brothers Ashkenazi*.

When I had an article in the *Jewish Chronicle* for the fiftieth anniversary of *Children of the Ghetto*, a correspondent wrote to the paper that he believed that "if Zangwill had been commissioned to write his masterpiece twenty-five years later, when his experience of human nature had widened, there is much in the *Children of the Ghetto* that he would have omitted. Since we are a much-criticised people our authors should be careful how they portray our collective character."

"Of course," I said, "Zangwill would have written a different book had he written *Children of the Ghetto* twenty-five years later, for as Zangwill grew older he learned and matured." "Nothing brought me more odium," he said, "than my habit of keeping my eyes open and trying to learn." He would certainly have omitted his remark that Yiddish was "the most hopelessly corrupt and hybrid jargon ever evolved." For he learned not many years after to have a better understanding of Yiddish, which he described as "a living language, the truest repository of specifically Jewish sociology." But it is not true, I said, that he would have portrayed the Jewish collective character in the later book more "carefully." *Children of the Ghetto* was effective precisely because it was not "careful." He "astonished Gentiles," said Holbrook Jackson, "by his fairness in recognising the evil as well as the good among the Jews. But that is no more an example of fairness than similar qualities in English or Scotch novelists. It is simply the faculty of observation and visualisation crystallised in art. Israel Zangwill sees the Jew steadily and sees him whole." Holbrook Jackson added: "The spiritual facts of Jewish history and of modern Jewish life, have received their highest and most convincing expression in English in *Children of the Ghetto*."

Whitechapel, the London Ghetto, London Jewry, the modern Jew live for the world in English and in world literature in Israel Zangwill's book, *Children of the Ghetto*.

Chapter II

CHILDREN OF THE GHETTO

WHEN Zangwill undertook to write *Children of the Ghetto*, he needed, his brother Louis said, "after years of work in Fleet Street to refresh his knowledge, and he made expeditions for the purpose." It is not strictly true, for in the years between Zangwill worked on the *Jewish Standard*, which appears in *Grandchildren of the Ghetto* as *The Flag of Judah*. And he wrote for the *Jewish Quarterly Review* the analysis of the Jewish Community which Lucien Wolf said impressed him so much that "when Judge Sulzberger sent Rabbi Krauskopf to tell me that they wanted a Jewish 'Robert Ellesmere,' and to ask me either to do it myself or to find somebody to do it I replied at once that there was only one man in England capable of the work and that was the author of *Satan Makatrig* and the article in the *Jewish Quarterly*."

Zangwill had maintained his contact with the life of the Whitechapel Ghetto even while he was winning what he called "my first laurels as a new humorist, with my friends Jerome K. Jerome, Eden Phillpotts and Barry Pain." "I do not believe it right to assert, as Mr. Leftwich does, that Zangwill at any time lost touch with the Ghetto. The call of Fleet Street was not so strong as to obliterate Zangwill's devotion and attachment to the scene of his youth," a correspondent wrote to the *Jewish Chronicle*. "He lived, taught, lectured and quarrelled in the Ghetto. Never could it have been absent from his mind." There is much truth in that; yet it is a fact that Zangwill had for a time left Whitechapel, and that his destiny as the writer of the Ghetto was not at all clear to him.

Mrs. Zangwill said that when Zangwill was a boy at the Jews' Free School he had refused Lord Rothschild's offer to send him to Eton and Oxford, because he couldn't afterwards criticise his would-be benefactor if he were under an obligation to him. In telling the story, she said that she had been surprised at his refusal, because she remembered he had often said to her that three years at a beautiful old University with nothing to do but study would have been to him a Paradise. In 1924, when he was sixty, Zangwill was invited to attend a World Congress of World Students held in Antwerp. He answered: "I am not a student, alas!—would that I were." It was an echo of his old dream. He had been winning scholarships at the Jews' Free School, and the Headmaster and Lord Rothschild, the

President of the School, thought he would make his mark as a student. He had a good deal of the student in him. Mrs. Zangwill relates that when he translated Ibn Gabirol, a noted Oriental scholar said to her: "It is astonishing. Your husband knows little Hebrew, yet he understands these poems better than I do." Rabbi David de Sola Pool, reviewing Zangwill's translation of Ibn Gabirol from "A Scholar's View" in the *Menorah Journal*, said "Mr. Zangwill's translations of poems by Ibn Gabirol are strikingly successful. Rarely has the translator slipped. He has enabled the English reader to look into the very soul of our lofty Hebrew poet, Solomon Ibn Gabirol." I remember seeing Zangwill in London while he was working at the Ibn Gabirol translation. I had brought David Herman, the producer of the Yiddish Vilna Troupe, to see him; he wanted to discuss with Herman a Yiddish production of *King of Schnorrers*. All through our talk he kept breaking in with questions about the proper translation of a Hebrew word or phrase in Ibn Gabirol. His mind was working on the translation all the time. Benjamin, in *Children of the Ghetto*, into whom as well as into his sister Esther, Zangwill projected something of himself, said to Esther: "I'm going to win a scholarship and go to the University." But scholarship at the time Zangwill left the Ghetto to go into Fleet Street, and to make his first success as a "new humorist," did not mean to him Jewish and Hebrew scholarship and Ibn Gabirol's religious poems. He was impatient of that sort of scholarship, to which his father was addicted. "I'll give father an allowance so that he can study beastly big books" (Hebrew books) "all day long," Benjamin says to Esther. "Does he still take a week to read a page?"

By the time he was Bar-mitzvah, thirteen years of age, Israel Zangwill had rebelled against his father's ways and his father's religion. His language and his literature were English. Of another member of the Ansell family Zangwill writes: "The literature and history Solomon really cared for was not of the Jews." "Why can't he speak English?" Benjamin asks irritably about his father. "I say it's a beastly disgrace. Look at the years he's been in England— just as long as we have." It sounds like Zangwill's father, Moses Zangwill. He spoke Yiddish. And he wanted his son to become a Rabbi. "Ugh! Tell him I'm going to write books." He could speak English—but badly. He lived "in a land of whose tongue he knew scarce more than the Saracen damsel married by legend to A'Becket's father."

He took to heathenish ways. He climbed the gallery stairs to the Brittania Theatre in neighbouring Gentile Shoreditch, once Shakespeare's home, "in sober boyish earnestness, elbowed of the gods and elbowing, and if I did not yield to the seductions of 'ginger-beer and Banbury' that filled up clamantly the entr'actes it was that I had not the coppers." "When to my fashionable friends," he said, "I have held forth on the glories and the humours of 'the Brit.,' they have taken it for granted, and I have lacked the courage or the energy to undeceive them, that my visits were expeditions of Haroun Al Raschid to the back streets." They were rather like those of that "graceless young fellow" in *Children of the Ghetto*, who had a book of tickets for the Oxbridge Music Hall, which I remember as the Cambridge, "and went there on Friday Nights," on the Sabbath. Zangwill was drawn to the ways of the world outside the Ghetto. Did he ever think, as one of his young men in *Children of the Ghetto* did, of denying that he was a Jew? Because to say that he was one "would be to produce a false impression. The conception of a Jew in the mind of the average Christian is a mixture of Fagin, Shylock, Rothschild, and the caricatures of the comic papers. I am certainly not like that, and I am not going to tell a lie and say I am."

Not everything in *Children of the Ghetto* happened to Israel Zangwill, but much or most of it did, to him or to someone to whom he saw it happen. That story in *Children of the Ghetto*, of Reb Shemuel searching for his son on Seder Night and finding him "coming out of an unclean place where he had violated the Passover" might have happened to him or to one of his friends. There is a reminiscent note—his own father in the house of Reb Shemuel's son-in-law, the real Dayan Susman Cohen, blotting out his son's name, Israel Zangwill's, the heretic, the sinner in Israel in Reb Shemuel in the book saying of his son: "Mention not his name. He is dead. He has become like a heathen!" It is typical of much that was happening in many Ghettos at that time, when young men were throwing off the yoke and the restraints of Judaism. The yoke of the Law is not light, and only the love of God makes it bearable. Those who have lost trust in God can only seek to ease the burden.

All his life Zangwill was torn between two desires, repelled and attracted by the life and faith and ways of his father. "Beware of the Goyim," he wrote many years later, repenting of the way he had once "worshipped the Gentiles, outgrowing the Ghetto." "Behold him to-day," he wrote, "with the Jew's haunted eyes, that have seen for themselves, seen history made on the old Gentile formula." "Back, back," he cried, "brethren, Back to the Ghetto, to our dream of Messiah, and our old Sabbath candles." There had of course been something else too. Zangwill had clearly resented his position at the Jews' Free School, where Lord Rothschild was a great person whom he approached with "a beating heart. He had been kind to me in the past, singling me out on account of some scholastic successes." The members of the School Committee belonged to what Louis Zangwill called "the great mass of prosperous Anglo-Judea who had assimilated to the British Philistinism of the day. Small wonder," he said, "that here and there a youth of sensibility turned from the barrenness of his own kin to what he deemed the light." It was happening in all the Ghettos of Eastern Europe.

When Zangwill pictured Esther Ansell having been taken up by some rich Jews, as he might have been, had he not refused, he made her reproach herself, because "with my temperament it was a mistake to fetter myself by obligations to anybody."

Louis Zangwill used to speak to me of their father and mother, the father, as Moses Ansell was, a man of piety, who "craved more for spiritual snacks than for physical," who was always praying and studying the sacred writings, unworldly, a saint, and his mother, like Mrs. Ansell, Esther's mother, whom Louis used to speak of as a "heathen." "There had indeed been a note of scepticism, of defiance in Esther's mother—a hankering after the customs of the heathen," Zangwill wrote in *Children of the Ghetto*. "She professed not to see the value to God, man or beast of the learned Rabbonim who sat shaking themselves all day in the Beth Hamidrash, and said they would be better occupied in supporting their families—primarily intended as a hint to Moses to study less and work longer."

"The father," Mrs. Zangwill wrote to me, "was rather a saintly person, from what my husband said. My husband, being the eldest son, was taken by his father to the Synagogue at a very early hour every morning. The poetry of it made a great impression on my husband, but I can imagine that in the domestic circle it must have been a little trying for the breadwinner to spend so much of his day in laying up treasure in heaven rather than on earth."

Their granddaughter, Primrose Horn, has written of them: "Grandmother Ellen Zangwill was brilliant and stormy, and did not find the uses of adversity at all sweet. She was as turbulent as her husband was tranquil. My memory of her is vivid, a fiery little woman, slender and upright, charged with great vitality, with luxuriant white hair, and darkly smouldering eyes. I was the first grandchild really accessible to her. I never knew Grandfather Zangwill, for he was so pious that he went to live in Jerusalem before I was born. Granny became much less religiously observant as the years went on, and so did her children, so that Grandfather ceased to feel spiritually at home in his home and longed for the Holy Land. I can't help feeling that there is a portrait of him in Moses Ansell, 'always living from hand to mouth, always praying when he had nothing better to do,' greatly respected for his piety by people who regarded him as otherwise a 'Shlemiel.'

"In his son Israel, my mother's brother, there was the complete swing of the pendulum, the change from rigid orthodoxy to complete heterodoxy, to a rejection of all forms of religion. The combination of his parents in Israel Zangwill produced the religious exaltation of his father Moses, his scholarship and his wisdom, the paganism, the fiery brilliance, the dramatic temperament, the wicked wit of his mother."

Israel Abrahams, who knew both Zangwill's parents, wrote: "I am not one of those who attribute all greatness to heredity. But that Israel Zangwill owes much to his mother is certain. She was no mere begetter of genius. She possessed genius herself. A part of him is due to his father also. He was in a sense a foil to his wife. Reticent where she was vocal, inefficient where she was competent, he belonged to the class which we designate the ineffectual saint. Pity that we lay so much stress on the adjective that we overlook the noun. For a saint he was. I saw him last in Jerusalem. He was passing a laborious student life on five shillings a week, bestowing on others the whole balance of an ample allowance. A saint truly, and devout; also a scholar of sorts, and above all a romantic. A wonderful couple."

Moses Zangwill tried to make Israel Zangwill a Jew like himself. He taught him all he could. Zangwill speaks in *Children of the Ghetto* of his father teaching his children "every Shabbos afternoon and Sunday. Solomon translates into Yiddish the whole Pentateuch with Rashi. He knows a little Gemorah too. I can't teach him at home, because I haven't got a Gemorah—it's so expensive. But he went with me to the Beth Hamidrash, and we learnt the whole of the Tractate Niddah. Solomon understands very well all about the Divorce Laws, and he could adjudicate on the duties of women to their husbands." There was a time when Israel Zangwill appeared (in 1911) as an expert before the High Court of Justice in an action brought by an East End Jewish butcher who disputed a decision by the Shechita Board which had advertised that his meat was not Kosher. "I have lived a good deal of my youth in orthodox communities," he told the Judge, "and I understand the spirit of the Jewish Law."

Zangwill put himself into all the Ansell children. He is Esther Ansell in the sense in which Flaubert could say that Emma Bovary was himself. He put more than himself into her. "In Esther Ansell I see not only my Uncle Israel, but also his sister, my aunt Leah Zangwill, who was about a year older than he was," Primrose has written. "Leah and Israel as tiny children knew all the hardships and privations of poor Jewish folk. I remember my aunt Leah telling me how very often they went hungry and cold."

Years later, in 1897, when Israel Zangwill was thirty-three and a famous author, Eliezer Ben Yehuda, the "father" of the Hebrew language in Israel, was excited by the news that "Israel Zangwill, the brilliant English author, was coming to visit Palestine. 'This is an opportunity such as we seldom get!' he exclaimed to his wife.

D

'Millions of people read what Zangwill writes. He is one of the most popular writers of the day. If we could only convince him and enlist him in our fight.' '' Ben Yehuda said to him: ''Zangwill, you have glorified the life of Jews in Ghettos in your many books. Now you have seen something of the life of Jews here in the place where they really belong. Why do you not make your home with us and glorify our new national life in your future books?'' Zangwill's next book, Ben Yehuda recorded with disappointment, was not about the Promised Land. It was *Dreamers of the Ghetto*.

''One hot afternoon Zangwill paid the first of many visits to Ben Yehuda's home in Jerusalem. His daughter Deborah who was barely four presented him with a rose she had picked. Zangwill bent over and kissed the child and tried to make conversation with her. The parents laughed and Ben Yehuda said—'it is no use, Zangwill. My children speak only Hebrew.' 'But I learned Hebrew myself as a child! Let me see if I can remember a few words,' said Zangwill. So with an accent so foreign that Deborah could hardly understand him the British writer tried to speak the language of his ancestors to the child.''

Zangwill's father, Moses Zangwill, was then living in Jerusalem. It was the year of the First Zionist Congress, which Zangwill described in *Dreamers of the Ghetto*. A year before, in 1896, on 2nd September 1896, less than a year after Herzl had come to him in London, with an introduction from Max Nordau to the author of *Children of the Ghetto*, to enlist his aid in his Zionist work, Israel Zangwill wrote to his cousin and friend, Dr. Eder, ''Father is, as you know, living in Jerusalem, and by latest accounts seems to be praying happily there.'' In *Children of the Ghetto* Old Hyams (who had in the first draft of the book been sketched in for what afterwards became Moses Answell, and the two were woven into a composite) finally goes to Jerusalem, ''which had been the dream of his life.'' In his story *To Die in Jerusalem*, Zangwill had his father in mind when he wrote of the old Maggid who had gone to Palestine, that ''such disappointment as often befalls the visionary when he sees the land of his dreams was spared to the Maggid, who remained a visionary even in the presence of the real. He lived enswathed as with heavenly love, waiting for the moment of his transition to the shining world-to-come.'' ''You sophisters of religion who cling to your creed because it is good for the poor, or a beautiful tradition, or a breath of respectability,'' he wrote, clearly with his father in mind, ''bow your heads before one who worshipped God as naïvely as a dog adores his master, who did not even know that he believed, who *was* belief; who went to Jerusalem not because he was a Zionist but because it was Zion, whose tears at the Wailing Wall were tinctured with never a thought of the wonder and picturesqueness of weeping over Zion lost eighteen hundred years before he was born. Poor pure fool! I have been privileged to see this *sancta simplicites* of the old Jewish pedlar."

Zangwill saw his father when he was in Jerusalem in 1897. When the old man heard he was coming to Jerusalem, he wrote: "I am already crying at the thought of parting with him." S. L. Bensusan, who was a member of the party that visited Jerusalem with Zangwill, told me that he met Zangwill's father in Jerusalem. He was, he said, "a shy, shrinkling little man, who seemed to be full of good will." But he had not enough good will to put up with the un-Jewish way in which his children were living. "Parting there had to be, for he simply could not live in a household so unorthodox," says his granddaughter. "English life had claimed his wife and children more and more." Rabbi Barnett Cohen, whose father, Dayan Susman Cohen, a great Rabbinical scholar, was a friend of Moses Zangwill, who used to come to his house to study and to discuss Rabbinical lore with him, told me that one day when Moses Zangwill had come to the house there were visitors, and Israel Zangwill being then at the height of his fame the Dayan had introduced Moses as Israel's father. Moses Zangwill did not say anything until the other people had gone, but then he reproached the Dayan. He was not proud of his son, he said. He did not want to be known as the father of a renegade. He used a bitter Hebrew phrase which means, blot out the name of the backslider and the sinner in Israel. Like Reb Shemuel in *Children of the Ghetto* mourning for his son's sin he said: "He lives like a heathen. My God, thou canst not say I did not teach him thy Law day and night. Whosoever is stubborn and disobedient, that soul shall surely be cut off from among his people." Yet in the end, Reb Shemuel forgave his son. "Perchance he will be restored to us," he said. So Israel Zangwill's father yearned to see his son Israel again when he came to the Holy Land. Israel Zangwill was indeed restored to his faith. Chief Rabbi Hertz gave him his Hechsher, his approbation: "He spoke and wrote out of the fulness of personal and historical knowledge of Judaism and the Jew."

But it took a long time before he returned to his faith. In his early Zionist days Zangwill had said that in a Jewish Parliament he would sit on the anti-clericalist benches. I am not sure that he ever altogether returned. His contribution, "My Religion," to a symposium in the *Daily Express* is not the avowal of a believing and practising Jew. "The Old Testament is as far from finality," he said, "as the New, which Judaism should now add to it." But he could also at other times laugh at those Jews who think that Judaism is Christianity minus Christ.

There were always conflicting moods and ideas in Israel Zangwill.

He was not a consistent man. When he was quite young he wrote: "I do not at all mind contradicting myself." Perhaps Chief Rabbi Hertz was right, or Rabbi de Sola Pool could not have found, as an Orthodox Rabbi, that he had carried over into English Ibn Gabirol's "religious yearnings, his spiritual passion, his loving awe." Whatever he might have thought for himself, he certainly had concluded already in 1915 that: "On the whole the Jews will have to go back to their religion if they wish to survive as an entity." Yet speaking for himself, he could describe himself five years later, in 1920, as religiously "the least orthodox of all."

There was always this dichotomy in Zangwill's mind. He married out of the Jewish faith. "Jewry thought," he said, "that I had made a mixed marriage, a form of union I utterly disapprove of, the fact being that the Englishwoman who honoured me by becoming my wife was essentially at one with me." He meant in religious views. Mrs. Zangwill wrote to me: "My husband used to say that my religious outlook was nearer to his own than that of any Jewess he had met." "Why shouldn't Jews without Judaism marry Christians without Christianity?" someone asks in *Children of the Ghetto*. "Must a Jew have a Jewess to help him break the Law?" Yet in the end, he won his wife so completely to his Jewish interests that Jacob de Haas, expressing the feeling of many people who knew her, wrote: "Though not a Jewess by race she is one by conviction." He did not circumcise his eldest son, but he had the younger circumcised, and explained that the doctor advised it. He said that he wanted to write of the great human life outside the Ghetto, and claimed that he was not interested in Jews as Jews, but in all suffering humanity. "Hitherto," he wrote, "I thought the crown of martyrdom had been Israel's. But I was mistaken. One people is suffering more. I bow before this higher majesty of sorrow. I take the crown of thorns from Israel's head and I place it upon Armenia's." Yet Zangwill did not sacrifice his life and his work for years for Armenia, as he did for the Jews.

Even while he thought he had turned his back on the Ghetto he was in it. His analysis of the Jewish Community in England in *The Jewish Quarterly Review* directed Jewish attention to him, and the Jewish Publication Society of America considered that analysis in deciding to approach him to write *Children of the Ghetto*. "*Children of the Ghetto*," it said, "presented in story form many of the ideas and observations which Zangwill had outlined in his *Jewish Quarterly Review* article." When Dr. Cyrus Adler spoke to him about writing *Children of the Ghetto*, he said he had no sympathy with the material; then he sent Dr. Adler his story *The Diary of a Meshumad*, and wrote: "Read the story; I think it will convince you that I have some sympathy with my material."

Zangwill was then editing *Ariel*, a comic paper, which Bensusan remembers as "a very bright weekly paper." Zangwill himself said he had then "sunk entirely into the slough of journalism (inter alia, editing a comic paper, *Ariel*) with a heavy heart." *Ariel* was started in 1890, a year before he was commissioned to write *Children of the Ghetto*. There was little Jewish in it. It had an advertisement of *The Cedar of Lebanon*, "a Centenary Psalm written on Sir Moses Montefiore attaining an hundred years of age," published at 4 Wine Office Court, Fleet Street, where *Ariel* was printed. There was a competition for a National Cycling Song, with Sir Frederick Cowen, the composer, as the adjudicator. "He will not award the prize unless the composition is genuinely worthy to become what *Ariel* will take steps to make the Marsellaise of the cycling world."

The Maccabeans, the club of Jewish professional men before which Dr. Herzl delivered his first public Zionist address, under Zangwill's chairmanship ("Zangwill called on me with a lightly satirical introduction," says Dr. Herzl in his *Diaries*) was formed in 1891, with Zangwill, Israel Abrahams, Elkan Adler, Sir Israel Gollancz, Solomon J. Solomon and Sir Frederick Cowen among the members. At the first meeting Zangwill suggested as its name "The Mosaics," "which appealed to a great many as sounding fittingly." It would have been before this that a small similar group, including Israel and Louis Zangwill ("my novelist-brother and brother-novelist"), Solomon J. Solomon, Lucien Wolf, Israel Abrahams and Joseph Jacobs met at the home of Dr. Schechter, and called themselves "The Wanderers," because one day, Louis Zangwill told me, Mrs. Schechter remarked how they were wandering from the subject, like a lot of wandering Jews, and Israel Zangwill exclaimed: "What an excellent name! Let's call ourselves that." "The spiritual fathers of the Maccabeans were the 'Wandering Jews,'" Israel Zangwill declared. I was puzzled by Lucien Wolf's remark in his Zangwill Memorial Address to the Jewish Historical Society in 1926 that "at the time," when Judge Sulzberger "sent Rabbi Krauskopf to tell me that they wanted a Jewish *Robert Ellesmere* I did not know Zangwill personally." For there is a reference in one of the "Letters from London of the 1880's" published by Dr. Mowshowitch, to a meeting "in the house of Lucien Wolf" at which Judge Sulzberger and Israel Zangwill were present. And there is an entry in Zangwill's diary for January 1889 about a long walk he took with Lucien Wolf and Joseph Jacobs, who thought "me more cynical than I am." *Robert Ellesmere* was published in 1888, the same year as Zangwill's *Premier and the Painter*. It is possible that the approach to Lucien Wolf which led to his acquaintance with Zangwill had been made that year, in the first months of the stir which *Robert Ellesmere* created. Zangwill had just been dismissed from Jews' Free School.

"Little guns like myself" he said, "can never go off of their own accord—we must wait to be discharged."

Dr. Cyrus Adler "on the same basis" formed a similar group in America called "The Wanderers," Schechter (in whose house in London the original "Wanderers" had first met), Louis Loeb, the artist, Adolph Ochs, the owner of the *New York Times*, Cyrus L. Sulzberger, Jacob Schiff, Louis Marshall and Oscar Strauss.

" 'The Maccabeans' is the result of an attempt to focus the Jewish forces: to gather not the celebrities, but the men of brains," Israel Zangwill said in an address to the Maccabeans in 1893. Then he turned to his main subject, the Jewish immigrants. "Desirable or not," he said, "the immigrants have in them the seeds of excellent English citizens. To exclude the children of the Ghetto is to keep out the grandchildren, from whom such blessings flow."

I assume that in *Ariel* the contributions signed Robin Goodfellow were Zangwill's. They are the sort of thing he was writing in *The Idler* and in the *Pall Mall Magazine*. He attacked Russia, because of the pogroms. "The only objection to styling the Government of Russia barbarous," he wrote, "is that it is rather too feeble an epithet." *Ariel's* Christmas Cards for 1890 include one to Baron de Hirsch, who was then colonising Russian Jews in South America: "Put not your trust in Princes." In the light of the approach made to him to write "a Jewish *Robert Ellesmere*," it is interesting to note his comment in *Ariel* that "The bad example of Mrs. Humphrey Ward's *Robert Ellesmere* has already produced two imitations."

He had his contact with the Ghetto in the *Jewish Standard*, published in 1888, the year he left the Jews' Free School. He put it into *Children of the Ghetto*, where he called it *The Flag of Judah*. Harry Lewis, who was the Editor of the *Jewish Standard*, seems to have been the original of Raphael Leon in the second part of *Children of the Ghetto*. Louis Zangwill, who also worked on the *Jewish Standard*, wrote: "The scenes laid by my brother Israel in the office of *The Flag of Judah* were suggested by the easy-going régime of the Vecht period." The reference is to Aaron Vecht, who had been the manager of the *Jewish Standard*. Israel Zangwill once wrote to Aaron Vecht: "You are not in my book. I wish you were. I quite spoiled some of the scenes we have laughed over together by leaving you out. A pale shadowy figure stands indeed in your shoes, but it is not you."

Israel Zangwill spread himself in the *Jewish Standard*. He was "Marshallik," which means a funny sort of Marshal, a jesting Master of Ceremonies, and he called his column "Morour and Charousoth," which are the bitter herbs and the sweet concoction of apple and wine eaten at the Seder table at Passover. "I am continually being annoyed by people who make jokes that I feel sure

I should have made myself some day or other, if they hadn't plagiarised by anticipation," he wrote. He could also be a savage, bitter jester. As when he wrote about the conversionists, who were conducting their campaign among the Jewish immigrant poor in Whitechapel: "Embracing Christianity is good. I like fine words. Even if they don't butter parsnips, they gloss over dirty actions: and 'embracing Christianity' sounds nicer than selling one's soul." Zangwill never liked the conversionists, nor converted Jews, though he was often proclaiming his own reverence for Jesus. "Why do I feel good when I read what Jesus said?" Esther asks in *Children of the Ghetto*. In *Dreamers of the Ghetto*, published after his visit to Jerusalem, his "modern scribe in Jerusalem," who was himself, visits the Wailing Wall and meets there "amid the mourners one stately figure, who turned his face to the Scribe, saying with outstretched hand and in a voice of ineffable love—'Shalom Aleichem.' And the Scribe was shaken, for lo! it was the face of Christ."

Zangwill contributed to the *Jewish Standard* verses like the following:

> "I'm an Anglo-Jewish Quaker,
> Moslem, Atheist and Shaker,
> Presbyterian, Papist,
> Comtist, Mormon, Darwin-Apist.
>
> Though I reverence the Mishna
> I can bend the knee to Vishna,
> And I'll be debarred by no Din
> From adoring Thor and Odin.
> Moses, Paul and Zoroaster
> Each to me is seer and master.
>
> I believe, from Jove to sun-god
> All at bottom cover one God.
> Him I worship—dropping Gammon—
> And his mighty name is MAMMON!"

He printed "A Jargon Lecture by Israel Zangwill," written in the Germanic Yiddish that was known as Congress-German.

> "Maine Shvester, Brueder, Greener
> Hoert zu mein vernunftig wort,
> Dass von dieser Grand Mediner
> Man shikt nich euch wider fort.
> Euch ist es genug bekannt
> Aingland's nich ein Yiddish Land.

Drum sollt ihr euch streng bestreben
Wie Ainglishmen zu leben.
Kuggel mussen sie vergessen.
Christmas Pudding sollt ihr fressen.
Wenn sie meine worte hoeren,
Wird sie sein geehrt, geschatzt.
Ainglishmanner vet ihr weren,
Und in Parliament gesetzt."

Which translated runs something like this:

My sisters, brothers, greenhorns,
Listen to what I say,
That from this mighty country
They don't send you away.
You must surely understand
England is not a Yiddish land.

You must make an effort then
To live like Englishmen.
Kuggel you must now forget.
Christmas Pudding you must eat.

If you listen to what I say
You will be respected in every way.
You will become Englishmen,
And will sit in Parliament then.

So though Zangwill no longer lived in the Ghetto—he lived in
Bloomsbury with Dr. Eder, and his mother was living in Victoria
Park, which was just outside the Ghetto—he maintained his contacts with the Ghetto, and with the ways and language of its people.
It was not however the same thing as living in the Ghetto, the old
day-by-day observation through participation in its life. He had to
return, as Esther did in his book, "to refresh her knowledge, she
made expeditions for the purpose." He too must have fancied
when he returned and heard "the great school bell ring"—that
"the last ten years were a dream. Were they indeed other children,
or were they not the same? *What* had he in common with all this
mean wretchedness? Why everything. This it was with which his
soul had intangible affinities."

Zangwill kept making such expeditions in after years. In 1915,
during the war, Zangwill went to Whitechapel to take the chair
at a meeting at the Jewish Working Men's Club, which he described
in *Children of the Ghetto*, the scene of the Purim Ball, and he said

that on his way to the Club he had passed through the Lane and a man thinking he was a stranger offered to show him round. A friend told me that in 1925, when Zangwill was running his disastrous theatrical season at Laurence Cowen's Fortune Theatre, little more than a year before he died, he saw Israel and Louis Zangwill get off a bus at Aldgate and walk along the Petticoat Lane side of the road, looking into the shop windows and talking as he overheard when he passed of changes that had taken place. No doubt, like all adults revisiting the scenes of childhood they found, as he said in *Children of the Ghetto*, "great magic shops where all things were to be had, had dwindled. But gradually, as the scene grew upon her she perceived that it was essentially unchanged."

Yet it was changed. When his father and mother came to London they were among the earliest immigrants from Russia and Poland. When he was a boy Whitechapel and the Lane were a stronghold of the Dutch Jews. Dutch Jews, Zangwill knew, were regarded by the Polish and Russian Jews as hardly Jews. Jacob de Haas, who became Dr. Herzl's secretary and his biographer, and then in his American period was the devoted follower and biographer of Judge Brandeis in his Jewish and Zionist activities, was one of those Dutch Jews who lived in the London Ghetto. He has written, "the Zangwills were among the first Russian Jews to invade our quiet English Square. These strange neighbours stirred my childish imagination. The boys were attending the Jews' Free School" (he attended the school of the Sephardic or Spanish and Portuguese Community, to which most of the Dutch Jews belonged). "Curiosity prompted me to cultivate these older boys."

There had been few Polish and Russian Jews in London before the wave of immigration from the lands of the Russian Czar after the oppression and pogroms of 1881, and then Israel Zangwill was eighteen. His father had come to London over thirty years earlier. When Zangwill came back in 1891 to study the Whitechapel Ghetto the tide of Jewish immigration from Russia and Poland had been flowing into it for ten years, and it had become a Russo-Polish Ghetto. He found Imber there, the poet who wrote the Zionist anthem Hatikvah, and Dayan Reinowitz, the father-in-law of Dayan Susman Cohen, and others who went into his book. He found Jewish trade unions and the beginnings of the pre-Herzlian Zionist movement.

Lucien Wolf claimed in his Israel Zangwill Memorial Address when Zangwill died in 1926 that he "was in a large measure responsible for the proposal" which was made to Zangwill "to write a big Jewish novel for the newly-started Jewish Publication Society of America," "a Jewish *Robert Ellesmere*."

Robert Ellesmere had been, Professor Ifor Evans wrote, looking back on it fifty years later, "swept by topical interest into every drawing room in England." Mrs. Humphrey Ward, its author, was everything that Israel Zangwill was not. She was the granddaughter of Arnold of Rugby, the niece of Matthew Arnold, and aunt to Aldous and Julian Huxley. She lived in Oxford, among scholars and intellectuals, when it was a battleground of thought, under the conflicting impacts of Newman and Darwin. *Robert Ellesmere* won praise from Henry James, Pater, Gladstone and Oliver Wendell Holmes, who said "*Robert Ellesmere* is I think beyond question the most effective and popular novel we have had since *Uncle Tom's Cabin.*" It was also an emancipating novel, seeking to liberate not the enslaved Negro, but what she considered the enslaved mind of man. A woman of advanced and liberal thought, she explained that she "wanted to show how a man of sensitive character, born for religion, comes to throw off the orthodoxies of his day and to go out into the wilderness, where spiritual life begins again. And with him I wished to contrast a type no less fine of the traditional and guided mind—and to imagine the clash of two such tendencies of thought, as it might affect all practical life, and especially the life of two people who loved each other"—the doubting clergyman and his believing wife. The book sold nearly a million copies. Sermons were preached on it. Robert Ellesmere's Settlement, which is described in the book, led to the establishment of a real settlement in London, the Mary Ward Settlement which is in Bloomsbury, and is named after her. "The scheme," she wrote, "had taken shape in my mind in 1889, and in the following year I was able to persuade Dr. Martineau, Mr. Stopford Brooke, Lord Carlisle and a group of other religious Liberals, to take part in its realisation." The idea was similar to that which led to the establishment of Toynbee Hall in Whitechapel, in memory of Arnold Toynbee. Mrs. Humphrey Ward related the two. "A spirit of fraternisation was in the air, a wish to break down the barriers that separated rich from poor, East End from West End." Mrs. Humphrey Ward knew Whitechapel. She visited it, and spoke of her absorbing interest in its Jewish population, and with Mrs. Sidney Webb she saw something of the sweating evils. She touched the Children of the Ghetto with the hem of her skirt, but she did not see their life, which Zangwill had lived.

She came from outside to the "dingy" East End streets, with "the recently erected blocks of workmen's dwellings, occupied by the workers in its innumerable floors." Zangwill could describe what was going on in these innumerable floors, with the knowledge and intimacy of one who had lived and been brought up on one of those floors. Mrs. Ward's parish was a little further away, among the dock labourers. Her book is that of the philanthropist, who wants to missionise, to bring the latest Christian thought to the poor, and art and culture, to bring it from outside, and to lift it up, to reform. Robert Ellesmere's "knowledge of the poor and of social questions attracted attention," and Robert "delighted in Society so far as his East End life allowed." Mrs. Ward's book is solid and earnest, and well-constructed, but not grown. Zangwill's book grew out of his inner self.

Zangwill confessed that "Mrs. Humphrey Ward—she terrifies me—she and her big cheques and her big country house and her big books. I shrink, I dwindle. One rises from a novel of hers distinctly older. In the middle of the second volume one wonders how many aeons ago one was reading the first. What a cosmic panorama, the town, the country, the mansion, the cottage, Belgravia, artisans' dwellings, the Fabian Society, the Houses of Parliament, the slums. Prodigious! In *Robert Ellesmere* the best things in it are not those the writer intended for such." Zangwill considered the idea suggested to him of a "Jewish *Robert Ellesmere*," and dismissed it. "A Jewish *Robert Ellesmere*," he wrote, "would have settled but the least of his problems when he decided to abandon the orthodox creed."

Years after, when Zangwill was an established writer and President of the Jewish Territorial Organisation, "which," he said, "was occupying all my energies," he wrote to a number of English writers, to ask them their opinion about the work of this organisation, "which had begun negotiating for a territory under British protection," to "build up an autonomous Jewish State out of the refugees from Russian persecution—a State which will likewise attract a number of prosperous and idealistic Jews." Mrs. Humphrey Ward replied that "in the midst of the horror and pity excited by the appalling news from Russia your appeal for the foundation of a new Jewish colony under the British flag naturally touches one's sympathies very strongly. I do not see how English sympathy can be wanting, however uncertain and difficult the scheme may appear to those unacquainted with the great practical problem involved. The present situation is a disgrace to Europe, and nothing venture nothing have." Mrs. Ward added her willingness to send a subscription to the funds. "Mrs. Humphrey Ward is the only writer," Zangwill commented, "who speaks of subscribing to the funds of the Ito as well as to its dogmas."

Zangwill came in touch again with Mrs. Humphrey Ward during his work for the women's Suffrage movement. Mrs. Humphrey Ward was a leader of the opposition to women's Suffrage, and Zangwill often spoke of her in this connection. "Mrs Humphrey Ward and the Anti-Suffragists may be trusted to continue tireless and ever-inventive." "Not even Christabel Pankhurst is a keener politician than Mrs. Humphrey Ward."

Both *Robert Ellesmere* and *Children of the Ghetto* were published by Heinemann; Frederic Whyte, William Heinemann's biographer, speaks of "*Robert Ellesmere's* unparalleled vogue," and says that *Children of the Ghetto* was one of the books Heinemann published "with more eclat than any of the rest." In writing the biography, he said, "the two men upon whom I counted most confidently for help were Sir George Lewis and Israel Zangwill. Throughout his business career William Heinemann was on very intimate terms with the younger Sir George Lewis." Zangwill had died shortly before; "I was disappointed," Mr. Whyte wrote, "not to have secured some of Zangwill's own recollections." He added that Sir George Lewis "surprised me a little, while showing himself fully alive to Zangwill's genius and to Heinemann's admiration for it, by expressing doubt whether the two men had much in common. Heinemann he regarded as a typical denizen of his own social world; Zangwill he placed in the world which borders upon Bohemia. He could not imagine Heinemann quite happy in Zangwill's modest little flat in the Temple, or in their secluded retreat near Worthing, nor could he see Israel in his element at Heinemann's Mayfair dinner parties. As a matter of fact," Mr. Whyte declared, "Heinemann had at least as much in common with Zangwill as with Sir George Lewis. He was more of a mixer than either of them. He seems to have got on equally well with both of them." Heinemann once published a play, and Zangwill commented: "O that mine enemy had written a book. Mr. Heinemann, my publisher-in-chief, has not indeed written a book, but his play, *The First Step*, having been prohibited by the Censor, he has had to publish it in a book. The Lord Chamberlain has delivered him into my hands. Why a work of art which is unfit for polite ears may be disseminated by respectable tradesmen I do not pretend to understand. What can have possessed Mr. Heinemann to have entered the lists of authorship?" Zangwill found the play "well-constructed, simply a piece of life put down objectively"—"but imagination has not touched it with its transfiguring finger. Mr. Heinemann is a man of culture, and it is his culture alone which has made his play an agreeable variation on the stock puppet-show. It is a pity he cannot see it damned on the boards."

Mrs. Zangwill spoke of meeting Heinemann in "the crush of my wedding reception. 'You don't know who I am,' he said smilingly. But I had caught the name. 'Yes, I do,' I contradicted. 'My publisher-in-law.' " Mrs. Zangwill's feeling about Heinemann seems to have been nearer to Sir George Lewis's. "We lived chiefly in the country," she continued, "and our simple life would hardly have appealed to Mr. Heinemann."

I think Zangwill wrote his own review of *Children of the Ghetto* in the book itself. "There is more actuality in it than in *Daniel*

Deronda and *Nathan der Weise* put together. It's a crude production, all the same; the writer's artistic gift seems handicapped by a dead weight of moral platitudes and high falutin. He not only presents his characters, but moralises over them—actually cares whether they are good or bad. It is all very young. Still, what he has done is good enough to make one hope his artistic instinct will shake off his moral." It sounds like the *Athenaeum's* later criticism—"good stuff ill-digested," and like Chesterton's feeling about Dickens's *Pickwick Papers*—"all the chaotic fancies and crude experiences of his boyhood."

"How could he have missed seeing?" cries Zangwill to the reader of his *Children of the Ghetto.* "Esther stared at him from every page. She was the heroine of her own book; yes and the hero too, for he was but another side of herself translated into the masculine. The whole book was Esther, the whole Esther, and nothing but Esther." It is self-confession. Zangwill is the heroine of his own book, as Flaubert said Madame Bovary was himself. He is Esther Ansell translated into the feminine. And the hero too, for he has put bits of himself into other characters. It is in the truest sense autobiography. As Thomas Mann says that Levin in Tolstoy's *Anna Karenina* is Tolstoy—"almost altogether Tolstoy," what he calls elsewhere "the assimilation of the hero to his creator." "It is beyond the power of man to 'create' individuals absolutely," H. G. Wells declared. "If we do not write from models, then we compile and fabricate. Every 'living' character in a novel is drawn, frankly or furtively, from life—is filched from biography, whole or in scraps, a portrait or a patch-up, and its actions are a reflection upon mere conduct."

When Louis Golding published his novel *Forward from Babylon,* Zangwill reviewed it, praised it highly, and premised "an element of autobiography." Golding wrote a letter thanking Zangwill for his "generous remarks," and said: "Mr. Zangwill may or may not be right in premising an element of autobiography, but his premiss remains totally irrelevant." Golding, of course, is right. The materials matter only for what the author makes of them. Yet when we see the author's own life-blood run through his story we feel, as Zangwill felt about Golding, "that when a man can tell his own story, it may be that this is the best story that he can tell." It means not the mere narration of events, but the story of the adventures of the man's own soul, his spiritual struggles, his doubts and triumphs, his agony, his labours and his faith, and his relations with his fellow-men, with his environment, the life to which he belongs, of which he is part. "I wrote about the Jew because I know the Jew," Zangwill confessed.

Louis Zangwill told me Lucien Wolf was mistaken in thinking that he had been responsible for suggesting Israel Zangwill to Judge

Sulzberger to write his "Jewish *Robert Ellesmere.*" Dr. Cyrus Adler
claimed it was he who "in November 1890," when he visited England,
and spent "ten days or so in England, carried the message from
Mayer Sulzberger to Israel Zangwill to ask him whether he would
undertake a book for the Jewish Publication Society. This resulted
in the famous *Children of the Ghetto.*" Louis Zangwill said Judge
Sulzberger had before that himself made a direct approach to his
brother, and that Cyrus Adler had been asked by the Judge to follow
it up. Mrs. Zangwill sent me a copy of a letter that Israel Zangwill
had written to Judge Sulzberger: "Your very kind and complim-
entary letter finds me immersed in work and complaining that only
twenty-four hours have been allotted to the day. It is obvious that
unless I drop some of my work (I would willingly drop some of the
journalism) I cannot undertake anything new; and speaking quite
frankly, since we are on the brutal question of money, the temptation
to do the Jewish novel *now* would be purely pecuniary. I certainly
intend, if I am spared, to write a Jewish novel; there is one inside
me, and it must come out some day; but I had not thought of doing
it at present, as I wished to make my first appeals in more catholic
form. As for my value in dollars, to tell the truth I am rather in the
dark at present. My publishers think that *The Bachelors' Club*
being of a popular nature will do for me what *The Premier and the
Painter* did not, e.g. give me as fancy a value as an author as my
friend Jerome K. Jerome. Whether they are right or not will be
determined in the next few months. I could easily work on the lines
you have indicated—very good ones too—only I could not undertake for any amount of dollars to write a novel which would appeal
exclusively to a section. You will remember I told you something of
the kind when I had the pleasure of meeting you in London, when
you broached the subject. Behind all the Jewish details there must
be the human interest which will raise it into that cosmopolitan
thing, a work of art. I want to put my best into everything I do."

So there had been a personal meeting in London between Judge
Sulzberger and Israel Zangwill at which Judge Sulzberger had
"broached the subject." Louis Zangwill knew of this meeting, had
probably been present, as he was present at the meeting with Herzl
in their home in Kilburn three years after *Children of the Ghetto*
was published, when Herzl arriving in London drove straight to
Zangwill only on the strength of what Nordau had told him of his
meeting with the author of *Children of the Ghetto.* So much in the
direction taken by Zionism might have been different but for the
fact that *Children of the Ghetto* was written, and brought Herzl to
Zangwill. Mrs. Zangwill wrote to me that she could not believe
Lucien Wolf "invented such a story. Yet certainly neither Israel nor
Louis knew of any contact having been made through Lucien Wolf.

Israel's letter to Judge Sulzberger, as I told you, is undated; it is possible that when Israel said that he did not want to do the Jewish book at that time, but first to write one or two books not dealing specifically with Jews, Judge Sulzberger accepted this refusal and then the rest followed as Mr. Lucien Wolf described. So doubtless when Mr. Lucien Wolf suggested to Judge Sulzberger that Israel was the only man to approach he thought he would make another effort, which this time succeeded."

Certainly, the prime mover in the matter was Judge Sulzberger. Zangwill said that of *Children of the Ghetto* Judge Sulzberger "was the main, if not 'the onlie begetter.' " "Perhaps in time we shall in England get a Jewish Publication Society like that which America possesses, and which primarily stimulated me to write *Children of the Ghetto*," Zangwill told the Maccabeans when they gave him a dinner for the publication of *Children of the Ghetto* (when he was too poor to have any dinner no one gave him dinner, he used to say. When he could afford to have all the dinners he wanted everyone was giving him dinner.). "I was extremely reluctant to write the book just now," he added, "but Judge Sulzberger overcame all my objections, and in the end the Society gave me *carte blanche* to write exactly what I pleased. I hope it will not repent its bargain."

There is a dedication to Judge Sulzberger in one of the editions of *Children of the Ghetto*, where Zangwill says: "It was under your direct impulsion that I wrote this Novel; but for you it might have been postponed till *manana*. Not that you are in any wise to be held responsible for its contents; there are, I feel sure, things you would wish away, altered, or added. But you are of the few who—assuming him honest—would leave the artist to himself."

In 1908 Judge Sulzberger explained what had happened. "In 1889, the Jewish Publication Society of America was beginning to work, but found it almost impossible to get English writers of Jewish books. In the *Jewish Quarterly Review* of London of 1889 there appeared an article entitled 'English Judaism.' Struck with its thoughtfulness and power, I asked my colleague, the late Rabbi Marcus Jastrow, to read it and give me his opinion whether he had not found the man who could write a worthy work on Jewish philosophy. His judgment was in the affirmative, and he asked me if the signature 'Israel Zangwill' was a pseudonym. All that I could answer was that I had never before heard the name. When in the summer of 1890 I spent some vacation weeks in England I fell in with the distinguished coterie, that subsequently formed the nucleus of the club called 'Maccabeans.' Zangwill was among them, and though I was waiting for a chance to sound him on the question of a book for the Publication Society, the opportunity did not at once present itself. Before the moment arrived I learned something of what he had already written, and in answer to my request he sent me next day one of his little stories that had been printed in a Jewish Annual. It was *Satan Mekatrig*, and it proved to be a real Mekatrig, for after reading it I decided to say nothing about a philosophical treatise. Somebody else would be found for that, while I felt that for what Zangwill could do, the second man would not soon appear. The upshot was that he finally wrote *Children of the Ghetto* and entered upon a prosperous career of literary workmanship which has placed him in the forefront of British and Jewish imaginative writers." Judge Sulzberger concluded by praising Zangwill, "the poet, the novelist, the playwright, but first and foremost Zangwill the man."

Years after, in 1925, when Mrs. Ben Zion Halper came to England on behalf of the Jewish Publication Society, and delivered an address to the Jewish Historical Society of which Zangwill was then President (he died in his year of office), Samuel Gordon, the Anglo-Jewish novelist, suggested to Zangwill the formation of an English Jewish Publication Society. Zangwill wrote to Gordon: "I am afraid you do not realise that unless I lie low at present, as my doctor insists, I may break down altogether. I have not the mental energy to grapple with the question of an English JPS. You are perhaps not aware that although America has three and a half million Jews and many millionaires to draw on, its JPS. is very hard up. I have often thought that the Arthur Davis Publication Society might be the nucleus of a larger effort, but that would mean a financial campaign for which I have not the strength. Possibly, too, the new literary and dramatic societies could be roped into a united effort. But all this needs constructive work, and if I had any strength just now I should want to devote it to a revival of the Ito now that the Jewish Colonisation question has, despite Zionism, become more insistent than ever."

It is characteristic of Zangwill that in the last year of his life, when he was desperately ill, he was thinking of a revival of the Ito and of Jewish immigration and colonisation needs.

How far is *Children of the Ghetto* autobiographical, drawn from Zangwill's own life, and from people he knew? "When George Eliot ceased to draw from models and fell back on intuition and her library, she produced *Daniel Deronda*," Israel Zangwill wrote, in the tone of one who would say—"And look at *Daniel Deronda*!" "Life is in the eye of the observer," he said. Take a number of people to the same street and, he went on, "each would take away a different impression from the street. All novels are written from the novelist's point of view. They are his vision of the world. The literary portrait involves both mind and body, practically a biography." Yet Zangwill thought "a real character could appear in a work of fiction and be entirely unrecognised either by the reader of the biography or its subject." "It is a common fallacy of inferior novelists," said

Zangwill, "to think their characters are living because they are drawn from people they know. They have not had the talent to transfer the life from the world of reality to the realm of art. Helen of Troy might sit to me, and I would only turn out a daub."

Rabbi Barnett Cohen, son of Dayan Susman Cohen, who was Moses Zangwill's friend, wrote to me in 1942, that the original of Zangwill's Reb Shemuel was his grandfather, known in the East End as Reb Yankele, Rabbi Jacob Reinowitz, also a Dayan, whom his father succeeded at his death in 1893 (Dayan Susman Cohen's son-in-law, Dayan Lazarus, too became a London Dayan). The same claim was made by his brother, Rabbi Harris Cohen, in an article in the *Jewish Chronicle*. "A frequent visitor to the house" (his grandfather's house), he wrote, "was a young Free School teacher named Israel Zangwill. He was then writing his *Children of the Ghetto*, and my grandfather was the prototype of Reb Shemuel in his novel."

Rabbi Barnett Cohen told me of other people in the Ghetto he recognised in Zangwill's book. Some, he said, were "occasionally overlapping." "I lived in the East End of London from 1893 till 1905," he said, "and was well acquainted with Simcha the Baker (Simon Cohen), Harry Lewis, of Toynbee Hall" (both of whom I also knew), "and Joseph Levy (the German Jewish 'astronomer' who lived and traded in Houndsditch). All three, and also the Cabbalist, Mr. L. D. Zimmer, were very well known in East London, where everybody recognised them as the originals of Zangwill's characters." The Jewish Encyclopedia agrees. Its note on Nathan Zimmer says: "He was one of the original founders of the Federation of Synagogues, and is the original of Karlkammer in Zangwill's *Children of the Ghetto*." Zimmer was a contributor to the *Jewish Standard*, Zangwill's *Flag of Judah*. He was in business in Bevis Marks as an "importer of foreign goods and toys," but his description is given "as scholar, pietist and gematriaist." Zangwill defines gematria as the mystic, numerical interpretation of Scripture. His Karlkammer was an adept at that. He "fervently believed that endless meanings were deducible from the numerical value of Biblical words." Karlkammer like Zimmer was "a businessman and had to earn his living by day."

I have been told that Rabbi Goodman Lipkind, who wrote the note on Zimmer in the Jewish Encyclopedia, served Zangwill for some of the characteristics of Joseph Strelitski, the Rabbi who emigrated to America. But he also drew on Harry Lewis, a Toynbee resident who became a Liberal Rabbi. Zangwill put things in Strelitski's mouth that the real Lewis said, like "modernise Judaism," to bring "the world the religion of the golden future." It found its way afterwards into Zangwill's play *The Next Religion*. Harry Lewis certainly was the original of Raphael Leon, the Editor of the *Flag of Judah*, as Melchitzedek Pinchas, the Hebrew poet was Naphtali Herz Imber, the author of *Hatikvah*, who described himself as the National Hebrew Poet. I have a copy of a book of Imber's poems, *Barkoi*, inscribed by Imber "To the famous Israel Zangwill as a token of gratitude by the author." I also had passed on to me by Mrs. Zangwill a booklet by Imber, this time describing himself as the "Jewish National Poet, author of *Barkoi* etc. called *Topics of To Day in the Talmud*. Reprinted from *The Jewish Standard*," and dedicated "To the Learned Men of All Nations," where he seeks to show that all things, even the most modern, like the methods discovered by Pasteur, and the Eiffel Tower, are in the Talmud. Zangwill has him in *Children of the Ghetto* proving "that Virgil stole all his ideas from the Talmud." Zangwill with characteristic audacity makes his Pinchas "pungently merry over" the real Imber's "pretensions to be the National Poet of Israel." In a later sketch he made Pinchas claim that he had created Zangwill, and commented: "Mr. Pinchas must be mistaken. We were under the impression that Mr. Zangwill created Mr. Pinchas."

There has been some controversy since Imber died over his identity with Pinchas. When he died it was taken for granted; though one writer in the *American Hebrew*, while saying "Imber was familiar to everybody as the prototype of Melchitzedek Pinchas" added Imber "strenuously denied that Zangwill had used him as a model and mentioned vaguely some 'low-down, beggarly chap in London as the real original.' " A story was told that he had in a frenzy of anger thrown a salt cellar at an actor playing Pinchas in a Yiddish dramatisation of *Children of the Ghetto* who had sedulously studied his mannerisms and tricks of speaking.

When Imber died, most of the obituary notices spoke of him as the original of Melchitzedek Pinchas. Twenty years later, when Bialik published in Palestine in 1928 a collection of Imber's Hebrew works, it was remarked that "in London he was associated with Israel Zangwill, who immortalised him in *Children of the Ghetto* as Melchitzedek Pinchas." Mr. Philip Cowen, who as Editor of the *American Hebrew* had Imber among his contributors—"he contributed a series of articles on the Talmud. He could find mention in the Talmud of anything under the sun: electricity, the bicycle, telegraphy etc."—wrote: "It was difficult to separate Imber from his bottle, much to the chagrin of his friends. He was always half-seas over. Whenever we wanted to find him it was only a question of which favourite tavern he was in. I shall never forget a Zionist meeting at Cooper Institute where Imber was thrown out because he was in his cups and had been obstreperous. I had come late to the meeting and he buttonholed me outside. As the meeting was about to close and they sang 'Hatikvah,' he opened the door and leered through the crack and said to those about him: 'They may kick me out, but they must sing my song.' "

Judge Mayer Sulzberger befriended Imber and, said Mr. Cowen, "he soon became absolutely dependent upon the Judge's bounty." It was said that Zangwill interested Sulzberger in Imber. When Imber died, Israel Zangwill wrote an obituary note in the *Jewish Chronicle* where he said: "His last years were redeemed from misery by the generosity of that Prince in Israel, Judge Mayer Sulzberger."

Zangwill placed Imber, when he added: "In him Jewry has found its Villon." Once in his diaries he had after a talk with Imber put him down as "a scoundrel," "a fraud," "thoroughly 'link' and immoral." He said that "Imber's passion for Palestine was purely literary. Imber had in fact far less belief in things than Heine, with whom his capacity for self-mockery and for flouting his own dis-eases would suggest a comparison. That such a poet should have written 'Hatikvah,' the Marseillaise of every Zionist meeting through-out the world, is one of the innumerable ironies of Jewish history." "To the general herd of well-to-do Jews," Zangwill concluded, "Imber was only a shabby, disreputable and unsavoury outcast."

Simon Woolf, the Labour leader, is modelled on Lewis Lyons, who organised a tailoring workers' association in London in 1884, when Zangwill was twenty and a teacher at the Free School. He was still active in the East End trade union and Labour movement in 1912; he died in 1915. George Lansbury, writing in his autobiography in 1935, of the great dockers' strike, paid a tribute to "Lewis Lyons, a working-class tailor who helped very materially to create the atmosphere which led to the dockers' fight." "The Jewish Journey-man tailor owes more to him," the *Jewish Chronicle* wrote, "than probably to any other man. His career was devoted to the betterment of the conditions of the Jewish working man."

Zangwill knew the Jewish workers in Whitechapel. "Their demands were moderate enough," he writes in *Children of the Ghetto* —"hours from eight to eight with an hour for dinner and half an hour for tea, and they might earn a pound a week." Zangwill knew not only the hard lot of the sweated worker. He also knew the life of those who "in Parliamentary Blue Books, English newspapers and the Berner Street Socialist Club were called sweaters." He gives a picture of the life of the sweater Belcovitch. "Black bread and potatoes and pickled herrings made up the bulk of the everyday diet. No one could accuse Bear Belcovitch of fattening on the entrails of his employees. The furniture was of the simplest and shabbiest. Bear Belcovitch had lived in much better style in Poland. But he brought nothing away except his bedding, and that was pawned in Germany on the route. When he arrived in London he had three groschen and a family." Zangwill knew these people, the Children of the Ghetto. He saw the sweater as a human being, as much as the sweated worker. It is not without knowledge of what really happened that he brought Simon Woolf, the Labour leader, to work in Mr. Belcovitch's workshop. "Woolf, who had a wife and six children, was grateful to Mr. Belcovitch in a dumb, sullen way."

They were terribly hard times in the East End of London then. At a literary dinner of the Maccabeans held in a West End hotel, Zangwill told them of the poverty among the East End Jews. He read an extract from a newspaper of the day reporting an inquest on a child that had died of starvation in Whitechapel. The father was a tailor, a new immigrant, who could not yet speak English.

Simcha the Baker, one of the men Rabbi Barnett Cohen recognised in *Children of the Ghetto*, played a great part in the movement to help the immigrants. Mr. Cohen Lask, whom Zangwill mentions in his *Watchman, What of the Night?* called him a man with "a great Jewish heart." He had been a bricklayer in Poland. In London he became a baker. "He is known all over the East End, to young and old, rich and poor as Simcha Baker—simply and lovingly without the Mr. or Reb. He held open house at the Synagogue which he founded in Back Church Lane. The Synagogue was on the first floor; the ground floor was given up entirely to a bath (mikvah), whose free use was of great practical value to the homeless Jews. His whole house was full, a centre where the forlorn and helpless found a haven, without the questioning and investigating which was the routine of the institutions. For many years he housed these unfortunates until the Jews' Shelter was established. "It was Herman Landau, himself an immigrant from Poland," according to an old *Jewish Chronicle*, "who had started it. In a private Beth Hamedrash in Back Church Lane" (Simcha Baker's Synagogue), "he found a number of refugees huddled together for want of a lodging. Its proprietor kept a bakery, and allowed the wanderers to rest their weary limbs on his sacks. Mr. Landau started the Shelter in one room in Great Garden Street, which soon came to occupy the whole house. At the outset the movement encountered considerable opposition from the Jewish Board of Guardians, to whom the fear presented itself that it would attract immigrants to this country, and congest the overstocked labour market."

Zangwill pictured the Jewish immigrant poor in his book in a series of vivid episodes, less a novel than a group of tales about the same people, connected and bound together. I am inclined to agree that Zangwill's book is not an architecturally designed structure on the grand plan, a story with what Henry James said of Mrs. Humphrey Ward's *Robert Ellesmere*—which Israel Zangwill was told to take as his model, but did not—"a great sweep." I think some of the best novels are short stories on a common theme, worked together. It was the way Zangwill did his best work; his unity was that of spirit, not of architecture. Mrs. Zangwill felt it too. "I have always felt," she wrote, "that he was a short story writer rather than a novelist, great as some of his novels were."

It may be that Zangwill's "Jews never were on land or sea," as one of his critics recently said. But he did not intend his Jews to be on land or sea. He exaggerated their characteristics, and their speech and their thought, he blended and composed, he obliterated and he invented. It is all larger than life, more real than reality. He lifted his men and women to poetry and immortality. They are not Jews on land or sea because they are universal. And they have not suffered from the changes that have taken place in Whitechapel, in the East End of London, in London as a whole since Zangwill wrote, any more than Dickens's people have suffered from the changes that modern life has effected. The details of life in the East End of London have changed, but the human spirit is the same. I went there a hundred times during the past year; I spent a whole morning or a whole afternoon there. I did not know that Zangwill had observed the same thing before I was born, when I wrote in an article about the London Blitz in 1942, that when I visited the East End after one of the big air raids, and found whole chunks of my boyhood and adolescence destroyed, I saw in the familiar streets old Jewish men and women, who had miraculously grown in the twenty-five and thirty years to look exactly like the old Jewish men and women whom I had seen there in my boyhood, so that I blinked and wondered if they were not the same—they were so exactly alike, even to their gait, even to their intonation. Re-reading *Children of the Ghetto* I found that Zangwill had written a year before I was born: "Were they, indeed, other children, or were they not the same? Surely those little girls in print frocks were her class-mates!" And "the shambling men and women" were the same. "It was essentially unchanged." Was it only because here I had, like Esther Ansell, like Israel Zangwill, "insensibly absorbed those heavy vapours that formed the background of my being?" There are less of them than there were in Zangwill's time, and in my boyhood, but they look and talk and behave the same, even if their English speech is more native. This is the permanence of life, and Zangwill has given it form and colour and words and lasting reality.

His scenes spring to life. The Soup Kitchen no longer plays that part in the life of the Ghetto that it did when I was a boy, but when I read that first chapter in *Children of the Ghetto* I see the cooks in white caps and blouses and I smell the steaming soup; just as though Bumble's workhouse has passed I can still see Oliver Twist asking for more.

The book grows as you read it. Some of the scenes have shifted to Golders Green and Maida Vale and Clapton and other parts of London; instead of riding in a gig the well-to-do drive their automobiles; Mr. Belcovitch, the sweater, runs a big model dressmaking factory, or has chain stores all over England; Simon Woolf, the Labour leader, sits in Parliament and in the next Labour Government may be a junior Minister, but their talk and their ways are very similar to the talk and ways of their parents and grandparents whom Zangwill depicted in *Children of the Ghetto*. He painted life that goes on still to-day.

In many places, in many parts of London, in Whitechapel and Stepney as much as in Hampstead and Stamford Hill, in Manchester and Glasgow, Leeds and Cardiff, in New York and Chicago, Montreal and Winnipeg, Johannesburg and Cape Town, Melbourne and Sydney (were not Malka's eldest a magistrate in Melbourne, and David Brandon from the Cape?), that life goes on. In many homes, in garrets or in rich villas or comfortable flats and apartment houses, the Children of the Ghetto sit, as Zangwill did, "in faith and hope," and their young children, like little Esther Ansell, sit with their hearts "full of a vague tender poetry, and penetrated by the beauties of Judaism, which please God, they will always cling to, looking forward hopefully to the larger life that the years will bring."

Zangwill knew the Ghetto life that he painted. He knew the workmen, the poor, the destitute, the humble and the arrogant, the domineering and the mad. He knew the idealists who read the *Arbeter Freint, The Friend of Labour*, as he translates it, the Day of Atonement pork eaters, embittered and inverted idealists, who were "disgusted with the commercialism of the believers," and he knew the pious Jews of the Sons of the Covenant, who "lived and died, sternly disciplined by voluntary and involuntary privation, hemmed and mewed in by iron walls of form and poverty, joyfully ground under the perpetual rotary wheel of ritualism, good-humoured withal —and a man is not half bad who does three fourths of his duty." He knew, before Herzl came to London to see him and they started the Zionist movement, the Zionist solution of the Jewish question which was proclaimed by his Holy Land League. Strelitski's speech is almost an anticipation of Herzl's pamphlet *The Jewish State*. "Give us back our country; this alone will solve the Jewish question. Between Russia and India there will be planted a people hating Russia for her wild-beast deeds. And if we cannot buy it back with gold, we must buy it back with steel."

Yet when Mendel Hyams is faced with the practical problem, where to go with his wife, Zangwill sends him to America, and it is the sweater, Belcovitch, who gives him the money for the fare. "And so Mendel and Beenah sailed away over the Atlantic." "The idea that Jews will go only to Palestine is a myth, which the presence of this great audience alone makes ridiculous," Zangwill told the big mass meeting of the American Jewish Congress in the Carnegie Hall in New York in 1923, more than thirty years after *Children of the Ghetto* was given to the public.

Zangwill's book is an epic of the Jewish immigrant, an epic of modern Jewish life, of the life of masses of people who form part of the life of Britain and America and South Africa and Canada and Australia, who live among their fellow-citizens, and whose story is told in that book, *Children of the Ghetto*, which brings to its readers an understanding of these people, and human sympathy for their problems and their ways of life.

Chapter III

THE ZANGWILLS

MOSES ANSELL in Israel Zangwill's *Children of the Ghetto* is his father, Moses Zangwill, as surely as Mr. Micawber was Dickens's father. Louis Zangwill often spoke to me about his father, Israel Zangwill's father and his own. Once after Louis had died, Mrs. Zangwill, Israel's widow, wrote to me: "I liked your account of Louis Zangwill's recollections of his boyhood. Certainly their father did peddling in this country." "My father as he went about the country was subjected to endless sneers and persecutions because he was a Jew. I wanted to end this situation of my people," Israel Zangwill said in New York in 1923. Louis Zangwill remembered their father as a packman going about the country peddling his wares; he told me the villagers respected him and looked out for his coming.

Israel Zangwill tells us in *Children of the Ghetto* that when Benjamin Ansell had to write an essay at school on travelling, he said one could travel with sponges, lemons, old clothes and so on. "To Moses," he writes in the book, " 'travelling' meant straying forlornly in strange towns and villages, given over to the worship of an alien deity and ever ready to avenge his crucifixion. It meant praying in crowded railway trains, winding his phylacteries round his left arm and on his forehead to the bewilderment or irritation of unsympathetic fellow-passengers. It meant living chiefly on dry bread and drinking black tea out of his own cup, with meat and fish and the good things of life utterly banned by the traditional law, even if he were flush. It meant passing months away from wife and children, in a solitude only occasionally alleviated by a Sabbath spent in a Synagogue-town. It meant being chaffed and gibed at in language of which he only understood that it was cruel. Once when he had been interrogated as to the locality of Moses when the light went out, he replied in Yiddish that the light could not go out, for 'it stands in the verse that round the head of Moses was a perpetual halo.' A German who happened to be there laughed, and translated the repartee, and the rough drinkers pressed bitter beer upon the temperate Jew. But as a rule, Moses Ansell drank the cup of affliction instead of hospitality. Yet Moses never despaired nor lost faith."

Louis Zangwill told me that story of the repartee to the old quiz —where was Moses when the light went out?—and said it had been his father who had made the repartee. It became one of the large stock of Zangwill family stories on which Israel Zangwill drew, and to which his brothers and sisters kept adding, as they heard or saw things which they thought would interest him for his writing. I remember Louis, who was a writer himself, making a note of a story someone had told us, and saying Israel would like it. Mark Zangwill did the same. Leah brought Israel the name Shosshi Shmendrik, which she had come upon, and Israel used it in *Children of the Ghetto*. Louis was not so bitter about his father's treatment by the villagers. He told me he took his own pots and dishes and cups with him as he travelled about the country, because he scrupulously observed the Jewish dietary laws about mixing prohibited foods with the kosher, or using the same utensils which had been used for prohibited foods, and said "everybody was very kind."

It was a hard life. Leah, who was a year older than Israel, used to speak of their hardships when they were children. The family waited for weeks for a postal order to come from the "traveller" and land-lords threatened to bundle them out; their mother's hands were worn to the bone slaving for her little ones. Israel never forgot it, and made it up to his mother when he could. "Her early life, until her children grew up, had been cruelly hard, and her children tried to make it up to her in after years," says her granddaughter. Israel Zangwill's diaries are full of references to his efforts to make it up to his mother.

"Things improved a little later," the author of *Children of the Ghetto* records, and Louis Zangwill who was younger, may not have remembered the worst poverty. But the family was still very poor. "It was as a hawker that Moses believed himself most gifted. Yet there was scarcely anything cheap with which he had not tramped the country," the chronicle of Moses Ansell relates. "Unquestionably Malka," who would in real life have been Moses's wife, Israel's mother, and not her cousin, as in the book, "was right in considering Moses a Shlemiel. He always made loyal efforts to find work. His versatility was marvellous. There was nothing he could not do badly. He had been glazier, Synagogue beadle, picture-frame manu-facturer, cantor, pedlar, shoemaker, circumciser, professional corpse-watcher, and now he was a tailor out of work."

"I have been out of work for three weeks," Moses Ansell ex-pounds. "What my silly cousin could see to marry in you," is Malka's answer to that exposition, and she goes on to suggest to Moses that for five shillings, which she gives him, he can get a basket of lemons, and sell them at a halfpenny each in the Lane, and make a profit, and "be able to live till the tailoring picks up a bit." I knew people who lived in and around the Lane who remembered Moses Zangwill selling lemons there, "verra good lemans, two a penny each." Jacob de Haas, a neighbour as a boy of the Zangwills, speaks of Moses Zangwill as a sponge pedlar, and says the family "touched the bottom of poverty."

In Israel Zangwill's birth certificate Moses Zangwill was put down as a glazier. That is the profession of old Hyams in *Children of the Ghetto*. Old Hyams too went travelling with his wares in the country, and said that if necessary he can always fall back upon glaziering.

Moses Zangwill had dreamed of ending his days in Jerusalem. His son, Israel Zangwill, was able to make that dream come true. So he went to Jerusalem, where he lived till his death in 1908, praying and studying and fasting, living abstemiously, doing good deeds, helping others with all he had. When he felt he was dying, he wrote to Israel. "I have had alarming news from my father, who lives in Jerusalem. He regards himself as dying," Israel Zangwill said in a letter to Joseph Fels in April, 1908. "I have abandoned my walking tour, and mean to get over to Palestine." But his father died before he could leave England.

Zangwill's mother had refused to leave the children, to go with her husband. I have been told that interpreting this as desertion, he sent her a "Get," a Jewish religious divorce, from Jerusalem. The records of the Jerusalem Jewish Community of that time, which are not completely preserved, have no confirmation of that. Old inhabitants of Jerusalem remember Moses Zangwill—Isaac Ben Zvi, the President of the State of Israel, Judge Gad Frumkin, Shalom Schwartz, Isaiah Press and others. They speak of him as Moshe ben Israel, Moses son of Israel, the name by which he went in Jerusalem. He had named his son after his own father, who had been Israel Zangwill in a small Latvian town Ravinisek, from which he himself had been snatched by the Czar's men to be conscripted into the Russian army as a lad, to escape to England, and give the world his son, Israel Zangwill.

In some of Israel Zangwill's correspondence there is reference to another Israel Zangwill, who was still living in Latvia, in Preili, probably a cousin, the son of a brother of his father's, who had also named his son after their father.

Moses Zangwill died on Ab 12th. 5668, and is buried on the Mount of Olives in Jerusalem. His last wish was that a Moses Zangwill bed should be endowed in the Bikhur Cholim Hospital in Jerusalem, and this was done by an unknown donor. He could hardly have left the money for it himself, for he gave all he had away. The donor was no doubt Israel Zangwill.

Louis Zangwill told me that though his father was never a Rabbi, people called him Rabbi, and he officiated at all family celebrations, as Old Hyams in *Children of the Ghetto* officiated at the Redemption of the Son. Moses Zangwill was "also a scholar of sorts," said Dr. Israel Abrahams.

The American Jewish Year book in 1926, the year Israel Zangwill died, said in its obituary article that "his parents had come to England from Ridenishki, a small town in Latvia, sixteen years before he was born." Mark Schweid, who translated *Dreamers of the Ghetto* into Yiddish, repeated in his foreword the legend that "Zangwill's parents came to London from the Lithuanian town Rishiniki." Jacob de Haas thought it was doubtful if Israel Zangwill was born in London. "The probabilities," he said, "are that he was born in Poland—his name is Polish—but if he was born in England it must have been Southampton or Portsmouth, for he lived in one of the South Coast towns as a child." His birth place has been variously reported as Bristol (where Louis was born) Portsmouth and Plymouth. He was born, as he always said he was, in London, a Cockney, within sound of Bow Bells. I have seen his birth certificate, which he kept among his papers. His parents did not come to England from Ridenishki in Latvia, nor from Rishiniki in Lithuania, nor from Poland—and the name Zangwill is not Polish but Hebrew, and means "ginger," what Imber means in Yiddish, the name of the poet who became Melchitzedek Pinchas in *Children of the Ghetto*. Or it might mean any kind of spice, in Hebrew-Chaldean. Mr. Myer Davis told a story in 1899 of passing a Synagogue, and hearing one of a knot of bearded Jews saying "Zangwill." "Then someone called out, 'No, three Zangwills.' We know three Zangwills," reflected Mr. Davis, "Israel, Louis and Mark." It turned out that these Zangwills were not members of the Zangwill family, but simply "three nails of spice" that were needed for a ceremony, "sweet herbs and spice." In Israel, I heard people speak normally in Hebrew of using Zangwill, meaning ginger.

But Israel Zangwill might have become known as Israel Samuel. He recalled that when he first came to the Jews' Free School, and was asked his name, the teacher mishcard and wrote him into the register as Israel Samuel. "And Samuel it was," said Zangwill, "till some time later, when I had summoned up the courage to protest."

Zangwill's parents did not come to England together, but separately, as children, not knowing of each other, from separate places, he from Latvia and she from Poland, both countries then under the rule of the Russian Czar, but as distant from each other as London from Vienna, or Paris from Warsaw. The father came to England sixteen years before Israel Zangwill was born, in 1848, the year of the big Revolutions in Europe, which brought a stream of refugees to England, including Dr. Schiller-Szinessy, who preceded Schechter and Israel Abrahams as Reader in Rabbinics at Cambridge, and was a contributor to Zangwill's *Jewish Standard*. But it was not the events of 1848 that brought Moses Zangwill to England. There are variants about his age when he arrived. Louis Zangwill told me his father was twelve when he landed in England. Mrs. Zangwill queried the age, thinking he must have been older, because he had already been in the Russian army. But he had been a Cantonist, one of the boy soldiers seized for the Russian army in those years, and some of those boys had been only eight or nine when they were press-ganged. The intention was not only to make life-long professional soldiers of them, which many became, but to take the children away from their Jewish homes, and in the barracks, under iron military discipline, make them forget their Jewish origin. The younger the children were, the more easy this was. Moses Zangwill was a stubborn boy, with that scrupulous regard for Jewish observance to which he adhered all his life, and he was put in solitary confinement because he refused to eat the pork served out in the barracks. An officer took pity on the boy, helped him to escape, and he found his way to England.

He arrived one of "the destitute alien in Great Britain," the name Arnold White used in his book *The Modern Jew*, also published by Heinemann in 1899, seven years after *Children of the Ghetto*. "Vessels are boarded at Gravesend by a customs officer and by a medical officer at the Port Sanitary Authority. Two lists are made out. One of these lists includes the names of those who are usually revolting in appearance," Mr. White wrote, asking for the exclusion of those "who are so filthy on arrival as to be recorded." In the same book Arnold White has a reference to "Mr. I. Zangwill's masterly book *Dreamers of the Ghetto*." If his idea of exclusion had been enforced when Moses Zangwill arrived, a young lad who had made his way penniless across Europe, fleeing from tyranny and military brutality, the masterly books by Mr. I. Zangwill would never have enriched English literature.

Jacob de Haas described Moses Zangwill afterwards as "a fairly tall, slightly bent figure, with long black hair and side-locks, extremely religious, one of that harsh, unyielding type that read well in books but made life difficult."

With the customs officer and the medical officer who boarded the incoming boat came Rabbi Shapiro, attached to the Great Synagogue in Dukes Place. He made a practice of meeting the immigrants, to help them by interpreting and putting them in touch with relatives and friends. Young Moses Zangwill knew no one in England, so Rabbi Shapiro took him to his home in Finsbury Circus, and kept him like his own son.

Moses Zangwill was born in Latvia, in Rivenishki, or Ravinisek, or Ravenishki, a small place where the Zangwills had lived quietly for generations, without causing any stir. There were Zangwills still living there when the Second World War began. Mrs. Zangwill

ISRAEL ZANGWILL

Portrait by Sickert

had kept in touch with them. "There used to be some Zangwills living in Russia," she wrote to me in August 1938, "whom my husband helped from time to time. I wonder if you happen to know anyone living at Preilos, Latvia, from whom I could get information about a family called Zangwill living there who claim to be relations. I sent them a little money. If these Zangwills are really relations and really in desperate need, I do not feel justified in doing nothing further for them; that is why I want to get into touch with some responsible person in Preilos." I was able through a friend to find someone in Preili (the official spelling). In January 1939 she again asked me if I could help her to trace the family, because she had not heard from them, and I obtained information that they were still in Preili. "I am so much obliged to you for making inquiries about the Zangwills in Latvia," Mrs. Zangwill wrote to me. One of the Latvian Zangwills wrote from Preili (in English) to Mrs. Zangwill: "Will you please let me know when your late husband died, as I want to know exactly the day. According to our religious ritual I want to bring a candle to the Synagogue and to do the praying."

Mrs. Zangwill wrote to me again about the Latvian Zangwills at the end of April 1939: "I sent the Latvia Zangwills a small gift, but I feel it is absolutely inadequate, and will be of no permanent help. As I simply cannot go on indefinitely sending them money, I feel one must try to put them on a better footing. If your friend does go to Preilos I should be so much obliged if he would look them up and let me know how matters really stand, and if he can suggest any permanent improvement in their status."

Zangwill's mother, who was born Ellen Hannah Marks (on Israel Zangwill's birth certificate, where the surname is spelled three times consistently Zangwiell, she is Anna, formerly Marks) was born at Zemiatchy or Siemyatche, a village near Brest Litovsk, on the road to Warsaw. Her father was a "Yeshuvnik," a farmer and miller. She came to England with a young cousin also named Ellen. The two Ellens, unlike Moses Zangwill, had relatives in England, an aunt in London, Mrs. Solomons, and an aunt in Plymouth. After they were married, Moses and Ellen Zangwill settled in Plymouth, and it was on a visit to London that Israel was born in London. Leah, the first child, and Mark, the third, were born in Plymouth. Afterwards they moved to Bristol, where Israel went to school, and Louis was born. Then they settled in London, where Dinah, the youngest child, was born, and Israel and the other children attended the Jews' Free School.

Ellen Marks stayed in London with her aunt, Mrs. Solomons. The other Ellen went to Plymouth, where in time she married a man named Cowen.

Why do I speak of Zangwill's family connections, his parents, his brothers and sisters, his cousins? Because I believe, as Havelock Ellis said, that to understand a man's life and work you must know something "of his origins, of his family and his early upbringing."

Ellen Marks's side of the family produced two notable men, besides her own Zangwill children, Dr. Eder and Joseph Cowen, who were not only Israel Zangwill's cousins, but also his intimate friends till the end of his life. I knew them both. Joseph Cowen was a bluff English-looking man, who became "one of the first English Jews who joined the Zionist movement," as Paul Goodman noted in his history of Zionism in England. He was a close friend and associate of Dr. Herzl, and was for some years President of the English Zionist Federation. "I went to the First Zionist Congress because my friend Zangwill told me I could just as well spend my holidays in Switzerland as anywhere else," he explained. "I am an Englishman born and bred, and to my shame, be it said, never concerned myself with my brother Jew until after the First Zionist Congress, to which you took me," Joseph Cowen wrote in a letter to Zangwill.

Despite their personal friendship Joseph Cowen and Israel Zangwill disagreed about Zionism. Cowen remained in the Zionist Organisation when Zangwill founded and led the Jewish Territorial Organisation (Ito). In 1915 Cowen said that when crossing to France he had talked to Lloyd George, who was on the boat. Lloyd George asked him if Zangwill was still an active Zionist. Cowen replied that Zangwill was busy with his own organisation, the Ito. This was before Lloyd George became Prime Minister, and head of the Government which issued the Balfour Declaration that led to the establishment of the Jewish State in Israel. In 1923, five years after the Balfour Declaration, Lloyd George was in America, after Zangwill had said that political Zionism was dead and Britain had not kept faith regarding her promise to the Jewish people. "Did Mr. Zangwill really say that?" Mr. Lloyd George exclaimed. "I cannot understand him. He is such a good old friend of mine. I don't agree with him. Political Zionism is not dead. Zangwill is a great writer, but not a great diplomat." Zangwill's retort was: "Diplomacy is only a second-rate job. The job of a writer is to tell the truth."

The two got together again in 1925 when Lloyd George took the chair for Philip Guedalla's lecture on "Napoleon and Palestine" to the Jewish Historical Society of England, and Zangwill as President of the Society, "introduced" Lloyd George. "The idea that he needs introducing to you by me is funnier than anything in Inge or Belloc," Zangwill said. "As regards the 'Jewish National Home,' which we owe to his premiership, I have no hesitation in saying that the Palestine Mandate would have been handled far more satisfactorily had he remained in office." He paid Lloyd George a much greater tribute: "He stands with Pitt as one who took the helm of England's fortunes in a terrible gale and brought her safely to port." He did not live to see Winston Churchill, whom too he knew, and in whose utterances, he said, he found "genius," repeat that great achievement. (He had found Churchill show "imaginative sympathy with the British-Jewish scheme" of his organisation, the Ito.)

Philip Guedalla, the lecturer on that occasion, seems to have been irritated by Zangwill's mannerisms in introducing Mr. Lloyd George as his Chairman. He found "something there in the alarming presence of a distinguished man of letters (now deceased) who was quite convinced that he and he alone must take the chair that evening. Nothing would turn him from his purpose. He led us, quacking faint protests, to the platform, grabbed the middle seat, and launched into a carefully prepared discourse complete with literary ornaments and a verse quotation. We were quite powerless to check his flow; and when it ended (and I had said my piece) Mr. Lloyd George was permitted to make the speech of the evening in the modest guise of a vote of thanks. Since that night I have always understood why the abundant hair of public men is nearly always white."

Mr. Guedalla forgot that Israel Zangwill's abundant hair was also white. Not everyone shared his opinion about the merits and demerits of Lloyd George's and Zangwill's speeches. G.K.'s Weekly for example wrote a few days later about "two speeches made recently at the same lecture, which was by Mr. Guedalla, at the Jewish Historical Society. The first was by Mr. Israel Zangwill and was quite admirably to the point, at any rate, up to a point. The second was by Mr. Lloyd George, and was perfectly pointless. Mr. Zangwill, being a mere man of letters is interested in his own ideas as ideas, and therefore enjoys stating them. They may not always be exactly the same; but they always obviously belong to the same man. The poet is not always posing like the politician; and Mr. Zangwill has always had something of the poet. But the point is that he states quite perfectly what would be the real case for the real Zionism. Mr. Zangwill's ideal at least is clear and rational enough; it is a self-contained Jewish nation, with Jews selling to Jews and buying from Jews, or employing Jews and working for Jews according to whatever social structure a community of Jews may desire for themselves and for nobody else. But it has no sort of relation to the state of things which Mr. Lloyd George described, so far as he described anything."

But Mr. Guedalla was right when he suggested that Zangwill was given to seize his occasions, to ram home what he wanted to say. "Why is Mr. Zangwill Allowed?" he once quoted a newspaper headline asking, and answered it: "Because he will not be silent," and underlined the word "silent."

He went about doing it, for instance to Stephen Graham, when he was defending Russia's treatment of the Jews during the First World War. He reprinted in his book *The War For the World* two letters he published at the time in *The Nation*—"Mr. Graham's whole article reads like an expansion of the dialogue which I put into the mouth of the Jew-baiting Russian baron in *The Melting Pot*. It is literary mine-sowing, and in a friendly area, for 350,000 Russian Jews are now fighting for their fatherland."

Zangwill went to a Stephen Graham meeting at the National Liberal Club, which according to a newspaper report of the time "was a very lively meeting, with Mr. Zangwill at the head and front of the liveliness. He has never been seen to better advantage." I have a letter Zangwill sent to Dr. Jochelman about this "onslaught I delivered on Stephen Graham before a very crowded audience. Unfortunately as the speaker of the evening he had the last word and made many mis-statements, some of which I challenged on the spot, but as this is a breach of etiquette, and the last speaker is permitted endless lies, I may have done as much harm as good by my interruptions. Still, there can be no doubt that as a whole I damaged Stephen Graham's credit with the National Liberal Club."

Zangwill would not be "silent," as he confessed. And at poor Mr. Guedalla's lecture he had come armed, using his official position as President of the Jewish Historical Society to which the lecture was delivered, to say a number of things both about British policy in Palestine and about some remarks that Dean Inge had made about Jews, that he considered "dangerous at a moment when antisemitism rages throughout the world." He had found that the Dean "persisted it was a joke," and "insisted that Jews had no sense of humour. I said I at least had never been accused of lack of it, but that I saw no wit in his observation. However, the upshot is that the Dean has empowered me to express to this great meeting his regret for his remark, which he never dreamed could be taken seriously." Zangwill had to get that off his chest, Mr. Guedalla's lecture and Mr. Lloyd George's chairmanship notwithstanding. It is all in the printed report of the meeting, published by George Allen and Unwin, "verse quotation" and all.

Dr. Eder, Zangwill's other cousin, was also brought into Zionism and Jewish activity by Zangwill. "I have often wondered how an assimilated internationalist in theory," Dr. Harry Roberts wrote of him, "he quite reconciled the nationalism in Zionism." He was a member of the Ito's expedition to Cyrenaica, and wrote a report for the Ito on the possibilities in Brazil. When the Balfour Declaration came Zangwill got him delegated to the Zionist Commission as the representative of the Ito. His appointment was not regarded favourably by many Zionists because of his Ito past. But Eder became a trusted Zionist leader. In 1932 he wrote of an offer made to the Ito "many years previously of some land in Brazil. Whatever a pioneer dreamed of was to be had in this favoured country. The stories were all quite true. There was only one thing lacking; the land was not in Palestine." When Eder died Dr. Weizmann said: "It is the loss of my best friend."

But Israel Zangwill remained the man Eder admired most. The memoir published after Eder's death says: "This intimate comradeship with Zangwill lasted without a personal cloud of any kind to the novelist's death in 1926." It was "the closest and most formative of Eder's male friendships in its influence on both men. With Joe Cowen there was a happy trio." "When exactly Joseph Cowen joined us I do not remember," Eder wrote of that trio, "but it was right in the early days of our friendship, and we three have remained intimate friends to this day."

D. H. Lawrence, who was a great friend of Eder's, urged him to "cease to be a Jew, and let Jewry disappear—much best." But Zangwill's influence was greater. "My friend whose body I saw cremated a few weeks ago," Eder said of him, "lives on through tens of thousands he had touched by his writings and his speech, and these in turn will reach out to others through the years to come. All life unto the remotest future becomes profoundly altered by an Israel Zangwill. This is immortality."

Eder was the son of Esther Solomons, the daughter of Ellen Marks's aunt, in whose house she lived until she married Moses Zangwill. The two girls had been brought up together. His father was a businessman, who came to London, Louis Zangwill told me, from Colombia, in South America, where the Eder family had been established. He was connected with a steamship line between South America and England and Eder spent some time in this business. Then he decided to do medicine, and got his cousin Louis Zangwill, who was then eighteen, to tutor him in mathematics. Afterwards, as I said, he was one of Freud's pupils, and the first and for a time the only doctor to practise the new therapy in England. In 1897 Eder went to South Africa, and the following year to Colombia, where his father came from, and where he had an uncle. He "landed 3,000 miles up the Amazon, £5 in my pocket, a shot gun, a few empty cartridges, some powder and shot, butterfly net and a cyanide bottle, surgical instruments and a Burroughs Wellcome tabloid case, a small kit bag." He was back in England in 1903. There was a revolution in Colombia while he was there, and he did work as a surgeon after the engagements. In England he served for a time as a medical officer in a mining village and then in practice in Commercial Road, in Whitechapel.

I remember Dr. Eder, heavy of build and a little bear-like,

F

completely un-Jewish looking by the standards of what is assumed to be the "Jewish type." Dr. Harry Roberts wrote of him: "He was of Russian-Jewish descent, but I always gave him as my example of that rare bird in England—the characteristic ideal Englishman." For all his being an "internationalist in theory," as Dr. Roberts said of him, he reconciled this not only with Zionism but also with a sturdy British nationalism and Imperialism, as did also his cousin Joseph Cowen, and Israel Zangwill too, who said that he had been "brought up in the Jingo faith."

Louis Zangwill too, who had emerged as a boy from Galton's composite photograph as the "Jewish type," grew to look like a distinguished English country-gentleman. He was so "un-Jewish" looking that when his sister Leah Zangwill died, and he went to the Synagogue to arrange for the funeral they could not believe that he was the brother. Yet Louis was attached to Jewish life and Jewish study and thought, and wrote much about Judaism. English ways and language and literature and interests had made the White-chapel-bred son of the Jewish immigrant pedlar, Moses Zangwill, with his long black hair and side-locks, an English gentleman, but retaining his love of Judaism and his interest in Jewish study and Jewish life.

He was a man who loved to sit alone, writing by night, "in these rooms over the Temple Gardens, in my tall armchair carved after the style of William and Mary, among my few cherished treasures." He loved and understood art better than Israel Zangwill did, and better I think than their painter-brother Mark Zangwill, who illustrated some of Israel Zangwill's books. He lived for a time in Paris and in Holland, about which he wrote a good novel, *A Drama in Dutch*. At one time he was a rising young writer under the pen-name "Z.Z.," and people were talking of the way the two Zangwills were occupying space in the review columns. But like Mark he lost ambition, and the two younger Zangwill brothers preferred to drop out of public notice. "What has become of Mr. Louis Zangwill?" Mr. L. G. Burgin asked in *To Day*. "At one time he did a good deal of literary work. Is it that he fears to clash with his elder brother?" There may be something frustrating to a man in being somebody's brother. "Too few remember Disraeli's father or Zangwill's brother," Louis Golding wrote.

In his early ambitious and successful years, before Israel Zangwill's marriage, Louis had been closely connected with his older brother. "Louis knows better than anyone who were my husband's friends in the 'nineties of last century," Mrs. Zangwill wrote to me. He was in the swim with them, together with Israel. Louis explained that he "was seduced from becoming a somebody by art and a roving freedom." There is self-revelation in an article Louis Zangwill wrote about a book on Japanese prints, of which he had some fine examples in his rooms: it had "succeeded in striking old chords in me, and stirring up memories and pictures other than Japanese. Pictures of bare gaunt studios in the Latin Quarter, warmed by enthusiasm rather than by the ungainly stoves. Figures of good Americans and good Saxons and good fellow-Semites rise before me; all compact of intellect and temperament, affecting the Gallic atmosphere and the Gallic cut of beard and dress. And endlessly we disputed fiercely the eternal question of the how and the what. Was Art how or was Art what? And in those early 'nineties all the clever ones—the present writer included, of course—went solid for 'the how.' Yet I hold to-day that in art the what is the thing. Such is my position though I do not know in the least by what route I arrived at it. Our minds have a way of working out things without consulting us."

Louis was disquieted by the growing acceptance of new methods in literature, and he found the position of a novelist like himself "most difficult." "He cannot go back to older types of work," he wrote. "He must suit the world of to-day with its outlook of to-day or be entirely silent." So he was, if not entirely, very largely silent.

Louis had also been a pupil teacher at the Jews' Free School, and had followed Israel into journalism and novel-writing. He told me how he came to write his first book. Israel was already famous, and there had been a gathering at their house of writers and artists. Israel had expected his young brother to be overawed, but he wasn't, and said that if those people could write books so could he; that night he wrote and produced by the morning the first chapter of his *Drama in Dutch*. In those years of his youth he was introduced to a gushing lady who when she heard his name asked if he was related to Israel Zangwill. "My brother," he said. "And do you write as well?" "Better, Madam."

Louis never married; he preferred his bachelor rooms in the Temple. He did not care to make new friends or to meet many people. So long as he had his competence he was happy in his quiet rooms in the Temple. But life dealt hard with Louis Zangwill, as it did with all the Zangwills, towards the end, financially and in health. The First World War in 1914 seems to have been the ebb point in their fortunes. I have a letter Israel Zangwill wrote to a friend in 1914: "I am afraid that you, like everybody else, must have been badly hit by the war. For my own part I looked to the American stage to recoup my losses here, instead of which my American managers have gone bankrupt with many thousands of my royalties. However, I have cheerfully written another comedy."

American and Canadian investments went badly for Louis and for the other members of his family. But it was after the American slump of 1929 that things became serious. He wrote to me: "I am personally in the full teeth of the economic gales—my investments have always been almost entirely in America." In 1932 he wrote to me: "Substantial revenue which my family got from one of the best U.S.A. sources has, after holding out finely, at last given way."

I knew Louis Zangwill when he lived in his rooms in the Temple. I don't know why he remained unmarried. He was a finely-built, handsome man, well-bred, beautifully-spoken, kind and considerate. He told me he had known and been fond of several women, but never enough to want to marry them. His trouble was no doubt in his character, which he diagnosed himself as a little "too isolated from the common run—a trifle too haughtily perhaps—living with his head in the skies. Why not come down to warm human earth sometimes?" He tried, but he confessed he was "of too severely intellectual a habit, too austerely aloof from ordinary humanity."

Israel Zangwill confessed that he would have liked to have been a student, a University Professor. Louis too would have liked it. "Fellow of a Cambridge College—now that would have been my dream."

In his last years Louis had trouble to make ends meet. He rarely spoke of it, and never to any but the most intimate friends. He sometimes lived on less, by the standards of the time, than his father, the pedlar, the packman, had earned, when they lived in Whitechapel. I thought of the packman when Louis used to come to my house in Highgate from the Temple, walking all the way, with a haversack strapped to his back. It was his favourite way of carrying his things, whether he walked to his sisters in Kilburn or to me in Highgate, or if he went tramping in the country. He sometimes went to the Authors' Club in Whitehall, where he kept up his membership, and came back to tell me that all he had heard was a list of several more old friends who had died. He made a brave effort to keep up appearances. He was the only one of the brothers who cared about dress. He had been a dandy in his day, with formal clothes, white waistcoats, silk hat and ebony knob stick. He was careful with his clothes to the end. But his treasured possessions, his carved oak, his silver, his Japanese prints, even his books became a burden, because he could not pay the rent for the room they needed, or for their storage. He disposed of most of them. He sold as much as he could, and gave some away. Someone he met in my house had said he was looking for a second-hand set of the Jewish Encyclopedia. He wrote to me next day to ask if I would tell him that he had Israel Zangwill's set, which he would sell. He had Israel Zangwill's working library, the books Israel used in his work, marked and annotated. Because he had no place where to keep it he loaned the library to the Mocatta Library of the Jewish Historical Society; it was destroyed when University College in Gower Street, where the Mocatta Library was housed, was bombed during the war.

He sighed with relief when the burden of paying for the housing of the books and other things he loved was lifted from him. He had learned that the fewer possessions a man has, he said, the easier it is to live—as much as a man can carry in a pack on his back.

Ambition, eagerness to do things, to succeed, to be talked about, he said, was foolish. He met a novelist in my house, who had just achieved a best seller and was unashamedly crowing over it. Louis kept quiet, but when he had gone he said to me: "I have known men who made bigger successes with their books, and to-day even I can't remember their names."

In 1936 he became ill, and could not come to me as often as before. "I wish you lived round the corner—in Utopia, it may be —so that I could show myself and explain how things are," he wrote to me. "I've had a request from Vienna to prepare the main formal speech for their Zangwill evening" (it was the tenth anniversary of Israel Zangwill's death, and memorial meetings were held in London, Vienna and other places). "Of course, I can't do it. Perhaps you could." "I had a heart attack," he wrote to me. "It caught me in Whitehall." (Going to the Authors' Club, there.) "Up to three and a half years ago I could tramp thirty miles nicely, but going up the stairs at the Temple one day I found I had become broken-winded and since then the one and only real trouble has been the central pump, which accounts for all else." His financial difficulties also continued, and he saw "difficulties and perplexities lie ahead."

In 1937 he went to live in Holland-on-Sea, with his sister, Dinah. He wrote to me in 1938: "A hefty youngster like yourself could not possibly realise the difficulty entailed for me in the simplest task. I have been reduced to an unimaginable state of absence of energy. Had I been in London at the time of Joan's" (my daughter's) "birthday I should have wished to join in, but I was not so much as able to move at all." A few weeks later I had a letter from his niece Primrose: "I had hoped to be able to tell you that my uncle was improving, and for this reason I deferred writing. I am sorry to tell you that he died yesterday, just after lunch, very suddenly. He had been growing increasingly feeble, as you know. We have lost a great friend, and you were his greatest."

Louis had been a brilliant chess player in his youth, and showed promise as a mathematician. In 1887, when he was seventeen, and a teacher at the Jews' Free School, he was winning prizes in chess tournaments. The *Morning Post* that year, published the game by which he won in a London tournament, and said: "Mr. Zangwill has this year made his mark in the City of London Chess Club as a brilliant and original player." Later he dropped chess-playing, because he found it took too much of his time and intellectual energy. He did brilliantly in mathematics. Towards the end of his life he presented his mathematical books to the Hebrew University in Jerusalem, and wrote to me that there were in the collection many rare and otherwise unobtainable works.

Louis Zangwill was present when Dr. Herzl arrived at the Zangwill home in London in November 1895 to say, as Israel Zangwill afterwards reported it: "I am Dr. Herzl. Help me to build the Jewish State." "His brother," Herzl recorded in his Diaries, "sat close to the fire, reading a book. Both made the impression of freezing Southerners who had strayed to the Ultima Thule." "I remember even my book—Matthew Arnold's *Essays on Criticism*," Louis explained, "which I was enjoying with a sense of rest and leisure, having just sent a book of my own to press after months of heavy labour. He was quite glad to find two auditors instead of one, and we settled round the fire. When we talked things over after Herzl's departure, the point arose whether it was an ideal or even right thing to contemplate the creation of one more political unit with boundaries and barriers of its own. While my brother conceived the utmost admiration for our visitor and was moved by the conception of an autonomous Jewish State, he had yet the whole weight of his spiritual outlook in general on the modern world to contend with. However, from the beginning, my brother was not without a certain faith in the possibility of Herzl's success."

By 1903, Louis had withdrawn from any active part in Jewish affairs. He spoke of "Anglo-Jewry clinging to the curious make-believe that the Ghetto and itself are of diverse derivation, and so continuing to despise its most honourable association—that Ghetto, which even the emergence of the Rothschilds has failed to ennoble. Anglo-Jewry will pay for a fire to warm its hands," he said, "but not to purge its soul."

He found himself increasingly out of touch and out of sympathy with his later world. "As I awake daily to a world grinding harshly in the economic process," he wrote, "so do I awake to the contemplation of a world which, in all further aspects is more unlike the sort of world I could contemplate with a full-spirited interest than it has ever been in my previous life-time. I have never been an optimist, in the sense of believing that we have been placed in the best, easiest and happiest of all possible schemes. The world, even at the best I have known it, in days when I could feel more akin to it, equally seemed to me as nothing else than essentially raw material. It was as if God had said to man: 'I give you only raw stuff. By transmutations of raw material, both without and within you, shall you live.'"

He saw the Jewish spirit at work in the world. "We may most simply recapture the spirit," he said, "in those pages of the Hebrew prayer book where are gathered the blessings for the varied occasions that may daily present themselves. Here we find a very jubilation of life—a spontaneous lyric appreciation of earth: joy in the fruits of the tree, the vine and the field; enchantment in the fragrant odours of barks, plants, fruits and spices; exaltation at the sight of stars, mountain, desert, sea and rainbow."

Moses Zangwill's life and teaching went deeper into his children than they had at first realised. Here perhaps is to be found the explanation of Israel Zangwill's life-long nostalgia for that religious Judaism to whose glorification he was continually going back from his rationalism and secularism. "The pious Jew's last words of prayer at night are: 'The Lord is with me and I will not fear,' " Louis Zangwill once wrote to me, quite in the spirit of his pious father. "If I may make a little midrash of my own, that means: 'I shall not fear, even though the Lord is with me. I shall not fear even though He is close to me—I shall not fear even in the presence of the Lord! So shall I fear him without fear!' The saint of the future will fear the Lord without fear!"

Israel Zangwill approached this feeling of his brother's and his father's in that majestic translation he made in the Jewish Festival Prayer Book of the Hymn of Glory: "I have not seen Thee, yet I tell Thy praise. Nor known Thee, yet I image forth Thy ways." And when he spoke of his father, "who did not even know that he believed, who was belief." Yet Louis felt it necessary to explain in a letter to the *Jewish Chronicle*, when his brother's religious views were under discussion, that "I disagree—and have always disagreed—more or less profoundly with some of the points of view expressed by Israel Zangwill in his writings, and in particular am unable to immerse myself exclusively in the extreme—and to me—somewhat inhuman universalistic position occupied by him. Fortunately, my brother's practice diverges in this respect from his formal thinking."

Ten years before Israel Zangwill was born in Whitechapel a girl was born in Portsea. Her name like that of his mother, was Marks. Her father too was a Jewish immigrant, also a pedlar. Her daughter, Mrs. Ayrton Gould, who became a Member of Parliament and the wife of the English poet and critic Gerald Gould and mother of the English artist, Michael Ayrton, kept the "licence for a hawker trading on foot" granted to Levi Marks, her grandfather, on 10th January 1860. Speaking at a meeting in the House of Commons I attended in 1935 she said, "my own grandfather was a Jewish-Polish refugee." Mrs. Gould's aunt, her mother's sister, Marion, married another Jewish immigrant, who came from France, also an observant Jew who, for a time, taught at Jews' College, London. When he died in his ninetieth year in 1904 the *Jewish Chronicle* wrote that he had "the simplicity of the Ghetto belief without questioning." His name was Alphonse Hartog. He wrote articles about Jewish communal affairs, and he translated into French Zangwill's short story, *The Sabbath Breaker*, which appeared in 1902 in *Le Temps*. Sir Philip Hartog, of London University, Israel Zangwill's friend, and for a time associated with him in the Ito, was one of his sons. His eldest son, Numa Hartog, was the first Jew to be Senior Wrangler—in 1869. His evidence before the Select Committee of the House of Lords, that he could not as a Jew become a candidate for a Fellowship, contributed to the passing of the Universities Test Act. Another son, was Professor Marcus Hartog.

Phoebe Sarah Marks, "afterwards to make her mark as Hertha Ayrton," as her biographer, Evelyn Sharp writes, married a widower, Professor W. E. Ayrton, F.R.S., and became step-mother to his young daughter Edith. In 1895, Mrs. Ayrton met Israel Zangwill at the house of her sister, Mrs. Hartog, and invited him to meet her husband, "who shared her admiration of his books." The result was that her young step-daughter, Edie, and Israel Zangwill "were great friends for some time before they became formally engaged"; they were married in 1903, when Zangwill was approaching forty.

There was a storm of protests against Zangwill's inter-marriage. Zangwill answered: "My wife who has the same Jewish ideals as those with which you credit me, was the child of parents who were not Christians, and was brought up by her father's second wife, the brilliant Jewish scientist, who is believed to have been the original of Mirah, in George Eliot's *Daniel Deronda*. Judaism is spiritual, but you appear to have forgotten the message of Moses." In her biography of Mrs. Ayrton Evelyn Sharp says: "It is often stated that she was the 'original' of Mirah in *Daniel Deronda*, but this assertion requires some modification. The probable truth is that the character was planned before her arrival on the scene. But George Eliot was then engaged in writing *Daniel Deronda*, and Hertha Marks, with her Jewish background and her pride of race, with her attractive Jewish personality, and her interesting way of singing or chanting the old Hebrew hymns she had learnt from her mother—she told a friend much later that once, under the influence of chloroform, she repeated these Hebrew hymns—must have provided just the touch of local colour that the novelist would find extremely useful, even if she had already planned the scheme of her book." In one of her letters to Israel Zangwill Mrs. Ayrton wrote: "The longer I live, the more convinced an agnostic I become, the more certain it seems that we know and can know nothing about the beginnings of things or their cause." Yet when the *Jewish Chronicle* referred to her as "a Jewess but not a co-religionist," Mrs. Ayrton got the paper to publish a statement that she had "never exchanged the faith in which I was born for any other." Israel Zangwill, in his "Watchman, What of the Night?" speech, spoke of her as "that distinguished Jewess, my wife's step-mother, Mrs. Ayrton." The relationship between Mrs. Ayrton and her step-daughter, Mrs. Israel Zangwill was described as "exceptionally happy."

While the other Miss Marks, Ellen Hannah Marks, who was to become the mother of Israel Zangwill, was living with her aunt, Mrs. Solomons, and her cousin Esther Solomons, who became Dr. Eder's mother, Moses Zangwill was living with Rabbi Shapiro, who was a friend of Mrs. Solomons, and a neighbour in Finsbury Circus. Moses Zangwill attended Rabbi Shapiro's classes at the Great Synagogue Beth Hamedrash, studying Talmud and Rashi. This was the life that would have suited Moses Zangwill. He would have loved to be the perpetual student, common at that time in Eastern Europe, spending his days and nights in the Beth Hamedrash, studying Talmud and Rashi, deriving no livelihood from it, but engaged in the pious exercise, praying and studying the sacred writings, while the wife earned the family living. "It is good to think that their passionate prayers brought them the happiness that a grim world refused otherwise to offer them," his son Louis Zangwill wrote of this kind of Jew. Israel Zangwill pointed out, "This focusing of all knowledge upon the Law did not lead to the mental poverty the irreflective reader might imagine." "Jewish education was like all Jewish life, Jewish religion."

It was a book that brought Israel Zangwill's parents together. Mrs. Solomons asked Rabbi Shapiro to lend her a book, and he sent young Moses Zangwill to take it round. That was their first meeting. They were married in 1861 at the Great Synagogue, in London (Duke's Place), by the Chief Rabbi, Dr. Nathan Marcus Adler.

The marriage certificate gives the date as 6th February 1861, the bride being Ellen Marks, in Hebrew Hannah Bath Mordecai (on Israel Zangwill's birth certificate she is Anna Zangwiell, formerly Marks) and the bridegroom Moses Zangweil, Moshe ben Israel. In the Hebrew Register at the Great Synagogue the name is spelled Zangweil. In the English Register it is Zangwiel. So the variations are Zangweil, Zangwiel, Zangwiell and Zangwill, which became the accepted form, though Israel Zangwill once produced another variation, Zangwell. In Tel Aviv where there is a Zangwill Street they spell it on the name plate with one "l."

It is difficult to say what their early married life was like. Louis could only guess that it was as hard as he remembered it in his childhood. There may be a clue in what Zangwill says about Mendel Hyams and his wife in *Children of the Ghetto*. The wife "did the housework unaided," while he "fell back on his religion, almost a profession in itself."

But the Hyamses were "a silent couple." Mrs. Zangwill could not have been silent, even at first. Louis described his mother as a very active woman, and rebellious. He said that she had guts. And no great religious piety. He called her a real pagan. A correspondent in the *Jewish Chronicle* once suggested that there must have been heated religious arguments in the Zangwill home. The domineering cousin Malka in *Children of the Ghetto* spoke to Moses Ansell something in the way that Mrs. Zangwill must have spoken to her husband, Moses Zangwill. With all her competence and brilliance, the old lady was a Tartar, and living with her must have been hard for Moses Zangwill, who wanted a quiet life, prayer and study. But always there was a softening of the voice when she had to tell him with a despairing gesture that he was a saint. She respected him no doubt, but she had no patience with his ineffectualness, with his being a Shlemiel, luckless and unachieving. The word Shlemiel must have been heard quite a lot in that poor household. When Israel Zangwill got out his first printed booklet, *Motso Kleis*, he gave the author's name as Ben Shlemiel, the son of the Shlemiel.

When Dr. Eder wrote that he "would like to counter the legend that seems to be springing up that Israel Zangwill's early boyhood was passed in penury and want. Nothing of the sort," he was thinking of a later period, when the boys were grown and earning a living. Though Zangwill's mother was his mother's first cousin, and the two had been brought up in the same home, they had not been much together since their marriage, for the Zangwills had gone to Plymouth and Portsmouth and Bristol, and when they came back to London they did not re-establish their relationship. Eder's mother married well. He was born in Endsleigh Gardens, in Bloomsbury, and their home was comfortable and bourgeois, while the Zangwills were poor and living in Whitechapel. Eder could not have known that the story of the Ansells taking soup from the Soup Kitchen described in the first chapter of *Children of the Ghetto* was the actual experience of the Zangwill children.

Old Mrs. Zangwill hated being reminded of their old poverty. Israel Zangwill noted in 1889, "one of the worst experiences in my life, mother taking a remark by Mark as a reflection on her past; she had donned bonnet and shawl to leave the house."

Zangwill's birth is everywhere stated to have been on 14th February 1864. Mrs. Zangwill once wrote to me that something I had sent her bore "by happy chance the date February 14th, the birthday of my husband." In fact Israel Zangwill was born, according to his birth certificate, on 21st January 1864. He "adopted" 14th February. He explained how he came to fix on 14th February in his foreword to a book called *This Is My Birthday*, by Anita Bartle, published in 1902. "I never had a birthday," he wrote. "When a young lady requested me to stand and deliver my birthday, I fell back upon the truth. She replied that if a man had no birthday it was necessary to invent one. With all my heart, I replied. One might at least commandeer a day on which no celebrity had planted his flagstaff. It appeared that more than one day was going abegging. It seemed an incredible negligence that the fourteenth of February should have remained unoccupied. St. Valentine's Day is the very day for a novelist."

Mark Zangwill started brilliantly as an artist and writer. He was spoken of as a coming artist. He had good notices. His painting, "The Student," which looks like a portrait of his father, and hangs in his son's house, was said when it was exhibited, to "merit the closest attention. Mr. Mark Zangwill is hardly less clever with his brush than are his two brothers with their pens. Wolmark, Rothenstein and Zangwill may be regarded as the founders of a new Jewish school of painters in this country." Then suddenly he decided that it was not worth while, and he sat back and looked at life, and did little. "Where will it get you?" he said to Wolmark, "always working, covering canvases? No one cares."

Unlike Louis, Mark married, and had a son, Louis Zangwill, who has a son of his own. But he kept his marriage secret. The family did not know till he died. He continued to live at the family house, where his mother and his sisters Leah and Dinah lived, at least most of the time. "The house at Kilburn Priory was taken for Dinah when she married," Mrs. Zangwill wrote to me. "Two or three years later the house at Elm Tree Road was given up and Mrs. Zangwill and Leah went to live with the Horns." (Dinah and her husband.) "Mark Zangwill lived there intermittently." I remember when the news of Mark Zangwill's widow and son first became known to the family and friends. None of us can understand why Mark concealed it, for Kitty Zangwill, his wife, is a charming person, "my favourite aunt after Leah Zangwill," Primrose says. My wife and I are fond of the lovely old lady, who has had a hard life, but has remained light and dainty and cheerfully witty. She was as Kitty Hyde on the musical comedy stage, and still dances beautifully. Her eyes sparkle with mischief under her white hair. I imagine Mrs. Israel Zangwill would have found Mrs. Mark Zangwill light-minded, and Mrs. Mark Zangwill may have been amused by Mrs. Israel Zangwill's earnestness. I expect she entered into the secret marriage with Mark Zangwill with a sense of fun, with something of the devil-may-care which she still has, and which must have been much greater when she was young. She must also have understood the difficulty of another Gentile daughter-in-law and sister-in-law coming into what was still, for all Moses Zangwill's consciousness of its Jewish shortcomings, a very Jewish household, and one where her husband had to live even if only "intermittently," while she was touring the country, a not very important stage artist, and both of them practically penniless. The old imperious matriarch, Israel and Mark and Louis's mother, would not have stood for it, and when she suspected it in her last years, and I am told finally had Mark confess it to her, she was furious, and used to taunt him about it without making her taunts so explicit that the others would understand what Mark and she knew. Mark and Kitty Zangwill's son, Louis Zangwill, is married to a Jewess, and considers himself Jewish.

Leah Zangwill her niece described as "the most unassuming and patient person I have ever met, full of humour and loving kindness. She was very small but beautifully proportioned and rounded, with masses of silvery, waving hair, twinkling brown eyes behind her pince-nez, and a mischievous smile that filled her lined, elderly face with charm. She battled against ill-health with great courage, and while she could still hold a needle she made and altered my clothes, till the last. Leah had always looked after the Zangwills, from an early age. She was a little older than Israel, and she had practically brought up my mother, who was the youngest, much younger than all of them." "Little unassuming Leah," her niece has written of her, "the eldest of the family, never thinks of herself as beautiful, but her quiet, intelligent little face beneath the masses of wavy hair has warm humanity and humour, and her brown eyes are so kindly and sympathetic. Her small rounded figure has the perfection of small Dresden china, and her feet are tiny. She and Dinah are always charmingly dressed, and few of their fashionable visitors know how patiently Leah shops for remnants and sits long hours sewing pretty dresses for her pretty little sister and herself, as well as doing all the family mending. Three menfolk to mend for, to help cater for, and a young sister to cherish, and a difficult, domineering mother to humour and obey—small wonder that Leah has not found time to marry. They would all be lost without her."

There may also have been other reasons for Leah not marrying. She had early trouble with her lungs. In 1896 Israel Zangwill wrote to Dr. Eder, then in South Africa, about a suggestion that Leah should go out there. "I have been told that by reason of its dust-storms Johannesburg is the worst possible place for Leah's lungs, whereas Natal would be favourable. However, on this point you are the best authority, as you would not ask her to come if it would kill her off. I should like her to go out if possible. I'm not myself in the best of health, though it is rather deficiency of vitality than any positive illness. I seem to have exhausted the first spurt of energy and perhaps only a very long rest or a complete change of conditions can give me my second wind."

Leah died in 1936, a few days after Dr. Eder died, ten years after Israel Zangwill. She had been ill for some years, and had lost touch with people. Louis wrote to me: "I am afraid there will not be much of a congregation. If you can send anyone along I shall be grateful. Would you telephone Dr. Yahuda, Leopold Kessler, Jochelman, Wolmark? I am worn out, and cannot write to these friends direct."

In the later years of the Zangwill menage, when they lived all together at Kilburn Priory, reduced once more to poverty, all their savings lost, Leah's needle made her largely the bread-winner of the family. She worked hard at her dressmaking, with a kindly good humour that was her character, not unlike Dutch Debby in *Children of the Ghetto*. Dinah gave music lessons. Louis and Mark were both sick men by that time, unable to do anything. Primrose's father too was ill, and things had not gone well with him. Primrose was too young to work. Israel was dead, and had died poor. And they did not know that Mark had an additional struggle to help to keep a wife and young son whose existence he kept from them.

I mentioned a letter from Mrs. Zangwill that she did not want a Life of Israel Zangwill written while she and Israel's brothers and sisters were alive. One reason was, she wrote, "that my husband stood in the position of bread-winner for his entire family. I am sure my husband would not like this fact made public, as it would hurt the feelings of his brothers and sisters. As they are all older than I am it is very unlikely that any of them should survive me."

Israel Zangwill's brothers and sisters are all dead. But Mrs. Zangwill's statement about them needs qualification. I knew Mrs. Zangwill best in the years of her widowhood, and to me she was a gentle, gracious, lovely, ethereal-looking woman, devoted to her husband's memory and work, and always very kind to me, so that I could not understand the bitterness with which Louis Zangwill sometimes spoke of her. There are family grudges and grievances in most families. He blamed her for some of the things that went wrong in Israel's life, and brought him many years of ill-health and maddening insomnia, his final collapse in physical and mental health, and led to his death.

But Israel Zangwill's ill-health started before his marriage, before he met Mrs. Zangwill. There is his letter to his cousin, Dr. Eder, written in 1896, seven years before he was married, complaining of deficiency of vitality, that he had exhausted his energy. Zangwill worked himself hard, and while Mrs. Zangwill felt that much of it was to help to keep his family, the family felt that much of it was due to the new standards of life his marriage imposed on him. Before the marriage the three brothers and two sisters had all lived together with their mother, a devoted and close-knit family. Naturally, his wife had taken Israel away. Even Israel must have felt it as a sort of desertion; for a long time after his marriage he had not the heart to take away his books from the common home. Nor is it true that the whole family, his brothers and sisters, simply sponged on Israel Zangwill. They all had their own work and earnings. Louis, Mark, Leah and Dinah were all at first like Israel pupil teachers at the Jews' Free School. Like Israel none of them continued in the teaching profession. Leah did dressmaking. Dinah was a music-teacher. But when Leah put a dressmaker's sign in the window the brothers objected and made her take it down. In the early days Dinah was also Israel's secretary, and did his typing.

Of course, Israel lived with the family before his marriage, and as he was the largest earner contributed the largest share to his mother's housekeeping account. In the whirl of his new life as a well-known writer he was often away from home, and reproached himself in his diary for "neglecting mother," and said he had "a thousand conscience pricks." He was a generous son. He maintained his father in Jerusalem. He considered himself under an obligation all the time to help the rest of the family. Even the Latvian Zangwills.

Dinah Zangwill was married in 1911 in London's most orthodox Synagogue, the Machzike Hadass, by Rabbi Werner. Israel Zangwill gave away the bride.

I first met Dinah's husband, Osias Frederick Horn, with Israel Zangwill. He had just arrived back in England from Palestine, where he spent many years. His father Frederick Horn had been one of the Palestine pioneers, one of the founders of Zichron Jacob, where there is an avenue named after him. "It is always interesting to track the source of a great river," Zangwill wrote about the beginnings of the Zionist movement. "The Horn and other pioneering families— they are the Pilgrim Fathers of the new Hebrew race. Unfortunately their descendants do not always live in Palestine."

Osias Horn had a business in Haifa, "Plant Protection Specialists and importers of chemical and organic manures, and shippers of citrus fruits." Palestine did not offer a commercial success for his enterprise, and he came home defeated. After that nothing went right. He died a sick man, in England, soon after the end of the Second World War, in which the family was evacuated from the sea coast into the rural parts of Essex. "When my father went to Palestine," Primrose told me, "he intended to have Mother and me settle in Palestine with him. But he never made good there; ill-health and misfortune dogged him. And he was not old when he died, a man of warm humanity and charm and much learning. When he talked of his travels his words burned with colour and he could hold his listeners. He had a paternal tenderness, which drew little children round him, Jewish children and Arab children in Palestine, and English children here. He had marvellous patience with them. Even Israel's children, Peggy and Oliver, who were wild and shy and inclined to run away from visiting relatives, came under my father's spell and loved him."

Dinah, the youngest of the Zangwill brothers and sisters, the last of them, died in August 1949, in her seventy-sixth year. She had been ill and bedridden for a long time. She had several strokes, which "struck her dumb, though she was left with her full intelligence and was able to express herself in writing," Primrose wrote to me. "The doctor gave her up, but I nursed my mother all through it. She was conscious of all that was going on, but she lay like a corpse, helpless."

To none of the Zangwills was death easy, except perhaps the tranquil-minded, simple, faith-possessed Moses Zangwill in Jerusalem. "In most biographies it is the subject's death which is most interesting," Somerset Maugham suggested. "It imports us as much to know how great men die as to know how they live." Israel Zangwill's death was hard and painful. Dr. Redcliffe Salaman wrote to me: "In the last year or two of his life, Zangwill was here a good deal and on the last occasion he was unfortunately very ill and irresponsible. Edie and I were with him at the time he left his home and was taken to a nursing home. It was the most painful scene I have ever witnessed, and it has always left me with the problem—does a man, when he is out of his mind, really suffer the agonising pains and terrors that from his wild talk he would appear to do? I think he does—which does not make the situation easier."

Mrs. Zangwill died in 1945. She was in Edinburgh at the time, to be near her son Oliver, who was attached as psychologist to a hospital near Edinburgh. "It may interest you to know in view of your long friendship with the Zangwill family," she wrote to me, "that Oliver is thinking of getting married. I am very happy about it. It is lovely to feel that there will be someone to care for Oliver when, in the course of nature, I am no longer here. I have been rather seriously ill." When she died Oliver Zangwill wrote to me: "One could hardly wish that my mother should have survived longer under the circumstances. She already felt her incapacity and invalidism acutely, and I am glad she did not have a further stage of even more complete incapacity."

When Oliver was born, Israel Zangwill wrote to Dr. Redcliffe Salaman, "that distinguished Mendelist," that he had looked at him with a "Redcliffian eye" and decided that he was "Jewish in type." He had him circumcised, unlike his elder brother, though he said he had done so only for health reasons. Oliver Zangwill is married to my friend Tom Moult's daughter—"my young friend Thomas Moult," Zangwill wrote of him before that daughter was born. Her mother, Bessie Moult, is Jewish.

When Oliver Zangwill was appointed to his Professorship at Cambridge, the *Jewish Chronicle* telephoned me to ask if I knew whether he considered himself a Jew, and would it be right to chronicle his appointment in the paper. I said I had never asked him, but I thought a mention of the fact that Israel Zangwill's son had received this appointment would be in order. After all, the general Press had reported that he was the son of "Israel Zangwill, the Jewish novelist." When I told Oliver this he said: "Of course you were right to reply to the *Jewish Chronicle* as you did. I don't really know whether I consider myself a Jew or not, but certainly I am flattered if other people see fit to consider me one."

It is hard to say what in terms of Jewishness this really means; but it would be good to know that Oliver Zangwill has given the answer to one of his father's critics who in 1925 wrote: "His sons will certainly not be Jews, and thus the name Zangwill will not be more than a memory among Jews." People in Oliver's circle turn to him for guidance when they approach Jewish subjects. When Dr. J. T. MacCurdy died, Oliver wrote an obituary notice in *The Times*, mentioning that "only two days before his death I was flattered to receive from him a chapter in manuscript from his latest work on social psychology. This is concerned in part with the problem of Zionism. 'What I hope you may be kind enough to read it for,' he wrote, 'is prejudice. Of course I am prejudiced in this field as is everyone who is human at all. What I am hoping to learn from you is where prejudice has caused me to distort or omit evidence. Can you help me?' "

When Oliver Zangwill's book *An Introduction to Modern Psychology* appeared, Dr. Emmanuel Miller started his review in the *Jewish Chronicle* with the words: "Readers of this paper will be gratified to see the name Zangwill as author of a book. Israel Zangwill's son promises to be a prominent figure in the field of psychology."

Israel Zangwill's daughter had a mental breakdown, and is in a Home. Zangwill was spared the knowledge of that tragedy. It happened five or six years after his death. Mrs. Zangwill once wrote to me, "I have very much slipped out of all social intercourse, owing to my daughter's illness." At one time she was in a Home in Switzerland, and Mrs. Zangwill visited her there. She meant to do so again in 1937, when she was in France and met Oliver there. "When he goes back to Cambridge I go on to my daughter." But the doctors advised her against it. They told her that "she is to have a new treatment during which they want to keep all emotion from her, even a pleasant one. So I am taking the opportunity to go out to Mexico to see my son there."

Ayrton or George Zangwill is a mining engineer in Mexico, married and with a daughter. "My son in Mexico is married to a charming girl," she wrote to me then, "and has a little daughter of a year old." And afterwards: "I had an interesting time in Mexico, and was very delighted to make the acquaintance of my daughter-in-law and my granddaughter."

During this visit to Mexico Mrs. Zangwill was driven by her interest in Zangwill's Ito work and the pressing need at that time of outlets for Jewish immigration from Hitler's Germany, as well as from Austria and Poland, to visit the plateau in Mexico which had been offered by President Obregon for Jewish settlement, an offer whose rejection by the American Jewish Congress had in the midst of his work on his last Jewish novel, left unfinished because of it, so infuriated Zangwill that he published his attack on the Congress, which in turn resulted in his acceptance of its invitation to address it, his "Watchman, What of the Night?" speech. Unfortunately, she found, "there is no question of the possibility of Jewish immigration into Mexico."

In her will Mrs. Zangwill left to her "daughter-in-law Sara, the wife of my elder son Ayrton Israel Zangwill my opal and diamond necklace together with the pastel portrait and charcoal sketch of Ayrton when he was a little boy," and she made bequests too to Peggy, "Margaret Ayrton Zangwill," but "if it appears unlikely that my daughter should have any use for same I authorise to sell my daughter's share of my personal chattels and transfer the proceeds of any such sale to Margaret's Trustees."

Ayrton Zangwill, or George as he preferred to be known, worked for a time as a chemist with Imperial Chemical Industries. He went to Mexico about 1930, and is at a big smelting works there. He seems to have acclimatised himself, and settled down. "My elder son," Mrs. Zangwill wrote to me in 1940, "has been in Mexico for the last ten years. He seems to have lost all touch with this country."

Israel Zangwill was thirty-seven when he first met his wife. Edith Ayrton had been a student at Bedford College, and was writing. Mrs. Ayrton said she had sent another of her manuscripts "to Mr. Zangwill; it is very good of him to look after them, and very nice of him to write to you every day, though I cannot say that he displays a large amount of self-denial in this. I have no doubt he gets some small modicum of enjoyment out of it too." This was in 1901.

Zangwill had known other women before he met his wife. Freud says a biographer who "really endeavours to penetrate the life of his hero must not, as happens in most biographies, through discretion or prudery, pass over in silence his sexual life." I know nothing scandalous about Zangwill's life. He was a fairly normal man, who was said to have an eye for a pretty girl. His early diaries are full of references to pretty girls at "jolly dances," and he confessed that he couldn't "eradicate the Old Adam." He made a point once of describing a lady who had interviewed him for a paper as "a pretty young woman; I must say that she is pretty," he said, "because she described me as ugly." The family legend is that "Israel had a fascination for lovely young ladies, who crowded round him." There were a number of women he was thought to be marrying. His friendship with several young actresses in his plays gave rise to rumours. There seemed something more tangible in his friendship with a young woman artist, Amy Stuart, with whom he went about a good deal. Once he showed her round Whitechapel, and took her into the Netherlands Club, in Bell Lane, near the Jews' Free School. They were given a great reception. About that time he was questioned about his views on intermarriage. He replied, quite wrongly, as he realised and admitted afterwards, only he was thinking then of his own loss of faith, that "Most Jews have no religion. I do not see why they should not marry the modern woman who has none either. I should personally find it difficult to marry a Jewess of my religion."

There were always women round him, but he was dilatory. It seemed he might stay unmarried, as Louis did, and Mark was believed to have done, and Leah did. He joked about the marriage rumours. "I was married at Ventnor," he said. "At least so I gather from the local newspapers, in whose visitors' lists there figures the entry, 'Mr. and Mrs. Zangwill.' I do not care to correct it, because the lady being my mother it is perfectly accurate. 'Why, she looks old enough to be his mother.' "

There may have been something more than the joke to this. For at this time, while he was writing "Without Prejudice" for the *Pall Mall Magazine*, he was friendly with Mrs. Burnett, the author of *Little Lord Fauntleroy*. Henry James, who called her "Most Heavenly of women," and Israel Zangwill seem to have been her closest friends in London. In 1894, when, according to her son, Vivian Burnett, who wrote her biography, "the real intimacy of her friendship with Israel Zangwill began," she was forty-five and he was thirty. She wrote to Zangwill: "I have not seen you often enough yet to have found out very much about you, have I? But I found out one thing, that you are kind and that that Beaconsfield brain of yours is not too brilliant to see." He sent her *Children of the Ghetto*, and she read to him from the manuscript her book, *A Lady of Quality*. Henry James also had this book read to him, and he wrote to the authoress about it: "I see her (the Lady of Quality) better than if I had made her. And what is better still, she sees me. She winks at me—distinctly." Zangwill invited her to read more of the book to him "over an afternoon cup of tea in my study, which has become bright and spring-like since you visited it." He praised it in his "Without Prejudice" pages in the *Pall Mall Magazine*.

In a letter to her son she wrote: "Mr. Zangwill has returned from a lecture tour and dropped in to dinner a few days ago. I read him the first chapter of *Tom de Willoughby*. When he shook hands with me he said in his odd way, 'I have great respect for you.' I care for his opinion of things. I care for all his thoughts and I believe in his mind enormously. If he respected a piece of work I should feel very reposeful about it. He is the only person I know at all intimately at present who fills that niche for me." When the Vagabonds Club (a club of writers) gave her a dinner in December 1895, "Zangwill sat on my right hand. When I had finished speaking he turned and took my hands in both his and said: 'It was perfect. It couldn't have been better.' "

Another woman friend was Nina Salaman, Dr. Redcliffe Salaman's first wife, who died in 1925, a year before Zangwill died. She married Dr. Salaman in 1901, two years before Zangwill married. Dr. Herbert Loewe, in his tribute to Nina Salaman, quoted one of her poems, in which she spoke of two friends with whom she went—

"Door after door, they open wide, But not alone.
They go before, but side by side, we face the Throne."

"These two friends," said Herbert Loewe, "were Israel Zangwill and Israel Abrahams, both of whom she had known since youth. With Israel Zangwill she had collaborated over the Machsor (the Festival Prayer Book.) "A voluminous correspondence passed between these two, whose deep friendship for each other was never dimmed by their diversity of views on Judaism or Zionism."

Zangwill said when she died that her book of poems came into print in 1901, the year of her marriage, by "curious chance." "The Jewish Publication Society wanted to foster Jewish talent," and he had recommended her first book, called *Songs of Exile*. "Dowered with every gift of soul and body," he wrote of her, "with every grace and charm, including a large unconsciousness of them, a poetess who found inspiration equally in Zionism and in Nature, she was the spiritual queen of Anglo-Jewry."

With Edith Ayrton who became his wife Israel Zangwill also had literary interests. He liked tinkering with her work. ("It was largely through his encouragement and help that she took steps to get her stories published and, indeed, realised that it was within her power to succeed as a writer," according to Evelyn Sharp's biography of her step-mother.)

How much Israel Zangwill had to do with the actual writing of her books one cannot say. He must have gone through them, and made suggestions and revisions, but more than that, ideas and characters came to her through their experiences, their meeting the same people in the same places, and discussing them and the problems they presented. Her first novel, *The First Mrs. Molivar*, is dedicated "To

Israel—in the Loving Hope that he may bring the Ideals for which we both care, a little Nearer—the Ideals which form the Bond that unites us." The book was published in 1905, two years after their marriage. Her Mrs. Molivar was not troubled by the question of the marriage service. The only time she had been to a chapel she had liked the simplicity of the worship, "and she was too lax or too broadminded a Churchwoman to be disturbed by the minor differences." Mrs. Molivar is the second wife, and she is everywhere tripped up by the first wife—the house "where she reigned, and which must be preserved as it is." The theme has since been exploited by a more successful woman novelist. "You have no right, Mr. Molivar," the second wife cries, "to put the dead before the living."

The influence of her life with Israel Zangwill, and her participation in his Jewish causes, is apparent in her much later book *The House* published in 1928, two years after his death, but no doubt, written in the last years of his life, and containing pictures of Jewish life in New York, that she must have seen when she was there with him in 1923-4, the East Side, Hester Street, and people who "aint got English very good yet, like me. She don't have no call to speak it, you see, for it's Yiddish all the day long, what we call Jargon."

Mrs. Zangwill brought Israel Zangwill into the Women Suffrage movement, in which she and her sister, Mrs. Ayrton Gould, and her step-mother, Mrs. Ayrton, were active. It happened to other literary men at the time. Jerome K. Jerome writing of W. W. Jacob's wife who became a militant suffragette, said: "Husbands lived in fear and trembling in those days." She also brought him into the Peace movement, where he played a considerable part, though in both movements, as in his own Jewish movements, he had and expressed doubts. He once confessed to a Women's Suffrage meeting that "instead of condoling with women upon their lack of votes I feel more like congratulating them upon it." And after the Peace movement, he could remind Mr. W. T. Stead, "when after a tour of the crowned heads of Europe he reported enthusiastically that the millennium was almost upon us that more good will be done by facing the brutal facts of life and the European situation than by allowing the wish that war shall cease to be father to the thought that it is ceasing." During the war he was "vastly obliged by the soldier and his rifle." "Worse than war," he said, "is the death of the soul of a people. For if there is a peace of God which passeth all understanding, there is a peace of the devil which passeth all endurance. It is a peace purchased by sacrificing to security every high national ideal, every generous instinct." "In a world of flux," he said, "the justice of to-day is the injustice of to-morrow."

When Bolshevism rose to power in Russia, and was attacked,

he could not forget the pogromist Czar and Government whom it had swept away, and the "antithetical glorification of the old Russia." But already in 1919 he was growing uneasy, as "an honest advocate of liberty," at what was happening in Russia. He feared it was encroaching too far upon individual liberty. "Has literature flourished more in Russia under the dictation of the Proletariat than under the Czardom?" he asked. In his play *The Forcing House*, written in 1922, he said: "If you are found with anything except the State organs, the *Red Worker* and the *International Republican*, you'll get very short shrift." "My handling of the theme would have been substantially the same had Russia been as imaginary a country as Valdania," he explained, "though I have of course profited by the Russian experience." He had thought of using Trotsky as a model for his revolutionary leader, but he felt his "Jewish psychology would have over-weighted the theme and I set him aside for a simpler type of leader." He described his *Forcing House* as "a tragi-comedy of Communism." He called what had been done in Russia "Socialism while you won't wait. Not a Paradise of blossoming brotherhood, not a natural growth under God's heaven, but a Socialism ripened prematurely under the heat of compulsion and watered with blood, a Socialism that can be perpetuated only by ever-renewed compulsion."

This was thirty-five years ago. Zangwill told the story of Rabbi Mase, "the only man in the Russian capital who dared to debate with Lunatcharsky, the Bolshevist Commissar for Education, the question 'Is there a God?' Not a single Russian pope dared to emulate this Jewish courage." He reminded the American Jewish Congress in 1923 of "the great trek of suffering Jewry from Bolshevist Russia, and of the kind of people who had come under Bolshevist rule, who had in the Ukraine bayonetted, bombed, buried alive hundreds of thousands of Jews, and who, if the Soviet Government should be overthrown, would massacre Russian Jewry." The Hitlerist war confirmed his fears. A Jewish Red Army soldier told what happened in the Soviet Ukraine during the German invasion. "The Nazis found little need of importing the seeds of racial prejudice; the native plant flourished under their approval and direction." "The Germans had little to do with the physical action of assembling and liquidating Jews in the Polish and Russian Ukraine; under their aegis the work was carried out by local enthusiasts."

Zangwill did not let himself be captivated by "the false romanticism of parrot phrases." He denounced evil wherever he found it. He saw "how the pressure of life overcomes ideas and even fixed idealisms." He believed that "there is no particular merit in being a 'what'; that men are not necessarily 'ists' or 'ites.' "

Yet though he could see beyond organisations and causes, he

worked hard for causes and organisations; and he brought his wife into his organisations and causes. She was welcomed into them, and she identified herself with them. Zangwill's cousin and friend Joseph Cowen speaking as a Zionist leader, said they had added a "Bath Zion," a daughter of Zion, to their Zionist ranks. L. J. Greenberg, another Zionist leader, who soon after entered on his great period as Editor of the *Jewish Chronicle*, said that she was "imbued with his ideals and had taken a noble part in Zionist work." Carmel Golds-mid, Colonel Goldsmid's daughter, said that "if all their ladies were such ardent Zionists as Mrs. Zangwill they would be a step nearer Zion." Many years later, towards the close of his life, when Mrs. Zangwill joined Zangwill in New York in 1924, she was given a reception, at which Miss Irma Kraft said that "speaking to this large body of Jewish women—Zionist enthusiasts all—Mrs. Zang-will had classified herself as 'ethically Jewish.' "

Israel Zangwill was married in a London registry office, on 26th November 1903. There was no religious ceremony. A reception was held at the home of the bride. Mrs. Ayrton her step-mother, wanted it to be a beautiful wedding. Mrs. Zangwill was described as wearing not bridal white, but a terra-cotta dress with embroidery, and a big hat of the same colour, "a dark, sweet looking girl with brown hair and the loveliest brown eyes." Israel Zangwill gave her as a wedding gift "three large cheques for her favourite causes, the Charity Organisation, Women's Suffrage and Zionism." The Zionist central organ, *Die Welt*, announced a contribution of ten guineas from Mrs. Zangwill to the Jewish National Fund. Soon after Mrs. Zangwill spoke at a Zionist meeting of the Hebrew that she was learning and made "kosher" puns, and urged a Jewish State where "the orthodox Jew could follow his own religion without let or hindrance."

Twenty years after their marriage Zangwill wrote: "Only where the Gentile has already been Judaised does intermarriage promote either harmony or the diffusion of Jewish ideals. But that with affinity of harmony and outlook intermarriage becomes possible has always been even the Rabbinical conception. The only trouble is that the Rabbis narrow down the concept of Judaism into too rigid and sectarian a form. It but remains with them to broaden out their principles." Zangwill even urged in defence of his wife that "she is a far better Jewess than I a Jew."

The marriage was nevertheless resented by some people. "Mr. Zangwill's bringing to America his non-Jewish wife when he comes on a Jewish mission would of itself estrange friends of his cause," the American correspondent of the *Jewish Chronicle* wrote in 1904. But the attitude of this correspondent is indicated by his opening sentence: "The coming of Mr. Zangwill has not raised a ripple of excitement outside certain Zionist circles. Of course," he went on, "we are all interested in him as a litterateur. But a self-constituted embassy to win us over to political Zionism is not likely to succeed." He repeated: "Mr. Zangwill's matrimonial venture will surely damage his usefulness as a Zionist propagandist." The feeling persisted after Mrs. Zangwill's death. There was Albert Hyamson, the Editor of the Jewish Year Book, who took the chair for my Zangwill Memorial Lecture at the Jewish Historical Society of England. I had reviewed the first post-war issue of the Jewish Year Book and said it contained no mention of Mrs. Zangwill's death. He replied in the *Jewish Chronicle*: "Mrs. Zangwill never was in any sense a Jewess, and the inclusion of her name in a list of Jewish obituaries would therefore be inappropriate."

I do not share that view. I am not sure to what extent Mrs. Zangwill became a Jewess by what we call religious conviction, but it seems that any test on such lines would equally exclude Israel Zangwill, whom Hyamson honoured. I once drew Mrs. Zangwill's attention to a remark by Jacob de Haas that she was a Jewess by conviction. She replied: "With regard to de Haas's remark that I am a 'Jewess by conviction' he may have referred to my deep sympathy with Jews, and my exceedingly great interest in Zionism and in the Ito. My husband used to say that my religious outlook was nearer to his own than that of any Jewess he had ever met." Strictly speaking, a non-Jewish wife who has not been admitted into the Jewish faith is not a Jewess. Zangwill knew it. He had written that "the only way in which Israel can be recruited from without is through conversion to Judaism and by a ceremony which is synagogal and which offers no analogy to naturalisation." Zangwill knew what it implied.

Mrs. Zangwill knew it too. What she said was that Zangwill considered her religious outlook very near his own. Which makes the question—what was Zangwill's religious outlook? If we accept Zangwill as a Jew—and I suppose no one will contest his right to be accepted as a Jew—she whose religious outlook was so near his own surely deserves to follow him into the fold. One thing is certain —no woman more definitely identified herself with her husband's belief and work. As truly as Ruth did, Mrs. Zangwill said—and acted all her life up to what she said—"Thy people shall be my people, and thy God my God." Edith Zangwill was certainly not a Christian. Once she wrote to me about the central figure of the Christian faith and Church in connection with an article of mine in which "you mention that Jewish sculptors and painters have in recent years been particularly interested in Christ as a subject matter. I think this is quite natural. They would naturally be interested in him as a great, probably the greatest Jewish prophet, quite apart from any religious aspect. The great trouble about the Christian world is that it has forgotten Christ. Otherwise things would not be in such a terrible state to-day." It is almost what Zangwill would have said.

Ever since Israel Zangwill died, for nearly twenty years, until her own death, she had been a perpetuation of himself, lending his name, "the name I am so proud to bear," she wrote to me, to organisations and activities with which he would have associated himself, so that the name Israel Zangwill, though prefixed by "Mrs.," still appeared in public form. "For years, my wife and I lived on an uncertain footing," Zangwill confessed twenty years after their marriage, in his speech to the American Jewish Congress in 1923, "because when I had hopes of the establishment of a Jewish State, whether in Palestine or elsewhere, it never occurred to me that I should not settle there. We never knew when the call would come, and if I had hesitated to answer it I am sure she would have gone off first."

When they married, Zangwill was at the height of his fame. *The Children of the Ghetto*, *The King of Schnorrers*, *Dreamers of the Ghetto*, *Ghetto Tragedies* and other books had already been written and published. "I did not know Israel Zangwill until his 'children' were several years old," she once said; "I made their acquaintance when he himself presented them to me, but I can at least claim to have stood in a pleasant step-motherly relation to them." Zangwill's book of poems, *Blind Children*, was published in the year of their marriage, and is dedicated to her. "I may be biased in its favour," she wrote to me, "for it was my own particular book." All Zangwill's books became her "own particular" books. "Could I be sufficiently impartial and critical, however hard I tried?" she wrote in her foreword to the Soncino Press volume of Zangwill's *Speeches, Articles and Letters* published in 1937. She regarded herself as his testatrix in all things. His books were her chief care. Everything that concerned his writings claimed her attention. Even the proper style of his translations. "I have received a letter from the Juedische Buch-Verein," she wrote to me, "imploring me to let them publish *The Sabbath-Breaker*. But I am uneasy about the translator. I would like your opinion upon it."

She was interested in everything that kept Zangwill's work and name alive. She followed everything that had to do with the plight of Jewish refugees, with Jewish immigration, with the history of the Ito, and with the activities of the Freeland movement, which considered itself an attempt to revive Zangwill's Ito. "It is shameful," she wrote to me in 1937, "the way these unfortunate Jewish refugees are hounded about from one country to another." It was the time of the Bermuda Conference on Immigration, at which the countries of the world discussed what to do to admit the refugees from Germany and elsewhere, and did almost nothing. "The real point," Mrs. Zangwill wrote to me, "is that the German and Polish Jews are in a desperate position and that there is nowhere for them to go. I am quite certain that Jewish immigration into Palestine will in practice be almost shut down for a considerable period, although I do not think the British Government will formally stop it, as the Arabs desire. I do not see how any one can maintain that the flight of the Jews is due to their not having struck root in any country, nor to any timidity on their part. It might as well be urged that the departure of the Pilgrim Fathers for America was due to their lack of stamina." When my book *What Will Happen to the Jews?* appeared, she wrote to me: "I want to thank you for your history of the Ito. It has never been done and it needed doing."

During the war she did voluntary war work. "It is possible even for an elderly and rather incapable woman to be of some use to the country," she wrote to me. "An elderly woman could and should take more risks than a younger one, for she can more easily be spared. If by dying she could preserve a young life that would be an end worth reaching." "I feel almost selfish," she went on, "in being here"—that is, not facing the dangers of the Blitz in London. "This place is really comparatively peaceful. There are often passing enemy aircraft overhead, but they do pass. I suppose they have been told not to waste their bombs on a small place like this."

When she became more ill, and could not continue her work she told me: "I am sick at heart at having to give up all my work. It was not very much, but at least one felt one was doing something. And even from a selfish point of view, work forms a sort of screen, keeping off a full realisation of the present miseries and horrors." "I have changed my pacifist point of view because of the monstrous cruelty of the Nazi Government," she wrote to me early in the war. "The overthrow of Hitlerism is the vital thing. Only will there be any European Jews left to deal with when this happens? Never was more need for the Jews to get together, dropping all minor differences in this, the most terrible crisis that there has probably ever been in the world's history."

When my friend Stefan Zweig committed suicide, she wrote to me: "It is another tragedy brought about by Hitler. Indeed, the whole world is full of them. When one thinks of the state of things just before Hitler came to power, and the present condition, it is almost incredible that one man could have wrought so much evil. Of course, there was a lot of unavoidable unhappiness before Hitler, as there was bound to be in a world that contains disease and death. Also there was a certain amount of injustice and cruelty of all sorts, but people taken as a whole seemed to be becoming more humane. I think the lapse into mental barbarism forms the greatest tragedy."

Then she wrote to me of her suffering because of "the nightmare that is going on in Poland, and which is haunting beyond description. I often wonder that we do not all commit suicide, like Stefan Zweig. Do not think," she hastened to add, "that I mean this seriously because, as you know, I consider such an action wrong." "I used to believe that the story of German atrocities was untrue, or largely exaggerated," she said in one of her letters, "but seeing the manner in which they now treat the Jews, probably these atrocities did take place."

Like Zangwill she had a high regard for Dr. Jochelman. The first idea of the Ito, she told me, came from Dr. Jochelman. Then she wrote to me: "When I told you that the first idea of the Ito came from Dr. Jochelman I should perhaps have worded the phrase differently. As you know, the Zionist Congress in 1905 turned down the offer of the British Government to give the Jews the Plateau in East Africa. Dr. Jochelman thereupon urged my husband to found an organisation to deal with the offer, and not to let the chance slip. My husband then founded the Ito. Dr. Jochelman did invaluable work in Russia to promote the Ito and he played a great part in the Galveston scheme."

Zangwill spoke of his wife as his "guardian angel." When he got into his big fight in America over his "Watchman, What of the Night?" speech, he had to "send an S.O.S. signal for my wife," and she joined him.

Yet with all her devotion and care for him, it is possible that Zangwill's family were not altogether wrong when they felt she was not enough homemaker for a man of such nervous tension as Zangwill was. She was busy with the Women's Suffrage movement, and with the Peace movement. She was often away on her own affairs. There were separate holidays. Zangwill wrote: "Mrs. Zangwill is away on a cycling tour; while I have come back from my little walking tour. I shall go again however for a week, as the sea (where he lived) does not agree with me." She did not feed him as his mother and sisters did. The house lacked the comforts of a home run by a woman whose sole or main interest was homemaking. Their niece Primrose may have put her finger on it when she spoke of Mrs. Zangwill having an unworldly innocence, a sweetness and single-mindedness that persisted her whole life through; "she moved upon this earth without really being of it or stained by its sinfulness." It is possible that Mrs. Zangwill was too busy with the things of the mind and the spirit to give more attention to Zangwill's creature comforts. And Zangwill himself not sufficiently concerned with such things, did not demand them. Louis Zangwill was interested in food. But Israel Zangwill when he was left alone never bothered about it. He was abstemious and self-forgetful. Dr. Jochelman, writing of a journey he made through Spain with Zangwill, said: "Zangwill was a generous man. In all the years I knew him I cannot recall one request for help that he refused. But when it came to himself he economised. He hated comfort and luxury. He believed it was sinful."

When Herzl first saw Zangwill in 1895, he remarked in his Diaries that it was a "somewhat poorish home." Louis Zangwill commented: "At that time, English writers all lived inexpensively and for the most part in modest suburban houses. Indeed, a writer making a great display externally would have then run the risk of having his talent thrown into question." Mrs. Zangwill wrote to me however about Herzl's remark: "I think the Zangwill home at Oxford Road was probably 'somewhat poor.' The best men of letters of that time did not live in Kilburn. Certainly all the most famous writers and actors of the time did visit the Zangwills in the 'nineties.'"

Mrs. Zangwill was concerned with other things than comfort, and I remember the Zangwill home, Far End, impressed me as stuffy, though children must have found it delightful. Primrose says that Far End when she was a child "was the ultimate paradise. I constantly found my way there in dreams. I have walked along London pavements and suddenly seen them transformed into a country lane shadowed by the dusky trees of Far End." But children could not have understood what a bundle of nervous tension Zangwill was, and how much special care he needed. "My younger children," he wrote less than a year before he died, "said to me recently: 'Daddy, if your insomnia really prevents you from ever writing again, we can offer you a job in our Indian Encampment'"

As long as I knew Zangwill he suffered from this terrible insomnia, that often made him long for the sleep from which there is no awakening. His diaries are full of entries: "Insomnia." He did not sleep properly for weeks. He said he had written *Merely Mary Ann* in a fortnight of insomnia, at night. He suggested in one of his last articles that "agonised incurables must be relieved of their agony." He spoke of the Kaddish which Jews say for the dead, the magnification of the Eternal, with its last word as the clods fall on the coffin, "May he come to his place in peace." Much of his insomnia must have come from his over-anxiety and his over-work, his preoccupation with his affairs and with Jewish interests, that would not let him rest, and that he could not get out of his mind enough to be able to sleep. When he went to America in 1923, and was writing and re-writing his "Watchman, What of the Night?" speech, he confessed afterwards that for a whole month "I never enjoyed one real night's sleep." He wrote to Dr. Jochelman after a meeting of the Ito Council: "I could not sleep after our Council meeting."

He also had some malady, that I think Louis too had in his last years, which would not let him digest his food properly. That, and his restless spirit which ate him up made him terribly thin, so that he looked taller than he was. With his mass of beautiful white hair he was an impressive figure. But when you saw his spindly legs you wondered how he could not only walk, but almost run. His eagerness carried him forward. A gossip writer once described him rushing along Fleet Street to his rooms in the Temple like the White Rabbit in *Alice in Wonderland,* stopping to pull out his watch to see the time. I remember him rushing along like that one day when I had an appointment with him at his rooms in the Temple, and then rushing me up the stairs at a pace that made me pant. I was once at a theatre with him, when the Vilna Players were in London. They sent someone to say they would like him to speak a few words from the stage. He grabbed my hand, and though I had nothing to do on the stage he rushed me along with him, down the stairs, up to the stage, still holding my hand, till he began to speak, and I could release myself and slip away in the wings. On another occasion, at a meeting where I was not on the list of speakers, and he was the Chairman, he pushed me on the stage, and announced me as the next speaker, and I had to speak. There was a dinner given to the Vilna Players at which I sat next to him. Without a word to me first about it, he announced in his speech that he would give his play *The King of Schnorrers* to the Company to produce, and that I would translate it into Yiddish.

Zangwill used to poke fun at his plain looks. But I remember him looking tremendously distinguished. When he sailed back from America in 1924, Cecil Roberts wrote: "There was a distinguished-looking Jew, with dilated nostrils, iron-grey hair, and a stoop, handsome in the manner of his race, bearing the impress of intellect, an intense personality, with great charm. He was a man with a hundred fights against poverty, prejudice and ill-health, but he had triumphed nobly. He had interpreted the Jews to a scornful world, displayed their poverty, revealed their poetry." There is a story of his resemblance to Sir Henry Irving, and to his son, H. B. Irving. Once Zangwill went to the British Museum Reading Room, and the librarian handed him a volume of Shakespeare which he said he had left there the previous day. Zangwill explained he had not been in the Reading Room for a long time; it turned out that the book had been left by H. B. Irving. There was a suggestion in *Harper's Weekly,* in 1896, that Israel Zangwill's likeness "to the late Lord Beaconsfield is more marked in real life than in any picture I have seen of him." His niece, without knowing this, wrote more than fifty years later: "When I saw George Arliss play Disraeli in the film of that name I was uncannily reminded of Israel Zangwill; there were the tall, thin, stooping figure, the curve of nose and lips, the soft ironic speech and the twinkle in the eye."

There is a description of Zangwill in the early years soon after the publication of *Children of the Ghetto* and his first acquaintance and friendship with Herzl, in an account by Herzl's friend and first biographer, Professor Leon Kellner, interesting not only for what it tells us about Zangwill, but also for what it tells us of Herzl and his home, and the life of the Jews of Vienna of his time and circle who regarded themselves as belonging to "good society." Zangwill was in Vienna, on his way home from Venice. Herzl had invited him to dinner at his house, and also invited Kellner. "Mrs. Herzl, who had been carefully informed by her husband how distinguished a visitor she was to receive, was visibly disappointed," Kellner wrote. "She had probably expected a tall, well-built man, carefully groomed, dressed in the latest English mode, and displaying perfect society manners. Instead there sat down at her festive table which had been prepared with such loving care an average-sized gentleman of grotesquely Jewish appearance and awkward behaviour, with ill-fitting and neglected clothes." "In honour of her guest Mrs. Herzl had prepared crabs for the first course. Zangwill did not know how to tackle the monster before him." (Crab is not permitted as food to observant Jews.) "He started back stiffly at the sight. He seized the crab with an effort at bravado and put it to his mouth. An outcry from Mrs. Herzl, a polite smile from the host—and we tried to show the impossible Englishman how to handle the beast on his plate. It was of no avail. Otherwise his table manners did not contrast too awkwardly with those of good society, and the meal continued under a barrage of intellectual fireworks between Herzl and Zangwill. But Mrs. Herzl did not wait a minute longer than was compatible with good manners, and when the dessert was being served she left the room without a word.

"Now," Kellner continued, "we were three men together, and I felt a childish pleasure at the thought of the forthcoming conversation. Zangwill discovered the chaise longue in the corner. Unceremoniously he stretched himself out at full length, saying that he was tired from the trip. Herzl was not exactly entranced by this lack of formality, but he let Zangwill do as he pleased. However, he was not altogether sorry when I carried the English guest off to the races."

It made no difference to Herzl's appreciation of Zangwill's genius. "That day, after the departure of Zangwill, as I was discussing the guest with Herzl and his wife—Mrs. Herzl was still distressed by his peculiarities"—Kellner went on, "Herzl said: 'Here we have a man who expends so much concern and thought on the care of his spirit that there remains nothing for externals.' The friendship between Herzl and Zangwill grew with each letter, and Zangwill's contributions to the first numbers of *Die Welt* were treasured by Herzl like jewels, as indeed they were."

Morris Waldman, later Secretary of the American Jewish Committee, who had been connected with the Galveston work, said that when he had first seen Zangwill "years before, he had left the impression on my mind of a young, restless, illmannered, ungainly product of the East End Ghetto of London. I was pleased to find him now (1908) nearly handsome in comparison, attractive, impressive in a well-built loosely-fitting Scotch grey suit that harmonised with his bushy iron grey hair and his somewhat ruddy complexion and more mellowed, though still sharp, hawk-like features." "Before his marriage he was probably one of the worst-dressed men in London," Zangwill's friend, Alfred Sutro, the playwright, said. "In season and out of season he wore a long and ill-cut frockcoat, over which his hair would straggle; with his flashing eyes he looked like a Hebrew prophet. When he became engaged, Mrs. Zangwill-to-be besought him to change his tailor—but in vain. 'I know he's a bad tailor,' said Israel, 'and being a bad tailor he has very few customers. He is a worthy man, with a family, and it would break his heart if I left him. And Mrs. Zangwill-to-be, who was troubled with a sense of duty herself, acquiesced."

The *Jewish Chronicle* in 1903, the year Zangwill married, described him as "an ungainly man, awkward and unconventional in his movements and in his dress, with dark, irregular features, a mop of curly dark hair and large nearsighted eyes." Earlier still, in 1895, a writer in *To Day* spoke of him "in his sombre habiliments. I see," he said, "his flowing sable locks, the pallid face. He is less a human being than an intellect, a dreamer among books, the admiration of literary fair ones." The same year, another note in *Harper's Weekly* spoke of Zangwill walking down Fleet Street, "peering with short-sighted vision into shop windows, with an abstracted air. He usually wears a long black frockcoat and his raven curls are surmounted by a curious little soft black hat. He is slightly round-shouldered, thin, without a particle of colour, stoops a little and scorns an umbrella in any weather."

So that Zangwill's thinness and pallid face and stoop were there when he was a young man, five or six years before he met Mrs. Zangwill. He seems to have been the same Zangwill from the start. He telephoned me one day, just before his last breakdown, and without stopping to say who it was, told me in a quick, almost incoherent rush of words that his doctors had ordered him to rest, and he was going back to Far End, but as soon as he was better he would come back and resume his fight for his place in the Theatre. But this rapid rush of speech was noted in him when he was much younger and was not heading for a serious nervous breakdown. He was always nervous, excitable and voluble. In 1908, when he was in his early forties, long before I knew him, he appeared as a witness before the Commission on the Censorship of Plays, and the report says that he spoke so quickly that the reporters could not keep up with him.

Dr. Redcliffe Salaman, who was a near friend for many years, and saw much of him at the end, told me that for the last two years of his life Zangwill was "not really *compos mentis*." He was certainly working under tremendous strain; but Bensusan and other friends who knew him from the early days and saw him till the end insist that he was as sane as any man. No other thought had crossed my own mind. But I do know that Zangwill looked terribly ill, and was heading for a nervous breakdown.

It started in 1923 when Zangwill was writing his last novel, *The Baron of Offenbach*, which he left unfinished; he was working at the British Museum Reading Room, collecting material about the period, which is that of Jacob Frank, the pseudo-Messiah who followed Sabbathai Zevi and who, as Sabbathai became a Moslem, turned Christian with his followers and, retiring to Offenbach, assumed the title of Baron of Offenbach.

He cast the story in the form of a supposed contemporary eye-witness account which, in a Head-Note, he claimed to have discovered, and he said he did not propose to give it to the British Museum where his typescript of the novel lies, but "as its legitimate place to the Mocatta Library" of the Jewish Historical Society of England, or "the Zionist Library at Jerusalem." Zangwill's method of writing was to put all he had into his book, and then cut, and work over the book three or four times before making the final version. He heaped his "Jewish Romance," as he called it in his letters to me, or his "Cabbalistic Romance," as he called it in the typescript, full of the material he had gathered in his historical researches. This successor of the Sabbathai Zevi whom he made one of his Dreamers of the Ghetto, and had introduced in his account of another Dreamer, the Baal Shem, "this Frank, who was by turns a Turk, a Jew and a Catholic," fascinated him, he and the cabbalistic sophistries by which his followers clung to the Messianic dream which he had revived and shattered by his apostasy. He linked Jacob Frank to his *Dreamers of the Ghetto* by making the Matron of a Home for the Jewish Aged in Philadelphia, who found the supposed contemporary eye-witness account left by one of the inmates, write to him that she sent him the manuscript because "you, dear Mr. Zangwill, had dealt with the subject, in my own copy of your beautiful *Dreamers of the Ghetto*, which I received when it first came out from the Jewish Publication Society of this city, of which I have always been a member. (May I say that this book, which I treasure side by side with my Longfellow and my Ella Wheeler Wilcox, deserves to be brought before a wider circle than our

Society?)" He was fascinated by the Frankist Jews, "a queer lot, with their long beards and their long kiss-curls and their long prayers and their Cabbalistic tricks." He was fascinated by a Jew with a military escort, then seeing "to my amaze that the soldiers—gallant lissom figures on spirited steeds—were Jews to a man." He fancied when he met Joseph Conrad that he had Jewish blood. "So many Polish Jews have been absorbed into Catholicism," he wrote, "especially of the Frankist sect." He found that Frank "pretended to have led his Hebrew flock to Holy Church, but it is to Holy Himself —that's his game, I'm sure." The history thrilled him—"the idea of being linked, so to speak, with Napoleon, and through a chain of hands with Voltaire, Dr. Johnson, Mozart, Marie Antoinette and Maria Theresa! The reader may not share my professional rapture."

One professional reader into whose hands he placed his manuscript, his brother-in-law, Gerald Gould, did not share his rapture. He reported against the book, and this, combining with other things —his American visit and the fight in which it landed him, and then his last fight over his play *We Moderns*, and his final luckless, fatal theatrical season—led Zangwill to abandon the book. There are 132 pages of typescript, 120 pages of which are the story proper, the first pages being his Introduction or Head-Note. I think Gould was right. The book is overloaded, crammed tight with dull evocation of dead history, as far as Zangwill could be dull. For there are sparkling passages and flashes of brilliant thought. But there is not enough action and movement. The narrator doesn't get to the point. He keeps skirting round it. "I knowing all the facts," he says, "from the beginning, see all the episodes lying spread out simultaneously like the dead in a cemetery, all equally dead, whenever it was they died." Zangwill would, as he worked, have cut out a lot of the dead history, introduced action and movement, made his people not only talk but live. But Gerald Gould disheartened him. Something else happened to distract him from his "Jewish Romance." The American Jewish Congress had invited him to come to New York to address its 1923 Session, and he had refused to go because he was busy with his new book. Then President Obregon made an offer of Jewish settlement in Mexico to the American Jewish Congress, which turned it down because "such a scheme of colonisation is quite beyond the scope of the investigation as understood by the Committee of the American Jewish Congress." Zangwill wrote to me that he was "boiling with indignation over the footling report of the American Jewish Congress re Mexico." He wrote an article which he sent me, where he said: "Had the Pilgrim Fathers trembled like the American Jewish Congress that Congress could not have deliberated under such comfortable conditions." "The only comfort I can find in the whole episode," he concluded, "is that it supplies yet another refutation of the calumny that 'the Elders of Zion' wish to conquer the world. Why, they would not have it as a gift.''

The American Jewish Congress replied to his article, and Zangwill wrote to me: "The reply was very feeble, merely reiterating the very neglect I accused them of.'' Then the American Jewish Congress repeated its invitation to Zangwill to address it. This time he accepted. "Yes, it is true,'' he wrote to me. "As the American Jewish Congress invited me *again* and *after* my attack I thought this *beau geste* demanded recognition. It is not however till October, by which time my new Jewish romance will be well advanced.''

So Zangwill went in 1923 to New York to deliver his great speech, "Watchman, What of the Night?'', and got himself into one of the fiercest fights of his life. A report found its way into the Press that he was making a lecture tour to America at a fee of 1,000 dollars for each lecture. "The fact that this proposition has been made to me—as often before—does not mean that I have accepted it,'' he wrote. "My object in visiting America remains simply to take advantage of the flattering invitation of the American Jewish Congress to expound my view of the Jewish situation from its platform. My address will thus be in line with the many 'lectures' given by me on Anglo-Jewish platforms, the only 'fee' for which has been misrepresentation or resentment.'' Max Nordau had fifteen years before, in 1908, said about Zangwill: "Think how easy his life would be if he only sat down and wrote his novels and dramas. Instead he chooses a kind of martyrdom without any possible reward except the satisfaction of his own conscience. An English patriot has the prospect of a seat in one part of Westminster or a tomb in another, but a Jewish patriot will be attacked, hated, slandered, libelled.''

The flood of abuse poured out on Zangwill after his 1923 speech in New York shocked me. I had published an article in the American Jewish Press about his coming visit to America, in which I spoke of one of the leading American Zionists then visiting England saying to me it was a pity so great a man as Zangwill stood outside the Zionist movement. I asked how a man like Zangwill could stand within any movement, since he straddled them all. Zangwill did not stand inside even the Ito, of which he was President. "The unhappy fact is,'' he said of his own Territorialist movement, "that Territorialism, while it can point out to the Diaspora that what is the matter with it is precisely that it is a Diaspora, can do little or nothing to do away with it.'' "The case for an Itoland as for Zionism, is unanswerable. The theory is all right. It is only in the realm of practice that they are assailable.'' Or speaking officially as President of the Ito at its third birthday celebration: "You see, I do not hide from you how high the mountain is, and how difficult it is to climb. Why should I deceive you?'' In his tragically ironic story "Samooborona,'' which means

"Self-Defence," in *Ghetto Comedies*, he does not omit to castigate together with all the other partisans his own followers, the Territorialists. The *Jewish Chronicle*, rebuking him for an attack on Zionism, "a movement of which he had once been a foremost champion," added: "But it is only fair to Mr. Zangwill to observe that his treatment of Territorialism is hardly less gracious." "I am not single-minded for Ito work," he noted in his 1911 diary.

I have read the Minutes of the Seventh Zionist Congress at which Zangwill stood for the acceptance of the British offer in East Africa. "Zangwill, get out!" was the reception he got when he rose to speak. "Please," Dr. Alexander Marmorek, who presided at the Session, pleaded with the delegates, "please let Mr. Zangwill speak. Mr. Zangwill is a delegate, and has a right to speak here." The cry went up: "No, he is not a Zionist!" In 1908, at a Conference of the Ito, Zangwill offered his resignation from the Presidency, because he felt "the necessity of dissociating so great a movement from a single personality, whose withdrawal from Jewish politics was demanded by many enemies."

After his 1923 speech in America, Mr. Samuel Untermyer protested against his "destructive and ill-balanced diatribe," and said: "Mr. Zangwill is not a Jewish leader. He has behind him no organisation and no followers." Dr. Shmarya Levin numbered him for that speech among the "detractors of the Jewish people." Dr. Weizmann said it was "bordering on national treason." The periodical *Palestine* said the speech belonged "to that class of speeches which enemies file away for production at a later opportunity." Zangwill himself insisted at the time that "some of my critics misconstrue me terribly." Ten years after his death Chief Rabbi Hertz held up that very speech for which he had been so attacked as one of his great Jewish utterances.

Zangwill was a grand fighter. He fought for his views with the vigorous pen of a brilliant and fearless journalist. Yet he had an idea that journalism was something lower than literature and art, and he kept denying that he was a journalist. When Max Nordau died in 1923, some of us who had known him in London, arranged a memorial meeting, and I was asked to send Zangwill a telegram to preside at the meeting. He replied: "Dear Leftwich, I was very sorry to refuse your request, but I am not really in place as a journalist, especially when there are men available like Lucien Wolf or Greenberg, who are an ornament to their profession. As your Bureau will probably be sending out articles about Nordau I send a small one (gratis). It might also be read at your Meeting when conveying my regrets at my inability to attend. I should like to add that, in my opinion, a protest against the confiscation of Nordau's resources by the French Government should be made, or at any rate, an appeal to that Government for the restitution of the same to the widow. Doubtless I shall be seeing you in London, so the other matters can keep." That note about the article (which is printed in the Soncino volume of Zangwill's speeches and articles as "Nordau and Abarbanel") being gratis, to what was a small and struggling agency, is characteristic of Zangwill. It was his regular practice. "The overwhelming part of my Jewish work is done for nothing, and it takes the greater part of my life," he wrote in 1919 to Henry Hurwitz, the Editor of the New York *Menorah Journal*. "All the more reason therefore that I should occasionally put in a stroke to earn my livelihood, especially in days when the Government takes away about a third of one's income and prices are rising all round." But the phrase I have in mind is that he is "not really in place as a journalist."

Was it because journalism had once been a hard struggle and a frustration? When his book *The Premier and the Painter* failed, he said that he "sank entirely in the slough of journalism." Then at the age of twenty-seven he was glad to take the opportunity *The Bachelors' Club* gave him to "cross Fleet Street" out of journalism back to writing books. He grew away from journalism in another way—as a younger man, in the early 1900s "Zangwill was fond of the atmosphere of the printing office" and, Mr. Philip Cowen said, "often dropped in" to the office of the *American Hebrew* while he was in New York. In later years he could not stand such noise. The study doors at Far End bore notices that no one was to "make a noise in the corridor" between certain hours. He had to have absolute silence and no disturbance while he was writing. At one time he had, as he related, been "working in odds and ends of time, correcting proofs of the first chapters while I was writing the last." He wrote his *Big Bow Mystery* like that, working out the plot while the first chapters were already in print, as a newspaper serial. His brother Louis did that too, with his mystery novel, *A Nineteenth Century Miracle*, which he gave me in copies of the *Star*, where it was serialised. So in America, at the end of his fight over his "Watchman, What of the Night?" speech, at the end of 1923, Israel Zangwill announced that he was now going "to retire to the Ivory Tower of Art." There he found time to complete and produce a new play *We Moderns*.

The play was produced in New York in March 1924, with Helen Hayes as Mary Sundale. It was a commercial failure. Possibly, the anti-Zangwill feeling in New York had much to do with it. "Jews raised no finger in New York to save this play," he wrote, "from the mendacity of local critics who were out to avenge—and prove—the statement that I had made in the Town Hall of their curious city, that America's sense of public honour was inferior to England's."

"Genuine failures are allowed to slip out quietly," he suggested.
"But as if to put their motives beyond dispute, some of my critics
devoted articles with big headlines to the obsequies, full of indecent
jubilation." "Here is a play of mine," he said, "produced in New
York, with the largest Jewish population any city has ever held, not
excluding Jerusalem at the height of its glory—and the Jewish
theatre proprietor and the Jewish public allow it to die in three
weeks. The only consolation is the blow it has given to the legend of
the Elders of Zion, among whom I have the honour to be one of the
most sinister figures."

"There was a moral bravery in the man," Jacob de Haas wrote of
that last speech of his in New York in 1923. It "created a still greater
storm because he criticised the Zionist Organisation. He was no
respecter of persons, and in America one of his great sins was that
he snubbed the rich, and pricked the bubble of much meaningless
oratory. Meeting him in New York after the American Jewish
Congress debacle I was impressed with his growing nervousness."
"Not long ago he had been in America," Zangwill said in London in
1925, "and had tried to teach there, with the result that he had got
into trouble."

On his return to England Zangwill found Robert Atkins, the
producer of the Old Vic, was leaving that theatre, and going into
management for himself. He decided to start off with Zangwill's
We Moderns. The play opened in the provinces, in Southport, in
April 1924, and came to London in July 1924, at the New Theatre.
It had a good London Press. *The Morning Post* said that the play
"has the weight and wit we expect from Mr. Zangwill. Its theme is
the familiar one of the clash between the older and the younger
generation. We are not fobbed off with the superficial marks of the
conflict. Mr. Zangwill's observation of these is shrewd, but his
comment on their underlying significances counts for more. For one
of the elders he shows a remarkable acquaintance with the moderns,
and sympathy as well." The *Manchester Guardian* thought "the play
should be popular. It has the sharp metallic Zangwill wit, and Mr.
Zangwill this time is on the popular side, hunting a popular quarry."
The *Daily Mail* described it as "a brilliant play, a play full-charged
with epigrammatic wit." The *Daily News*, now the *News Chronicle*,
expected "more from Israel Zangwill than he has given us in *We
Moderns*," but thought that "probably he has managed to write a
best seller."

The *Daily Telegraph* was almost alone in sensing the trouble.
"Mr. Zangwill has done far fresher and better work," it said. "The
play would be better for a good deal of compression." A more valid
objection was made in *G.K.'s Weekly* by its dramatic critic, Mr. J. K.
Prothero, who found the play (already then) "dated," because it

seemed inspired by "one small period—that of the Suffragist. Now
that the vote has been won by women, the creatures of Mr. Zangwill's
brain speak with hollow voices as from a very narrow tomb. The
author, as it seems to me, at a most impressionable age was caught
up by the Suffrage movement and still moves in the Pankhurst
orbit. But the author still retains his sense of wit and occasionally
flashes out an epigram. It was sad to recall that delicious, if unequal
comedy *Merely Mary Ann*, and to realise that between this play and
We Moderns there has been no period of growth. In his next work for
the theatre more than one of his admirers cherishes the hope that
Mr. Zangwill will go back to his race for inspiration. The author of
Stories of the Ghetto should still have much to say of vital moment on
the stage." Mr. Prothero went from *We Moderns* to see a revival of
The Wild Duck, and found Ibsen immortal. He also saw St. John
Ervine's *Anthony and Anna*, and his criticism of that play provoked
St. John Ervine to make a protest. "No one has less right to com-
plain of harsh criticism than I have," he wrote, "nor do I complain
of it. Nor do I complain of Mr. Prothero's suggestion that I wrote
Anthony and Anna for money. I write all my plays for money. If Mr.
Prothero was able to write plays he too would write them for
money. But I do complain of his suggestion that I corruptly write for
money. I put it to you, Sir, that this is not a charge which should
be made against a man merely because he has written a play which
Mr. Prothero happens to despise." Zangwill too wrote to *G.K.'s
Weekly* about "Mr. Prothero's not unkindly notice of my comedy
We Moderns," to point out that the real modern girl of the play is
not Mary but Dolly. "I am amused," he said, "by your critic's
recognition of 'delicious qualities' in my ancient comedy *Merely
Mary Ann*. They were certainly not recognised by the critics of the
day." The Editor added a note to the letter: "We appreciate very
highly the compliment of a letter from Mr. Zangwill; the points
raised are not within our immediate department."

The mention of Zangwill's "ancient comedy, *Merely Mary Ann*,"
brings to mind his other ancient play *Children of the Ghetto*, to which
he referred in his pamphlet about the failure of *We Moderns*.
"In a recent editorial," he said, "the *New York Times* pleaded with
the Theatre Guild to revive that 'masterpiece of our national drama,'
my *Children of the Ghetto*. No wonder Mr. Tyler wrote to the journal
to remind it that in 1899 when he produced this 'masterpiece' with a
wonderful cast only one critic had a good word for it. Possibly
twenty-five years hence—when I shall be beyond caring—*We
Moderns* too will have grown into a masterpiece." Mr. Prothero's
reference to Ibsen prompts a mention of Dr. Edwards, the London
correspondent of the Berlin *Vossische Zeitung* who saw *We Moderns*,
and wrote that he wished that "the whole play could be done in

Germany, and have such a production as the unforgettable latest rendering of Ibsen's *League of Youth* at the Deutsches Theatre. Only the very best representation could," in his opinion, "do full justice to the fineness of the structure and the dialogue." The wish was fulfilled. "I suppose," Zangwill wrote to me on 21st April 1926, a year later, "you will have heard that last night Reinhardt produced my *We Moderns* at the Deutsches Theatre, Berlin. I had a wire this morning that it was a great success, but between ourselves, it is so badly mutilated by the translator that I have no faith in its future."

At first Zangwill had meant to go back to writing his novel, *The Baron of Offenbach*. Soon after his return to England, on 12th May 1924, he wrote to me: "I am going abroad for a month to study material for my new Jewish novel." But it was never completed. The Theatre took possession of him. Mrs. Zangwill placed it on record "that the typescript of an unfinished novel by my late husband entitled *The Baron of Offenbach* is now deposited at the British Museum and if at any time there should arise a suitable and fitting appreciation of my late husband's work I desire such typescript to be published."

The trouble was that Robert Atkins had decided that to succeed *We Moderns* must undergo certain changes. Zangwill who had written in *The Idler* in 1893, when he was not yet thirty, that he had "never been able to endure the slightest arbitrary interference with my work" refused to allow any changes to be made. Robert Atkins told me afterwards that they were not drastic changes that he had proposed, and he was sure that if Zangwill had agreed to them the play would have been a box-office success, and Zangwill need not have plunged into his last disastrous struggle as a theatre manager, which cost him his money, his health, perhaps his reason and his life. As it was, "But for my own financial help," Zangwill wrote, describing himself "as the sole financier of my season," "the play would not have survived its first fortnight in London." Among the letters he wrote at that time was one to Mrs. Nordau, in which he said: "My success in the theatre has been only moral and I have had to pay heavily for it."

Yet even in the midst of his theatrical difficulties Zangwill still, in that last year of his life, was turning over in his mind offers to go abroad lecturing. He was approached on all sides. He was regarded as the only English Jew of world-importance. People abroad had got into the habit of attributing everything in Anglo-Jewish life to Zangwill. In December 1914 Zangwill had written to the *Jewish Chronicle* to disclaim something the *Frankfurter Zeitung* had said was "obviously due to the inspiration of the Hon. Herr Zangwill, that if the Rumanian Jews had not yet obtained their rights it was because England was kept back by Germany from insisting on the fulfilment of the provisions of the Berlin Congress." "I seem to remember some such suggestion in your columns, whether your own or a correspondent's I cannot recall," Zangwill wrote, "but I shall be glad if you, Sir, will state (and the Jewish American Press will copy) that I have not the faintest responsibility for anything that appears in your columns except what appears over my own signature. I note, however, not without pleasure," he went on, "that although my services to England may not be appreciated by British Jewry, Germany understands so well my patriotic zeal, and has followed so closely my championship of England in neutral lands, that she thinks me even capable of mendacity in my country's cause. That is, of course, the sort of mistake Germany is always making. An English Jew will die for England if occasion calls, but he will not lie for her—or even for her Jews."

The Editor of the *Jewish Chronicle* added a note: "We are most happy to accede to Mr. Zangwill's very reasonable—and very kindly —request. It may interest him and our readers to know that a letter recently sent by us to *The Times* was printed by an American journal as his handiwork, and, on the other hand, a Dutch paper, quite characteristically, attributed something he had written 'to the author of the *Children of the Ghetto*, who is now Chief Rabbi of England, and the Editor of the *Jewish Chronicle*.' "

Zangwill refused the lecturing offers, "as my health would not permit it." I hadn't realised how ill he was, and in April 1925 I sent him a letter I had received from Zalman Reisen, in Vilna, suggesting a visit by Zangwill to Poland. It would have been a great thing after his speech eighteen months before in New York, for Zangwill to speak to the Jews of that three-million Polish Jewry which Hitler annihilated between fifteen and twenty years later, the Jews of Warsaw and Vilna and Bialystock and Brest-Litovsk, near where his mother was born. "As to Mr. Reisen," he wrote to me, "your recommendation induces me to meet his demands to some extent; but I had already refused the offer of a leading agent to visit Poland, as my health would not permit it. I can only attend a few rehearsals of my new play. Apropos I send you a paragraph about it; but I want you to hold it up for an hour or two as I have sent a copy to Mr. Robert Atkins, who might not approve of it. I have told him to ring you up, if it is all right, and whether he would like anything added."

His trouble with Robert Atkins had already started. Holbrook Jackson told me he passed the Fortune Theatre about this time, and saw Zangwill and Atkins outside the theatre in fierce argument. Then Zangwill sent me a letter dated "August Bank Holiday 1925," exactly a year before he died on August Bank Holiday 1926, from Dr. Redcliffe Salaman's home at Royston, near Cambridge, to tell me that "*We Moderns* is moving to another West End London theatre, the name of which cannot yet be disclosed. The general fact plus the news it is leaving the New Theatre at the end of this week will probably appear ere you get this, but to counteract any impression of failure I have warned the theatre it must not announce 'Last Week' without adding 'At This Theatre' or 'Resuming Elsewhere.' This is the moment for publishing the Bishop's letter and I should be particularly glad if you could get it over to America when it would co-operate with Colleen Moore's return from filming *We Moderns* to prove New York had failed to kill it. Of course seats or a box for the New Theatre are at your disposal. I shall be at the Wednesday matinee (in the lobby about 2.25). My address otherwise up to Friday is c/o Thomas Moult. The letter you forwarded came as the last straw. I return it that you may—at your leisure—tell me why I am thus plagued. In future please open any letters c/o you and let me have a synopsis, Then I shall be Yours Gratefully Israel Zangwill."

First National Pictures Inc. of New York had acquired the world film rights of *We Moderns* for Miss Colleen Moore. The Bishop was Dr. Garbett, later Archbishop of York, who saw *We Moderns* and wrote to him to praise it. I haven't heard of *We Moderns* being shown as a film, but old films disappear quickly. Zangwill wrote to me, in 1925: "My *Children of the Ghetto* and *The Melting Pot* have been filmed all over the States, and the former was even presented in the very latest hall in New York. Also both have been done throughout Great Britain."

Zangwill transferred *We Moderns* to the Fortune Theatre, built and owned by his friend of Jews' Free School days, Laurence Cowen, brother of Louis Cowen, his collaborator in *Premier and the Painter*. "*Punch* pictured me years ago," he said, "as Lord Zion, and later many have believed that I aimed to be King of Jerusalem, with the Arabs expelled. But that I should ever become manager of a West End theatre has never entered into my wildest dreams." "Without the generous sympathy and co-operation of my old friend Laurence Cowen, proprietor of the Fortune Theatre, it could not have been possible. Being a Jew I am not out for money." " 'Box office draws' will play no part in the casting." "During my season at the Fortune I hope to give most of my plays by making the popular pay for the highbrow." "I shall be my own producer, for neither Robert Atkin nor the critics understand."

An odd thing about Laurence Cowen's relations with Israel Zangwill is that according to Laurence Cowen they persisted after Zangwill's death. In 1936, ten years after Zangwill had died, Mr. Maurice Barbanel, the spiritualist, wrote that Laurence Cowen had come into the spiritualist movement "because of the evidence received from his old friend Israel Zangwill," from whom Mr. Barbanel also claimed to have received a "spirit extra." The Zangwill family had no spirit communication with Zangwill, and knew nothing of the "evidence." Zangwill during his life did not seem impressed with the "evidence" of spiritualism. He had in fact written very strongly against spiritualism. "If Moses came to London he would have been very disgusted with it," he wrote. "For that supremely sane and sage legislator made one clean sweep of all the festering superstitions that fascinate the silly and the scientific to-day, as much as they did three thousand years ago. Deuteronomy is most definite —'There shall not be found in thee a consulter with a familiar spirit.' "

Zangwill had made some experiments as a young man with "spirits." He didn't really believe in them, he explained. He just wanted to try out a theory he had. He tried them about the date of his death, and he found "they did not contradict each other. There was a cheerful unanimity about the Author's dying at fifty-seven. But this did not perturb the Author." The spirits were wrong by five years. Zangwill died at sixty-two. We should have lost a good deal had Zangwill died in 1921, instead of 1926, including his great speech in 1923, "Watchman, What of the Night?" and of course his play We Moderns, about which his last years turned.

Mr. Prothero's reminder in G.K.'s Weekly of Merely Mary Ann may have led Zangwill to announce that We Moderns would be followed by Merely Mary Ann, "which, though played all over the world, has not been seen in London since 1905, when Henry Ainley, Gerald du Maurier and Miss Eleanor Robson made a brilliant trio in it at the Duke of York's Theatre." "Following these," it was announced, "Mr. Zangwill will revive Too Much Money and The Melting Pot, and will stage two other plays—The King of Schnorrers and (if Censorship permits) his still prohibited play The Next Religion." It was to be a season of Zangwill plays. But Zangwill found theatre management a very involved business. It took him beyond his own plays. "It was never my intention on assuming management to do any but my own works," he said, "but the inducement came in the shape of a play which reached me from a totally unknown source. When I had finished the reading of Gloriana, I was so impressed by its literary and dramatic qualities that I felt, come what may, I just had to produce it. Gloriana is in my opinion the greatest drama ever written by a woman." Gloriana is a play of the Tudor Queen Elizabeth, by Miss Gwen John, which was published by the British Drama League in 1923, under the title The Prince. "This is a study of character, based on contemporary evidence," she said in her Foreword to the play. "It is a series of impressions rather than dramatic happenings, and the more obviously dramatic events have been avoided." But there are dramatic scenes and dramatic speeches in the play that must have stirred Zangwill's heart, like Elizabeth ordering Drake to sail for the Spanish waters, "to the end which God may appoint." "To the breaking of tyranny—to the new day!"

Zangwill discovered that he was what he himself called "a green-horn" in theatre management. There was a law suit over scenery and properties supplied for *We Moderns* and *Merely Mary Ann*. Zangwill counter-claimed for alleged overcharges and for scenery he had to supply because of the alleged inadequacy of that supplied. The Judge said he was sorry for Mr. Zangwill, but he would have to give judgment against him. The whole experiment unnerved him. "I have had a nervous breakdown," he wrote to Mrs. Nordau on 1st April 1926. His health had been bad before that. While *We Moderns* was still in rehearsal with Robert Atkins, before there was any suggestion of changes or any quarrel, he wrote to me: "I can only attend a few rehearsals of my play, as my health would not permit it." It was just after the judgment against him that he telephoned me, and in a quick rush of words told me that his doctor had ordered him to rest, and he was going back to Far End, but as soon as he was better he would return and resume his fight for his place in the theatre. He never came back. I had a letter from Mrs. Zangwill in June 1926 telling me that the doctors had ordered him a complete rest and had sent him to a nursing home. "He is already a little better," she wrote, "so I hope that his health will with sufficient time be completely restored." On 1st August Zangwill died. I still have the telegram from Mrs. Zangwill telling me of his death.

Primrose was at Far End, on the lawn with her cousins, Israel Zangwill's three children, that first of August 1926, when Zangwill died. "It was a flawless summer's day," she wrote afterwards. "A taxi drew up outside the house; their mother had returned from the nursing home. They rushed to her for news of their father. As I walked across the grass the sudden awareness of tragedy clutched at my heart. After twenty-five years that moment is as fresh and poignant in my memory as if it had happened yesterday. The next morning when I read the long obituary columns, I was even proud of my sense of bereavement, as Aunt Leah tied a black sash round my white dress. Aunt Leah was beyond tears. There was not much outward expression of sorrow; it went too deep for that. The children tried to be as stoical as their elders. My cousin Peggy said to me thoughtfully: 'If Daddy had lived, he wouldn't have been able to do any more work.' I was a little shocked that Uncle Israel was to be cremated. It was a new thing in our family. But Uncle Louis's explanation made a deep impression on my mind: His brother's mortal remains would vanish into air like a spirit, leaving nothing to decay."

"Undoubtedly the launching of a West End season of his own plays was the most tragic blunder Uncle Israel ever made," Primrose wrote, reflecting the feeling in the family about that last period in his life. In the last two years, she said, bearing out in a way what Dr. Redcliffe Salaman put more forcibly when he told me that for the last two years of his life he was not really *compos mentis*, "he looked burnt out." "His insomnia was terrible. His nerves were torn to shreds. He quarrelled with the dramatic critics; he fought gruelling law suits over stage scenery; he worried everyone dreadfully. He was a weary man, thinner and frailer than ever before. He used to lie in a chaise longue in the sunshine. He drank hot water. Nothing could relieve his terrible insomnia. He could find no rest. Yet he still made puns and gleams of his old self showed through his weariness."

He lost thousands of pounds on his theatrical venture. His will, made in 1920, did not take account of those heavy losses which came six years later. He left all his literary and dramatic rights, all manuscripts, letters and papers to his wife, and she at her death left all these rights to be dealt with by their son, Oliver Zangwill. Mrs. Zangwill explained after the publication of the will that the discrepancy between the amount bequeathed and the value of the estate was due to heavy theatrical losses.

Dr. Stephen Wise, who as Chairman of the American Jewish Congress when Zangwill delivered his "Watchman, What of the Night?" speech, had repudiated him as a Jewish spokesman, declaring that he spoke not for Israel, but for Israel Zangwill, was in London when Zangwill died, and officiated at the cremation. Now Stephen Wise spoke in his officiating address of that speech as "a weighty message, the one fault of which lay in its too daring hope and its too audacious truth-speaking." He said of him that "the occasionally loyal of Israel are treated with deference and the sacrificially loyal too often go without reverence." "But not since the death of Herzl has the passing of any Jew evoked such grief throughout the Diaspora. Because of his courage he did not always please men, least of all his fellow-Jews who sat in high places. Fate has made the Jew impatient of the critic, of the self-critic, particularly. Therefore the potent leaders of Israel sometimes love peace better than the right. Zangwill will be remembered," he declared, "when the puny protestants of his day shall have been forgotten. Now he belongs to the ages. Zangwill belongs to the Jewish ages, enduring and unforgetting."

In those days there was no paper shortage in England, and the *Jewish Chronicle* had an Editorial on Zangwill's death, as well as a special article by the Editor, L. J. Greenberg, writing as "Mentor," and a five-page obituary. "Only now," the Editor said, "can we begin to know what his sojourn among us really meant for us. Jews of this generation the world over have grown up as part of their lives with the man whose life came to an untimely end on Sunday. The spirit that animated him is not dead; it will live on and on and on. Time will write with no uncertain finger of the career and character of Israel Zangwill. Regarding his life as a whole Jews never had a more splendid champion."

But Zangwill was a champion not only of Jews. When H. G. Wells complained that "the whole of Mr. Zangwill's political outlook is dominated by the problem of Zionism," he replied: "Let us see. At a dubious moment of the war Mr. Balfour promised Palestine to the Jews in the event of a British victory. The whole of the period that intervened between that declaration and the victory I was crying 'Stop the War!' For I felt that Germany was sufficiently checked and no British victory would be worth the loss that would accrue—even to Britain—from the impending collapse of Europe. Obviously on your hypothesis, I ought to have egged on England and let Europe go to the devil, if only the Jews could get their bit of Asia." The same charge that during the war, "Zangwill and the Jewish spokesmen were most elaborately and energetically demonstrating that they cared not a rap for the troubles and dangers of English, French, Germans, Russians, Americans or any other people but their own," was made by H. G. Wells in his book, *In Search of Hot Water*. The book went out of print, and Mrs. Zangwill decided that as it was not in circulation, it would be "better to let sleeping dogs lie."

Wells afterwards explained that Zangwill had provoked him by always pushing forward the Jewish cause in season and out of season. There are many stories of Zangwill's stubbornness and his persistence in pushing his ideas upon people, "in season and out of season," his frequent fits of exasperation when people could not understand him when he was being driven frantic by some act of injustice or savagery. He was often in the position of the Jew whom he described, "having seen these things," as sitting in his room "writing appeals to the rulers and potentates of the nations, begging them to make an end of the sufferings of the Jews. You perceive," he said pointedly, "that he is mad." Oliver Wendell Holmes said there are things which if they don't drive people mad, those people ought to be ashamed of themselves. I always found Zangwill kindly and good natured. But then I shared his fury because of the terrible reports that kept pouring in to my office about the treatment of Jews in one country or another. There is a speech of Zangwill's printed in *The Voice of Jerusalem* which ends with a number of such reports taken from the Jewish Telegraphic Agency Bulletin which I was then editing—"Another Ukrainian Massacre," "Riot at Kovno," "Rioting in Galicia," "Outrage upon Hungarian Jewesses,"

"Jewish Exodus from Poland," "The White Terror in Hungary"—
"The Chronicle," he said, "flows on to another page. A pogrom in
Jerusalem. But enough! This, be it marked, is by no means a bad
page of Jewish news of the week. It is an average example of the
continuous pogrom in action, the vast majority of the episodes in
which never even find their way into print. Such is the background of
the Zionist rejoicings. Infinitely more important and urgent therefore
than any pseudo-Restoration to Palestine is the problem of the
Diaspora."

I was with Zangwill when the news arrived of the pogrom in
Jerusalem in 1921, and Jabotinsky's arrest for organising a self-
defence. I remember how excited, how indignant he became, and how
he stood telephoning in all directions, in an attempt not only to get
the news widely published, but to rouse opinion, and to move the
authorities to act.

I have been reading Anatole France on Flaubert, and I think
he described something that Flaubert had in common with Zangwill.
"Gustave Flaubert was very good-natured," says Anatole France.
"He had a prodigious capacity for enthusiasm and sympathy. That
is why he was always in a rage. He went to war on every possible
occasion, having continually an insult to avenge. He was in the same
case as Don Quixote. If Don Quixote had cared less for justice and
felt less pity for weakness, he would not have broken the Biscayan
mule-driver's head, nor run his lance through the innocent sheep."
It may have bearing on Zangwill's "madness." "I say madness, and
not insanity," Anatole France wrote. "Insanity is the loss of the
intellectual faculties. Madness is only a strange and singular use of
those faculties."

Zangwill had friendships with Lloyd George and Winston
Churchill and Joseph Chamberlain, whom "I converted to the con-
ception of British East Africa turned into a British Judea." He spoke
of "my friends Maeterlinck, Shaw and Wells." There was a time when
"I was living with Maeterlinck." He had his disagreements with
Wells, but when Turkey came into the war on Germany's side in
1914, it was to Zangwill that Wells addressed his query: "And now
what is to prevent the Jews having Palestine and restoring a real
Judea?" He spoke of "My friend Bernard Shaw." He said. "Mr.
Kipling confided to me." G. K. Chesterton referred to "great Jews
like Zangwill." "It seems only yesterday," said Zangwill, "since
Walter Pater sat by my side." He knew John Davidson, "a great
poet." He knew Gissing. He hunted up Verlaine. "Oscar Wilde," he
wrote, "once said to me." "I once expressed to Whistler my conviction that . . ." "My friend Sir James Frazer." Barrie and Galsworthy spoke of him as their friend. When Reuben Brainin, a leading
Hebrew journalist and an early Zionist, interviewed Shaw and the

question of Zionism came up, Shaw said: "My friend Zangwill is also a Zionist, and has greatly interested me in the movement."

Louis Golding speaks of Zangwill sometimes putting on side, and of "the preparatory school arrogance with which he told me he had beaten Colonel So-and-So at croquet. And whereas he was no more than a scion of the sunless and grassless Ghetto, the gallant Colonel was sprung from the loins of generations of University blues." It is true. Zangwill did put on side, sometimes. He loved to recall his meetings with the great, forgetting that he was a great man himself. "When I first met Meredith, he said to me . . . " *"The King of Schnorrers* was read aloud by Oscar Wilde to a duchess." "I won over the great Joseph Chamberlain and Winston Churchill." "I met Lord Robert Cecil, and this time he greeted me 'My dear friend.' Lord Robert Cecil comes from the oldest English nobility and I, after all, was only the son of a Russian pedlar." In 1889, when he was twenty-five, he wrote in his diary: "I do not care for 'fame'—at least not much."

But Zangwill could also be humble. When he published his translation of Gabirol's poems poets and scholars praised his work. Rabbi Dr. David de Sola Pool said that "rarely has the translator slipped up," and in dealing specifically with one of his mistranslations he said "this is one of the rare errors into which he has fallen." He found it was "a task for even Mr. Zangwill's ingenuity to transfer to an English version the pedantically subtle allusiveness which characterises so much of Hebrew poetry." When another scholar, Dr. Wolfson of Harvard, corrected Zangwill about some things he had said in an essay on Gabirol, he wrote: "I do not in the least mind being corrected. I welcome it. I have no first-hand learning whatever, but I understand what I am about with second-hand material. As a rule I sit humbly at the feet of savants, among whom I have never ranged myself. But I have begun to notice a pedantic itch for correction. I object to being pedantically misread."

Golding saw him put on side about his prowess at croquet; he was the same about his other games. I find it difficult to see Zangwill, as I knew him in his older, frail years, as a sportsman. He rode. Harry Greenwall, the journalist, says that, as a boy in Maida Vale he used to see Israel Zangwill riding a horse past his house. There are descriptions of Zangwill riding in Rotten Row. He used to go riding from East Preston to Littlehampton. When he was in Jerusalem, he said, he rode on horseback all round the City. He was a swimmer. His cousin Dr. Eder said he gave Israel Zangwill his first swimming lesson in the Baths at Goulston Street, off Whitechapel High Street; swimming "throughout his life," he added, was to him "a most joyful pastime. Swimming in the sea became to him the passionate enjoyment it was to Swinburne. It must have been a little later that he had

his first bicycle lesson on an old boneshaker I somehow possessed."
His niece Primrose says he prided himself on being an athlete. He
cycled with his wife through Alpine Switzerland. He strode down
Zangwill Lane at Far End to swim strongly in the sea. "He looked an
odd figure striding out into the sea, so bent and emaciated, as if the
vigorous breeze must be too strong for him. But he withstood it and
battled against it." His brothers, Louis and Mark, too, were good
swimmers. "Unlike Israel, Louis had a fine physique. It was Uncle
Israel who first taught me to swim." "Louis was not a cyclist like
Israel, but he was a great walker, and he often went on walking tours
with Israel. When he was at Far End he loved to join Israel and his
friends in a game of croquet." Jerome K. Jerome said "Zangwill
used to be keen on croquet but never had the makings of a great
player." Herman Bernstein wrote that when he stayed at Far End
Zangwill woke him in the morning, "and we went out for a swim.
Then we played his favourite game of golf-croquet on his beautiful
lawn. He played an excellent game and seemed quite proud of it."
He also spoke of Zangwill after dinner playing the piano (it was the
pianola Zangwill played) in his study, "with deep emotion, his head
thrown back, his frail form swaying violently, his dreamy eyes half-
closed. He played with the same exaltation with which some chassidic
rabbis pray." Louis Golding suggests that if Zangwill "had achieved
the championship of croquet over all Surrey and Sussex, he would
have been twenty times more conceited about it than if the Nobel
Prize had been conferred on him." I remember Louis Zangwill
telling me of their games of croquet, and their walking tours. Israel
Zangwill also played tennis, and he shot—he kept a record of the
number of pheasants he shot.

Zangwill's habit of punning and jesting which persisted even in his
last illness, when he lay in the chaise longue at Far End, sipping hot
water, thin and frail and worn out with sleeplessness, always kept
breaking out. As far back as 1893 he had made a New Year resolution "never to joke again." But that must have been a joke. He
punned on his name. Speaking at a dinner, he said that on the list
his name was printed as Zangwell. Perhaps they had thought to let
well alone. He had thought himself that his name had an "ill"
ending, but "All's well that ends well."

To Andrew Lang, the critic, he wrote:

> If Andrew Lang will
> Israel Zangwill.

Someone reviewing a book of Zangwill's said it was full of Sweet
Williams and Zangwilliams. Professor Smertenko told me that when
Zangwill was in America he printed an article criticising him.

Zangwill responded by inviting him to lunch. At the end of the meal Smertenko helped Zangwill on with his coat, and Zangwill remarked: "Now I understand. No man is a hero to his valet."

Zangwill told the story of a Jew who asked to see him. He came and sat looking at Zangwill, who finally asked what he could do for him. "Thank you," said the man, "you haf done for me." He illustrated the importance of faith by a story of what happened to him during the war. He had three sovereigns in his sovereign case, and decided to leave them there for eventualities. He did not open his sovereign case all during the war. At the end he found it empty. But all those years he had felt he had the security of the gold in his case.

It takes two to make one brother, he reminded us. And to the Immigration restrictionists he suggested that we are all immigrants to this planet. He asked what would have happened if Eve had not accepted Adam. When he was a teacher and a boy came to school and said he hadn't been able to do his home work, he reminded him that cane came after Abel.

In his early *Mantle of Elijah*, he had concluded that "Life is a dull business. Seventy years is a long time to go on dressing and undressing oneself." When he spoke of immortality, he wondered why it should be thought of only as in the future, and why people did not want to live also in the past—in the Stone Age, and in the days of Creation. Yet he concluded: "A future life is unthinkable, but not therefore impossible, and there are not a few people I should love to see again or to atone to."

Israel Zangwill was a doubter who was always wondering whether there might not be something after all in the things he doubted, the reverse of that old Jew of whom he told, that lying on his death bed after a long life spent in faith, and rigid observance and piety he was heard to laugh. "Wouldn't it be funny," he said, "if there were no future life after all, no punishment and reward." He was always trying to escape from the narrowness of Judaism to the universal, and always ended by singing new hymns to Judaism. He told H. G. Wells in search, like himself, of a new religion, that what he sought was there in Judaism. "We are back in the derided Old Testament. The fact is that Mr. Wells has all the stigmata of Hebrew prophecy. Mr. Wells even unconsciously accepts in principle the dietary and sexual regimen of Judaism," the same regimen that he himself had found narrow and tribal, and had suggested cutting away. "What has Judaism been about," he asks at the end of his pamphlet *Chosen Peoples*, "that Lincoln did not know that there was (in Judaism) such a Church" as he was seeking? "Too long," he cries, "has Israel been silent."

The *Next Religion* is his own interpretation of Judaism. "If there were only a single God, and He a God of Justice and the world, how could He be confined to Israel?" "Religion, not race, has always been the guiding principle in Jewish history." "The Talmud defined a non-idolater as a Jew, and ranked a Gentile learned in the Torah as greater than the High Priest." He had drawn the conclusion from the Dreyfus case that "the non-Jew Zola was a truer Jew than many a born, married and buried Hebrew." Even his approaches to Christianity—and they went so far as to suggest that "the Old Testament is as far from finality as the New, which Judaism should now add to it"—were inspired by his feeling that "both are compounded of the same elements, only in different proportions. This is not to deny that the result is different. But it is to affirm that their affinities are minor and adjustable compared with their common antagonism to atheism, polytheism and pragmatic pluralism." What he feared was the resurrection of the "old German gods with their racial Valhallas," and the spread of "the Futurist morals—that there is no objective gauge of right or wrong, no standard but the individual whim." He quoted against that doctrine the Jewish proclamation: "Let Judgment run down as waters and righteousness as a mighty stream." What inspired him was "the millennial dream of Judaism," the message of the Alenu prayer, with which "every service ends— 'And all the children of flesh will call upon Thy name . . . In that day the Lord shall be One and His name One.' " "Israel disappears altogether," he pointed out, "in this diurnal aspiration." "Our whole war-ravaged world," he said, "will have to turn back to the old Jewish ideals—'To do justice, love mercy, and walk humbly with thy God.' The claims of the Jewish race do not rest on its separate blood but on its quality and its history."

Yet this universalist could also preach Jewish nationalism— "to re-nationalise Judaism," could argue that "internationalism must be rooted in nationalism, that there cannot be a brotherhood of peoples without peoples to be brothers. When we have a country of our own we can begin to talk brotherhood." Nor was his nationalism only Jewish. "As an English-born citizen I am proud that my country England deserves it of us, and our lives are at her call." He was proud that he was an English Jew, who could speak to the British Government as an Englishman, not as an outsider, overawed or antagonistic. "There must be some mean between Erskine Childers and Uriah Heap." "A people cannot be saved by 'bated breath and whispering humbleness.' "

It made the pacifist and universalist declare during the war that "the victory of England is desirable—even for the outside world— because she is England." It made him work for the Jewish Legion, and ask Herman Bernstein when he came from America in 1915 "to cable to the American newspapers an appeal to the Jewish youth of America to enlist in the Jewish Legion." "I shall be glad to hear

I

from any able-bodied young men," he said in an appeal he issued, "who are ready to promote the cause of this country and the honour of the Jewish name." Before the Jewish Legion was formed, when Colonel Patterson was leading the Zion Mule Corps, Zangwill was writing in a letter: "I have a cable from Patterson, from Alexandria. 'Can you recruit and send to Alexandria 1,000 useful Jews for Zion Corps?' Now Jabotinsky is gone, and I no longer know whether he can get the recruits. I will see the War Office to understand the conditions." Herman Bernstein reported that Zangwill "had just received a letter from one of the British commanders at the Dardanelles, in which he wrote in high praise of the bravery and fighting qualities of the Jewish boys, and said that he felt confident Palestine would be liberated by Great Britain and that it would be but a case of historic justice and a fine gesture if Zangwill, the leading British Jew, were to lead the British procession into Palestine, and enter Jerusalem on horseback."

When the Balfour Declaration was issued in 1917, Zangwill deliberately stood aside, "to give the diplomacy of the Zionist leaders and the bona fides of the British politicians the benefit of the doubt." "It was a wise instinct," he had said, "that led to our shores the immortal founder of Zionism, Dr. Herzl; here he first delivered his message."

"Clear thinking upon the Jewish question is as uncommon as upon any other human question," Zangwill confessed. He walked, like all normal men on two legs, and now the weight of him rested on one leg, and now on the other. He was Jew and Englishman, nationalist and universalist. Even at the First Zionist Congress he saw the delegates as "types that once sought to slough their Jewish skins." He had sought to do that himself. "Two opposing forces are at work upon the Jew—the wind and the sun," he said. "The gaberdine, thrown open for a moment in the burst of heat, is buttoned tighter the next before the biting blast." Other Anglo-Jewish writers of his day had thrown off the gaberdine in the English sunshine. Zangwill threw it open, but always kept it on. They despised their fellow Jews, and painted them balefully, and then departed from the Jewish scene. Zangwill remained with the Jews to the end, a painter of the Jewish scene, without malice and without flummery, portraying credible human figures, good and bad, tragic and humorous. He stood in the midst of Jewish life, as a Jewish teacher and a Jewish leader. He had his doubts, and he often tried to escape from the bonds of Judaism, but I do not remember him ever saying as an American Jewish writer, Meyer Levin, has said, that "my dominant childhood memory is of fear and shame at being a Jew."

Zangwill had no such feeling. He often deplored that he had given to the Ghetto what he wanted to give to mankind, and to

Jewish politics what he wanted to give to literature. But however much he tried to get away he kept coming back—he stayed till the end of his life. Even when he was attacked for what he said in his "Watchman, What of the Night?" speech, his critics based their attack on their disappointment that the things they objected to had been said by "Israel Zangwill, once the acclaimed leader not only of English Jewry, but of world Jewry as well." History is not written by ifs, but it is interesting to speculate what might have happened in Zionism and Israel and Jewish life and the world if Israel Zangwill had not stood aside in favour of the Zionist Organisation and Dr. Weizmann and Dr. Sokolov, or even if he had instead of delegating his friend and cousin Dr. Eder, joined the Zionist Commission and the Zionist Executive as the representative of the Ito. "For the Ito to oppose any really practicable plan for a Jewish territory would be not only treason to the Jewish people, but to its own programme." he said when the Balfour Declaration was issued. "I shall always remain persuaded," he declared, "that a Jewish State was possible at the moment when the Arab was a defeated enemy. I shall always believe that the Zionist leadership, perhaps even content with Achad Ha'amism, failed in nerve and will power. The Palestinian was then perfectly ready for a Jewish regime." The Peel Royal Commission which issued the Palestine Partition Report in 1937 confirmed his view seventeen years later, when it said: "If the new frontier had at once been drawn and the new Jewish State at once established, it is possible perhaps that the Arabs would by now have acquiesced."

Zangwill remained convinced of that. He kept saying it to the end of his life. His feeling was that Dr. Weizmann and Lord Samuel were not the people to press their point and to insist on promises being kept. They were, he said, well-meaning, but weak. "As weak a man as my friend Samuel," he said. "The British Empire was never built up by Herbert Samuel or Weizmann. They were too civilised."

"At the beginning of the war Dr. Weizmann came to me," Zangwill recalled, "and asked me—he was not then leader; he was an important figure, but he was not the leader—he came to me and said: 'The organisation (the Zionist Organisation) is broken up through the war; it is in a bad position. If some chance occurs or other that we want somebody of some prestige in England, will you not take over the leadership?' There Dr. Weizmann," said Zangwill, "was absolutely unselfish. He had no idea of course that he would become leader. He asked me out of real, genuine interest in Palestine, to take over the leadership. I replied, 'I am not *persona grata* with a great many of the Zionists; they don't like my ideas and my organisation. If I were to say "Yes, I will take over the leadership," it may only split the organisation still more; but if you would like to, take counsel among them—you seem to have done this off your own bat. Get international opinion, find out whether my coming would split the party, or whether it would really fuse the party, then I will give you my answer.'

"Well," Zangwill went on, "I never heard any further from Dr. Weizmann. He seemed to have found some possibility of going on, and apparently he then thought he could dispense with my assistance." Sir Leon Simon, who was a member of the Zionist Commission set up after the issue of the Balfour Declaration, which Zangwill's cousin, Dr. Eder, joined as the representative of Zangwill's Ito, said that the suggestion of even Eder's appointment to the Commission made him "inclined to resent in principle the inclusion of a representative of the Ito in a Zionist Commission."

Speaking of the Balfour Declaration, Zangwill said that after Dr. Weizmann's early approach to him at the beginning of the war, "I heard nothing directly further until about a week before the Balfour Declaration Sokolov and Tschlenov came down to me and brought me a copy, but then it was too late to do anything. Had they asked my assistance earlier I am sure I would have got a real document, but they did not ask my assistance. After my speech the other day Dr. Weizmann said my speech was a betrayal of the Jewish people; it is one of those romantic things that people say on those occasions, but as a matter of fact I was the only one who guarded the interests of the Jewish people, because when this Balfour Declaration came out it was in the middle of the war, and it took no notice of the interests of the Austrian or Turkish or German Jews. What a terrible situation for the Austrian, Turkish and German Jews! I delivered a speech in the presence of Sir Robert Cecil (Viscount Cecil of Chelwood), Mark Sykes and various other Government representatives, and I brought out this point very clearly. I said: 'Whatever the general Jewish gratitude for this extension of the principle of nationalities, the Jews in Turkey and other now enemy countries are as loyal to their fatherland as we are to ours, and we who stand here have no claim to pledge the race to any power or powers.' You see I guarded the interests of those Jews in the enemy countries, and no one else did then. So I ask, who betrayed the Jewish people, I or Dr. Weizmann?"

Zangwill spoke of how he met Viscount Cecil of Chelwood at a meeting, and he said: "You have forgotten me, Mr. Zangwill." On another occasion, he greeted him as "My dear friend." "I was proud," he said, "because he comes from the oldest English nobility; not only was his father Prime Minister, but his family goes back to Elizabeth and earlier, and I after all was only the son of a Russian pedlar." He spoke of Lloyd George, and how a fortnight before the war he invited Zangwill to breakfast at his house, and "in the course of this breakfast many topics were discussed, and

I said to him: 'I take it for granted that if there is any possibility of a Jewish autonomous State arising, whether in Palestine or anywhere else, it would have your sympathy,' and he said 'Certainly.' Immediately afterwards there was a meeting of my organisation, and I told them that, and it is recorded in the minutes to witness if I lie. Therefore, you see I had begun already before Dr. Weizmann to get Lloyd George's sympathy." "I knew Lloyd George well enough not to have tried to get behind Weizmann and Sokolov, and interfere with their negotiations," Zangwill explained, "knowing that the trouble in Jewish history is that someone always tries to interfere. I simply stood aside and let them run the show."

Dr. Weizmann called Zangwill "our D'Annunzio." It is possible he had something of that quality, which Jabotinsky also had. But a Zionist leadership in the years immediately after the Balfour Declaration and the Mandate consisting of Israel Zangwill, Max Nordau and Jabotinsky might have written history differently.

At the same period, in the spring of 1918, Ab Cahan, the Editor of the New York Yiddish daily *Forward*, hearing a report that the first Governor of Palestine would be a prominent British Jew interpreted it in his paper into a forecast that it would be Israel Zangwill, not thinking of Lord Samuel, to whom the post went. Zangwill might have considered the offer. He had a liking for such marks of distinction. He used to refer to the *Punch* cartoon of himself as Lord Zion. "*Punch* pictured me years ago as Lord Zion," he wrote in one of the last things he did, his attempt to vindicate himself after the failure of his play *We Moderns*, not long before he died. "And lately many have believed," he went on, "that I aimed to be King of Jerusalem." He was flattered by the description of himself as "the leading British Jew," and the suggestion that he (who used to ride horseback in Maida Vale and Rotten Row, and round Sussex, and rode all round Jerusalem on horseback when he was on a visit there) should as "the leading British Jew" enter Jerusalem on horseback, At the head of the British Army.

It is the sort of thing his King of Schnorrers would have loved, "Manasseh the Great, first beggar in Europe," Manasseh Bueno da Costa. "There go my soldiers," he said, with swelling breast, when he heard martial music, and saw a squad of recruits marching with mounted officers, gallant in blue surtouts and scarlet-striped trousers, and fell in step with the military air. Emanuel Romano, looking at the King of Schnorrers with a painter's eye, sees him as a brave, swaggering figure, full of robust humour and a healthy scorn for the conventional successes, making a mockery of riches and conceit. He calls him brother to Don Quixote. This is what the dramatic critic of the London *Daily Telegraph* said when *The King of Schnorrers* was played in the West End in 1950, "a cross between Don Quixote

and Baron Munchausen." Unfortunately, the casting was not successful, and Ernest Milton made him a Shakespearean Benedick, and
strutted and declaimed, instead of making him a confident, arrogant
bravado, who demands his contribution as a right. For he was
conferring a gift, not taking it—giving the rich their opportunity to
win heaven by their alms. Yet I think Zangwill had a sneaking
sympathy also for the dingier, clumsy, stooping Polish Schnorrer,
Yankele, who is more like his pedlar-father, Moses Zangwill. Da
Costa, brilliant, commanding, energetic, not suffering fools gladly,
seems to be Zangwill's heritage from his mother. And Yankele, loom-
ing meekly in the shadow, is his heritage from his father.

"The only Jewish work I have done since *Children of the Ghetto*
is a short serial in the *Idler*, called *The King of Schnorrers*, which is
entirely flippant," Israel Zangwill wrote in 1893 to Mr. Philip Cowen
in New York; "it is merely attempting to seize and express the
humour of that delightful being, the Jewish professional beggar."
Elsewhere he explained: "I wrote *The King of Schnorrers* merely to
amuse myself and to amuse idlers" (it appeared in the *Idler*) "by
incarnating the floating tradition of the Jewish Schnorrer." But he
afterwards read a deeper meaning and purpose into his Schnorrer.
Louis Zangwill often spoke to me of how he had discussed *The King
of Schnorrers* with his brother Israel. "The London critics of *The
King of Schnorrers*," he wrote, "could not take in the forbearance
and tolerant understanding of the old-time Jew of wealth and character, who had some sense of humour, too, in the self-asserting
presence of the poor magnificent one: could not take in this patient
sense of brotherhood—'Why does he not kick him downstairs?
It is all incredible—outside the pale of reality!' they exclaimed. They
had forgotten that even for Christianity poverty had once been a living ideal!"

Always Israel Zangwill's life and work were woven with the double
thread—the Ghetto and the wider world, Judaism and the universe,
pity and pride, laughter and admonition—he was the Marshallik,
the name he adopted for himself and translated as "licenced jester,"
dispensing "morour and chorosouth," bitter and sweet—and he was
teacher and preacher. "Always," he said in the last year of his life,
"I have been a teacher, and always was punished for it." He was, he
said, "brilliant and flippant and even smart," but he had "high
aspiration." He had acceptance, and defiance, and daring—his
father's bookworm saintliness and desire for peace, and his mother's
fighting Maccabean turbulence.

Among his books his favourite was *The Master*, where he thought
he had got away from the Jewish field, for an author does not always
see where his own strength lies, and he was sometimes resentful of
"becoming identified with the Ghetto." He believed it was a book in

which he had more than in any other painted human feeling and human experience. There is fine writing in the Proem, and descriptions of rural life almost as good as in his later and much better book *Jinny the Carrier*. But he was never able to get far away from things Jewish. His central figure, the artist, Matt Strang, was inspired by his friend Solomon J. Solomon R.A. (which does not mean that drawing his character from that model he also drew on his life for his story). Solomon J. Solomon himself spoke of being "the foster-father of *The Master*," for another reason, "as a great portion of it was written in my studio." Solomon J. Solomon did not have to struggle with poverty, as Matt Strang did, until he married a woman with no understanding of art, but with a little money, which enabled him to work, and achieve success. Thrown into the society of artists and cultured people Strang left his unattractive home and wife, until on the point of throwing over everything for a beautiful and understanding woman he renounced it all and went back to his wife and home. Here he continues to work and becomes the "Master" not only of his art but of his soul.

There is good character-drawing in the book, and there are fine pictures of scenery in Nova Scotia and in England. But what made him go for the opening of his book to Nova Scotia, which he had never seen, and made no attempt in later life to see, to those "simple communities," in that "wild land"? Did he warm to the stories of those cold regions that were told to him by his much-travelled friend and colleague Burgin, who had been there? Did he think he could tell Burgin's stories better than Burgin did? He deplored of Burgin that "so charming a talent should run to seed. If Mr. Burgin could learn," he wrote, "that blague is not literature!" But why did he have to write about a second-hand locale? Was it to "see the world," as he said, "with other eyes than one's fellows, yet express the vision of one's race?" To transplant the experiences of people he knew to other climes and other communities, and show that those experiences are common to all people, are universal? "The simple communities" of Annapolis County had also "shut out the world and time, marrying their own," and "their sons and heirs did not always cling to their fathers' tradition of piety and perseverance."

Was it to try out his theory of fiction, that it need not derive from a man's own experience, that an author can create his world by imaginative evocation? He did better work when he painted the scenes that were around him, were part of himself, his own background and his own life, were inside him and not inside someone else. Yet Flaubert could evoke in *Salambo* scenes from a Carthage distant from his own life not only in space but in time. That is a magic evocation. Zangwill could not achieve that magic. His genius lay in painting the life that he knew from intimate contact, with insight, humour, compassion, with a Dickensian comprehension and love.

"It is true I have myself walked over the ruins of Carthage," said Zangwill. But he was never moved to write of it. In *The Master* Zangwill came to "think I've lived in every place and time under the sun. In Jerusalem with the Jews I was back in the B.C. ages. I really think all the centuries live side by side." That was an idea he had discussed with Maeterlinck. My feeling is that even where *The Master* succeeds, it succeeds by invention, by the power of the scribe, instead of by feeling and the power of the poet. Zangwill said himself in *The Master* that "the essence of all art is emotion, feeling, the medium by which the artist passes on his emotion, his feeling for nature, his sadness, his aspiration, even his view of life." In Nova Scotia he was only a visitor, and the "empty birch-bark troughs" that he found there "scattered about" created for me, as for him, "an air of desolation," instead of that air of warm human bustle that is in *Children of the Ghetto*.

I found interest in Matt's uncle and in the uncle's son. But even the London scenes are not out of his own living, only out of his observation, and his reconstruction of things he saw and heard and I have no doubt felt in his friend Solomon's studio. I had the impression that much of it was contrived, and there is the conventional romantic about his hero and heroine. Sir William Rothenstein, writing when the book appeared in 1894, found it already then "a disappointment. No novelist," he wrote, "not even Henry James, has to my mind done a convincing study of a painter or sculptor." There is a lot of dated artistic talk: "How can you have Art and the English Sunday together? Don't talk to me of the middle classes. They will never be saved till Boccaccio is read aloud in every parlour on Sunday afternoons." "Likeness is the last thing a portrait painter goes for. Values, colour-schemes, all sorts of things take precedence of the likeness in their importance for art. The likeness is irrelevant to art." Presented brightly as though they were new discoveries, as they may have been then, they have the outdated effect of Oscar Wilde's inversions of the expected. When he depicted the people he knew, his own life and background, Zangwill produced work that is more lasting.

He could not keep the Jew in him out of even *The Master*. He speaks there of saying the benediction over pork. One of his characters says: "I pretended to be a Jew; and it was great fun when he became a Jew to tell him that I was a Christian. I don't know which was the biggest lie." He has phrases like these: "Church and State arose where only Faith and Freedom had been." "The islands of Arcadia are riddled with pits where men have burrowed for Captain Kidd's Treasure, and found nothing but holes." "Life is too long for ideals; the unending procession of the days depress the finest enthusiasm."

The Mantle of Elijah is a better book than *The Master*. It might almost have been written by Disraeli, by "Dizzy," who was probably in Zangwill's mind when he called one of his characters "Fizzy," entitling one of his chapters "Fizzy M.P.," and described him as "dapper and brilliant and dandified, never at a loss for an answer, not being limited by truth." It is a later book than *Children of the Ghetto*, by seven years. It is full of the inside of politics, society balls, country-houses and duchesses, hardly the life Zangwill had grown up in, and knew from his own experience. His title refers to Sir Donald Bagnall, who looked for promising young men to marry his daughters and carry on his interests, to inherit his Mantle.

Into this non-Jewish book too Zangwill's Jewish thoughts and his Jews and half-Jews keep intruding. Raphael Domineck had a Jewish mother and a Christian father. "The father was drowned, and the mother saved from the shipwreck by a French cattle-boat, on which Raphael was born prematurely. Mother and child had been passed on by charitable Jewish committees to London. Here they had undergone terrible poverty till the boy grew up." "She will never be happy until I admit that the Messiah has come; I who do not even share the Jewish belief that he will come," he says. And "What have I to be ashamed of? That my wife ran away with a Jew?"

The Jew creeps in even in *Jinny the Carrier*—"Oi'll tell her sow to her head the next time she's at me to be a Jew!" "Gloves were unknown to the ancient Hebrews. Not a single patriarch, priest, shepherd, apostle, publican or sinner had ever sported gloves. The Pharisees covered their foreheads with phylacteries, but left their hands bare. Yet Rebekah 'put the skins of the kids of the goats upon Jacob's hands.' "

Zangwill was pleased with "the flattering welcome accorded to *The Master*, which deals with art, to *The Mantle of Elijah*, whose theme is politics, or to a novel so remote from the Ghetto as *Jinny the Carrier*." But when time has done its work, the book that will stand out will be *Children of the Ghetto*, the quintessential Zangwill. Not because it is Jewish and I am a Jew, but because drawing the Jews of London he had drawn a picture of London, a part of England, of the world, of humanity, that he has lifted to the plane of the shoreless, the timeless, the truly human and universal. In this book, where he has painted both Jew and London he has revealed himself not only as a Jew but as a Londoner, a Cockney, an English writer, the Englishman.

Chapter IV

THE ENGLISHMAN

THERE is a sense in which English literature includes everything written in (not translated into) English. Though even there we must consider the influence of translated work on the course of native literature. The translated Hebrew Bible has become the English Bible, and the Hebrew thought that fashioned it made the English mind and English speech and the English-speaking world, our common Anglo-Saxon civilisation, whose tradition continues to shape American life and American literature as much as it shapes English life and English literature. America grew from the English-Hebrew Bible mind as surely as England did. Without its English literary history American literature, even when it rebels against it, is not to be understood. Language is tradition, and the English language shapes not only the words but the thought of those who write it. I have in front of me a book called *The Spirit of American Literature*, by John Macy; its first words are: "American literature is a branch of English literature, as truly as are English books written in Scotland or South Africa. In literature," it goes on, "nationality is determined by language rather than by blood or geography. Dickens who writes of London influences Bret Harte, who writes of California, and Bret Harte influences Kipling, who writes of India." Mr. Henry Canby tells of a talk in Dublin in 1918, with an Irish writer who vowed to give up the English language and write only Gaelic. "In his heart," he says, "he knew how mad he would have been to give up the only literary tradition which, thanks to language, could be his own." Yeats writes of the companions of his youth, when he lived in London, "They were my close companions many a year, A portion of my mind and life, as it were"—they and their English speech and the life and people of English London. When he dreamed of Ireland it was against the reality of London—"the grey corner of a cloud slanting its rain upon Cheapside called to mind the clouds rushing and falling on the seaward steep of a mountain north of Ballah. Delayed by a crush in the Strand he heard a faint trickling of water near by that suggested a cataract at Ballah. He was set dreaming a whole day by walking down to the border of the Thames."

Yet considering this business of English words and English literature, Ford Madox Ford, to whom Joseph Conrad is a great English writer, can still speak of him because of his Polish birth as an "alien." It is the description Conrad uses for himself: "I am an alien." Ford Madox Ford is talking of Thomas Hardy, George Meredith, Henry James, Joseph Conrad and Mark Twain, who were all living simultaneously—"two solitary Englishmen, two Americans, and one alien." He speaks of the triad, Henry James, Stephen Crane and Joseph Conrad, who "lived in the same corner of England, saw each other often and discussed literary methods more thoroughly and more frequently than can ever at any other time in England have been the case. Not one of the three was English. Indeed," he recalls, "my friend Wells wrote that in the first decade of this century a group of foreigners occupied that corner of England." But it was not long ago that a London paper described Shaw as an "alien" and Wells himself, for all his English birth, as a "counter-jumping genius" with an "alien mentality." "For all I know," Wells said, "I am of Jewish lineage. I do not know anything of my great-great grandparents." "I'm an extensive sceptic," Wells wrote of himself—"no God, no King, no nationality."

There was a time, in 1891, a year before *Children of the Ghetto* appeared, when the *Athenaeum*, reviewing Zangwill's *Bachelors' Club*, was not sure "if the author is himself an American." The reviewer was worried because so "many recent English writers have been mere imitators of the American humorists," and as Zangwill's book seemed to him "not modelled on that form of American humour of which Mark Twain's earlier works are the type," he wondered if Zangwill might not be in that way "asserting for himself a claim to originality."

So that when Cecil Chesterton declared at a meeting held during the First World War, at which Shaw, Zangwill and Hyndman were the other speakers, that "he did not look upon Mr. Zangwill as an Englishman, but as a Jew," it does not follow that Zangwill was thereby deprived of his rights as an Englishman. Mr. Chesterton "disavowed on his honour being an antisemite. He thought the Jews a different nation and wished them to return to Palestine. Being a separate nation they had no claim to enjoy equal rights in other countries." It is the argument of the G. K. Chesterton-Cecil Chesterton-Hilaire Belloc group, that the Jews should have a Jewish State to which all Jews should go, so that "the Zionist experiment will relax the strain created by the presence of the Jews in the midst of a non-Jewish world." "So far goes the arrogance of this little group that it still boasts of its 'hospitality' even to British-born Jews," was Zangwill's retort. "And even other Englishmen, free from anti-semitism," he went on, "appear to expect the enfranchised Jew to go abroad to the third and fourth generation exuding gratitude like a Uriah Heep." He refused to surrender his rights as an Englishman and as a Jew. "The Jew cannot surrender even his right to criticise

Christianity," he said, in this connection—"indeed, to criticise it is the sole *raison d'etre* of his separateness. For my own part," he continued, "I hold that the highest patriotic service a writer can render to the country of his birth is to offer it his truest thinking and his deepest race-heritage, and to try to make it worthier of his love." "The poet Cowper, a Bigger Englander than Kipling, since he valued the greatness of England by its value to all humanity," he said, "boasted that the slave who touched our soil was free. That freedom, more than her wealth, gave England the leadership of the world."

The cry of "alien" pursued Zangwill. He speaks of Stephen Graham saying in his presence " 'Of course, Mr. Zangwill does not speak as an Englishman,' upon which I interrupted with 'You are not an Englishman, you are a Scotchman.' " In some moods Zangwill equated Scotchman with Jew among the components making up the population of the British Isles. "Our own little island embraces besides Scotch and Welsh, persistent Manx and Jewish elements," he said. But that is not what Zangwill wanted to emphasise—the distinction between the Jew and the Englishman on the basis of the distinction between the Englishman and the Scotchman. The Jewish child brought up in a Christian home is a Christian. "Russo-Jewish children orphaned by the war and swept into Christian villages," he said, "begin to throw stones, like the other children, at passing Jews." He and the Chestertons and Belloc placed the distinction on what was different between the Jew and the Christian. It was the stand taken before them by Matthew Arnold, who wrote ten years before Zangwill was born: "I want to take my stand on my favourite principle that the world is made up of Christians and non-Christians; with all of the former we should be one, with none of the latter. I think the Jews have no claim whatever of political right. England is the land of Englishmen, not of Jews. The Jews have no claim to become citizens, but by conforming to our moral law, which is the Gospel." That puts the distinction squarely. There would be many who are not Jews who would be deprived of citizenship if Matthew Arnold's principle were acted upon, that only Christians may be citizens. Indeed, the right of the Roman Catholic Chestertons and Belloc might be questioned. Dean Inge quoted with some approval George Santayana's belief that "an Englishman who becomes a Catholic ceases to be an Englishman." Dean Inge thought "this is overstated," but he felt that "the typical Englishman" dislikes "the Catholic system," which is "decidedly Latin." The quarrel between the two branches of the Christian Church is not my concern, but it is interesting to have it so stated, though G. K. Chesterton had in return some harsh things to say of Dean Inge "as a superstitious person" because he worships something "called Protestant

Christianity." "I am an Englishman," Chesterton said, and I can't see how his claim to be one can be disputed. Nor can I see how the same claim can be denied to Zangwill.

Zangwill replied more explicitly to Cecil Chesterton and Stephen Graham and the others when an unnamed interrupter called out at a public meeting he addressed in London, that he was "an alien Jew." "I am a Jew, of course, and I am proud of it," he said. "But I am not an alien. I am a pure Cockney. I was born in London, within the sound of Bow Bells." That commonsense Scotch Cockney Ian Mackay said: "There are streaks and strains in all of us which prove that we are 'all Jock Tamson's bairns,' or Adam's children. It may be true that Chaplin is a Jew" (I am not sure he is) "but surely the thing that matters about him is that he is a Cockney." Zangwill described himself as a Cockney. Others spoke of him as a Cockney. Some—he himself as well—used the term "Cockney Jew." He was willing to have that as his designation: "A Cockney Jew." His niece, Primrose, accepted the designation for him, and applied it also to me. Urging me to write about Zangwill, she said: "Aren't you, too, like him, a Cockney Jew?"

But the *Manchester Courier* during the war objected "even to a Cockney Jew speaking otherwise than Imperially in the centre of the Empire." In his reply, Zangwill quoted: "Here and here did England help me; how can I help England, say?" "Surely," he said, "it is by helping her to remain England." "I am a native, not a guest," he explained. "I and mine have paid, fought and suffered for England." Zangwill, indeed, suffered for England during the war. For whilst he was rousing the fury of Cecil Chesterton, Stephen Graham and others because he demanded that Britain should insist her ally Russia should emancipate her Jews, he was infuriating the German Jews, who were in the war against Britain and Russia, and neutral American Jewry, by his British patriotism. "As a patriotic Englishman Zangwill is naturally standing up for his own country in its time of trial," wrote the *American Hebrew*. "That however does not add convincing power to his effort to make American Jews who distrust the promises of Russia see that matter from his point of view."

"From America I receive a constant stream of letters of abuse, saying I have entirely forfeited my position by asking Jews to embrace Russia," Zangwill said in the early part of the war. That was because "To American Jewry and other neutral Jewries I issued the following appeal in the early days of the war: 'Although the most monstrous war in human history was "made in Germany," and although Germany's behaviour in war is as barbarous as her temper in peace, I note with regret that a certain section of Jewry in America and other neutral countries seems to withhold sympathy for Britain and her allies. In so far as these Jews are German-born, their feeling for Germany is as intelligible as mine for England. But in so far as they are swayed by consideration for the interests of the Russian Jews (to whom Germany and Austria are offering equal rights) let me tell them that it were better for the Jewish minority to continue to suffer, and that I would far sooner lose my own rights as an English citizen, than that the great interests of civilisation should be submerged by the triumph of Prussian militarism.' "

As for the Jews in Germany, who could not have foreseen Hitler, they accused Zangwill of "treason to the Jews." One who made that charge against him was the great philosopher, Professor Hermann Cohen. The *Ulk*, "the German *Punch*" had a poem called "Pogrom," "dedicated to Zangwill."

> Cossacks plunder the house of the Jew.
> What is the poor Jew to do?
> England, land of the free!
> Hear my cry, and stop the thief.
> England is deaf.
>
> Cossacks pull out the Jew's hair.
> The Jew cries in despair.
> England, land of the free!
> Where shall my child refuge find?
> England is blind.
>
> Cossacks rape the wife of the Jew.
> What is the poor Jew to do?
> England, land of the free!
> Speak, let deliverance come.
> England is dumb.

"I have urged upon the neutral Jew to trust in the influence of France and England upon Russia," Zangwill said. "It is not as a Jew that I stand asking for justice. Both our ideal interests as Englishmen and our practical interests as belligerents demand the immediate emancipation of the Russian Jew, as of every other oppressed nationality in the Russian Empire. It will help to win the war. Why is national unity less vital to Russia than to England and France?"

But on the broad issue Zangwill was entirely on the side of England in the war. "Vain for Germany to cry that it is Russia which is the enemy of civilisation," he said. "The Cossack is only a wild beast, the German a wilful beast. The Briton is a beast neither by nature nor design." He could not follow Shaw's reasoning, when "irritated by the attempt to paint Germany as a wolf and England as a lamb, Mr.

Shaw paints England as a lion, with Germany apparently as the lamb." He had no patience with "apologists for Germany." "Much as I sympathise with Mr. Morel's campaign against secret diplomacy," he said, "I cannot follow him in his vindication of Germany." "There are soldiers, not chocolate, but iron," he reminded us, "there are traitors and bullies." Even G. K. Chesterton puzzled him, when he wrote "a characteristic book, called *more suo The Crimes of England*, the point of which is, I gather, that this is the first war in which England has been right. That is further than even Coleridge (who once cursed this country), or Cowper (who bade her cease to 'grind India'), or Wordsworth (on whom the 'freight' of her offences lay heavy) has ever gone." "The victory of England is desirable—even for the outside world," Zangwill declared, "not because she is 'right,' but because she is England, because she represents a freer and less selfish civilisation. She may be no better than Germany in her lust of Empire, but once her rule is accepted she will rule with justice, with sympathy, with generosity."

Israel Zangwill was in fact that normal being who loves his own land and his own people. When he went *Walking in War-Time*, and asked his way of a "brawny farm-lounger, a studgroom," who turned out to be a special constable, "who to test if the German spy thought the information worth buying asked, "How much will you give me to tell you?", he was "taken aback. In a goodly experience of tramping my native land I had never been asked for money before by any human finger-post."

Zangwill knew and loved his native land, the London streets to which he was born, and the little Sussex village which he made his home from the time he took his young wife there in 1903 till he died in 1926, the lovely Temple, where he had his rooms, near his brother Louis's, and where he heard the "glorious music soar up to my tree shadowed study from the Temple Church, where I would willingly sit, though I was born a Jew, and know that the original Templars on the day they recaptured Jerusalem slew every Jew, man, woman and child." Mrs. Humphrey Ward dwelt with no greater love in *Robert Ellesmere* on the Westmorland and Surrey scene than Zangwill in *Jinny the Carrier* on the quiet rural Essex countryside, whose "landscape, character and dialect" he had "absorbed." "How often," he wrote, "have I passed over High Field and seen the opulent valley—tilth and pasture and ancient country seats—stretching before me like a great poem, with its glint of winding water, and the exquisite blue of its distance, and Bassets awaiting me below, snuggling under its mellow moss-stained tiles, a true English home, the beautiful country in which my lot has been cast, with its many lovable customs and simple, kindly people."

Those of us who have lived our lives in the streets of the great

English cities and in the English countryside have absorbed into our bodies and our souls the landscape, the character, the spirit and the speech. It is part of us. It moulded us. We belong to the English scene as much as the houses that stand along the roads we pass through day after day, along which we could find our way blindfolded, guided by memory, by sounds in the air, by the voices of those who dwell there and ply their business there, by the feel of our tread on the familiar pavements, as much as the trees and the hedgerows in our lovely English country lanes. I spoke on the day I wrote this to an Englishwoman living in America for many years and, with the noise of the New York traffic outside the windows, she closed her eyes and told me she could see the country lanes of Kent, could smell the scents of the apple orchards, and the hop-fields, and hear the lark mounting and singing over the English fields. There is magic in memory, but the magic will not work if you have not left your heart in those English lanes and English streets. Zangwill's heart was always there, in the London streets and the English countryside. "On that human palimpsest which has borne the inscriptions of all languages and all epochs was writ large the sign-manual of England," he wrote of the way in which the Jewish immigrants in England blurred "into the uniform grey of English middle-class life." He knew "the London street picture, the narrow thoroughfares in the East End of London, connecting Spitalfields with Whitechapel, the courts and alleys and squares, and the Park, Victoria Park, which was 'The Park to the Ghetto,'" where "the birds twittered in the leafy trees" and where children from the Ghetto streets, like himself, and myself, would throw themselves "down on the thick grass and look up in mystic rapture at the brooding blue sky." He knew the peace of "the shady quadrangles that branch out of the bustle of Fleet Street" and the strange ancient gardens and fragments of fields in the backways of Holborn, the "quaint waterside alleys and old-world churches in out-of-the-way turnings." He knew "the sunny weald that circles for miles around and ends to the south in the downs that hide the English Channel." He knew "the village and the villagers, and the Parson and the Squire, and the stalwart farmer," and he could wonder if George Eliot "ever wrote a pure description of scenery without psychological or mythological allusions." He could laugh, too, at the Cockney who couldn't "bide in a place where there wasn't a neighbour to speak to except a silly shepherd who was never at home." He himself loved "the misty magnificence of great spaces, whose gentle undulations could not counteract a sublime flatness," and the "winding and much halting way to Clipstone, and the remoter woodland regions," the English countryside with "sheep lying in the wide fields and great, newly-ploughed spaces of red, freshly turned earth."

Zangwill knew "what makes a nation is a common spirit, and this spirit exercises a hypnotic effect over all that comes within its range, moulding and transforming. The nation makes the national spirit, and the national spirit makes the nation. The flag, the constitution, the national anthems, the national prejudices, the language, the proverbs—these are the product of the people they produce." Zangwill had a dream of England, of London and of the English countryside, that though he was the son of immigrant Jews, was distinctly English. "Nowhere have I found more ardent patriots than among the Jews," he said. "The test of life in a nation would be its power of transforming its immigrants into patriots."

It was the most natural thing when the British offer of an area for Jewish autonomous settlement in East Africa was read to the Sixth Zionist Congress that Zangwill should jump to his feet and lead the cheering for England. When he said that English Jews had become Zionists largely because England held the Mandate for Palestine, he was aware that there was a great deal of that feeling in himself. As soon as Turkey came into the war on Germany's side he saw the opportunity, and declared: "If Britain took Palestine, she could make no greater stroke of policy than to call in the Jews to regenerate it for her." In his work in the Ito he emphasised: "In our quest for a territory we wish, if possible, to take advantage of England's offer of a virgin soil under British suzerainty." "The British order and success which Dr. Herzl witnessed in Egypt," he said, "convinced him that under the aegis of Britain, which alone understands to leave other races to their own Kultur, the dream of a Jewish State had the best chance of achieving substance." "British Judea," he wanted to call it, a "loyal link in that mighty chain of Imperial Britain which binds together so many races, creeds and colours."

Zangwill's fear was lest England under the stress of war conditions might restrict and curtail those liberties which to him made England stand out as the greatest among the nations of the world. He dreaded, he said, as he saw Magna Charta, Parliament, the Press, all her great historic landmarks disappearing, "that our young men who have gone out to fight for England will find no England to return to," and he held therefore that "it is the duty of us who are beyond the age for foreign service to go to the front for the defence of England, to preserve England for her absent sons. For what is a nation?" he asked. "What is England? What Germany? What Russia? These are living and therefore perpetually shifting concepts, always expanding, diminishing, changing."

Yet he saw little change in Germany. He confessed himself "an obdurate anti-German." He had "an instinctive loathing," he said "for the Bismarckised State." He had encountered German mentality in "the callous handling of the thousands of poor Jews whom for

K

many years it was a function of an organisation over which I
presided, to emigrate via Germany. Once the brutality was so
palpable that I actually succeeded in getting a couple of naval officers
dismissed. But as a rule it was less acts of tyranny than a pervasive
atmosphere of harshness and contempt, embittering the lot of the
steerage passengers, already suffering sufficiently from exile, poverty
and sea-sickness. To dispense with German lines in favour, for
example, of Dutch was impossible, because Germany simply forbade
emigrants to pass through her territory unless provided with sailing
tickets for her vessels." He had many other reasons for detesting the
Germans, even his experiences with his German translators, one of
whom "rendered a nursery reference to Baby Bunting into Baby's
flag," which he interpreted as another sign of German militarism.
He hated the Germans, he said, "from a reasonable antipathy to
spiritual swagger and medieval militarism, accompanied by bump-
tiousness and cruelty."

As he saw the struggle as "a perpetual beating of the waves of
barbarism against the dykes of civilisation," he appointed himself
"at the post of national duty as a dyke-custodian, a trustee of
civilisation—self-appointed." So that when he came to speak of
"the struggle of the Jew to get or preserve his civil rights," he explained that "this struggle is important less for the Jew's sake than the
world's sake, inasmuch as the position of minorities is the high-
water mark of civilisation." He wrote:

"If e'er I doubt of England, I recall
   Gentle Will Shakespeare, her authentic son
   Whose tears and laughter hold the world in thrall,
   Impartial bard of Briton, Roman, Gaul,
   Jew, Gentile, white or black. His sovereign art embraces all.

   Such too is England's Empire—hers the art
   To hold all faiths and races 'neath her sway.
   Thus comes it all beside her fight and pray."

Zangwill was a universalist also in his love of England. He wanted
England's Empire to extend, "to hold all faiths and races ' 'neath
her sway.' " When he said that Mr. Edwin Montagu, who was then
the Minister for India, "could exhibit no finer patriotism than to
contribute the Jew's ethical mentality to the intellectual assets of
England," he added he would thus "save India for England," and
suggested that "he has, in fact, been doing truer Jewish work than
any his relative, Sir Herbert (Lord) Samuel, can accomplish in
Palestine." The interesting thing, considering Zangwill's Zionism,
is that Samuel was the Zionist, while Edwin Montagu had fought

fiercely in the Cabinet against the policy which resulted in the issue of the Balfour Declaration, and his memory is execrated by Zionists.

In his dual striving to extend universally the boundaries of both the ideas that he loved, the Jewish and the English, Zangwill was as truly as Blake, struggling to build Jerusalem "in England's green and pleasant land." All writers have their spiritual lineage. Lazarus Aaronson, the poet, who, like Isaac Rosenberg was one of my boyhood friends in Whitechapel, wrote to me: "We are Jewish writers in England, maybe, but indeed, we must, particularly the poets, have our proper language-lineage, and mine is undoubtedly English: Chaucer, Shakespeare, Donne. And if there be any extra language lineage it is for me French—Baudelaire, Verlaine, Mallarme and Valery—none outside Europe." Zangwill's language-lineage, with all his knowledge of Jewish literature, and his translations from the Hebrew, was English. If we say he walked on two legs, he was firm on both, the English and the Jewish. When he wrote his poem "The Hebrew's Friday Night," welcoming the Sabbath Bride, he marked it "After Burns," shaping it in his memory of "The Cottar's Saturday night," "even to the metre." He saw, in the spirit of Burns: "The Jew's ideals, The simple love of home and child and wife, The sweet humanities which make our higher life." In his Prologue to *Children of the Ghetto* he saw Jewish life linked "to the purple past of Babylon and Egypt, all the vast Enchantment of the ancient Orient, And yet with London and New York blent." When he laid down to dream, his dream was not only of Jews and Zion and the Messiah, but also of "Ariel and Puck, Titania and Oberon and Robin Hood and Little John." He said: "The human heart is large enough to hold many loyalties."

There is more that gets through a man's skin than seems credible. His whole land is in him. All England is in the Englishman. The air he breathes, the soil he treads, the sights and sounds that strike his eye and ear are different from those he would have found elsewhere and they make us different men and women. It is more than a word when my friend Isaac Rosenberg writes of his hand in his poem "Break of Day in the Trenches," "This English hand." Even a cosmopolitan Englishman is English in a distinctive way. "For all his cosmopolitanism," I have said of Wells, "Wells is really a good Englishman, whose cosmopolitanism is a desire to have the whole world English like himself." It is not for nothing that one of his books appeared under the title *An Englishman Looks at the World*. When Wells put forward the idea of a world language *The Times Literary Supplement* could not help remarking: "Mr. H. G. Wells has lately given expression to his belief that what the world needs is a world language, and that world language, he thinks, should be English." Even the Little Englander wants his Little England, not France or Bulgaria.

I came upon a report in an old issue of the *Jewish Chronicle*, of Israel Zangwill presiding at a dinner of the Maccabeans. Proposing "The Queen," he said: "If we Jews join in the heartfelt adoration of the Queen, it is not because of any special Jewish reason, not because the Queen's reign has been co-incident with Jewish emancipation, but simply because we are animated by the general feeling of the inhabitants of this country. It is not for any specifically Jewish reasons that we are in sympathy with the rest of her subjects." He added "even George Washington could have proposed the toast of Queen Victoria," whatever he thought of her predecessors, and he quoted *The Times*, which had said that "on no occasion had it said a word of praise of George IV, even when he died."

There is an Americanism which imagines it has turned its back on its English and European origins, has flung them away, and started completely afresh. Yet from what I have seen from my visits to America I am inclined to accept Holbrook Jackson's thesis in his book *Dreamers of Dreams*, where he links together three Englishmen, Carlyle, Ruskin and William Morris, and three Americans, Emerson, Thoreau and Walt Whitman, on the basis of "ideas which are common to each of the six writers," and emphasises their affinity with England.

Zangwill, who might have been an American had his parents had the money for the fare, and remained an Englishman with a great love and admiration of America, also linked England with America. He remembered America's English beginnings. "Once upon a time," he said, "some of us threw up our country and sailed away in the *Mayflower*." "I have often striven to bring home this truth to my fellow-citizens," he wrote—"if you knew how the thought of England lives and glows in the hearts of the oppressed— as the sun of liberty, the ark of refuge—then you would be more careful than you are to keep this great vision, this splendid ideal untarnished, even by foreign misunderstandings." He applied his vision and his admonition equally to America—in the words of John Bright—"over all that vast continent the home of freedom, and a refuge for the oppressed of every race and of every clime." "Lest the superior person, lifting an eyebrow at my admiration for America," he wrote, "dismiss me as a belated doctrinaire democrat, let me remark that I have always defined myself as 'a democrat with a profound mistrust of the people.' But democracy tempered by Tammany, is better than autocracy tempered by assassination." He sought in his *Melting Pot*, he said, "to bring home to America her manifest mission that she carried humanity and its fortunes. The twentieth century, I wrote, will be America's critical century. Will she develop on the clear lines laid down by her great founders? That all men are created free and equal is a noble proposition, if 'free' be interpreted as having a right to one's own body and soul, and 'equal' as having a right to develop one's own body and soul to their highest. America became the exponent of these ideals. If America breaks away from her ideals, humanity's last chance will be gone. O if America were less conscious of her greatness and more conscious of the greatness of her opportunity!

"But let it be remembered that Liberty, Equality, Fraternity, do not belong to the world of facts, but to the world of ideals. They are the way man's aspiration shapes the facts, as man's will cuts tunnels through the dumb mountains and lays cables beneath the blind seas."

He repeated his call in *The Melting Pot*: "A fig for your feuds and vendettas! Germans and Frenchmen, Irishmen and Englishmen, Jews and Russians—into the crucible with you all. God is making the American!" When Zangwill was accused because of his phrase, "Into the crucible with you all," of preaching intermarriage between Jew and Christian and so the disappearance of Judaism, he explained that what he advocated was a politically homogeneous America— "actual physical fusion was not even necessary, any more than it is necessary in Britain for Welshmen to marry Highland women or countesses to wed costermongers." Or for the American negro and white to mate. "White and black are yet too far apart," Zangwill wrote, "for profitable fusion. Fear of the black may be pragmatically as valuable a racial defence for the white as the counter-instinct, love of the white, is a force of racial uplifting for the black. The action of the crucible is thus not exclusively physical—a consideration particularly important as regards the Jew. The Jew may be Americanised and the American Judaised without any gamic interaction."

Zangwill regarded Britain and the British Dominions too as "Melting Pots." "The British Empire, the greatest motley of creeds, races and colours that has ever been brought under one standard of justice, lives by the harmonisation of its measureless diversity," he wrote. He saw Canada "only second as a 'Melting Pot' to the United States. Canada will be a United States," he said, "a Melting Pot of every people under the sun. The same with Australia." The whole "world has always been and always will be a melting pot." "Though half my manhood has been devoted to the quest for a Jewish State," he confessed, "I have never regarded racial differences as a final goal," and "were the landlessness of the Jews the only obstacle to universal peace, I should be the first to waive their claim." "The Biblical Palestine, like all other countries, was a melting pot, a blend of races." The Jews to-day are themselves, he said, a "melting pot." His own parents came from different countries, as distant from each other as France from Russia, though both were at the time of their birth ruled by the Russian Czar. He portrayed the intermarriage of Sephardic and Ashkenazic Jews. He gave a picture of the President of the Sephardic Community in London rebuking Manasseh da Costa, "in tones of righteous indignation" for daring "to meditate giving your daughter in marriage to a Polish Jew. What! A Sephardi marry a Tedesco! Shameful!"

In one of his last public declarations Zangwill said: "For my part, I doubt whether Jewish segregation does not always remain religious." By which he meant that where there are no religious differences between Jew and Christian to justify it, the segregation is pointless. "Why keep up a form of separation when the life of it is fled?" he quoted Charles Lamb. "It is beyond question," he said, "that at the best the Jewish race must long look for its foothold to religion. But when I say religion is a rock for the feet and a frontier for the soul of a people, I mean a real religion, not a seat in the synagogue and a grave in a Jewish cemetery, but a faith like that which made our fathers sit Shivah for faithless children. It was not the faith that moves mountains, but it was the faith that makes mountains immovable. And so far it has found no successor."

G. K. Chesterton was a Catholic, yet he found a superiority in the Irish Protestant rioters—"the Irish Protestant rioters really believe in Protestant theology." "The eternal duel between Judaism and Nationalism is the drama of Jewish history," said Zangwill. "But you cannot reduce a people whose faith and literature have nourished continents to the category of a mere political nationality." He repeated the image of the father mourning for his faithless child. "You have only to remember how an orthodox Jew sat seven days on the ground for a child married out of the faith, to see that no effective conserving substitute can be found in a pseudo-American ideal of life, liberty and the pursuit of happiness. Even the Ku Klux Klan, with all its absurdities, is to me more respectable than a racial Jewry that has lost its soul. It has no legitimate place in America, for the genius of America is to give a square deal to the individual, not to the group, and those Jews who emigrated to America knew or should have known that they were coming to a land where only religious unity was constitutional."

Zangwill rebuked a certain type of "muddle-heads" whom he found in the American Zionist movement, who thought they "could cohere in a political unity or that any of them could be linked politically with Palestine." "If they mean seriously," he said, "that they are not merely sentimental sympathisers with the Palestinian Jewry, as Irish-Americans are with Ireland, but that they are actual subjects of the Jewish National Home, they must naturally give up their American citizenship and all rights save those appertaining to resident aliens; a status which when proposed by a Belloc they are the first to cry out against. The only way of being a Zionist is to be in Zion."

Then turning to the problem of America, he said: "America still calls herself God's own country, but let her beware lest God emigrate." He warned against the spirit that manifested itself in the Ku Klux Klan and other organisations, "not because it is a menace to Jews, but because it is a menace to America. You must fight it by all moral weapons, not so much because of impugned Judaism, but because of its insults to the Catholic Church which, when all is said, has to its credit more noble and beautiful achievements of the human spirit than anything the Klan can boast of." He urged America not to forget or to misunderstand "the richness produced by the diversity of her peoples, as of her scenery." "It is time we Jews reasserted the Universal God and the unity of civilisation," he said. " 'Back to Christ' is the cry of the despairing thinkers of Europe. But Reason and Justice, Love and Mercy were in the world before Christ, and our cry is not so much 'back to Moses,' as back to these and their source."

Zangwill saw that source behind the impulse of America, and of Britain. "I do not know exactly when America began to call herself 'God's own country,' " he said, "but her National Anthem, 'My Country, 'tis of thee,' dating from 1832, fixes the date when America consciously felt herself as a Holy Land. The Pilgrim Fathers went to America merely for their own freedom of religious worship. From a sectarian patriotism developed what I have called 'The Melting Pot,' with its high universal mission, first at home and now over the world at large." He found "the stages of growth still more clearly marked in English history, that national self-consciousness which to-day gives itself undaunted and indomitable." In both he traced the Jewish Biblical heritage, the universal mission in which Jews standing by Judaism, and Britain and America fight "that 'mental fight,' " he wrote, "from which that English poet Blake declared he would not cease till he had 'built Jerusalem in England's green and pleasant land.' " As he did for his friend Joseph Jacobs, Zangwill would have written for his own epitaph, "not merely that he was a great Jew, but that he was also—and perhaps the two are really one —a great humanist." He could not forget that "underneath and through it all goes the same flesh and blood," and that "human nature reasserts itself in all its divine identity. Vain," he cries, "to sunder the human family by the artificial boundaries of States, religions, countries, ambitions, hatreds."

Yet he kept coming back to the mission of the Jewish religion, of Judaism, and its prayer " 'Alenu,' with which every Synagogue service ends—the prayer for the coming of the Kingdom of God, 'when Thou wilt remove the abominations from the earth, and the idols will be utterly cut off, and all the children of flesh will call upon Thy name.' " He found the Jewish note in England and America in the word "Recessional," in a sense of "humility" still to be seen in the liturgy of the Church, which ascribes its victories not to the might of the English arm, but to the favour of God." "National missions," he proclaimed, "become false only when nations are false to them." It is what Lord Bryce meant when he said in his book *Modern Democracies*, "Democracy is based on the expectation of certain virtues in the people."

It was in that sense of refusal to become complacent, or worse, boastful and swaggering, aggressive and contemptuous, in the realisation of what he called "not only the sense of mission, but also the sense of sin," that Zangwill defined himself as "a democrat with a profound mistrust of the people." He feared that "King Demos, like other monarchs, hears only what tickles the royal ear." He was afraid of the rule of majorities, as much as of any other undisputed rule, against all of which "a free, thoughtful man must rebel. Who are they that make up the majority of a country?" he asked. "Is it the wise men or the foolish?" Yet he was not sure "the wise men would agree." He thought "they would split up." Besides, the democracy did not really put forward ideas; "its whole power is that of choice between the ideas put forward by its would-be leaders." So that speaking while "the value of democracy is being questioned —materially by men like Mussolini, intellectually by men like Dean Inge and Bernard Shaw"—he recognised that "Democracy is the least bad form of Government. It is of course," he said, "liable to be exploited by demagogues. But whereas there is no way of correcting a maleficent autocracy save by smashing it, a maleficent Democracy contains the cure for its own evils. For the people has a sound instinct in the long run. But whether Democracy is the best form of governing man or not, for good or ill, America is founded on it." And England, likewise, from whom the American founding fathers, who were all Englishmen, took their ideas and convictions.

In spite of his doubts of democracy, with all his mistrust of "the people," Zangwill was sure that democracy, representative Government, was the best form of Government that could be found. "It requires no great philosopher," he said, "to explain it. The ideal ruler should be all-knowing, so as to be aware of all social facts; all-wise, so as to understand how to better them; and all-good, so as to wish to do so. Such a combination cannot be found on earth in any man, King or Pope, nor even in any group, noble or plebian, but the nearest approximation to it lies in the whole people. And if it is not all-wise, all-knowing, and all-good, it compensates for its inferiority to the ideal autocrat by promoting a healthy spiritual and educational activity among the ruled, instead of turning them into perfectly governed puppets."

Israel Zangwill, born in England, where he lived all his life, and died, was brought up on English constitutional usage. The methods of election and of Government that he knew, were those of England. Even where he doubted and contrasted them, they were his standard and his norm. As a social scientist and a politician, wherever he turned, to the Zionist movement and the coming Jewish State, as much as to France and Germany and Russia, it was by English customs and methods he measured and judged. His doubts of democracy are something he learned from the English and American thinkers of the generation that preceded him, who were still writing when he was already winning his own reading public. Holbrook Jackson, writing on Carlyle, Ruskin, William Morris (whose *News from Nowhere* appeared in 1891, the year when Zangwill was writing *Children of the Ghetto*) Emerson, Thoreau and Walt Whitman, says: "All of them, with the possible exception of William Morris who calls himself a social-democrat, doubt or else are opposed to democratic rule. Carlyle, Emerson and Ruskin believe in leadership rather than the counting of votes." Yet Zangwill did not accept them completely. He came to the conclusion that "Popular suffrage is much maligned." He found a lot to argue in its favour. "The strength of the British Constitution," to him, "lies in its inherent absurdity. Our Constitution was not made, but 'growed,' and that which grows is never logically perfect." "It is like an old tree, strangely gnarled, with countless abrasions and mutilations, and sometimes even curious grafts. Here the lightning struck it, and yonder branch was snapped in the great gale. Machine-made schemes may be theoretically perfect, but they will never suit human nature, which is a soil for living growths, not a concrete foundation for elegant architecture. Perfect things are dead things: the law of life is imperfection and movement. Politics is a great educative force. Politics sets the humblest at the centre of great cross-roads of history, and enables the poorest—on polling day at least—to know himself the equal of the greatest. Even the most illiterate is spared the mortification of being reminded that he cannot sign his name (by making a cross, like everyone else). An election comforts, gives a new lease of hope. Even the beaten party feels that it has won a moral victory, and confidently looks forward to victory at the next turn of the wheel."

Who that is not an Englishman, brought up on English ways, amid English institutions, could have written thus? Or have confessed, as Zangwill did, that he "always loved fireworks, from boyhood, and would rather have had dry bread and fireworks than cake with jam"? "I have put crackers under doors," he said, "and I have listened with demoniac joy to the shrieks from behind. I have seen fireworks, at the Brittania Theatre; and I have listened to the long-drawn ecstatic 'aw' of the Crystal Palace crowd." It all went into his books. It is in *Children of the Ghetto*, with his other boyhood memories. Benjy Ansell, at the Orphanage, is quite near the Crystal Palace. "We can see the fireworks." He has "a field to play in, with balls. . . . It's all country all round about, with trees and flowers and birds. Why, I've helped to make hay in the autumn."

Zangwill's mother and father both came from small town or village in the Russian Czar's domains. His mother was the daughter of a Jewish farmer and miller, and had known the fields and the growing corn. In Israel Zangwill it became love of the English countryside. He could dwell happily on the "wide horizons—great ploughed lands or meadows with grazing cattle—the level broken only by ricks, roofs, and trees, mainly witch-elms, with a few poplars. To the right was a delicious sense of the saltings and of mewing sea-birds. And where the road mounted a glimpse of the Blackwater, and ships floating, and the dim, blue shore beyond."

When the Editor of the *Morning Post*, Mr. H. A. Gwynne, wrote the foreword to one of S. L. Bensusan's volumes of East Anglian countryside sketches, he said: "The simple people of East Anglia have been highly favoured in their interpreters. In *Jinny the Carrier* Mr. Zangwill reproduces East Anglian life with accuracy and a wonderful sympathy. Following close behind him comes Mr. Bensusan." Zangwill loved that East Anglian countryside. Bensusan told me how they roamed it together, and Zangwill stayed at Bassets, to whose Mistress *Jinny the Carrier* is dedicated. The house, he said, "is at Great Baddow, in Essex." At Little Baddow lived Professor Gregory, who led several Ito expeditions; Zangwill often stayed with him. I was at Colchester with Bensusan when the Essex floods of 1952 came almost to Colchester, and Bensusan reminded me of the Essex floods Zangwill has in *Jinny the Carrier*; he had taken Zangwill to see them when he was writing the book. "Not as bad as Noah's flood in the Bible," was Zangwill's comment, and he put it into the book.

Mr. Gwynne's foreword was written two years after Zangwill had died; one of the last things Zangwill wrote was a foreword in 1926 to another volume of Bensusan's Essex village tales. He wondered there why Wells and Bennett who lived in Essex had not written about the life of its countryside. As for himself, "I have essayed," he said, "to add Essex to my literary provinces, though Mr. Bensusan remains undisputed master of it."

That is Zangwill, the Englishman, the English writer, who knew and loved the English scene, the city streets, and the countryside, with "a goodly experience of tramping my native land." He was

another Cockney who had by his work secured the means to emancipate himself from the streets of London and, loving them no less,
and returning to them often, yet loved too the countryside landscape,
the extension of Victoria Park, where he had as a youngster thrown
himself "down on the thick grass and looked up in mystic rapture at
the brooding blue sky." He had dreamed of helping in the hay-
making; he loved to see the lonely farmyards, the cottages, the
hayricks, the barns. Yet, city-bred, he could wonder "what country-
children do for a holiday?" "So that their lives that stretch on from
year to year with never a whiff of town fog, never a glimpse of
buses or dangerous crossings or furnace-smoke, may be expanded
and elevated." "There are old yokels whose lives have always moved
within a four miles radius, women who have grown grey without ever
knowing what lay beyond the blue hills that girdled their native
village. A glimpse of the town in youth might also do good in check-
ing the perpetual urban immigration, which, alas, removes so many
of the rustic population from the soil and places them under it."

But always it was English soil he had in mind. And if at times the
other Zangwill, the Jewish Zangwill, confronts him from the opposite
side of the road, why, says he, "We agree to differ—I and myself."
In such a mood he can despise that other great Jew, Disraeli, Jewish
at least by birth and early upbringing, who has like himself—I think
the only other—entered world literature as an English writer, for
lying in the Church of Hughenden, buried as a Christian. "A sense of
something shoddy oppresses me," he says, "of tinsel and glitter,
and flamboyance. A Napoleonic vulgarity coarsens the features,
there is a Mephistophelian wrinkle in the corner of the lips. I think
of his books," he goes on, "of his grandiose style, gorgeous as his
early waistcoats, the prose often made up of bad blank verse, leavings
from his long coxcombical strain to be a poet; of his false-sublime
and his false-romantic, of his rococo personages, monotonously
magnificent; of his pseudo-Jewish stories, and his braggart assertions
of blood, with a politic perseverance to be more English than the
English—The Ghetto parvenu."

Yet he can reverse his verdict. He can see Disraeli giving the British
Empire a spirit, a mission, inspired by the ideals of Zion, perceiving
"with Heine that Puritan Britain is the heir of ancient Palestine, and
its State Church the guardian of the semitic principle. He is caught by
the fascination of the vastness of the Empire, of its magnificent
possibilities. And he binds England closer to her colonies."

Yet why does he call him an outsider? Disraeli, who was not only,
like himself, born in London, a Cockney, but was, unlike himself, the
son of a native-born English Jew? If Disraeli was an outsider, why
did he deny that he was an alien? For all his fighting against it,
Zangwill felt that "the notion that Jews form an alien section of the

nation cannot be eradicated. They may call themselves Englishmen, Frenchmen, Germans and Italians, but the question is not what they call themselves, but what Englishmen, Frenchmen, Germans and Italians call them." Indeed, "we agree to differ—I and myself. I do not at all mind contradicting myself," Zangwill said. "If it were some one else, I might hesitate, but between equals——"

"I know," he said, "that I am cleverer than the man in the street, though I take no credit for it; it is a mere accident of birth, and on the whole a regrettable one. I recently proposed the toast of literature, coupled with the name of Mr. Zangwill. I said that I could wish that someone more competent and distinguished than myself had been chosen to do justice to such a toast and to such a distinguished man of letters. When I rose to reply, I began by saying that I could wish that someone more competent and distinguished than myself had been chosen to respond to so important a toast—the last speaker had considerably overrated my humble achievements in the fields of literature." But this is just his fun. "All my I," he punned.

Zangwill considered himself an English writer. He numbered himself, and felt he belonged among the English novelists, with "Wells, Shaw and Bennett, Jerome, Galsworthy, Hall Caine, Chesterton." When England's "eminent authors" were called into conference by the Government at the start of the 1914 war, Bennett who was there, mentioned those present—"Hall Caine, Zangwill, Parker, Wells, Thomas Hardy, Barrie, Chesterton, Gilbert Murray, R. H. Benson." Zangwill did not feel out of place in this group of England's "eminent novelists," nor did Bennett think he was, though he found that "Zangwill talked too much," which suggests that he felt he belonged there very much, and had a lot of points to put. Bennett was "rather disappointed in Gilbert Murray," too. "Thomas Hardy was all right. The sense was talked by Wells and Chesterton." All in all, he says, "I was much pleased with the serious, confident and kind demeanour of everyone." Zangwill explained it nine years after, this meeting of authors which the British Government called to get them "to use their literary power to help the cause against Germany." "Well, these authors proved rather a mum lot; they had very little to say; they had not the experience of politics which I had had with my Jewish Territorial Organisation. So as nothing was forthcoming I got up and said: 'The Germans said all sorts of things against England, which are untrue, but they are saying one thing which is true, namely, that England is in alliance with disgraceful Russia. And so if you want to get the sympathy of the world, if you are going to say that you are fighting a battle for democracy, for righteous ideals, you have got to straighten out your position with Russia.'"

"I believe I could have done better for the Jews had I accepted

LORD ZION.

By courtesy of the proprietors of Punch

FROM MR. PUNCH'S REFORMED HOUSE OF LORDS

offers to go into British politics," Zangwill said, who knows with what wistful thought of a real "Lord Zion," not just a *Punch* cartoon, and a dual career in literature and politics like Disraeli's. But most of all he thought of himself as an English writer, "with my friends Jerome K. Jerome, Eden Phillpotts and Barry Pain." "The bulk of my work has nothing to do with the Ghetto," he claimed, "but belongs to the general human life."

When he wrote of the English coast, he spoke of it as "our cozy eastern coast." "We," he said, "have saltings which may be grazed over at certain times. We have pasture land which gradually improves into arable land." Britain was to him "our country," the British Empire "our great Empire," the British Army's victories were "our victories," English history "our history," and the English poets were "our poets." When he went abroad, whether to Hungary or Italy or America, and he had something there to compare with what obtained at home, it was always "we English." When he said, "let us educate our schoolboys in true Imperialism," he meant English schoolboys, all English schoolboys, not just those who went to the Jews' Free School, and to other Jewish schools in England.

Yet in an odd way, the English novelist who is also a Jew seems to invite from some critics a reminder that he is not as entirely and solely an English novelist as are those who are not Jews. André Gide denied that a Jew could be a European writer, French or English. "It is absurd, it is even dangerous," he wrote, "to deny the good points of Jewish literature; but it is important to recognise that there is to-day in France a Jewish literature that is not French literature, that has its own virtues, its own meanings and its own tendencies. What does it matter to me," he asked, "that the literature of my country should be enriched if it is at the expense of its significance?" He found the plays of Porto-Riche, for instance, "of great worth," but Jewish, not French works. I came upon a review by Michael Sadleir of Robert Henriques's novel *Through the Valley*, which "presents a slice of English social history from 1926 to 1948, following the melancholy fortunes of a great estate situated in the Cotswold Hills." "He" (Mr. Henriques) "knows and loves the Cotswolds," Mr. Sadleir says. "The picture of England is painted with compassion, at times with fond despair, and always with affection. But it is not an English picture; it is the work of a sensitive onlooker." He finds in this very British Jew, of a long line of British-born Jews, and with a distinguished war record, a "cosmopolitan quality." The book is "written in an opulent style," and "is the product of a European rather than an English mind." Is it only because this book is also "deeply concerned to explore the place of the Jews, the sufferings, failings, feelings and secret hesitations of the Jew in a non-Jewish society?"

Chapter V

THE JEW

"SECRET hesitations of the Jew in a non-Jewish society" was something Zangwill did not know. Whatever he thought and said about Jews and their place in the land to which they belong, and in the world, there was never anything secret or hesitant about it. He asserted the difference between Jew and Christian, and he found "one thing certain: the Jew will not yield to the Christian. He will not be worsted in the age-long fight." That age-long fight is the battle of the creeds, Judaism or Christianity. "Judaism," he said, "aims at influencing character through conduct, Christianity at influencing conduct through emotion. If Judaism is in danger of formalism, Christianity runs the risk of an empty spiritualism. If I were asked to sum up the intellectual tendency of Israel, I should say it was a tendency to unification. The unity of God, which is the declaration of the dying Israelite, is but the theological expression of this tendency. There is one God who unifies the cosmos, and one creed to which all the world will come."

He claimed that "the great movement of the modern mind is away from the Trinity. What trace of Trinitarianism," he asked, "is there in Browning, Tennyson, Matthew Arnold, George Meredith, George Eliot, Carlyle, Emerson, Whitman, Holmes, Kipling, Hardy, Henry James and a score of others? This part of Christianity is crumbling away even while Judaism looks idly on. And while the negative side of Judaism is thus being approached by the internal movement of Christianity, so is the positive side of Judaism likewise being arrived at by the thinkers of Christendom."

Certainly there are many born Christians who agree with him about the movement away from the Trinity. St. John Ervine says that once travelling by ship he asked about a dozen laymen on board, none of whom was an "intellectual," "whether or not he believed in the doctrine of the Trinity. Not one of them did. They shared my belief that the largest single sect in Great Britain is composed of unofficial Unitarians who are to be found in almost every Christian organisation." It is not on the dogmatic and the institutional side that Dean Inge saw England still as a Christian nation, but on the ethical. "Theology and dogma have decayed," he said, "and the superficial test of Church-attendance has made many people think that Christianity is declining; but ethically we are still a

Christian nation." Yet on the ethical side, Zangwill's comment on
another pronouncement by Dean Inge was: "I agree with the Dean—
it is nonsense to talk of the failure of Christianity when Christianity
has never been tried." "The bulk of this volume does not concern
the Christian problem," Zangwill said in his book, *The War for the
World*; "it is occupied or pre-occupied with problems which belong
equally to Judaism or religion generally." But he emphasised his
point that Christianity had never been tried. "The Sermon on the
Mount was meant to be the inspiration of a few—the salt of the
earth, the yeast to leaven the lump. Its spiritual extremism is
necessary to offset the grossness of the body politic. It is 'minority
Ethics.' Although it appeals to all mankind it is aware that only the
elect will vibrate to its teaching. Christianity is a religion for losers.
The attempt to fit this tragic universe of ours into a comfortable
Church establishment is hopeless. The function of a Christian is to
struggle and suffer. And hence in every great crisis the real Christian
will be found not in the Church, but outside it." He went on to
quote the Bishop of Carlisle confessing "that the Church is more
Jewish and Pagan than Christian, but he does not seem to see," he
remarked, "that a National Faith cannot be otherwise."

"While Christian history with its countless blood-spillings and
mutual burnings, that are a constituent even of its religious record,
is almost insufferable in the reading to any man of sympathy or
imagination," he went on, "it is impossible, despite the sordid stains
as upon old clo', to read Jewish history since the fall of Jerusalem
without being purged by pity and terror. For here no blood is shed
but that of Israel, and if the epic is defaced by meanness and squalor,
and if the tragedy comes not seldom from a betrayal, by what is false
within, there remains enough to make it an eternal epic of the
triumph of the spirit." Zangwill saw Rabbi Jochanan ben Zakkai, at
the time of the Roman conquest of Judea, as the man who "dis-
entangled the religion from the locale. He may have felt already that
Israel's greatness was spiritual," he said, "belonged to a category of
force that could not and should not be measured against Rome's
material might. The unifying centre was no longer geographical, and
the Jews became 'the People of the Book.' A book substituted for
a geographical centre, and a condition of spirit for a point of space."
What bound the Jews together was their faith, and God had "selected
Israel to make known his name to the world."

Yet Zangwill was a Zionist, active in the Zionist movement, a
political Zionist, who spoke of "Jewish nationalism." "To deny that
the Jews were once a political people is as foolish," he said, "as to
assert that they have maintained that character for two thousand
years, and that the comparative religious unity of the Diaspora was a
political nationalism." He believed that "once Jews have a territory

again, they can take their political nationalism out of storage, and restore it to its soil." But "for my part, I doubt," he said, "whether Jewish segregation does not always remain religious."

He could not agree with the use made by a leading Zionist, Dr. Shmarya Levin, "of the term 'Nationality' for a phenomenon which in its Jewish aspect is of a complexity utterly transcending our existing political vocabulary. 'Nationality' is a very dubious word to express what all Jews have in common," he said. Sometimes he could be very impatient with Zionism because it acted as a brake on his ideal movement of abolishing sects and nations and establishing a brotherhood of man. Dr. Claude Montefiore was a passionate anti-Zionist, but his insistence that Liberal Judaism is a movement for Jews made Zangwill exclaim: "O lame and impotent conclusion! Only intelligible if Mr. Montefiore is really the most secret and passionate of Zionists. For what reasons Mr. Montefiore having evolved for himself a religion so noble and sustaining, so rational and universal, yet addresses his ministrations to the Jews exclusively, I have never been able to make out." "In the case of Jewry," he pointed out, "the human atoms who cherish this corporate con-sciousness have in every country entered into a new and ever-varying geographic relation. The result is a series of crosses betwixt Jewish and Gentile psychology. Sometimes these groups have no language but that of their environment; always they have no other political allegiance—and in war they kill one another. If any in-ternational bond persisted ámong all these variants, it was felt as the expression of a religious connection, not a political." "The Jewish martyrs," he said, "went to the stake not for the unity of Jewry, but for the unity of God." Zangwill would have approved the declaration of his friend, Dr. Schechter, that "Judaism is, in the first instance, a divine religion, not a mere complex of racial peculiarities and tribal customs." And that "Judaism is a proselytising religion, being the mission to bring God's kingdom on earth, and to include in that kingdom all mankind." I think he would have agreed too with Schechter's repudiation of the "Jewish atheist," when he said: "If there is anything sure, it is that the highest motives which worked through the history of Judaism are the strong belief in God and the unshaken confidence that at last this God, the God of Israel, will be the God of the whole world."

Zangwill had no great bias in favour of Jewish atheists, though he had himself been one. Incidentally, apropos that monstrosity the atheist Jew, I knew an English journalist of some distinction, born into a Roman Catholic family who spoke of himself as an atheist Roman Catholic. It sounds strange, but people speak strangely. As for all atheists being good ethical folk, Zangwill said: "I know an atheist who is extremely vicious, and an orthodox Jew who is a

saint." "The Jewish Freethinkers, who dine together on the Day of
Atonement" were to him only "the natural reaction against the Jews
who merely fast together on the Day of Atonement. Vulgarity
avenges vulgarity." He didn't agree with "the Jewish Atheists who
think we ought to be taken in hand by the Society for the Preservation of Ancient Ruins." "Judaism I regard as a reduction to practice
of Hebrew ideals," he said, "and I by no means look on Jewish ideals
as played out. Judaism grapples honestly and wisely with many social
problems. It is a sociological system, a way of living, the physical
and moral interblent, which is far from being a failure, and which
contains much more besides sanitation and meat inspection which
Jewish thinkers might well press upon the attention of the modern
world. I am afraid too many Jewish reformers confound Judaism
with Hebraism and think that Judaism is merely Christianity minus
Christ. It is something far more positive."

Hillaire Belloc, in his book *The Jews,* said rightly that the Jewish
problem "cannot be avoided. It must be met." How did he as a
Roman Catholic meet it? Speaking of "the sharp distinction
between the Jew and ourselves," he said: "The Rationalist would
say that this distinction was racial, and that it only found religious
expression on account of its racial quality. His opponent would say
that the origin of the quarrel was mainly religious; that it was a
difference in religious tradition which formed the contrast between
the Jew and Christendom." When he spoke of intermarriage, he
spoke of it as "marriage between Christian and Jew," not "English
and Jew."

Zangwill said he had "long pondered between our triple names,
Hebrew, Jew and Israelite"; by the Hebrew he meant "the idealist,"
which would be Zionist, striving for the regeneration of the Jewish
nation; "the Jew the adherent of an historical system," which is
Judaism; and "the Israelite, the Jew by birth, our lowest common
factor." He returned years later to this distinction. "When I talk
about the race," he said, "I mean the word 'Hebrew'; when I talk
of the Jew, I mean the Jew as a religion." "I put Judaism first," he
declared, "because since the fall of Jerusalem the Jewish race has been
preserved by its religion. If there has been in every age and country a
large leakage from the race, it has always been through the conduit
of religious conversion or religious indifference. What threatens
the existence of the race is the decay of Judaism. So long as Judaism
flourishes among Jews there is no need to talk of safeguarding race or
nationality; both are automatically preserved by the religion." It
was certainly in the sense of being a Jew by religion that he once
asked Joseph Jacobs "whether I was a Jew. He said, 'Certainly. You
go further than I.' " Zangwill tried "to explain his mistake to him."
He was less observant than Joseph Jacobs thought. "I see some crank

has been lecturing about me, and he said, 'Zangwill is a Jew only in name.' Well, if you will allow me to make a little pun, if he had said, 'Only in aim,' he would have been nearer the truth." He had a distaste for the Jew who tried to conceal the fact that he was a Jew. "Marranoism," he called it. "Sailing under false religious colours." He spoke of it in his Introduction to a book called *The Real Jew*. "In our own epoch, among Jews who have no faith to conceal," he said, "Marranoism has taken the shape of sailing under false racial colours. That is still more degrading and vulgar." He hated also that Marranoism, which while "openly practising Judaism," "lurks shyly in the background of civilisation." He wanted Judaism to proclaim itself proudly. The Jewish problem, for all his belief in universalism, was not something that would pass. Neither Zionism nor the "melting pot" would solve it. "Neither in the gathering place of Palestine nor in the melting pots of the Diaspora," he wrote, "can the Jew and his problem disappear. Not of course, that there is any Jewish problem, except for the Jew. For the races with whom the Jew lives there is nothing but advantage in his persistence. Every country is enriched by his intelligence and industry; and as a whipping-boy he is indispensable." He went on to consider the differences between Judaism and Christianity. "In directing its attention too exclusively to individual salvation Christianity," he said, "has neglected the spirit of that Law to fulfil which its founder claimed to have come." He concluded, as he repeatedly concluded: "In so far as our age is striving for justice on earth and goodwill to all peoples, it is returning to essential Judaism."

His idea of the Jew was an ethical not an ethnical being, the bearer of a religious mission, distinct from those around him because of his Jewish religious beliefs, observances and way of life. Thus when he was asked to express himself about the Hebrew University in Jerusalem, he said that in his view it ought to be a Jewish religious Seminary, an authoritative centre of Jewish religious teaching, not a secular University. "The perpetuation of the Jewish people is neither desirable nor possible," he said, "except on a religious basis." At the same time he could not get out of his head the need of a Jewish territorial settlement, where Jews could live.

Zangwill could not tie himself down to one point of view. He kept seeing both sides of a question. Asked what he believed, he invoked for his answer Renan, who had "urged that only drama, giving through its personages even opposite answers can give the full reply to any real human question." In him there were forever two souls struggling in one breast. He kept expressing his father's belief and his mother's unbelief. He looked back wistfully to his father's contentment with his religion. "Orthodoxy makes for happiness," he said, "and with all my larger opportunities and means my life has probably been less enviable than that of my penurious father who, in his old age left his home and family 'to die in Jerusalem.' " Yet disbelief shook him. Not only was he a natural sceptic. He had been brought up in the scientific age, and how could he believe in Genesis? —"I who know that the sun is only one of the twenty million stars of the Milky Way, and the Milky Way itself only a pin-point in the endless universe," how could he believe in "the creation of Adam and his rib on this pokery little planet"?

Zangwill was always inconsistent and contradictory. He could "see no good in making death a bogey as Orthodox Judaism does," and "say we must bear everything with a stout heart." But he could also recoil at the thought of dead bodies.

Yet whatever we say of Zangwill, and of his changing attitudes as he grew older or looked at life from different points of view, or in different moods, whatever we say of his inconsistencies—he said that he did not believe in "consistent lying"—he had no "secret hesitations" in respect of "the Jew in a non-Jewish society," nor of the Jew in a Jewish society, in his different Jewish organisations and movements, nor in anything with which he was connected. He may indeed have been too outspoken, and too voluble, not tactful, not reticent enough; but he was honest, and without "secret hesitations." His wife spoke of his "devastating frankness. 'Honesty was a very difficult feat,' he said of himself, but he tried to be honest. If they might judge honesty by the number of times one got into a row, he must be very honest indeed, because he got into more rows than anybody he knew."

His view on Zionism was that "the national restoration for which the Jew prayed was inseparable from the re-establishment of the Judaism of the Temple." Even in his early Zionist days, as far back as 1899, while Herzl lived and Zangwill adoring him worked at his side, before the Uganda split drove him into opposition to official Zionism, Zangwill had already come to suspect some of the purely "national Jews" who repudiated any religious connection with their Jewish national feeling. "We shall I think find as much lip-profession of irreligion as of religion," he said, "and there is no need to take either Dr. Herzl or Dr. Nordau at their own estimate as unbelievers. Herzl's tears at the sight of the Holy Land held perhaps as much religion as those of any of the weepers at the Wailing Wall."

It is a vital mistake, he said, to regard externals like intermarriage as threatening the existence of the race. What threatens the existence of the race is the decay of Judaism, of which intermarriage is a mere symptom. So long as Judaism flourishes among Jews there is no need to talk of safeguarding race or nationality; both are automatically preserved by the religion. "The Jewish nationality had been preserved not as a nationality but as a religion," he told the Race Congress in

London in 1911. "Where they did not believe in the religion the only force that could keep the Jews together was violent pressure," by which he meant "the pressure of anti-semitism." He had seen dangers in Zionism even in the early years of his championship of the Zionist cause. He said: "It is contended that Zionism is dangerous, plays into the hands of the antisemites, with their cry of unpatriotism; that it is religiously a blasphemous attempt to force the hand of Providence; spiritually a misconception of the true future and mission of Israel; intellectually a mere caricature of the exaggerated nationalism which has temporarily replaced the eighteenth-century cosmopolitanism; and politically an undoing of all the constitutional rights Israel has won so painfully from civilised communities." He took up the suggestion that Zionism aimed at clearing all the Jews out of the countries in which they live. "That the Jews are to migrate *en masse* has never been suggested," he said. "A recognised centre of Jewish life is to be set up, which will be left to its own evolutionary impetus, a centre of gravity which may be trusted to attract the persecuted and the patriotic." He was echoing Herzl: "An exodus of all Jews is not contemplated."

As he formulated it later in the programme of the Jewish Territorial Organisation, "Only for those who cannot or will not stay." It made him reply to H. G. Wells in 1914, when Turkey went into the war against Britain, and Wells wrote to him: "And now, what is to prevent the Jews having Palestine and restoring a real Judea?"— "Grateful as all true Jews would be, they could only accept it if its motive was pro-Jewish, not anti-Jewish, justice and not Jew-hate. An offer of Palestine, coupled with an inspiration, or worse, a policy for the clearance of other countries of Jews, would be a trap from which I should do my best to dissuade my fellow-Jews." He was working to help to establish a home for Jews in Palestine or in some other new Judea, but he was even more concerned to maintain and secure equal rights for those Jews who live and want to live in other countries. That was to him a greater prerequisite of civilisation.

Yet however you defined it, there were Jews, a body of people who hold certain beliefs and observances in common, even if it is only a common religion. "All religious bodies have organisations," Zangwill said, "for protection and self-expression." "Whoever heard of a religious sect that did not yearn to live as compactly as possible, whether for communion or for self-defence." "Judaism as a religion has a right to organise itself nationally and even internationally, no less than Catholicism." Even if Jews had no common descent, and he knew that the millions of Jews in Russia, who were oppressed and pogromed in Russia were the same people in origin as his father and mother, and that he still had relatives living there, they had a duty to protect the rights of those people in foreign lands who observed the same common Judaism. You could not assert the rights of Judaism in a Christian world and not battle for those rights and for the human dignity of those who believed in and practised Judaism. He drew the lesson from the answer attributed to Pobiedonostseff, the head of the Russian Holy Synod, to the question "what would become of the Jews in Russia": "One third will emigrate, one third will be baptised, and one third will starve." He liked none of the three solutions, though he was an advocate of emigration. Three millions or two millions "are a tough number to emigrate," he said. He hated the idea of baptism as much as the idea of starvation.

He knew the kin of those Russian Jews, who were the Children of his Ghetto, of Whitechapel, in the East End of London, and he knew their kin who had emigrated, in New York and other places in America. He regarded himself as one of them. "I can never forget," he said, "that I am one of the Children of the Ghetto."

So though Zangwill was dubious about the form of Dr. Herzl's "Solution of the Jewish Question"—Herzl's biographer, Jacob de Haas says Zangwill had observed that his sponsorship of Herzl "did not involve him in approval of his ideas"—any plan of work that might help the Jews of Russia had his support. Even after Herzl's death, at the height of his quarrel with the Zionists, Zangwill was prepared, according to Dr. Nahum Sokolov, the Zionist leader, in 1912, to go to Russia "to intervene with its Government on behalf of the Jews generally, and in particular to endeavour to secure from the Russian Government a more sympathetic attitude towards Zionism." Sokolov recalled Zangwill's services to Zionism when he presided in 1927 at the Zionist Congress. "Israel Zangwill was the third," he said, "in the link of Herzl and Nordau."

During the First World War when Zangwill conducted a campaign for the emancipation of the Russian Jews, he could not help adding: "I should be giving a false perspective if I failed to point out that the Jews, though the worst, are not the only victims of the Russian bureaucracy. Every religious and racial minority was oppressed in turn." "All these oppressed minorities of religion and race have, like the Jews, brethren in other lands," he went on, "and some, like the Moslem, infinitely more powerful brethren than the Jews."

In the first weeks of the war, early in September 1914, Zangwill received from Sir Edward Grey, the Foreign Minister, "the assurance that he is very fully aware of the importance of the subject of Jewish emancipation in Russia, and would neglect no opportunity of encouraging the reform in question." Britain failed however to influence her Russian ally, and the oppressions of Jews and others in Russia continued. In July 1915 Zangwill wrote to the British Foreign Office drawing attention to this oppression of "Poles, Jews, Finns,

Ukrainians, Socialists and Liberals." "I have kept silence," he said, "for England's sake, but now I see it is precisely for England's sake that I should not have held my peace. Millions in Russia now look to Russia's defeat as the only chance of liberty. The barbarities are therefore no longer a mere breach of the moral law and of the political liberties we profess to defend; they are a serious national danger to England." Zangwill's representations impressed the British Foreign Office. He received a reply from the Foreign Office: "You may be assured that we will see that your views on the Russian question are put forward in the proper quarter. The matter is no doubt one of great gravity, and if I learn anything that would be of interest to you I will write to you again."

Zangwill then turned to Palestine. He saw the forces in Russia working not only for Jewish emancipation, but " 'under the Divinity that shapes our ends' even making for the rise of a Jewish land." (This was before the Balfour Declaration.) "The idea of Palestine or some other territory for the Jew is at last in the air. Even in the British Cabinet powerful elements favour the claims of the Jews upon Palestine. The return of the Jews to Palestine was always to be the immediate sequel of the Great World War."

That led Zangwill to the idea of the Jewish Army, which became in the First World War the Jewish Legion, or the Jewish Battalions, raised under the inspiration of Trumpeldor and Jabotinsky and Colonel Patterson, in which Ben Gurion, the Prime Minister of Israel, and Ben Zvi, the President of Israel, served as privates. When the Zion Mule Corps was formed to fight in the Dardenelles, Zangwill issued an appeal in London "to any young man who might care to join the Zion Mule Corps at the Dardanelles," telling them "how anxious the Commander, Colonel Patterson, is to have more Jewish recruits, owing to the splendid service this Jewish corps—the only one in the world—had rendered to the British and French forces. He says that the Commander-in-Chief, Sir Ian Hamilton, is most anxious to keep this corps up to its full strength. Young Jews who are not yet British subjects and wish to show their gratitude to England, can join this corps. I should be glad to hear from any able-bodied young men who are ready to promote the cause of this country and the honour of the Jewish name."

The Zion Mule Corps appeal was made in March 1915, in the first months of the war. In a letter accompanying the appeal Zangwill said: "I had a cable from the Governor of Alexandria, who has taken Zionist refugees into the British service. I welcomed the omen of a British protectorate in Palestine."

I was actively engaged in the movement for a Jewish Army in the Second World War, so I am specially interested in what Zangwill said and did in the First World War for the Jewish Legion. Zangwill was dead seven years before Hitler became the ruler of Germany, and turned the Bismarckised State that he hated into something much more hateful. I can imagine how Zangwill would have thundered for volunteers to fight in a recognisably Jewish force against the Hitler forces which were exterminating millions of Jewish men, women and children in the death camps and the crematoriums. Mrs. Zangwill helped us in the movement; and his friend, Dr. Redcliffe Salaman, who had been the Medical Officer in the Jewish Regiment of the First World War, suggested the idea "not only as the natural development of the Jewish Regiment of the last war, but as the Jews' natural and logical answer to the forces of Evil." Some Jews objected to the idea of a Jewish Army, some because they said it was a Zionist idea; others because they considered it a Ghetto idea and said it meant segregation, keeping Jews separate from their comrades.

"This instinctive shrinking from solidarity is doubtless a heritage of the tragic centuries," Zangwill said, speaking of the Jewish opposition that he encountered then, as we encountered it later.

Zangwill understood that there were ordinary Jewish reasons for Jews keeping together. His own father had suffered and finally fled from the Russian army because he could not keep the Jewish dietary and other practices there. "The Anglo-Jewish volunteer who might easily stipulate for special treatment accepts the very disregard of his dietary and ritual that constitutes the tragedy of Russo-Jewish conscription," he said. "While the Indian troops are scrupulously safeguarded in their dietary, while the Mohamedan, Sikh and Hindoo have each their slaughterer, the Jewish soldiers are limited to chaplains." He understood that observant Jews could not eat "in Gentile hotels." He quoted Charles Lamb with approval: "If they can sit with us at table why do they keck at our cookery?" "Soldiers in the fighting line, under the ever-present shadow of death, are naturally susceptible to their childish memories," he wrote. They need "the consolations of their neglected religion" more than they can get from their "army chaplains who distribute prayer books and administer to the dying (when they chance to come upon them). 'On Seder night,' wrote an English recruit from the trenches," he quoted, "'I could picture everyone at home sitting round the Passover table, and the thought made me feel as if I could cry my eyes out.' A Jewish battalion," he concluded, "would have attracted volunteers both racially and spiritually. Yet the Anglo-Jewish Community frowned upon the suggestion, and the Jewish chaplain himself, whose labours would have been so lightened by concentration, did his best to keep his flock sundered and dispersed."

People sometimes speculate what a man might have been if he were born and brought up somewhere else, had different friends and different associations. But then he would have been someone else of the same name. "If a man could be drained of his blood, and yet go about with every vital function absolutely unimpaired," said Zangwill, "if an eagle could have its pinions amputated and yet sail aloft as superbly as ever, we should come to the conclusion that the blood and the wings played no real part in the life of the man or the bird, but were mere ornamental appendages." But they are not mere appendages. The soil on which a man lives, the language he speaks, the traditions of his country, his friends and neighbours, his reading, his religion, all shape a man, make him a different man than he would have been with a different soil and language and traditions, friends and neighbours, reading and religion.

If Zangwill's parents had gone to America when they went to Bristol, and he had become an American; or if he had stayed there when he undertook his successful lecture tour in America as a young man, and lecture agents and editors and others clamoured for him to remain; if his father had not been such a scrupulously observant Jew, so that he absorbed such knowledge and love of Judaism and Jewish ways that even when he rebelled against them and wanted to escape it was like trying to escape from himself, and he kept coming back; if Herzl had not come to summon him to the Zionist flag at the very beginning of the Zionist movement; if Judge Sulzberger had not kept persuading him to do the Jewish book that became *Children of the Ghetto*, when he was reluctant to leave his newly-found success as an English humorist, until he finally agreed to do it, then Israel Zangwill would not have been Israel Zangwill, but an English or an American writer of Jewish birth, of that name, but not the man he became, who lives in English literature and in Jewish history. Zangwill might have been another Leonard Merrick, an English Jew born in London in the same year that Zangwill was born, and a writer of considerable importance, whom some good judges held to be more important purely as a writer than Zangwill. Zangwill might, if he had stuck to literature only, as Holbrook Jackson and others asked him to do, have become a greater and more accepted literary figure as such. But he would not have been Israel Zangwill, worthy to stand as one of his *Dreamers of the Ghetto*. Mark Schweid, writing of Zangwill, in the 1950-1 volume of the Jewish Book Annual, issued by the Jewish Book Council of America, speaks of Israel Zangwill being little known to Yiddish and Hebrew readers, because not much of his work was translated into Yiddish and Hebrew, "yet," he says, "his name was known and loved in every Jewish home. He was considered a great writer and a great Jew. He owed much of his popularity to his work as a Zionist and a Territorialist, but he would soon have been forgotten if he were only a politician and a public worker."

Zangwill did not of course stand still in his opinions. He published his article "The Position of Judaism" in 1895; twenty-five years later he wrote: "In the quarter of a century that have elapsed there have been such changes in thought—in my own doubtless as well as in that of Christians—that there are not a few passages that I should express differently to-day. But I have not tampered with it. Were I once to begin altering I should refrigerate rather than recapture that first lyric rapture. Doubtless," he went on challengingly, "were I writing the article now, I should be tempted to dwell on the supplementary proof which the great war has afforded of the incapacity of Christianity to maintain itself in the real human environment, or to equate itself to life save nominally." Yet "through Christianity and Islam, the moral impulse of Judaism," he wrote, "was communicated through the greater part of the civilised world, and each of these great religions has sent out missionaries even to those polytheistic savages which have remained outside the great currents of history. In the very year that the Jews were expelled from Spain, a Spaniard won a new world—America—for the Jewish Bible. And from century to century, to this day, the Bible written entirely by Jews, dominates existence, its vision of life moulds States and societies, its texts confront us on every hand, it is an inexhaustible treasury of themes for music and pictures. Its psalms are more popular in every country than the poems of the nation's own poets. Beside this one book, with all the good and ill it has done, all other national literature seem 'trifles light as air.' "

Always to Zangwill Judaism reached its consummation with the Alenu prayer: "When the world will be perfected under the Kingdom of the Almighty, and all the children of flesh will call upon thy name." That was after all the idea too behind his *Melting Pot*—"God's crucible." He was obsessed by "the mission of Israel." "How," he asked, "are we to reconcile the conception of a nation destined to be 'God's witnesses' among the heathen, with a thousand years of unobtrusive stagnation?", by which he meant Judaism's cessation of active proselytisation. "Well," he answered his own question, " 'they also serve who only stand and wait.' And in a sense, the mere obstinate survival of Israel may still be deemed a witness to 'the finger of God.' Moreover," he said, "the Jewish idea of a 'mission' is not of that fussy activity which Christianity connects with the word; of imposing verbal beliefs upon savages, whose vision of life is quite other. It is in fact the Rabbi's duty to dissuade the would-be proselyte. One may influence one's time by simply being; each righteous soul is a radiation of good."

By the time he wrote this, less than three years after *Children of the Ghetto* appeared, Israel Zangwill had travelled a long way back to the position held by his father, the quiet, unfussy, good, saintly soul, whose good influence was "simply by being, who did not believe, but was belief." "A new current of thought has been set going in my mind," he makes one of his characters say for him. "If a religion that I thought all formalism is capable of producing such types of abnegation as my dear father, then it must, too, somewhere or other, hold in solution all those ennobling ingredients, all those stimuli to self-sacrifice, which the world calls Christianity. Perhaps I have always misunderstood. Perhaps the prosaic epoch of Judaism into which I was born" (by which he meant "the great mass of prosperous Anglo-Judea who had assimilated to the British Philistinism of the day"), "is only transitional, perhaps it only belongs to the middle classes, for I know I felt more of its poetry in my childhood." He came to express it finally in this way: "In Judaism proper there is no philosophy. Sufficient to obey and adore the unknowable Creator." Yet he always knew there was more than that to Judaism. He could not forget his father's strict observance of all the minutiae of Jewish practice. Judaism is a religion, indeed, but it is also a way of life, of daily conduct. He had known that when he wrote *Children of the Ghetto* as a young man of twenty-seven. He described Judaism there as "a religion in which eating, drinking, every act of life is holy, is sanctified by some relation to Heaven." "We will not divorce some portions of life from religion, and say these are of the world."

Zangwill realised the conflict between the scrupulous observance of the minutiae of Jewish orthodox practice and his mission idea of a universalistic Judaism to which all people could adhere. But he would have accepted G. K. Chesterton's "paradox by which two opposite cords of truth become entangled in an inextricable knot. It is often this knot which ties safely together the whole bundle of human life." It had become fashionable in the circles to which Zangwill belonged to sneer at the "Jewish Mission." The later generation, that has realised Zionism, is more attracted by the mission idea. Mr. Ben Gurion has said "the setting up of the State of Israel guaranteed the principal condition of fulfilment. But each one of us, however, is entitled to hug the chauvinistic belief that merely to be like all other people is not enough. We may aspire to bring true the words of the prophet—'I the Lord . . . give thee for a covenant of the people to the Gentiles.' "

Zangwill's book, *The Voice of Jerusalem*, is a passionate plea for the Jewish Mission. "The Jew," he said, "has lived with every people, and by his ability to share the life of them all has proved indirectly that they are all brothers. One touch of Jewry makes the whole world kin." "The history of Israel forbids us to think that the end is any nearer now than when Pharaoh engraved his vain inscription." On the point of dispersion or ingathering, he felt that "a people that has learned to live without a country is unconquerable. Might is baffled when opposed to the ubiquitous." He called upon Jews to live up to a higher standard than other people—like Herzl, Nordau, Baron Hirsch, Jacob Schiff, Mayer Sulzberger. "The trouble with the Jewish Missioners," he concluded, "is that they do not function. Had they been as devoted to their mission as the Zionists to their territorial concept, the war for Jewry—and perhaps for the world— might have gone differently. In practice the Jewish Mission has never appeared except as a stick to beat the Zionists with."

He spoke of it in his stories. Sir Asher Aaronsberg, in *The Jewish Trinity*, believes that "we have a mission to the nations. We must," he says, "be dispersed. We have to preach the unity of God." "I have never heard you preach it," objects Barstein. "We have to preach silently," answers Sir Asher, "by our example. Merely by keeping our religion we convert the world." To Zangwill the true carrying out of the Mission idea was a noble thing. "But I fear," he said, "that the mission-preaching Jews would be seriously disturbed if one proposed to take 'the mission of Israel' seriously."

He explained: "If Judaism is to be a universal religion, it must be universalised, and de-nationalised, and race-Jews, like the early Christians and the pioneer Mohamedans, must be lost in the multitude of their converts, white, black and yellow. This universalism," he added, "is not incapable, however, of arising through a territorial Judaism, which if it gave markedly valuable results would inspire the heathen to go and do likewise. Likewise, not identically: that is, to infuse analogous ideas and practices into their respective national religions. Here lies one solution of the controversy, Mission v. Territory." "If Judaism is to be a universal religion, it must not be too hard for the mass of ordinary people to observe."

Zangwill had sung the praise of the Jewish Sabbath, "the essential verity of the Jews' Sabbath." "This is the sanctified rest day; happy the man who observes it." "Sweet Sabbath-bride, the Hebrew's theme of praise." "There is Sabbath magic in the very bread." "A holy light the Sabbath candles shed." Even when "the candles gutter out—is not Sabbath its own self-sufficient light?" He realised the hold which the Sabbath has on the Jews. Speaking of his Galveston immigration work, he said: "The bait here was bread. Could we have added also the Jewish folk-life and the Jewish Sabbath we should have had a rush like that to the gold-fields." He would have agreed that "more than the Jews have kept the Sabbath, the Sabbath has kept the Jews." Yet he began to worry that the Saturday-Sabbath observance was running "against the stream of general life." He went so far as to say that in the Diaspora it was "almost impossible to keep it." And "a Palestine Jewry which could not help keeping it would be useless as a model for Jewries where it was almost impossible to keep it." So he seriously put forward the idea that

Jews should keep the Sabbath on Sunday. He did not mean a Sunday-Sabbath, but a "Sunday-Shabbos," he said. "What has been tried is a Sunday-Sabbath. There have been Reform services on Sunday—not unlike Church services—but there have been no orthodox services on Sunday. Nobody has turned Saturday night into the old-fashioned Friday night. Once a single Shabbos was slipped over into Sunday, once Lechah Dodi was sung on Sunday night and Kiddush said over the Challos, the change would not again be noticed. And orthodoxy would be established solidly for centuries."

I wonder what his friend Chief Rabbi Hertz, who fought so strenuously against the attempt of the Calendar reformers to get a new Calendar accepted which would change the sequence of days, and make Saturday a different day each year, thought of Zangwill's proposal.

Zangwill showed in his story *The Sabbath Breaker* that he knew with what tenacity Jews cling to the observance of the Sabbath, even to death, even "to be martyred for the honour of the Sabbath." But he also believed, and he illustrated it in *The Sabbath Question in Sudminster*, that as Barstein says to Sir Asher Aaronsberg, "Dispersion among Sunday-keeping peoples makes our very Sabbath an economic impossibility." Mr. Samuels in Sudminster, who keeps his shop open on Saturday, tells his fellow-Jews that "By the Act of Charles I the Sabbath is defined as the Sunday, and as a British subject I take my stand upon the British Constitution." It is true, as Israel Abrahams said, that "mixing with the world, and sharing the world's pursuits, the Jews began to find it hard to observe the Saturday as of old," and that "the difficulty has increased," so that with "the growing laxity in observance this is one of the most pressing problems that face the Jewish community to-day." It speaks for Zangwill's constant concern with Jewish problems that he was moved to suggest a solution, though he pointed out that it was not originally his own, but Judge Sulzberger's, who had "fruitlessly proposed it a good many years ago—the Shabbos Sheini—keeping Shabbos on Sunday while in the Christian Diaspora." He saw that the Shabbos is something more than a Sunday service in a Temple; that Lechah Dodi and Kiddush and Challos are part of it, and that Judaism does not grow by cutting away its observances. "The story of Shylock seems to me to have a Jewish significance," he said, "of which Shakespeare did not dream. Shylock was the Jewish Reformer who thought that pounds of flesh could be cut away; but that is a very dangerous way of reducing unhealthy obesity. Fasting and prayer would be a better therapeutic." He wanted the "American Rabbi, if he believed in Judaism at all," to "cling desperately to the historical and domestic poetry. The modern Jewish agnostics I understand," he said, "and in some moods sympathise with; but the

professing believers who tear away the better half of their heritage
—these puzzle me."

Yet Zangwill in another mood could preach the very thing he had
condemned. "Cutting away pounds of flesh was a very dangerous
way of reducing obesity," he had said of the reducing methods of the
Reformers. Then he urged "Judaism, if it is ever to create the world
of its dream," to "perform a surgical operation on itself and cut
away all that clogs and hinders its vitalising activity." In such a
mood the Reformers did not cut away enough to please him. Not
even Dr. Claude Montefiore, who "instead of dynamically expounding the new," he complained, "is perpetually wrestling with
this or that bit of the old system." The Sabbath question, for instance. Why keep it on Saturday? he asked again.

It is characteristic of Zangwill's dichotomy that he could also laud
the Jews for their "proud clinging to their Sabbath, their refusal to
fight upon it which lost them Jerusalem on two separate occasions."
He compared it with the Christian readiness to abolish Sunday—
"handing over the Lord's Day to the King." It is the same with his
conflicting views about Zionism. He could advocate putting all
our eggs in one basket and standing watch over it. And he could say
that the only way of preserving the Jews was not to put all the eggs
in one basket. It was Zangwill's everlasting pro and con.

I mentioned how Zangwill took it upon himself in 1911 to appear
in the High Court as an expert witness on Jewish orthodox practice.
He said he had studied the customs of the Jews, "not as a Rabbi
would, but I have studied them generally and have a general acquaintance with them. I have lived a good deal of my youth in
orthodox communities." The *Jewish Chronicle* had an editorial that
year complaining that Zangwill has "assumed the mantle of some
ultra-orthodox Golus Rabbi and gravely warns his correspondents
that in Judaism, in the observance of our religion and faith, is to be
found the only salvation of the Jewish people. Now, we do not
quarrel in the least with Mr. Zangwill's opinions as to the value of
religious renaissance in the redemption of Israel," it went on. "It is
a view we have never ceased to impress in these columns. But nothing
now, be it noted, about the necessity of a centrum for the Jewish
people so that Jews may be given the best chance of maintaining
Judaism in practice. What Mr. Zangwill is now at pains alone to
point to as balm for Jewish wounds is strict Jewish observance."
Zangwill once presided at a lecture by Israel Abrahams on Jewish
table customs, and in his own speech drew "attention to the hygienic
value of the Jewish form of Grace. Doctors," he said, "trace a great
deal of the evils of modern life to dyspepsia and a great deal of
dyspepsia to the irrational method of taking food. It is possible," he
suggested, "that the post-prandial recitation of a prayer which should

in decency occupy ten minutes would be of considerable indirect value as a digestive." The Jewish Grace after meals is called "Benching," which is probably a derivation from the root of "benediction"; when Zangwill was called on to propose the toast of the Bar at a Maccabean dinner to Lord Reading, who was then Lord Chief Justice, he indulged in "Benching the Bar," which pun may be translated as "Blessing the Bar."

In 1911 Zangwill was invited to address the Race Congress held in London. His thesis was one he was always repeating, which was the kernel of his *Melting Pot*, that "the Jew demonstrates the comparative superficiality of all human differences. Like the Colonel's lady and Judy O'Grady all these peoples are the same under their skins—as even Bismarck was once constrained to remark when he saw Prussians and Frenchmen lying side by side in the community of death." Speaking of Jewish assimilation, he asked, "should Jews so readily assimilate to all these types, were these types fundamentally different? Not only is every race akin to every other, but every people is a hotch-potch of races." "To preserve the Jews, whether as a race or as a religious community," he went on, "is no part of the world's duty, nor would artificial preservation preserve anything of value. Their salvation must come from themselves. Civilisation is not called upon to save the Jews, but it is called upon to save itself. And by its treatment of the Jews it is destroying itself." He was the President of the Jewish Territorial Organisation, and he was busy wrestling with the problem of the Russian Jews.

So Zangwill drew the attention of the Congress to the plight of the Russian Jews, five or six million in number, shut up in the Pale. "In insisting that Russia abolish the Jewish Pale I am pleading for the regeneration of Russia, not of the Russian Jew," he said. He quoted a Russian Liberal who had said: "Russia cannot enter the Temple of Freedom as long as there exists a Pale of Settlement for the Jews." Then he pleaded for the creation of a Jewish State, or at least a Jewish land of refuge upon a basis of local autonomy, to which, in the course of the centuries, all that was truly Jewish would gravitate." Even that weighed more with him because it would mean for "the world getting rid of the Jewish problem," and because it would "foster world-peace and establish in the heart of the Old World a bridge of civilisation between the East and the West, and a symbol of hope for the future of mankind." When Zangwill joined Herzl in the Zionist movement, he confessed afterwards, the universal idea was uppermost with him. He found Herzl, "though an incarnation of all that is best in the Jewish type, curiously ignorant of Judaism, and content to accept a Jew as a phenomenon purely biological. If in the end I endorsed his political conception, it was partly because of sympathy with a great man, and partly because I saw there was no real contradiction between the spiritual ideal and a definite locale for it, which locale could be at once a land of refuge for the oppressed and a working model of a socially just common-wealth."

More than the fulfilment of Zionism, more than a Jewish land, he wanted universal Peace and human brotherhood. "Were the landlessness of the Jews the only obstacle to universal peace I should be the first," he said, "to waive their claim. Jerusalem, which means the heritage of peace, would be better built so than by actual restora-tion. The mere fact that a group of people hates its neighbours affords no basis for reverence." He not only foresaw and disliked the Jewish State born out of hatred for the British; he, who had been a rebel from his father's Judaism, also declared himself utterly opposed to the new Godless Jewish nationalism which believes Jewish attach-ment adequately fulfilled in devotion to the nation and State. "What would make the old Jews turn in their graves would be to read atheistic articles by Jerusalem journalists," he wrote, "or to witness the crusades of the young colonists of Palestine against the Holy Sabbath. Political Zionist though I am," he said, "I cannot share the intolerance for the Jews of the old type who live in Jerusalem," of whom his father was one. "I feel more strongly than ever," he declared, "that in these frowsy greybeards poring over their obsolete Talmuds and hugging their worm-eaten traditions to their caftaned breasts, we have a finer type of humanity than the Prussian Junker, in all his bravery, and that it pays a people better to keep up such a standing army of mystics and students than to nourish the insolence of a military caste. If the purpose of Zionism was merely to beget another national type of the Western pattern, it would not be worth the striving."

Zangwill even came to respect his father's "Six hundred and thirteen precepts of the Mosaic code, a sanctified sociology, an order in human affairs, an attempt at practical idealism." He realised that "there is in fact no real contradiction between the spirit and a letter which codifies it for practical purposes." As he said of Wells, Zangwill "had all the stigmata of Hebrew prophecy—lips touched with the burning coal can speak no otherwise." It is true that he regarded himself as "spiritually adult," and therefore himself not needing to adhere rigidly to each letter of the code, which was rather for "spiritual minors." "The spirit that has come of age will auto-matically do what the immature spirit has to be commanded to do," he said. It was also, as with many people, a matter of mood. "The modern Jewish agnostics I understand, and in some moods sym-pathise with," he said.

I don't think Zangwill observed the Jewish fasts and feasts. His friend L. J. Greenberg, who once attacked Zangwill for not being religiously observant, agreed afterwards that he was himself not "orthodox." And when Zangwill, on one of his visits to America was accused of not keeping the dietary laws, someone pointed out that the accuser did not keep them either. But Zangwill was careful about how other Jews felt about Jewish observances. Thus he wrote to ask that a meeting should be postponed, because the date fixed for it was Shevuoth, which is the feast of the Giving of the Law on Mount Sinai. He wrote to Dr. Jochelman, and dated his letter, "Erev Rosh Hashonah," which is "the Eve of the New Year." There is a copy of the Rosh Hashonah Machzor, the Prayer Book for the Jewish New Year, which he gave to Jacob Schiff, now in the Jewish Theological Seminary in New York. He inscribed it with the Hebrew date, Tishri 5667. This is one of the books of the Synagogue Festival Service Prayers which, the British Museum Catalogue records, has "an English translation in prose and verse by I. Zangwill and others." One of his translations in that New Year Prayer Book, over which he must have pondered as he translated it, reads:

> "For He who knows each action and its aim,
> Will mercifully moderate our blame."

He knew the Jewish New Year from his childhood, when he "felt more of its poetry." "The New Year dawned upon the Ghetto," he wrote in the *Children of the Ghetto*, "heralded by a month of special matins and the long-sustained note of the ram's horn," and followed by "the Ten Days of Repentance which find their awful climax in the Day of Atonement." "The New Year itself was the most sacred of the Festivals, provided with prayers half a day long, and made terrible by peals on the ram's horn," he wrote in *A Child of the Ghetto*. "The sinner was warned to repent, for the New Year marked the Day of Judgment." He knew the meaning of the prayers, "passionate bursts of prayer," and of "the three kinds of calls on the primitive trumpet" (the Shofar) "plain, trembling, wailing." Then at the end of the Ten Days of Repentance came "the great White Fast, the terrible Day of Atonement commanded in the Bible." "Many of the male worshippers were clad in their grave-clothes, and the extreme zealots remained standing all day long, swaying to and fro and beating their breasts at the confession of sin." The last chapter of *Children of the Ghetto*, the closing of the book, recounts Esther Ansell's—his own—experience in the little Synagogue of the Sons of the Covenant, where his father had taken him when he was a small boy. "She was overwhelmed by the thought of its sons in every corner of the earth proclaiming to the sombre twilight sky the belief for which its generations had lived and died. They seemed like a great army of the sheeted dead risen to testify to the Unity. The magnetic tremor that ran through the Synagogue thrilled her to the core; once again her dead self woke, her dead ancestors that would not be shaken off lived and moved in her. She was sucked up into the great wave of passionate faith."

Zangwill had experienced it so that he could never forget it. Whether he worked and ate on the Day of Atonement, or sat reliving its memories, before "the strange sounds" had drawn him away, "the magnetic tremor" that ran through the Synagogue of his boyhood thrilled him "to the core," and his "dead ancestors that would not be shaken off lived and moved in him." "God and the God of our fathers," he translated an ancient hymn in the Day of Atonement Prayer Book, "Honoured and terrible Name, Pardon the sin of this people, gathered Thy praise to proclaim. Turn from Thy fierceness of anger, turn from Thy fury and flame; Thus shall the whole world acknowledge Thee and shall call on Thy Name."

In the midst of his Uganda fight in Zionism, Zangwill spoke at a London Zionist meeting on the eve of Rosh Hashonah 1904; he said he hoped "the New Year will bring more light on our path and blessing on our work, and that the Day of Atonement, by reminding some of us that the slander of opponents is a sin, may conduce to our Atonement." The following year, 1905, the year of the formation of the Jewish Territorial Organisation, he issued a Rosh Hashonah message, calling upon all Jews, "all of our race or religion," to "listen to that 'Tekiyo Gedolo,' that great call, the bitter cry of our homeless and persecuted brothers." According to Rabbi Dr. Henry Cohen of Galveston, who had known Zangwill in London when he was a young teacher at the Jews' Free School, Zangwill always carried a mezuza with him. Moved by an article I wrote in 1945 when Mrs. Zangwill died, he wrote to me that "after Israel died, Edith Zangwill sent me the mezuza that her husband always carried with him." It seems a strange thing to do with a mezuza. I have seen Jewish girls wear a mezuza-shaped ornament, as many Christian girls and women wear a cross. But the commandment about the mezuza, in Deuteronomy, is that it should be "upon the door posts of thy house and upon thy gate." Zangwill may have been thinking of the injunction that the words in the mezuza "shall be upon thy heart." Louis Zangwill said "my brother's practice diverges in this respect from his formal thinking."

Zangwill was in his time not only a rebel from Jewish orthodox practice and from Jewish religious belief, a rationalist, an "irreligious person," a "heathen," but as he kept glancing backward nostalgically towards the Judaism of his father, he also kept turning towards the figure of Jesus, and he was, like Sholem Asch to-day, accused by some of "Christianising." In 1903, a correspondent in the *Jewish Chronicle* objected to an article by Zangwill in the *Daily Mail*, on

"The Future of the Jew," in which he said "the Jew tends towards the acceptance of Christ in the apostolic chain of Hebrew prophets." Zangwill repeated the passage nearly twenty years later in *The Voice of Jerusalem*: "The freer the Jew is left the more he tends, if not towards Christianity, towards a broader view of it, and towards the acceptance of Christ in the Apostolic chain of Hebrew prophets." When Zangwill died, in August 1926, there was an article in the *Jewish Chronicle* asserting of Zangwill that "In religion he veered to Christianity."

It is true that Jesus attracted Zangwill as he has attracted many other Jews, who have not, however, joined the Church. Professor Morris Raphael Cohen, the philosopher, who spoke of "Rabbi Jesus," pointed out that one who believes in the ethical commands of Jesus would not be considered a Christian "if he had not been baptised into any Church, and did not subscribe to the doctrine of the Trinity or the Virgin Birth." What attracted Zangwill was his belief that Jesus had always remained a Jew, and that his teachings were Jewish. Rabbi Louis Finkelstein, the head of the Jewish Theological Seminary of America, seems to have the same feeling. "It is generally recognised," he wrote, "that Jesus was a faithful, observant Jew who followed the Law and believed in its divine inspiration." What Zangwill could not understand was the mentality that "calmly labels all the Old Testament virtues as 'Christian' (as though before the advent of Jesus the world was a nest of vipers, and God the Father had lived utterly withdrawn)." To him Jesus was a Jew; "Two Jews," he called "Moses and Jesus" in his poem of that name. But he confessed that Christian missionaries "had been anathema to me since childhood; conceived as a sort of spiritual spider in wait for the Jewish soul. Indeed, maturer acquaintance with the missionary methods had not enhanced my respect." "I know how these devils set their baits for the helpless immigrant, offering bread in return for lip conversion," Reb Shemuel said in his *Children of the Ghetto*. During the war, when Christians were fighting Christians, and "British and German missionaries were divided in their work in Africa," he trusted "that at least the Society for the Conversion of the Jews will have the grace or the humour to cease from troubling now."

He had another objection to Christianity. "While Judaism inspires life, Christianity inspires to negation of life," he wrote. "Valuable as a counsel of perfection, Christianity can only stimulate chosen spirits, making saints of the few and hypocrites of the many. Judaism does not despise the world, it accepts it. This acceptance of the world is the very note of 'modernity.' Judaism aims at influencing character through conduct, Christianity at influencing conduct through emotion. Souls cannot rise above their level. It is true that in working through the figure of Christ, Christianity stands on a basis of sound psychology, for nothing affects character like character. But there must be already a latent affinity between the two characters. There is no such thing as 'conversion,' no sudden fire, without prior accumulation of inflammable matter.'' It did not lessen his feeling for Jesus. He went so far as to say that "If Christians are ready to abandon the doctrines of the Incarnation and the Atonement, there is no reason why Jews should not admit that the heroic tragedy of the great Galilean illumines the cosmic problem of suffering.''

Zangwill, who, in his sceptic mood, can scoff in *Italian Fantasies* that "not even Lot's wife supplies sufficient salt to swallow Genesis with,'' finds in the same book that "the dying cry of Jesus stamps him with authenticity, as the complaints of the Israelites against their leader guarantee Moses and the Exodus.'' On his travels in Italy, Zangwill met Mary, almost in the way of those who claim to have had Visitations. He thought her an Italian peasant, and asked her his way to Vicenza, but she spoke to him of Jerusalem. She told him her Yeshua had gone to Jerusalem. Then suddenly she shrieked: "They have killed my Yeshua!'' But, being Zangwill and a Jew, he had another vision, this time in Siena, where they were burning Jews. "I could now distinguish the Hebrew death cries of the victims, 'Hear, O Israel, the Lord our God is One.' I perceive, dragged along to the pyre, a little olive-eyed Jewish mother, whose worn face I seemed to recognise: 'Viva Maria! Viva la Madre di Dio.' With a shudder I shook off these visions.''

As always, his Judaism reasserted itself: "It was Moses who more voluntarily than Jesus offered his life that the equilibrium of this righteous universe should not be shaken. 'I will go up unto the Lord; peradventure I shall make an atonement for your sin.' And the atonement offered ran: 'Blot me, I pray Thee, out of Thy Book which Thou hast written!' Here in the Old Testament, not in the New,'' says Zangwill, "first appears the notion of the vicarious atonement. But the Old Testament sternly rejects it: 'Whoever hath sinned against Me him will I blot out of My Book.' '' For all that he kept speaking of Jesus, Moses was to him "the greatest figure in all history.''

Zangwill, in this matter of his religious beliefs, is like a bark that cruises past foreign lands, but always returns to discharge crew and cargo in the home port. Yet much in those foreign lands and seas attracted him. He found a kindred spirit in the people and much that was familiar in the view. Something of the spirit he knew and loved had been taken by previous travellers to those foreign parts and had been planted and bore fruit. Cruising about the seven seas he had come to see that "Mosaism is no longer a solitary lighthouse dominating a sea of darkness. It is not, as perhaps in Pharaoh's day, the one safeguard against the rocks of idolatry and the reefs of immorality. Other beacons warn, other lights shine, and the stars are for all steersmen."

Yet the flower from which all the other flowers sprang was the flower of Judaism. Christianity and Mohamedanism were later growths from the Jewish tree. They were doing the work of God, to bring the whole world under the dominion of the Almighty, when "all the children of flesh will call upon the One God, when the Lord shall be One, and his Name One."

He wondered why a religion like Judaism was not better known and more widely observed, why "even in Palestine the young generation of Haluzim regards it as obsolete. Yet in essence, Judaism is so modern," he said, "that Mr. H. G. Wells has been proposing the extraction of it—history, literature, dietary code, League of Nations, lock, stock and barrel—as a Gospel for the world. Is there no way of revivifying it," he asked, "for the Jews themselves?" He wanted people to live their religion. "The truth of religions can only be proved," Zangwill said, "through the lives of their followers. Judaism needs to live in its own spirit, true to its ardent belief in life. For people refrain from wrong in proportion to their power of sympathy, of imagining the consequences to others. The larger the heart," he said, "the less the wrong-doing."

Everywhere, in all his ideals and his dreams of the future, he saw the spirit and the message and the hope of Judaism, the coming of the Messiah, the turning of all people, of "all the children of flesh," to the One God. When he spoke of his friend Dr. Schechter's departure for America to become President of the Jewish Theological Seminary in New York, he did not forget to pay tribute to him because "Dr. Schechter rightly regards Judaism as a missionary religion." He wanted Jewish thought to "help to shape the world's thought." When he stood in doubt between his two ideals, of the Jewish people resurrected, and of the Kingdom of God extended over all mankind, he resolved his doubt by explaining that they were "the two Hebraic dreams, the major and the minor." "The repossession of Palestine" was for Judaism, he said, "a minor traditional hope." He looked forward to a time when "the two Hebraic dreams, the major and the minor, would be fused in one, and the Hebrew metropolis—that meeting-point of three religions—would become at once the centre and symbol of the new era." It is the dream of the "Alenu" prayer: "when the Lord shall be King over all the earth, when all the children of flesh will call upon Thy Name."

"I was born into Judaism," Zangwill said shortly before he died. "When I came to years of reflection I looked forward to finding one religion for the whole world, when all men should be brothers. Perhaps that is the real Judaism."

Chapter VI

THE ZIONIST

"MODERN Zionism began when Herzl entered Zangwill's study," Dr. Josef Fraenkel says in his biography of Herzl. It was November 1895 when, Zangwill relates, "Herzl came to me and said: 'I am Theodor Herzl. Help me to build the Jewish State.'" Herzl's Diaries, where he records the beginning of the movement, opened in the spring of 1895. The only important things that had happened since he wrote his *Jewish State*, which was not published till 1896, were his meetings with Baron de Hirsch, which brought him no support, and with Dr. Max Nordau, who told him to go to Zangwill. "It was under my chairmanship," Zangwill afterwards declared, "that Dr. Herzl first broached his idea to the Jewish public." "I was the first person that Dr. Herzl came to in London," Zangwill said. "He came with an introduction from Max Nordau. I worked for him loyally as a perfect slave for a great many years, so it is not true that I am an obstinate person and cannot work with anybody. When I meet a great person, I know it."

When Zangwill was in New York in 1923, Dr. Stephen Wise said: "Just before he died, Theodor Herzl spoke to me in Vienna of what Zangwill had done in the effort to help him to bear his—Herzl's —heavy, crushing burdens." Zangwill quoted impishly Joseph Jacob's remark to him when he first saw Herzl: "I know how to kill Zionism. Cut off Herzl's beard." Zangwill knew that Herzl was "picturesque" with his beard. He could understand that Joseph Jacobs could have a real "repugnance to Herzl," "that of the profound student of Jewish problems to the man who approached them superficially as a race-Jew; who occupied solely with Real-politik was—at first, at least—quite out of touch with the soul of the people or the faith. And Jacobs was not wrong," he said, "in ever keeping steadfastly before the fanatics of race that a narrow inter-pretation of their ideal might not be a culmination but an anti-climax of Jewish history."

But he saw above and beyond that, beyond the picturesque beard and the magnetism of his eyes and presence, the stature of an Assyrian King, the force that was Herzl, the Jewish need that drove him, the spirit that when he died at the age of forty-four, made him give this death-bed message, as he lay coughing and bringing up blood: "Tell them that I gave my heart's blood for my people."

"A majestic figure dominating the assembly with eyes that brood and glow," Zangwill wrote in *Dreamers of the Ghetto*, describing Herzl at the First Zionist Congress. "There will never arise one like unto him, no one with his fiery energy, his magnificent dash, his inspired impatience," Zangwill said when Herzl died on 3rd July 1904. On 16th March 1904, Zangwill, being then in Seville, had written what he called "A Lost Chapter of Numbers," which is the Fourth Book of the Pentateuch, but which is more apposite to his purpose under the Hebrew name "Bamidbor," which means "the Desert," the wanderings of the children of Israel in the Desert, the wilderness. It appeared in the Passover issue of Herzl's paper, the *Welt*, the official publication of the Zionist Organisation, which Herzl founded and led. The Editors explained in a footnote: "We asked our celebrated colleague, Israel Zangwill, a long time ago, to let us have a contribution for our Passover issue. Zangwill has been so kind as to send us this humorous fantasy, whose blithe ruthlessness intends no affront to anyone." But Zangwill's article *was* intended to affront more than one person. It was aimed deliberately at Herzl's opponents and detractors, especially at Ussischkin. "Ussischkin," says de Haas in his biography of Herzl, "came to the First Congress as an opponent. He and his colleagues, quite apart from principles in which they devoutly believed, had always rebelled against a leader who had little personal sympathy for them and over-awed them, and to whom, owing to the force of public opinion, they were always compelled to yield." Ussischkin was at that moment challenging Herzl's leadership. "There are many," Herzl replied to Ussischkin, "who have either never been seen at our councils, or for some reason have sulkily withdrawn because their vanity or their ambition has not been satisfied, who imagined that the moment had arrived when they could step into other people's shoes because my friends and I proposed to the Congress sending an expedition to investigate the splendid offer of the British Government. They were in error. Their time has not come." So at this moment, when Ussischkin and his friends were challenging Herzl's leadership, Zangwill published in the *Welt* his "ruthless fantasy," describing the revolt of the Sons of Charkov against Moses, "because the whole Congress consists of none other than holy men, so why do you, Moses, make yourself a Prince over us?"

Almost as the article appeared, Herzl fell ill, and felt he was dying. "Why fool ourselves?" he said. "I have heard the ringing of the third bell. I am no coward. I look at death composedly. This is bitter earnest." He never recovered.

"Not dead, because immortal," Zangwill said when Herzl died. And in the poem which he wrote for Herzl's death: "Farewell, O Prince. You dreamed a dream and you have paid the cost. To save

a people leaders must be lost. The noblest soul in Judah is not dust,
but fire that works in every vein and must reshape our life. Death
has but fixed him in immortal life." When my friend Hans Herzl,
Dr. Herzl's son, died, I found among his papers this poem of Zangwill's copied out in his handwriting, which looked so much like his
father's. "It may be a little comfort to you and to Hans (as to
Pauline and Trude)," Zangwill wrote to Mrs. Herzl when her
husband died, "to hear of the thousands and thousands of Jews I
saw weeping for your sake, but also for their own sake, and for the
great cause which your dear husband brought into the world. Our
love for him and our devotion will be everlasting." "Without Herzl
there would have been no Zionist movement," Zangwill said. "This
Herzl stands to-day among the makers of history."

After the storm raised by Zangwill's "Watchman What of the
Night?" speech, Dr. Stephen Wise, who had been in the chair—
"mine was the personal responsibility," he said, "of having invited
him"—said: "Zangwill criticised, not as an anti-Zionist, but as a
Zionist of Zionists, as a Herzlian Zionist. As far as Zangwill has
any quarrel, it is not with the fundamental ideals and principles of
Zionism, but with policies of the present Zionist leadership with
respect to which there may be honest differences of opinion. In one
word, Zangwill's protest is against minimum, not maximum Zionism,
for Zangwill is a maximum Zionist. Zionist he long has been; as
Zionist we claim him."

But Israel Zangwill cannot be claimed so completely and un-
questioningly as a Zionist. I am not sure Herzl himself could be.
A year after Herzl died, his close friend, Dr. York-Steiner, wrote: "If
a second Herzl came, he would be broken on the political machine.
Even if Herzl himself came back and as we know him, found a good
deal that has been done since his death against which he would
protest, he would run the danger of being expelled from the Party
as a non-Zionist."

It was not just blindness or stupidity that made Zionists sometimes
accuse Zangwill of treason to their cause. From the point of view of
their cause they were right. Zangwill was not a Zionist in their sense.
"It is not from the ground of a party organisation that the intricacies,
the heights and depths of the Jewish problem can be accurately
perceived," he said. "All organisations cling to life, especially when
they own funds. But humanity must not become a parasite on its own
machinery, and the proudest will must sometimes acknowledge
honourable defeat." "The pressure of life," he confessed, "overcomes fixed ideas and even fixed idealisms." When Zangwill presided
at the meeting which decided to close the activities of the Ito, he
quoted: "Not failure, but low aim is crime." It was because "in the
Ito there were no people interested in keeping it going," he said,

because "in the Ito we never had anybody drawing salaries, because there was no person, from the beginning to the end of its existence who received any salary or even travelling expenses, except strangers sent out on scientific expeditions that the Ito had been wound up so easily" when after the British conquest of Palestine and the Balfour Declaration Jewish settlement in Palestine became practical politics, which it had not been under Turkish rule.

The *Jewish Chronicle* published an interview in 1911 with a Turkish politician, Dr. Riza Tewfik, who said: "I can never make Mr. Zangwill understand the state of affairs in Turkey. He is a great novelist, but I must declare emphatically that his methods are dangerous. Only yesterday there was no anti-semitism in Turkey. To my deep regret I cannot say the same of conditions to-day. Mr. Zangwill and various Zionists have openly claimed parts of Turkey for the Jews." The Zionist Congress that year, the newly-elected Zionist Executive, even Nordau had been trying to assure the Turkish Government that the Zionists did not seek to establish a separate Jewish State in Palestine, but wanted the Jewish settlers to become loyal Ottoman subjects. That was the line the pre-Herzlian Chovevei Zion had taken. In 1891 the Chovevei Zion had through Sir Samuel Montagu, M.P. (later the first Lord Swaythling), transmitted a petition to Lord Rosebery, the Prime Minister, to be forwarded to the Sultan of Turkey, assuring the Sultan that it "wishes to send to your Imperial Majesty's dominions only such men with their families as will with God's help and under your Imperial Majesty's protection, increase the prosperity of your Imperial Majesty's dominions and become faithful subjects of your Imperial Majesty." Herzl himself, speaking in London in 1899, explained his plan in these words: "Our desire is to obtain from the Turkish Government a Charter for the colonisation of Palestine under the sovereignty of the Sultan. Turkey will gain unheard-of profit when she permits the industrious, peaceful and commercially-equipped Jews to develop the natural riches of the country. The Jews will bring modern art and industry to Turkey. What the realisation of our plan means to Europe—it would be the end of the bitter, hateful Jewish question, though none of us suppose that all Jews will go to Palestine. Only those who so desire to improve their lot will go."

Wolffsohn, who succeeded Herzl as President of the Zionist Organisation, repudiated at the 1911 Zionist Congress "the malicious talk that the Zionists want to tear away Palestine from the Ottoman Empire, that we want to establish an independent Jewish State." Wolffsohn was rightly concerned with the future of the large Jewish communities who were living under Turkish rule. There were still big Jewish populations then in Salonica, Constantinople, Bagdad, Adrianople, Aleppo and Damascus. These were all Turkish subjects.

Wolffsohn, in his speech, dwelt on "the only ray of light that we see anywhere, the improvement in the position of our brethren in Turkey. The equality of citizenship rights which has been secured to the Jews there seems to be seriously intended."

Fifty years ago, when the Uganda issue agitated Zionist and Jewish public opinion, people could not have foreseen the end of Turkish rule in Palestine. Turkish rule in Palestine was intolerant of the Jewish State aspirations which many of the colonists cherished. Laurence Oliphant, who interested himself in the Jewish colonisation of Palestine, came up against Turkish hostility. He was optimistic. "The opposition of the Turkish Government to the establishment of foreign colonies cannot last for ever," he wrote. But it did last. The Zionist Organisation published in 1921 *A Record of the Preservation of the Jewish Settlements in Palestine*, in which it spoke of its disappointed hopes of the Turkish Revolution. "The young Turks," it said, "adopted an imperialistic policy, and aimed at establishing a Turkish State with the suppression of other nationalities, so that the Jews could not look to them for fulfilment of their national aspirations." When Turkey came into the war on the side of Germany in 1914, "the Turks," says the Report, "believed that the day had come when they could sweep all foreigners out of the Ottoman Empire. In respect of the Jews this purpose revealed itself in a series of persecutions and repressive acts. Jemal Pasha came to the country with the idea of fully Ottomanising all Turkish provinces, to root out all foreign subjects. He was inflexibly opposed to the idea of an extension of the Jewish Yishub. Jemal Pasha made a special point of persecuting the Zionists. Jemal's period of office was marked by a whole series of Jewish trials. His first official act, which threw the Jewish population into a state of terror, was the house search in Tel Aviv and the arrest of Zionist leaders. This search was expected to provide proof that the Zionists were pursuing separatist aims, detrimental to the integrity of the Turkish State."

"Jemal Pasha had formally announced his determination to stamp out Zionism," *Palestine* wrote in an account of what was happening in Palestine, published in 1917. If he did not succeed, "it was due to the British advance." "Just before General Allenby's onward sweep, murder was let loose by Jemal Pasha." "The persecution to which the Jewish population of Palestine had been exposed made them all the more thankful for the liberation of the country by the British troops," said the official Zionist Organisation Report.

Nor was Turkey the only obstacle in those years. Russia was still planning to drive towards Constantinople, to Alexandretta and Jerusalem. Germany had her drive to the East, to Bagdad and Damascus and Jerusalem. German Imperialism had brought the Kaiser to Jerusalem, where Herzl interviewed him. Turkey was

Germany's ally in the war, and it was a German General, von der Goltz, whom Allenby drove out of Palestine. In the Second World War, Hitler had designs on Palestine, and appointed the Mufti of Jerusalem, the arch-enemy of the Jews, as his Gauleiter there.

There was also France. I once found Zangwill in a very pessimistic mood soon after the war, because he had received information that Britain might yield to French pressure that Syria as a whole, including Palestine, should go to France. To France, Palestine did not exist. It was part of Syria, with its centre in Antioch, with Jerusalem as its subsidiary, the old Latin Kingdom. It would have altered the course of history. "The Turkish Empire knows not Palestine," said Zangwill. "In the same spirit France would submerge it in Syria." If the Mandate for the United Syria had gone to France, there would have been no Jewish National Home, from which, under British administration, the State of Israel grew. I can think of no other country, except, perhaps, America, under which Israel could have arisen.

At the time of the Uganda crisis Turkey was firmly in control in Palestine, and the Zionists had to shape their policy according to the reality of the time. That was why the Zionist Executive elected at the 1911 Zionist Congress declared in its statement of policy that it sought "the progressive development of the Ottoman Empire, and is conscious that our efforts accord with its well-understood interests."

Zangwill was a Herzlian Zionist in the sense that he agreed with the attitude Herzl expressed in his address to the Uganda Congress, explaining why he put forward the British offer. "Scattered, divided colonies in various parts of the Turkish Empire do not satisfy our national requirements." "Either Mr. Ussischkin knows a shorter way and a better way of giving the Jews the publicly and legally assured possession of Palestine—in which case it is not proper for so good a Zionist to withhold it; or he knows none." Herzl did not consider buying plots of land in Palestine was Zionism, or that it could "solve the Jewish problem." That was the cause of his quarrel with the Chovevei Zion. The Chovevei Zion movement would have welcomed Herzl if he could have accepted its programme.

After Zangwill left the Zionist Congress and the Zionist Organisation, the *Jewish Chronicle* wrote: "Zionist policy has rolled over heavily from that which Herzl enunciated, and if the meaning of Zionism could be safely translated from the proceedings of the last Congress, so far as they directly concerned Palestine, it would be practically indistinguishable from the sort of Zionism Herzl was supposed to have substituted. He hated and despised what was known as Chovevei Zionism; he would not have Jews sneak into Palestine."

Zangwill disliked the methods of the Chovevei Zion. "As I

understand Dr. Herzl," he said, "he is strongly opposed to any continuance of the present immigration into Palestine, without legal recognition of the Jew's position. Let us come into Palestine, he says in effect, as into a State in which we are not regarded as Uitlanders."

Ussischkin certainly regarded the Tenth Congress as a victory of Chovevei Zionism over Herzlianism. Soon after the Tenth Congress he reported to the Conference of the Russian Chovevei Zion held in Odessa, that now "positive work in Palestine was no longer the sole interest of the Russian Zionists, but had the support of the German, English and even the American Zionists." "The Chovevei Zion, which was founded more than twenty years ago," he went on (in contrast to the Zionist Organisation, which Herzl founded ten years later), "had the same aim as Zionism. The main work of the Zionist Organisation consisted now," he said, "in land purchase in Palestine. To obtain a charter for the whole of Palestine was out of the question, and all their efforts and energies must therefore be directed to gain small allowances and small charters."

Dr. Weizmann reporting to Manchester Zionists in 1911, "both as a Manchester delegate and as a member of the Greater Actions Committee," said "the Tenth Congress was a turning point in the history of Zionism. The tone of the speeches, the character of the resolutions, and the result of the elections showed that practical work was now regarded as forming the essence of the Zionist movement. The best argument to use with non-Jews was that of practical achievement in Palestine." It was diametrically opposed to Herzl's fundamental conception.

"There are two kinds of Zionists," Herzl said in 1900, "and you know that there are differences of opinion between them. I am one of the political Zionists. The practical Zionists want to start at once to go to Palestine, before it belongs to the Jewish people. The political Zionists say that it must belong to us before we go there. If the practical colonists imagine they can bring a large number of Jews to Palestine and that they will then demand rights for these Jews from the Turkish Government to whom the country belongs, they are reckoning without their host. Do they think the immigration of ten thousand people in Palestine would pass unnoticed by the Government? Let us assume there is a house I want to occupy. Would I just take my furniture there without asking the owner? He could simply eject me with my furniture, and perhaps break my neck. Anyway, if I remain I have to accept whatever conditions he imposes. No, that is not our way. We must first come to an understanding with the owner, to obtain the right to live in the house. Then I shall move in. Till then I remain in my present home, even if I don't feel comfortable there."

I wonder what many later Zionists who were too young to participate in the Uganda Congress would have said to the sort of thing Ussischkin was urging, "land purchase in Palestine; to gain small allowances and small charters." That was the issue of the Uganda Congress—Chovevei Zionism, small "practical" settlement in Palestine under Turkish rule, with no Jewish political rights, or settlement in East Africa with Jewish rights and political autonomy under the aegis of Britain. It was because, as Zangwill pointed out, "the Sultan would not give in, would not give Palestine for the Jews, I went on with the separate activities of the Jewish Territorial Organisation." "The region really offered to the Zionists by Joseph Chamberlain was not in Uganda, but in the adjoining province of East Africa," Zangwill pointed out. He quoted Winston Churchill, writing about that offer in 1906: "I agree most heartily with the spirit of Mr. Zangwill's letter to *The Times*, of 12th December 1905. There should be room within the world-wide limits of the British Empire for the self-development and peculiar growth of many races and many traditions and of many creeds."

Zangwill quoted Nordau at the critical Zionist Congress retorting to a speaker who cried ("shrieked," says Zangwill), "We have Palestine. Why do we want Uganda?"—"Have you Palestine? Give it to us then." Zangwill pointed out that when East Africa was offered, Palestine was closed to Jewish immigration.

"Let us assume," Herzl said in an open letter to Ussischkin, who had circularised the delegates to the Zionist Congress against the decision of the Sixth Congress accepting Herzl's proposal to send an expedition to investigate East Africa, declaring "I do not consider this decision binding on me," "Let us assume," Herzl said, "that I want to buy a house; even if it were the house of my fathers that had fallen into other hands I would not subject myself to the present owner's favour or disfavour. I would move into a house near by. It seems to me more practical than Mr. Ussischkin's 'activity in the hills of Israel.' " Herzl meant the need to find homes for the victims of Kishinev. He had in mind the misery of the victims of the Russian pogroms. Zangwill too was concerned with this misery, with a practical outlet for it, a place where the Jews of Russia could go. If Palestine was closed, he must find another place. If Palestine were suddenly to sink under the sea, he said the Jewish National Fund boxes would go on rattling as though nothing had happened.

But he was immediately sensitive to the change that came with the war in Palestine. As early as 12th March 1915 Zangwill called a meeting of the Ito Council "to determine its attitude in the present crisis, especially in view of possible changes in the political status of Palestine." In 1917, Zangwill wrote: "The Ottoman Empire is threatened with disintegration, and if this chance—one in a thousand years—is not seized to restore it to the Jew, who is to have it?" He urged that Palestine should be constituted "a province of the British Empire, manned by sturdy Jewish settlers." In 1922, the year of the Palestine Mandate, Zangwill sent out a letter in which he said: "At our last Council meeting we decided to co-operate with the Zionist Organisation provided Palestine could be acquired on the terms of our programme. The Palestine Mandate and its governing document, Mr. Churchill's White Paper, being at last before us, we must decide whether to absorb ourselves in the Zionist Organisation or to continue our independent activity, or whether it would be best to dissolve the Organisation."

"For the Ito to oppose any really practicable plan for a Jewish territory would be not only treason to the Jewish people, but to its own programme," Zangwill declared in 1917, welcoming the issue of the Balfour Declaration.

In an article in *The Menorah Journal*, in February 1918, he said: "The establishment of a Jewish national home in Palestine is a policy I have been urging upon my country for two years, and there can be no surprise therefore that the Jewish Territorial Organisation, of which I have the honour to be President, has agreed to co-operate with the Zionist movement, provided the settlement be made upon an autonomous basis, according to our programme. Small colonisation in Palestine," he said, with a backward glance at Ussischkin and his colleagues, "may have its appeal—but not to the Ito." He added the Ito formula: "The political status of the Palestine Jews and of the Jews of the Diaspora must be absolutely distinct. The territory must be only for those unable or unwilling to remain in the lands in which they at present live."

Zangwill insisted that when Dr. Herzl came to him with his Zionist idea he had wanted "a Jewish State anywhere." Dr. Herzl said so himself: "I began as a believer in the Jewish State, no importance where; and later I took hold of the Zionist flag. Palestine is the only land where our people can find rest. But it is essential to provide immediate succour for the hundreds of thousands in need of a place of refuge." "What would Zionists like Mr. Bentwich have said if—which God forbid!—worse horrors should arise than at Kishinev," Zangwill said after the Sixth Congress, "and the Jews flying wildly in search of some refuge should learn that Dr. Herzl had received this offer and had refused it without even saying a word to them? Why, Mr. Bentwich raged against the Fourth Congress because it did not do enough for the Roumanian refugees. Dr. Herzl naturally hesitated to reject a scheme for the salvation of our suffering masses. It is not that he loves Palestine less, but because he loves his people more."

People cannot easily realise now how immense the need of

immigration openings for the Jews of the Russian Empire was at that time. " 'Wohin,' 'Where to,' is the dominating question for Jews the world over," said a *Jewish Chronicle* Editorial, in January 1905, the year of the Zionist Congress which rejected the Uganda offer. "In this year, 1905, the Continent is thronged with Jews plodding along in their perpetual search for freedom. The Jewish fugitives stream incessantly over the frontier, to be sneered at here, threatened there, or held up in thousands, as at this moment, while their brethren sustain them with charity. The 'luftmenshen' crowd the ships that traverse the Atlantic in search of a new home. The whole history of the world contains no companion picture to this astonishing scene of many millions of men condemned either to the cruellest oppression or to wander about among nations who close their doors as they see them coming. For mercy's sake, and leaving aside all question of the Jewish dignity, we cannot allow the emigrants to be driven from pillar to post, to the accompaniment of a popular hue and cry."

The experience was repeated in our time after the Hitler régime came into power and made the Russian Pharaoh appear a mild tyrant by contrast. Zionist leaders and Zionist organisations devoted themselves to the question of finding places of refuge for the masses of refugees fleeing from Hitler, and for those larger masses who never managed to get out and were forced to stay behind, and were massacred in millions. It was not, it could not be, with the immigration laws then in force in Palestine, an immigration to Palestine only. The *Jewish Chronicle* in October 1938 quoted Dr. Weizmann saying at a "Zionist meeting 'one million Jews are in Europe virtually in a concentration camp.' They will want to get out," said the *Jewish Chronicle*. "As Nazism continues its successful march their numbers will grow. The refugee has passed beyond the control of Jews, beyond the power of Jewish agencies alone. It has become for them an unmanageable problem." That was the time of the Evian Conference on the Refugee Problem.

It is an indication of the feeling in official Zionist quarters at that time that the American Labour Zionist paper, *The Jewish Frontier*, complained in March 1937 of Jabotinsky and his Revisionists who, "at a time when all Zionist energy is bent on preserving the principle of economic absorptive capacity as the criterion for Jewish immigration—a principle which is now seriously threatened—Jabotinsky clamours for a 'Jewish State.' " When the Evian Conference on Emigration was called, *The Jewish Frontier* did not speak of "Palestine only." "This Conference has one task before it," it wrote. "It must devise a method of salvation for the hundreds of thousands of tortured beings in Central Europe. The civilised world cannot wash its hands of the fate of the Jews of Germany and Austria. The lines of desperate men and women stretching before every Consular office in Vienna or Berlin cannot be dismissed with a shrug or a sigh. The International Conference has two courses before it. It must either make it possible for persecuted Jews and Christians to live in their native lands with a full restitution of civil rights, or it must find other countries in which refugees may dwell in peace." It even urged ordinary immigration under the quota into the United States. It saw no reason "for keeping the gates shut. We do not shove the drowning back into the water."

It was a natural human reaction to the desperate need. Several Zionists were among those who revived Zangwill's idea of Territorial settlements, only this time not because Palestine was unobtainable, as it had been under the Turks, but because under the British Mandate Jewish immigration was being kept down to the "absorptive capacity," and even lower, according to "the principle of high political level." Dr. Arthur Ruppin, a member of the Zionist World Executive, who succeeded Dr. Weizmann as Director of the Jewish Agency Central Bureau for the Settlement of German Jews, visited South America in 1935, and drew up an official Jewish Agency memorandum for the settlement of 200,000 German Jews, half in Palestine and half in other countries. Dr. Nahum Goldmann, a member of the Zionist World Executive, suggested before the League of Nations Committee on Refugees Questions that 25,000 Jews from Germany could be settled, half in Palestine and the other half in various other countries. Meer Grossman, the leader of the Jewish State Party, advanced the idea of "Jewish mass colonisation on a definite territory, while emphasising the priority of Palestine as the country destined to become the Jewish Homeland." He thought of the other territories as "colonies of Palestine." Other Zionists, notably Dr. Julius Brutzkus, took a leading part in Jewish emigration and Territorial work. They were moved by the urgency of the need.

The same urgency existed when the Uganda offer occupied the attention not only of the Zionist world but of all Jewry. The Russian Jews were driven by their need blindly, anywhere they could see an open door. In England, in June 1906, less than a year after the Uganda Congress, the Zionist Organisation had joined with the Jewish Territorial Organisation in an appeal to "the fortunate Jews in England and America," signed by Sir Francis Montefiore, President of the English Zionist Federation, and L. J. Greenberg, the Honorary Secretary, and by Israel Zangwill, President of the Ito and Clement I. Salaman, the Honorary Secretary. "The recrudescence of massacres in Russia unhappily justifies the contention of the Zionists and the Territorialists," they said, "that any hope of a speedy cessation of the sufferings of the Russian Jews is as vain as the generous attempt to grapple with them by charity collections. Nearly half a million of money was collected a few months ago under the auspices of the leading Jewish philanthropists, and almost another quarter of a million in Russia itself. This immense sum, whilst it served its temporary purpose of alleviating some small fraction of the distress, has disappeared 'like the snowfall on the river' without leaving any trace of permanent improvement in the Jewish situation. We do not suppose that anyone will now maintain that the collecting-box can follow on the heels of every massacre. The only feasible policy is to acquire for Jews a home which, while raising generally the status of Jews throughout the world, shall provide the Russian Jews in particular with a means of gradually releasing themselves from their present desperate environment."

Wolffsohn, Herzl's successor as President of the Zionist Organisation, and Jacobus Kann, his closest colleague in the Zionist Organisation joined Zangwill a few weeks later, in July 1906, with L. J. Greenberg, Joseph Cowen, Lucien Wolf and others, to endeavour to find a plan on which they could agree to help the Jews of Russia to settle elsewhere.

People have forgotten to-day how the Uganda offer affected many Russian Jews and Russian Zionists. I have in front of me a report in the *Jewish Chronicle* of 13th October 1905 from its correspondent in St. Petersburg on "The Jewish Territorial Organisation and the Jews in Russia." "English readers will be interested to learn what attitude is taken by their Russian co-religionists towards the newly-formed Jewish Territorial Organisation, whose manifesto was recently issued by Mr. Israel Zangwill," it begins. "The impression which the document has made on the thinking classes of Russian Jewry is highly favourable. The fundamental idea of this Organisation— the founding of an autonomous settlement for the oppressed Jewries of Eastern Europe under the suzerainty of England—does not strike the intellectual class of Russian Jews as objectionable or visionary. Emigration remains the one and only means of salvation for myriads of Russian Jews. An autonomous colony under English suzerainty would be quite another matter. The few prominent personalities who were to be found in the ranks of the Russian Zionists, such as Professor Mandelstamm, of Kiev, Jassinowsky, of Warsaw, Dr. Jelsky, of Lodz, and others, have gone over to the Territorial Organisation. Israel Zangwill is *persona grata* with the Russian Jews, in whom he inspires complete confidence."

Jacob de Haas deals with this period in his biography of Herzl. "Opinion in Russia, according to outsiders, was generally favourable to the East African plan," he says. "One outsider wrote: 'Never before did the Basle Congress excite so much interest in Russia. On the whole, opinion is decidedly in favour of the project. It must sorrowfully be admitted that Zionism in Russia has not been fortunate in many of its leading mouthpieces'" (those who voted against the British offer). "Indeed it would be unfair were we to judge the movement in this Empire by some of its representatives at the Basle Congress." De Haas continues: "The Mizrachi in Russia were the first to accept the taunt that they were 'Zionists without Zion.' And they answered: 'The creation of a Jewish State promises to be more speedily realised in Uganda than in Zion; that is why we voted for it.' Mandelstamm, Jassinowsky and others in Russia besides the Mizrachi were supporting Herzl." De Haas suggests that Ussischkin organised the Russian opposition because he saw it as a chance to overthrow Herzl. "Ussischkin, it will be recalled, came to the First Congress as an opponent," he says. "Now that there was a real issue they were ready to struggle for control of the Zionist forces." Incidentally, they were, as de Haas points out, "rebels," and as Zangwill said, "dissentients," for as Zangwill recalled, the Zionist Congress had by "a majority of 295 against 177 voted in favour of sending an expedition to British East Africa. There was some attempt to make out there was not a real majority on our side. I forget the reason. The majority in favour of East Africa was a real majority." "Herzl regarded what Ussischkin and his colleagues were doing as open mutiny," says Dr. Bein in his biography of Herzl. Herzl himself called it "war declared against me, the agitation against me. I impugn the competence of the Charkov Conference," Herzl said. "They" (the Charkov Zionists) "introduced a canker into the movement." Dr. Weizmann's fellow-delegate from Manchester to the 1911 Zionist Congress, Mr. Wassilevsky (whom Louis Golding used as his model for *Mr. Emanuel*) said in his report on the Congress to a Manchester Zionist meeting that apparently because "they took seriously the threat of Dr. Weizmann that he and his followers would leave the movement if they did not obtain the management in their hands, the followers of the political Zionism of the late Dr. Herzl although in a majority handed over the management to the opposition."

Ussischkin's friend and colleague, Dr. Tchlenov, who came to London during the war to join Dr. Weizmann and Dr. Sokolov as the third member of the Zionist world leadership which negotiated the Balfour Declaration—he died in London in 1918—admitted what had happened in 1905 when he spoke at the 1911 Congress. "I want to remind you of the Uganda period," he said. "It was in this hall, from this platform that after the historic vote I walked out, and a large number of delegates walked out with me. We did not know if we would return, or if there had come a breach in our ranks that could never be healed." Dr. Tchlenov agreed that his opposition to Uganda and that of his friends was based on their old Chovevei Zion ideology. "It was said here that we Zion-Zionists are Chovevei

Zionists. I do not consider it a shame to be a Chovevei Zionist. We were that long before political Zionism began."

Not all the Russian Zionist delegates shared Tchlenov's and Ussischkin's view. Dr. Nachman Syrkin, one of the founders and the leading spokesman of the Zionist Labour movement, speaking after Dr. Tchlenov at the 1905 Congress, said: "In the name of the Congress group of the Zionist-Socialist Labour Party, which consists of 28 delegates, I make the following declaration—The Zionist-Socialists have always regarded the Zionist ideal as the expression of the historic problem and the vital interests of the Jewish masses. The Zionist-Socialists see the fixation of the Zionist programme on Palestine, which cannot show the necessary conditions for the realisation of our ideal, and all the consequences which follow from it, as small-colonisation, a narrowing down in fact and in principle of the Zionist programme. It is in complete contradiction to the interests of the Jewish proletariat and of the Jewish masses. The Zion-Zionists have exploited their privileged position at the Seventh Congress to force a programme on the entire Zionist Organisation that is not in accordance with the spirit and the aim of Zionism. We therefore declare that we consider the programme of the Zion-Zionists as a hindrance to the cause of our national liberation, and regard our further participation in this Congress, which has become disloyal to itself and to our people, as impossible." A later Zionist Labour leader, Berl Locker, has written of "the split in the Poale Zion movement over the Uganda question and afterwards over the question of Palestine or a territory anywhere."

Jabotinsky and the Revisionists were not the first to walk out of the Zionist Organisation. Before the Territorialists seceded the Zion-Zionists with Ussischkin, Tchlenov, Dr. Weizmann and others had laid their plans to walk out if the decision of the Zionist Congress would have been in favour of accepting the Uganda offer. Zangwill saw that as the first secession. "When after a tense hour of voting, in which each delegate's 'yes' or 'no' sounded like the hammer-strokes of destiny, forging the future of the Jewish people," he said in his report after the Sixth Congress, which had decided to send the expedition to East Africa, "it was found that those who said 'no' were beaten by 295 to 177, the defeated minority, instead of accepting the ruling of the majority, left the Congress." Jacob de Haas carries the story of this defiance of Herzl further. He gives the text of a secret declaration drafted by Ussischkin and eight of his associates (the "Nine," as they became known), which included among its points, "the refusal to send further moneys to Vienna" (Herzl's headquarters), "the development of an independent Zionist Organisation without Dr. Herzl," and "the transference of the final centre of the movement in Russia, which has hitherto been under the administration of Dr. Mandelstamm of Kiev to another person and place, probably Vilna. The decisions arrived at were to be kept secret and not communicated to the authorities in Vienna." "These nine men had practically committed themselves to a revolution in Zionism," is de Haas's comment. "They were all old Chovevei-Zionists, and they apparently saw an opportunity to dethrone Herzl and swing the movement back to the policy they had supported prior to the publication of the *Jewish State*."

Professor Mandelstamm, who was to be deposed, and joined Zangwill in the Territorialist movement, was the one man in Russian Zionism on whom Herzl had most relied. When Herzl saw Plehve, the Russian Minister of the Interior, in Petersburg, and was questioned about the Zionist leaders in Russia, he said (recorded in his diaries): "The most important is Professor Mandelstamm in Kiev."

In 1906 Dr. Mandelstamm spoke in London at an Ito meeting, at the Great Assembly Hall, in Mile End, with Israel Zangwill in the chair. He said the situation in Russia was "appalling." Another speaker at that meeting was Oscar Straus, former U.S. Ambassador to Turkey and later U.S. Minister of Commerce. "He could not help admiring," he said, "and extolling the splendid enthusiasm, the brilliant genius, the whole-hearted devotion which the 'Dreamer of the Ghetto' gave to this problem."

"The Dreamer of the Ghetto" must have been much heartened also by the support of Judge Mayer Sulzberger, who had commissioned him to write *Children of the Ghetto*. Immediately the Ito was founded, Judge Sulzberger wrote to Zangwill: "I heartily support the Jewish Territorial Organisation. You know that I have always been revolted by anything that savoured of anti-Zionism, though the Zionistic scheme of obtaining the Government of Palestine under present conditions has never seemed practicable to me. The project of the Jewish Territorial Organisation, however difficult to carry out, is well worth the most earnest trial. So far from being antagonistic to Zionism it rather supplements it, and if at all successful, will assist in its fulfilment and final realisation."

Since much of the discussion at that time turned about the relationship of Territorialism to Zionism, Zangwill read a letter he had received from Dr. Nordau. "My dear Zangwill," he wrote, "Last week I had an opportunity, in the presence of Mr. Greenberg and five hundred Parisian Zionists, to give my opinion of the relations of Territorialism and Zionism, an opinion which I since repeated in letters to the Federation of the Roumanian Zionists, and to Dr. Katzenelson of Libau. I maintain that one can be a Territorialist and a Zionist at the same time, Territorialism aiming only at immediate relief, while Zionism strives for the final solution of the

Jewish problem which, in my opinion, can only be found in Palestine.
I am most happy to note the hopeful view you take of the prospects
of Territorialism. I wish you God-speed with all my heart." "As to
the relations between Zionism and Territorialists he took his cue from
Dr. Nordau," Zangwill said when he had read the letter.

Many Zionists followed Dr. Nordau's line and worked in the
Ito. Even Ben Yehuda, the regenerator of the Hebrew language,
who lived in Palestine, was ready to go to Uganda, though "there
would be nothing more difficult," he said, "than to leave Jerusalem.
But if our national life demands it I am ready to make the sacrifice.
This is a great ray of light. At last we shall have a shelter, free from
persecution: a home where England will protect us in our yearning
for self-government and peace. We will be able to gather there from
our exile and prepare ourselves for the time when we shall receive
the land of Israel." Dr. Syrkin said much the same thing. "Even
strong Palestinians," he urged at a Poale Zion meeting held in
London, "should for the present prefer East Africa as a stepping
stone to Palestine. From the point of view of freedom and progress
English rule was equally preferable to that of Turkey. The insistence
on Palestine only when this could not be obtained was calculated to
perpetuate the present bitter golus and those who contemplated
preventing the East African project from being carried at the forthcoming Congress would be doing great harm to the Jewish cause."

Rabbi Reines, the leader of the Mizrachi, speaking in London in
1906, a few months after the rejection of the Uganda offer by the
Tenth Zionist Congress, said: "Zionism does not compete with
Territorialism. If it did I would not be a Territorialist. I cannot
understand why people should oppose Territorialism. Surely, having
regard to the situation in Russia they should accept any territory
we can get."

That was Zangwill's attitude. If Palestine was unobtainable at the
time, and all that could be done there was to establish what he
called "toy colonies where you can count your chickens as soon as
they are hatched," and another territory was offered, he felt that
Jews who could not or would not stay in Russia and wanted to
settle in a Jewish territory should be given the chance to go there.
If East Africa was not suitable, negotiations should be continued
with the British Government for a more suitable territory. He wanted
"a real live country, which shall exert upon the Jewish emigrant as
potent an attraction as New York." Nordau had the same feeling
about accepting a suitable territory. Shortly before the decisive
Tenth Zionist Congress met, he gave an interview to Israel Cohen,
which appeared in the London *Jewish World*, where he said: "On
the pressing question of to-day, East Africa, the Commission will be
back in March. Its report will be considered at the next Congress,

and if it is favourable then the British offer must be accepted." It was not the view of Ussischkin and Tchlenov, and those who felt as they did. Dr. Tchlenov said so very bluntly. "Our problem can be solved only in Palestine," he declared at the Tenth Congress. Addressing himself to Zangwill, he went on: "Now, Mr. Zangwill, if you ask us about other countries, you will understand our answer. For our purpose there is only one country. Therefore we Zionists cannot accept any other country. Mr. Zangwill says—'I am also inclined to think that Uganda is not altogether suitable for us. But we may be offered a better, larger country. What will your answer be then?' I shall tell you, Mr. Zangwill, in the name of all Zion-Zionists, clearly and emphatically—No! No other country can be and will be acceptable to us."

That was the attitude also of Dr. Weizmann, who belonged to the Tchlenov-Ussischkin group. Thirty years after, in his statement before the Palestine Royal Commission in 1936, Dr. Weizmann recalled what had happened. "The Jewish position grew worse from day to day; in 1903 there was a massacre in Kishinev which started a wave of pogroms that swept the whole of Russia. The position of the Jews became desperate. The hope of ever obtaining anything definite from the Turkish Government dwindled. Joseph Chamberlain made the Jews an offer of a country which was then called Uganda. Here we were—a Movement far from any practical realisation of its aspirations, treated very seriously by the mightiest Government in the world, which had made a generous offer of a territory which is almost as big as Mandatory Palestine. As far as I know it was good land. We had the rope round our necks, and yet when this offer was brought to the Zionist Congress a great discussion ensued, and finally the offer was accepted in this form: that a Commission should be sent to the country to see what it was. But that was carried by a small majority." (The vote was 295 for, 177 against; majority 118. De Haas in his Herzl biography says, "The majority was distinct. Two-thirds of the Congress said yes.") "The minority, a very important minority, consisted primarily of Jews from Eastern Europe (I myself was among them)," Dr. Weizmann went on, "and they refused the offer for one reason only: 'It is not Palestine, and it never will be Palestine.' We said, 'We have waited two thousand years, and we shall wait a few more years.'" Significantly, Dr. Weizmann linked the rejection of the offer at the next Congress by his minority grown to be a majority, with the death of Herzl. His very next sentence was: "The leader died, the offer was refused."

Zangwill's attitude was fundamentally different. "I had decided," he said, "that since Mr. Chamberlain and Mr. Balfour both appeared to favour a Jewish settlement on a large scale" (Winston Churchill, who became a junior Minister soon after—in 1906—agreed with the idea, and wrote to one of Zangwill's supporters, Dr. Dulberg, of Manchester, "There should be room within the world-wide limits of the British Empire for the self-development and peculiar growth of many races and of many traditions and many creeds. I do not feel that the noble vision you behold ought to be allowed to fade, and I will do what I can to preserve it and fulfil it"), "we had only to ask for a suitable territory to get it, and I had come to the Congress prepared to move a resolution to that effect." When the vote went against him and his supporters, he advised them to "remain in the Party to form the nucleus of a victorious majority in the next Congress. I pointed out the evils of a split. My Territorialist consulters replied however that there was already a split made by the Zion-Zionists who had already forced many of the Territorialists out of Zionism by refusing to take the shekels of their supporters, and thus seriously limiting the number of Territorialist delegates. The Territorialists said to me, 'Even if we are not shut out yet, the Seventh Congress will shut us out. Let us therefore break off at once, with you as our leader.' I did all in my power to keep all nationalist forces inside Zionism."

Zangwill's attitude expressed at that Seventh Congress was simply the realistic facing of the position in the Turkish Empire. "Ussischkin imagines," he said, "that General Ussischkin has a great army of Ussischkins behind him, and that the Sultan of Turkey is a fool. Do you think the Sultan will let us take with folded arms what he has refused to give us? All Europe cannot force the Sultan to do anything. Do you know that the Jewish Colonial Trust in Jerusalem could be entered by Turkish soldiers and that our Bank could be closed down if we could not fly the British flag over it?" (The Bank was registered in London as a British Company.) "We hear a lot of sarcastic laughter and criticism of what the British Government is doing for Zionism, but if the British Government were not here, Zionism would not be able to do anything in Palestine." Dr. Tchlenov, following Zangwill, accepted his point about the British Government. "We know," he said, "that we are not liked in many countries. The nations till now apply always one method—to oppress and persecute us. Britain is the first nation that has understood that the best way is to help the Jewish people to its own homeland. We hope that Britain will realise that we can attain our aim only in Palestine, and that she will assist us in this purpose."

The British Prime Minister at this time, the Prime Minister of the Government in which Joseph Chamberlain, who made the Uganda offer to Herzl was Colonial Secretary, was Arthur James Balfour, later Lord Balfour, who as Foreign Secretary issued the Balfour Declaration in 1918. At this 1905 Zionist Congress Balfour was attacked as an antisemite. He was the head of the Government which had introduced and enforced the Aliens Act, restricting Jewish immigration to the British Isles. Zangwill rose to repudiate the charge of antisemitism that had been made against the British Government. "Faced with our dilemma" he said, "I go to the grave of Herzl, and I ask him what we should do. Herzl's plan of campaign included some other autonomous land as a means towards his end. Herzl was not for waiting, but for acting. That is why he tried to get the El-Arish territory. Then came the East Africa offer. Though his heart yearned for Palestine his common sense turned to East Africa. We must not reject any means that can help us towards our goal. Remember," and he quoted in Hebrew: "Even Moassu Habonim Hoiso Lerosh Pinoh"—"The stone which the builders rejected is become the headstone of the corner."

But at the 1905 Congress the vote went against Zangwill and his supporters, and all Zangwill could do after the vote was to tell the Congress: "You will be charged before the bar of history."

Replying to someone who had reproached him for deserting the Zionist flag under which Herzl had enrolled him, Zangwill said it was "not the fact. Many years ago," he recalled, "a tall, dark gentleman called at my study and handed in a card which bore a name I had never heard of before—'Dr. Theodor Herzl.' During the interview Dr. Herzl asked me to help him to secure for the Jewish people independence and a territory of their own. It was that which, after long consideration, induced me to come into the movement. If we could not get Palestine I was not going to sit in the mud and cry about it. While waiting I would work for another territory, for the soul is greater than the soil."

Zangwill took as one of the subjects for his *Ghetto Tragedies* the story of an earlier Territorialist, Mordecai Noah, an American Jew who tried in 1825 to found a Jewish city of refuge on Grand Island, New York State, near Buffalo, close to the Niagara Falls, in which Zangwill's hero, Peloni, plunges to his death when the plan fails." " 'Noah's Ark,' " the name of his story, "stands on the firmer Ararat of history, my invention being confined to the figure of Peloni (the Hebrew for 'nobody')," Zangwill wrote in his Preface.

In the *Voice of Jerusalem* Zangwill wrote: "Had the European ghettos to which he addressed his appeal been sufficiently prepared by propaganda, the great city of Buffalo would by now have been Jewish, with a Jewish majority in New York State. When after the pogroms of the '80s the great stream of Jewish emigration to America began Judge Sulzberger suggested that instead of receiving it into the cities it should be diverted to a sparsely-populated territory, which would then automatically, under the Constitution, evolve into a Jewish State. Perhaps it is even now not too late to pour a steam of Jewish migration upon a thinly occupied territory in America— North or South—or in Australia. In the past, when new continents lay practically unpopulated, a Jewish State could have been carved out with comparative facility. If only the exiles from Spain had followed in the wake of Columbus!"

Uganda, or British East Africa, with the political safeguards he considered essential, was more important to Herzl than Palestine without political safeguards. "This British East African beginning is politically a Rishon-le-Zion and therefore nearer to a national Palestine than Edmond de Rothschild's Palestine colonies," Herzl said. "Our first political colony would be the settlement between Kilimanjaro and Kenya. If we can't begin in Palestine we must reverse the process. Begin with colonies elsewhere and use them as political national points of support on the way to Palestine."

In his Diary Herzl wrote that he thought the Sultan would be impressed "when he sees our colonising successes in Africa. He would be more inclined to do something with us." "I had already opened contact with the British Government," he explained on the same page, "and submitted to the Cabinet Minister, Lord James of Hereford, my proposals for the establishment of a Jewish colony in Africa. England," he added, "wants no money sacrifices from us; will indeed rather give us all facilities."

When Herzl interviewed Baron de Hirsch his objections were to Hirsch's philanthropic methods, not to his choice of the Argentine for Jewish settlement. When Herzl laid his plans for Jewish settlement he contemplated the Society of Jews that he wanted to found calling a conference of Jewish geographers, and asking them "wohin wir auswandern," where shall we go? "I shall tell them of the Promised Land, but not where it is. That is to be decided after considering all the geological, climatic and all other natural conditions. When we have decided on what part of the world and which country we have in mind we shall begin to take careful diplomatic steps. Let us think for instance of the Argentine," he said. "I thought for a long time," he went on, "of Palestine. This has the recommendation that it was the seat of our people and the name itself is a programme. But most Jews are no longer Orientals, and my transplantation system would be difficult to carry out there. It is also too near to Europe, and for the first quarter of a century of our existence we must have rest from Europe and from its war and other complications. In principle I am neither against Palestine nor the Argentine. The experts will advise us. And the Administrative Council will decide." Indeed, Herzl was a Territorialist. It was Colonel Goldsmid, the Chovevei Zionist who, Herzl records in his Diaries, "would not think of the Argentine. He wants Palestine."

There was also a great deal of personal antipathy that divided the Herzlian Zionists, among whom Zangwill numbered himself, from those Zionists who, Herzl's biographer de Haas says, had "quite apart from principles always rebelled against a leader who had little personal sympathy for them." "We Zionists have something to bury in Herzl's grave," Zangwill said when Herzl died, "all that venom of factions and foolish accusations which divided brother from brother and embittered our leader's last days."

Herzl's death precipitated the crisis. His authority would have prevented the split. Zangwill would never have left a Zionist Organisation under Herzl's leadership. And Herzl could have dealt with the Ussischkin opposition. Had he been alive during the 1905 Zionist Congress, we know what he would have said, and what decision he would have urged on the Congress. It would not have been the decision which the Congress in his absence adopted. At the end of the Sixth Congress in 1903, to which he had submitted the British offer of Uganda, Herzl outlined to "my friends Zangwill, Nordau and Cowen" the speech which he meant to deliver at the Seventh Congress of 1905. He recorded it in his Diary: "When I returned with my friends Zangwill, Nordau and Cowen after the closing session of the Sixth Congress, I said to them: 'I shall tell you my speech at the Seventh Congress—if I live till then. My speech will read: It was not possible. The final goal has not been reached. But an intermediate result lies before us—this land in which we can settle our suffering masses on a national basis, with an autonomous administration. I do not believe that we have the right because of a beautiful dream or a legitimate flag, to withhold this relief from the unfortunates." "I agree with Herzl," Zangwill said at the 1905 Congress, "that an East African territory may be accepted as a means to obtain Palestine." Herzl had felt sure that the 1905 Congress would accept the East African offer. "How could I possibly reject the British offer without giving it the fullest consideration?" he said. "I have not thought of the cleavage that may result. I have devoted myself to the African offer because it appeals to my innermost convictions, and had the majority been against me, including my dearest colleagues, it would not have made me swerve from my position. But you see, the majority supported me and I am not without hope that the vast mass of Jewry will confirm what the Congress has decided."

Even Zionism, even a Jewish State in Palestine, even an Itoland "will not bring the millennium—no more than England or France brings it," Zangwill said. And his belief was that "Zion is where the Jew lives as a Jew." "It would be a happy coincidence," Zangwill said, "if the two ideals of Itoism and Zionism could materialise in one and the same territory. That was the original aim of the founder of modern Zionism, the immortal Dr. Herzl. When this aim appeared to be unrealisable there were two alternatives. Either to give up Zion or to give up Zionism. Dr. Herzl and myself gave up Zion; the bulk of the movement gave up Zionism. "Palestine without

Jewish rights is Golus," he said. So "leaving it to others to develop
the present Palestine colonies I should be inclined to turn elsewhere
for a Provisional Palestine. Any territory which was Jewish, under a
Jewish flag, would save the Jews' body and the Jews' soul, and
become a rallying point for Zionism, a training school in self-government, a fulcrum of political influence and a nursery of agriculturists
for Palestine when obtained."

Kaplansky, a Poale Zion leader, who later became Principal
of the Haifa Technion, told me how at the Seventh Zionist Congress
in 1905, he had after the vote which rejected the Uganda offer, come
upon a delegate weeping at the foot of Glicenstein's statue of the
Messiah, exhibited at that Congress. He had seen the Uganda
offer, Kaplansky said, as the Messiah come to lead out thousands
of Jews from the Russian oppression, and the Congress had rejected
the Messiah. Zangwill spoke of Glicenstein's Messiah as his symbol
at a London meeting held immediately after the 1905 Congress. He
spoke of it again fifteen years after the 1905 Congress, at a public
meeting held to welcome Glicenstein on his arrival in London.
"Perhaps you will expect me to answer the question how far the
Messiah has really awakened," he said. It was the time of the
pogroms in Palestine. "You will remember that in Jerusalem after
the San Remo Conference Ussischkin had the Shofar sounded to
proclaim that the Messiah had actually arrived. I fear that these
rosy visions have changed into red—the red of Jewish blood. The
dreamers of the ghetto thought they could have a country without
being killed or worse, killing others. The world's rewards are
given not to those who break stones but to those who break heads."

"The Zionists have tried to take Palestine without an army,"
Zangwill said, nearly thirty years ahead of his time in this matter of
a Jewish army. He was ahead of his time also when he said it was
impossible to build a Jewish State in Palestine if the Arab population
remained in possession. He argued that the Arabs liberated by the
British from the Turks had been given several States, but the Jews
in Palestine had been given only a state of friction. "People talk of
the removal of the Arabs from Palestine as an unimaginable atrocity,"
he said, "yet France is at this moment expelling thousands of
Germans from Alsace-Lorraine, and England's expulsion of the
French-Canadians of Acadia in 1755 forms the subject of Longfellow's poem 'Evangeline.' "

His proposal was considered dangerous at that time by the
Zionists. I have a letter from Zangwill where he speaks of a visit
he had from Aaron Aaronsohn, who had been attending the Paris
Peace Conference in the Zionist interest. "He said my article in
Pearson's Magazine, pointing out the Arab population difficulty in
Palestine was read by the Arabs (when he was in Egypt) and produced

great agitation among them. The Zionists have now begged me not to raise the question and I have consented for the moment." But the problem kept worrying him. "The trouble comes," he said, "from the large existing population, roughly classified as Arab, about 600,000 in number. If Poland protests that 14 per cent. of Jews constitute too great an alloy for a nationality to bear, how then establish a National Home in face of an alien 86 per cent. ?" He spoke of "the wilful myopia cultivated by official Zionism towards this aspect of its problem." Even Jabotinsky was not sure about the justice of Zangwill's idea. "Jabotinsky is beginning to veer round to my idea of the expropriation of the Arabs," Zangwill noted, "though he thought that Judaism stood for social justice."

The Israel War of Independence realised Zangwill's idea of a trek of the Arab population of Palestine. Mr. Sharett, who became Prime Minister and Foreign Minister of Israel, called it "just a piece of unexpected good fortune that the development of the State is not complicated by the presence of a hostile Arab minority."

It was not because he was anti-Arab that Zangwill put forward the idea of an Arab trek from Palestine. He explained that he was in favour of Arab rights. He was a member, he said, of the English Parliamentary Committee for Egyptian Home Rule, so how could he deny the rights of the Arabs of Palestine? "If the Arabs will not fold their tents and silently steal away, if they elect to remain in Palestine, then," he said, "as I have emphasised in my speeches, 'their welfare must be as dear to us as our own.' But even so," he went on (in 1920), "painful though the necessity be, they should come at once under a Jewish Government, and Sir Herbert Samuel should represent the Zionists rather than the British Foreign Office. The Arabs should recognise that the road of their renewed national glory lies through Bagdad, Damascus and Mecca, and all the vast territory freed for them from the Turks, and be content as far as Palestine is concerned to be politically submerged. The Powers which freed it and them have surely the right to ask them not to grudge the petty strip necessary for the renaissance of a still more downtrodden people."

He faced the problem of an Arab refusal to "submit to the Jewish Government or trek." What, he asked, could Britain do to "handle the problem more fairly than she has done?" He referred to Lord Balfour speaking at the Albert Hall in July 1920 at a Zionist demonstration, and "appealing to the Arabs of Palestine in the very language which I had used a week or so earlier echo: 'Remember we have freed you from the Turk, that we are setting up Arab States in the Hedjaz and Mesopotamia. Do not begrudge that small notch in the Arab territory being given to the people which for hundreds of years has been separated from it.' But a plea to the Arabs which is all very well from a humble penman with no power but words, becomes ridiculous," Zangwill said, "in the statesman responsible for the project, in the depository of the Allied Power, which in return for services without which neither Syria nor Palestine could have been wrested from the Turk undertook to shape both the Arab and the Jewish future. Mr. Balfour should have made the necessary provision for the rise of a Jewish State when he dealt with Feisal and the Arab leaders: their consent to the sequestration of this 'small notch in the Arab territory' should have been stipulated in advance, at the moment when they were plunging their fists into bags of British gold."

"The smallness of the Jewish population is transient," Zangwill pointed out. "The very object of the scheme is to find a place for millions. Had the Jews not been a minority in Palestine there would have been no need of special Balfourian manifestos on their behalf; even under the Turkish Constitution they would have dominated automatically. This is a scheme 'dealing in futures'; what we have to look at is the race of fourteen or fifteen millions from which streams of immigration are to pour. It is doubtful if 'safety first' is a safe principle for the establishment of States. There is more hope in the desperate and undisciplined stampede which would ensue from the shambles of Europe were the Nordau scheme adopted. The Jewish future now turns more upon Jabotinsky than upon the admirable and official Samuel."

"Without force of a kind there can be no 'Jewish National Home,' " Zangwill insisted in the first years of British rule. He was convinced that if Palestine was to be the Jewish National Home something would have to be done to remove the Arab population. He believed that "a bargain could be struck by the Powers with Prince Feisal for recognising Palestine as a Jewish State," and that "my whole conception of an amicable Arab trek into Syria or other of the new and neighbouring Arab States" was possible.

In ignoring the Arab problem, "the Zionist movement had not come to grips with reality," he said. As late as 1928, Lord Samuel in his foreword to Lord Balfour's *Speeches on Zionism*, wrote: "The presence in Palestine of half a million Moslem Arabs should not be regarded as an absolute bar to Jewish settlement in a country which is capable of maintaining a population four times or six times as great." Dr. Weizmann, speaking at the 1929 Zionist Congress, on the eve of the Arab attacks on the Jews in Palestine, said: "We feel sure that the causes of these conflicts can be put aside, and we shall do everything on our side to bring about an understanding with the Arabs of Palestine."

Zangwill on the other hand wrote in 1921 that his "step on the road to reality in the Arab question was taken—so far as documents easily at hand testify—in 1904, when I appear to have become fully aware of the Arab peril, and in a speech in New York to have honestly drawn attention to it as the outstanding obstacle to Zionism. 'There is a difficulty from which the Zionist dares not avert his eyes, though he rarely likes to face it,' " he had said in that speech. "Palestine proper already has its inhabitants. The pashalik of Jerusalem is already twice as thickly populated as the United States, having fifty-two souls to every square mile, and not 25 per cent. of them Jews; so we must be prepared either to drive out by the sword the tribes in possession as our forefathers did, or to grapple with the problem of a large alien population. This is an infinitely graver difficulty than the stock anti-Zionist taunt that nobody would go to Palestine if we got it." "Here," he said, "is the crux of the situation."

At the very time, in 1920, when Zangwill was calling for an Arab trek from Palestine, Dr. Weizmann published an article in the Palestine Hebrew paper *Haaretz*, repudiating the idea. "When the Arabs read the speeches of our D'Annunzio—Mr. Zangwill"— he wrote, "they may well believe that the Jews will come suddenly in their millions to conquer the land and turn out the Arabs. But responsible Zionists have never said or desired such a thing." Mr. Ormsby-Gore (later Lord Harlech), taking the chair at a lecture delivered by Dr. Weizmann, echoed the charge against Zangwill. "Speaking as a British politician," he complained that "all the trouble arising in regard to the question of Arabs and Jews in Palestine was due to Mr. Zangwill." That was only a few years after Dr. Weizmann, speaking at a meeting in December 1916, at which Zangwill was in the chair, had called Zangwill "a great Jew." "A great Jew like Zangwill," he said, "would not stay away when the moment arrived for the Zionist ideal to be realised. It was unimaginable that then Israel Zangwill should not be there."

On the Arab question Dr. Weizmann remained an optimist. As late as 1942, during the war, he said: "Though our work in Palestine has for its object primarily the welfare of the Jews, the benefits derived from it by the Arabs are incontestable. The Arab population of Palestine has increased—by natural growth and through immigration—far more rapidly than in Transjordan or in wealthy Egypt. The increase has been greatest precisely in those parts of Palestine where Jewish activity has been most intense. Arab wages are higher in Palestine than in any Arab country, and this accounts for a very considerable Arab influx." He had of course to consider the role of the Mufti of Jerusalem, whom he described as "an implacable enemy of both the Jews and the British," but he believed "the Mufti has never represented the whole of the Palestine Arabs." He insisted that "in the early stages of our work there were distinct possibilities

of reaching a reasonable *modus vivendi* with the Arabs, and he
promised them that in the Jewish State "the Arabs will enjoy full
autonomy." Yet then he accepted Zangwill's idea of the Arab trek.
"If any Arabs do not wish to remain in a Jewish State, every facility
will be given to them to transfer to one of the many and vast Arab
countries."

In his statement in 1946 before the Anglo-American Committee
of Inquiry on Palestine, Dr. Weizmann used almost the same words
that Zangwill had used in 1920, more than a quarter of a century
earlier, of "how the Arabs have emerged out of this war, with so
many kingdoms, at any rate, two kingdoms, four republics; they
will have six seats in the UNO, one in the Security Council." He was
even ready to agree that "some slight injustice there may be, politically, if Palestine is made a Jewish State, but individually," he assured
the Commission, "the Arabs will not suffer. On the contrary,
economically, culturally, religiously the Arabs will not be affected.
The Arabs have a perfect guarantee; whatever Palestine may be, it
will only be an island in an Arab sea, and the Arabs will not need to
appeal or to have separate guarantees inserted in the treaties; the
mere weight of their existence in organised States would prevent any
Jew from doing them injustice even if he wanted to. Their national
sentiments can find full expression in Damascus, Cairo and Bagdad.
Palestine is to the Jews what Bagdad, Cairo and Damascus are to
the Arabs." Judge Singleton, the Chairman of the Commission,
asked Dr. Weizmann about a statement attributed to him in 1918,
that "there was room in Palestine for both Jews and Arabs to work
side by side. Let his hearers beware the treacherous insinuations
that Zionists were seeking political power. Rather let both progress
together until they were ready for a joint autonomy." "It is absolutely correct," Dr. Weizmann answered, in 1946. "I said it, and I
still adhere to it."

Even now, after the Arab flight, there is still an Arab problem in
Israel. Not all the Arabs fled. "Of the 1,550,000 inhabitants of Israel
at the end of 1951, between 170,000 and 180,000 were Arabs,"
Professor Norman Bentwich wrote. They formed about 12 per cent.
of the population, which is about the same proportion that the Jews
were to the total population of Palestine at the beginning of the
Mandate." It is also about the same proportion as the Jews were to
the total population of Poland, that great Polish Jewry which
Hitler's forces murdered in the ghettos and the death camps. It is a
factor in the life of a country. "The attitude of Israel to the Arabs in
its country is marked by a certain ambivalence, as though it could
not make up its mind whether to be guided by faith or by fear,"
says Professor Bentwich. "Equal political and civil rights are granted,
but economic discrimination, denial of the rights of property, and

security measures which involve hardships diminish the virtue of political assurances. A section believes that the best and simplest solution would be to encourage the Arab minority to leave Israel. Mapam, on the other hand, champions equal rights for the Arabs. Conscience is often stronger in opposition; but within the Government Coalition also a section believes in carrying out the Biblical maxim, 'dwell in the land and cherish faith.' "

Zangwill realised the danger to Jews in Palestine of assimilation to Arab or Oriental life, which is now emphasised in the demands for larger immigration of Western Jews to offset the increasing immigration of Jews from the Arab countries. When Zangwill was in America in 1923 he told the American Zionists that "the only way of being a Zionist is to be in Zion. Believe me," he said, "when I had hopes of the establishment of a Jewish State, whether in Palestine or elsewhere, it never occurred to me that I should not settle there. Though Zionism is practically financed from America only sixty-six Jews left America for Palestine in 1922." Now, over thirty years later, I read that "not half a dozen American Zionist families have left their American homes and settled in Israel since the establishment of the State." Forty years ago Zangwill was worried by Dr. Joseph Klausner writing, "assimilation to the Arabs has already begun." "What guarantee," Zangwill asked, "is there that Palestine will produce real Jews rather than Arabs of the Jewish persuasion?" We are told to-day that "the failure of Western immigration is viewed with gravity by the Government of Israel."

Yet Zangwill was a realist, and even while he reproached Zionists for not going to Zion, he "remembered that a thorough going Zionism in the sense of a thorough going of Zionists to Palestine would be impracticable inasmuch as Palestine is too small to hold the Zionists, not to mention the millions of other Jews. So a Zionist," he conceded, "may reconcile it with his conscience to deport his money rather than his person to Palestine." He knew how important money is. How important it is to have this large and wealthy American Jewry, so that "Zionism is practically financed from America." When he spoke of the danger of Jewish assimilation in Palestine to the surrounding Arab world, he did not forget the assimilation in Europe and America. "Wherever the Jews have perfect equality and have been tempted out of the Ghetto, there the beginnings of disintegration are manifest. The bulk of American Jewry knows more of Christian Science than of the Talmud," he complained. "In the small new towns of the West the poor Jew drifts into the Church as easily as the rich Jew in the Eastern towns. Thousands of the rising generation have never seen phylacteries." He instanced an immigrant who had joined an Episcopelian congregation. " 'In the Church,' he said, 'I am told to be good. In the

Temple I am told to be good. In the Church the organ is playing. In
the Temple the organ is playing. In the Church Christian choir girls
are singing. In the Temple Christian choir girls are singing. Why
should we not all davven together?' Asked how he could believe
in Jesus, he replied that a Jewish Rabbi had preached that Jesus
was a great prophet, and the reassurance he received from the
Episcopelian Rabbi that stress was no longer laid on the immaculate
conception had set his conscience completely at rest." At such times
Zangwill thought that only in a Jewish land could the Jew "be at
one with himself."

But the Jewish land could not hold all the Jewish millions. Also
the need of financing the Jewish land from outside required a large,
strong and prosperous Jewry in America and in the Diaspora generally. And in order to develop commercially Palestine must turn to
Jews in the Diaspora who could buy from Palestine. More than
twenty years before—he wrote in 1920, that is before 1900, when
Palestine had been, he said, "veiled in pietistic clouds"—he had
already drawn up a report on "The Commercial Future of Palestine,"
"urging its commercial and industrial development, to absorb a large
Jewish immigration." Yet Zangwill, with his continual pro and con,
even while he spoke of Palestine absorbing a large Jewish immigration, wanted the mass of the Jews to stay where they are. He cherished
the belief that conditions were improving for them. "Glicenstein's
Messiah is not altogether asleep," he said. "An immense improvement has taken place in the position of the Jews—despite all the
antisemitism and the massacres—since my boyhood. Imagine the
dullness of Europe without its Jews. Perhaps the reason the Goyim
won't let the Messiah come is that they would be lost without us."
It was a jest of Zangwill's that he kept repeating, that the nations
would not let the Jews go because they need them. He spoke of a
member of the United States Government, the Secretary for the
Navy, threatening at a Jewish meeting in New York, that he would
have the guns of the Navy trained on any attempt by the American
Jews to depart from the United States to Palestine. He felt that
the Jews need to live in the Diaspora, that it is good for the Jews,
and good for the Gentiles. He believed in the value to the world as a
whole of this cross-influence and cross-fertilisation. "The Jewish
people was interfused," he said, "with almost every people on the
planet. It lived in contact with every nation, it underwent the influence of every environment, it played a part in every history. A
people that has learned to live without a country is unconquerable.
For never will the combined people break into an attack upon the
Jews. There are always plenty of other Jews elsewhere. Here indeed is
the secret of immortality." He had decided against putting all our
eggs into one basket.

This is the other, the non-Zionist side of Zangwill; for he displayed a polarity at every point. He always saw and defended the opposite of everything that he believed in and advocated. He believed that the reverse of everything must be shown. To be one-sided was to him deliberately to gouge out one eye, and go about the world like a cyclop. He was terribly concerned about the plight of the masses of oppressed Jews in Russia and elsewhere who were denied civilised conditions in their own land and wanted to go elsewhere. For these he wanted Zionism, Territorialism, the widest possible facilities for immigration, a Jewish State in Palestine or elsewhere, immigration to America, Canada, South America, planned immigration through Galveston. But only for "those who cannot or will not stay in the lands where they live." Not for others. It is the very antithesis of the doctrine of the "Ingathering of the Exiles," the mass exodus to the Jewish State, and the emptying and disappearance of the Diaspora. Zangwill was not even certain that the re-creation of the Jewish State for which he worked would really be a good thing. He quoted Longfellow's poem "The Jewish Cemetery at Newport" "But ah, what once has been shall be no more. The dead nations never rise again."

He agreed "that Time never retraces its steps. Even if Judea is re-established in Palestine it can never be the old Judea over again." He was not sure it would not be a dangerous thing to restore the Jewish State. He recalled a story by H. G. Wells of a man who hatches out the egg of an extinct bird. "At first all is charm and idyll, but in a few years the creature grown colossal and terrible, kicks and pummels its foster-father as with the foot of a cart-horse and a beak like a sledge-hammer. It is the fate that awaits all who play with the past and revive the intellectually extinct."

He wondered if perhaps to the Jewish problem "there is no remedy. Even this," he said, "would not be a word of unique despair: as much might be said of the countless other tragic problems that beset the thinker—for the Judenschmerz is only a fraction of the world's suffering." He thought perhaps the only way for the Jew was disappearance or "a religious regeneration." Zangwill turned from Zionism to his favourite theme—Judaism. He spoke of "some extremists for Jewish race and soil who have sought to dispense with a religious bond," and said that "Herzl had a glimpse of the truth when he declared that the return to Judaism must precede the return to Zion. Zion is not a mere place; to rebuild it is not like rebuilding Belgium or Serbia."

It is understandable that Zionists should denounce such a man as an anti-Zionist. There was indeed a time when Zangwill concentrating on his own method of dealing with the Jewish problem could not help opposing the Zionist activities which were working in a different

o

direction, and Mrs. Zangwill agreed that during this period "he was an anti-Zionist."

Even in his Zionist period the Zionists had responded to his writings when they disliked them, by refusing to publish what he said. I suppose the official organ of a political Party can justify its refusal to print opinions which run counter to the official programme. So when Zangwill, asked for another contribution for the Passover number of the Zionist official organ *Die Welt*, sent an essay which questioned the wisdom of a people after some nineteen centuries had changed the face of the world still clinging to the dream of restoring their ancient homeland, *Die Welt* did not print it. Zangwill's comment was "that even before Palestine is re-established it should already be necessary to establish a Jewish censorship is another illustration of the evils of the False Romantic." Years after, in 1922, Zangwill sent me an article for distribution, which he called "The Betrayal of Zionism." Few of the American Jewish publications which took our service used the article. "I am very interested to hear," Zangwill wrote, "that the bulk of your American journals would not publish my article, because it shows that Zionism has already established a censorship in Israel, and will not hear the truth." "A profound legend makes Balaam's ass die the moment it has seen the truth and spoken," said Zangwill. "If the truth-speaker does not always escape the consequences so deftly, there always remains the resource of calling him an ass."

Yet Zangwill was a Zionist too. He was always tossing the two balls, Zionism and anti-Zionism, into the air simultaneously, and catching them deftly. Before Herzl had come to enlist his sympathy for the Zionist movement, Zangwill had already shown that he knew the Zionist movement, the pre-Herzlian movement, the Chovevei Zion, which he translated in *Children of the Ghetto*, published before he met Herzl, as Holy Land League. It was not a small movement, nor a silent one. Its largest activity was in East London, which Zangwill knew and depicted. The East London Tent of the Chovevei Zion had been formed in 1885, ten years before Herzl wrote the *Jewish State*, before he had begun to think out his Zionist problem. In May 1891, while Zangwill was writing *Children of the Ghetto*, the Chovevei Zion held a meeting at the Great Assembly Hall, Mile End, of which it was said: "It was no doubt the largest meeting of Jews ever held in England, the audience being estimated at over 4,000 people." Colonel Goldsmid, who spoke of himself as Daniel Deronda, and whose daughter, Carmel Goldsmid, became one of Zangwill's followers in the Ito, was in the chair. Zangwill knew him well enough to send him a telegram when Herzl arrived, to arrange for him to receive Herzl. One of the speakers at the meeting was Aaron Vecht, the manager of the *Jewish Standard*—the *Flag of*

Judah in *Children of the Ghetto*—on which Zangwill was a leading contributor. One of the founders of the East London Tent was Val Finkelstein, whom I knew. He had made the English translation of Pinsker's *Auto-Emancipation*, out of which the Chovevei Zion movement had grown; and afterwards he was the Secretary of Zangwill's Ito. Zangwill knew the movement, and he must have had sympathy with it to write of it as he did, to put into his book such a Zionist speech as Strelitsky's, and to translate Imber's anthem *The Watch on the Jordan*, as he did; even, with his doubts, to respond to Herzl's call as he did.

Zionist politics created in recent years a legend of a "perfidious Britain," of an anti-Jewish Britain even, certainly of an anti-Zionist Britain. But Zangwill recalled that "the first embryonic stirrings of practical Zionism did not antedate British sympathy with the cause. Long before the first Jewish colony was founded in Palestine, Lord Shaftesbury had been memorialising Palmerston to set up the Jews in Palestine, and while the colonists were contenting themselves per-force with Turkish rule, Laurence Oliphant was planning for them an autonomous concession from the Porte. No Jew had interpreted Zionism with such depth and poetry as George Eliot in *Daniel Deronda*. Even when Herzl twenty years later founded the Zionist movement, England remained its spiritual home. Herzl was an Anglophil. Mr. Chamberlain's East Africa offer and Sinai projects were logical episodes in the evolution of British-Jewish history." Sir Moses Montefiore, an English Jew, was the pioneer of Jewish colonisation in Palestine. "There is a Jew in England, Colonel Goldsmid," Herzl had noted in his Diaries, "who is an enthusiastic Zionist. I must mark this Colonel." When through Zangwill he met the Colonel, Herzl recorded their talk: "I am an orthodox Jew. My children are brought up strictly religious; learned Hebrew. The Christians in England will help us to go to Palestine. For they expect after the return of the Jews the coming of the Messiah. He thinks like Montagu (later Lord Swaythling, Lord Samuel's uncle) of a greater Palestine. I suddenly stand in a different world with Goldsmid."

The clash came later, with the Clerkenwell Conference in London, soon after the First Zionist Congress, when the practical Zionists and the cultural Zionists, Achad Ha'am's followers, were defeated by the new political Zionists led by Herzl. Zangwill stood with Herzl. "There are not two Zionisms: there is only one Zionism," he said when Herzl died, "the Zionism that was laid down in Herzl's *Jewish State*." To that extent Dr. Stephen Wise was right when he said that Zangwill's "Watchman, What of the Night?" speech was the speech of a Herzlian Zionist. Zangwill might doubt Zionism, might doubt the realisation or the ultimate form and value of the Jewish State, might place higher another ideal that he believed greater and more lasting, Judaism, universalism, but when he spoke of Zionism or thought of Zionism it was Herzlian Zionism, Jewish State Zionism. "I came over here some twenty years ago to try to convert American Jews to Zionism. In my absence you seem to have become converted so thoroughly that you think you are better Zionists than I am," Zangwill told the Carnegie Hall meeting of the American Jewish Congress. His own feeling, he said, was that "you are not Zionists; you are playing at Zionism." Because one argument put forward, he said, was that "it is going to be a land of refuge for millions," and another argument was that "it was small and could be developed better. Well, if it is small it is not going to be a land of refuge for millions," Zangwill said, "and if it is going to be a land of refuge for millions, then you cannot congratulate yourself that it is small. What you have to do is to decide what you are going to do in Palestine, whether you want it for millions or not—whether it is quantity or quality you want. Always I hear nothing except the words 'give money,' and I say you will get much more money when you have considered what the old Hebrew word 'Tachlis' means."

When Zangwill said, "I hear nothing except the words 'give money,'" he did not mean that the work could be done without money. His use immediately after of the word "Tachlis," which means, the end, the goal, getting on with the job, securing the funds and everything else needed for it makes that clear. "They keep crying that nothing is wanted save money; whereas what is first necessary," he said, "is a solid political foundation." Not only a political foundation, but also an economic foundation. "The financing of Zionism by charity," he objected in 1923, "has the drawback that it tends for a long time to conceal the rottenness in the economic fabric."

Zangwill had never been unaware of the need of money for the work in Palestine. From his first association with Herzl he had pressed on him and on the Zionist movement the need of money to realise their plans. He conducted a fierce campaign to try to get the millions bequeathed by Baron de Hirsch to the Jewish Colonisation Association (Ica) diverted to Palestine colonisation. "These millions were left for the salvation of the Jewish people," he said, "and the Directors cannot stand haughtily over their treasure, leaving Israel to sweat and agonise." He took a leading part in the fight which Herzl started over the Ica Bill in Parliament, in the attempt to have Ica funds made available for the Palestine work. He was with Herzl in his approaches to Andrew Carnegie and to Cecil Rhodes. When Herzl wrote his letter to Rhodes he asked Zangwill to translate it for him into English. "This movement," the letter said, "cries out in vain for money. Why? Because the Jewish big financiers are against us." In his Diary, Herzl notes immediately after this entry: "Zangwill is trying with Lord Suffield's help to build up a financial group. Then I may perhaps reach Edward VII through Lord Suffield, whom Zangwill has won." He wrote to "My dear friends Zangwill and Joe" (Zangwill's cousin and friend, Joseph Cowen): "You ask me to set out a financial plan. Here it is." He concludes: "If your effort succeeds, my dear friends, you have done the highest service to our immortal cause." Zangwill was always aware of Zionism's need of money, and he kept approaching Jewish and other financiers. "The trouble," he said afterwards, "was that they were all physically deaf. Lord Rothschild was deaf. Then there was Jacob Schiff. I tried to talk Zionism to him. But he was deaf. In Paris there is Baron Edmond Rothschild. He too is deaf. To all those I have tried to talk Zionism. Lord Rothschild, sitting in his great office in New Court, and supposed to be the leading financier of the world, said to me once, 'It is so difficult to get Palestine.' I thought to myself, 'If I were only sitting in your chair, I wouldn't find it so difficult to get Palestine.' "

Afterwards, when Zangwill became the leader of the Ito he made an attempt in the High Court to prevent the Jewish Colonial Trust altering its objects to restrict them to Palestine and adjoining countries, in the hope of securing some of the funds for Jewish settlement in an Itoland. But he confessed in his speech in Court during that action: "I have no hope of getting money from the Zionists."

Zangwill had a sense of reality. I have a copy of *The Menorah Journal*, in which Zangwill had annotated an article on "The Jew and Trans-National America." "As I understand it," said the author, "the Jewish State which Zionists are building is a non-military, a non-chauvinistic State." Zangwill could not understand such an abstraction in a human world. "If not a full State," he commented in the margin, "it is no more a model than a Catholic priest."

Zangwill looked to Zionism to solve a need. "The Ito," he said, "has always declared its readiness to co-operate in developing Palestine if the Zionists could guarantee the political safeguards." That was in 1907, when he showed "the acquisition of Palestine is uncertain." "By a territory," he explained, "we do not mean a toy colony. We mean a real country which shall ultimately exert upon the Jewish emigrants as potent an attraction as New York exercises to-day, and be as able to receive them in their thousands and their tens of thousands." He realised the possible cost. "This is not a world," he said, "in which everything can be bought for money. It may be that ere a Jewish State arises part of the price will have to be paid in blood."

Even at that, "a new Judea," Zangwill held, "cannot supplant the Diaspora, it can only supplement it. If the question were to be asked, What will become of the Jews of the Diaspora, the answer would have to be: 'Ten per cent. will emigrate to the Jewish State, 20 per cent. will be baptised or otherwise lost to Jewry, and 70 per cent. will remain in the Diaspora." Again, as always, Zangwill returned to Judaism as the only Jewish hope. "So long as the Diaspora believes in Judaism, it has no need of a spiritual centre. The Torah is its spiritual centre. To replace the religion which has kept the Diaspora alive nearly two thousand years, and which is a solid reality coming home to the Jew at every hour of the day, by an absentee nationalism so tenuous that another and a nearer nationalism can occupy his heart simultaneously and claim even the sacrifice of his blood, this is a conception which could occur only to visionaries ignorant of life. A spiritual centre in Zion may suffice to hold the first generation of absentee Zionists minus Judaism; without either political or religious substance it will not avail to keep their children Jewish. The young generation will crave less windy nourishment and a more solid ground for separation from the general life. No minority in history has ever sustained itself in the bosom of a majority unless fortified by a burning faith." "History which is largely a record of the melting of minorities in majorities, records no instance—except that of the Gypsies who are nomads outside civilisation—of the survival of a group not segregated in space or not protected by a burning faith as by a frontier of fire."

He was sure the Diaspora would survive "the completest possible triumph of Zionism." And he held fast to his "ideal of human brotherhood." If the Jews would use their dispersion, their "ubiquity," to preach this ideal, "to stand out staunchly for Israel's mission, thus linking up the nations, the evils due to the absence of a territory would cease to count. The glow of apostolic faith and ardour would preserve the Jewish spirit in more than its pristine vitality, while antisemitism would be welcomed as at once the price of prophesying and the tribute which the lower pays to the higher. The nation of martyrs and pioneers would then wear persecution as a crown and welcome death as a privilege. The Diaspora would either be wiped out—a glorious ending—or it would survive in prophetic splendour." When prophecy "marks a man for its own" no adherence to any political party or movement or dogma can keep him from breaking out into such rapturous glorification of the Hebrew spirit and the Jewish ideal. Zangwill's lips were indeed "touched with the burning coal," and as he said, "could speak no otherwise."

In such a mood "race-Zionism" was to Zangwill "a superstition." Yet he kept coming back all the time to the Jewish need. There were Jews, race-Jews, or religious Jews, but whichever they were, people discriminated against and suffering because they were, by whatever definition, Jews, people "who cannot or will not stay in the lands in which they live at present." Their plight and their need weighed heavily on him. Three months after the Jewish Territorial Organisation had dissolved, in September 1925, when Zangwill had less than a year left to live, he spoke at a Conference of the Federation of Ukrainian Jews, with Chief Rabbi Hertz, Haham Dr. Gaster and Dr. Jochelman, and the theme of his speech was the "closed doors" that "everywhere confront the Jewish emigrant." By the end of the year, in November 1925, he was concerned with a number of calls that were coming to him from Continental groups of the Ito to restart the organisation in order to find outlets for Jewish immigration. A few years later, when the restrictions made Jewish immigration to Palestine difficult, some active Zionists tried to help in a movement on Ito lines to establish Jewish autonomous settlement in other countries, to find room for Jewish refugees. Jewish need, not Zionist romanticism, inspired Zangwill's Zionist work. "The rift that suddenly opened at the so-called Uganda Conference was not a brand-new chasm made by the earthquake of the British offer," Zangwill said. "It was the exposure of an abyss which had yawned between them from the first. Zionism takes it vision and ideal from the past; Territorialism places them in the future. The one looks back, the other forward. Probably no nation now lives in its original habitat." "We who struggle, who desire to translate dreams into deeds," he urged, "let us beware how we fall into the false romanticism of parrot phrases and ancient images. The holy Land was not holy while it belonged to the Perizites and the Jebuzites, and any land in which Israel should find his soul again would be also a Holy Land." "Zion is where the Jew lives as a Jew."

When Herzl found it was impossible at that time under Turkish rule to realise Zionism in Zion "Dr. Herzl and myself gave up Zion." "Colonies in Palestine, a university in Jerusalem, a spiritual centre, Jewish culture, any method except the normal method of numerical preponderance in Palestine is not Zionism." He insisted that he had always been concerned with a land of refuge for Jews in need, not with colonisation and Jewish culture in Palestine. "In April 1899," he said, "I wrote to the *Jewish Chronicle*, 'I hope Dr. Herzl has retained the option of making his State outside Palestine if necessary'—that meant if it was impracticable otherwise." And "I say positively," he declared, "that Dr. Herzl's idea was simply to found a Jewish State anywhere. But it was natural that he should try first for Palestine."

Chapter VII

THE JEWISH TERRITORIAL ORGANISATION

I HAVE quoted Shaw's remark to Reuben Brainin, a Hebrew writer and early Zionist who interviewed him in 1909, that "my friend Zangwill is also a Zionist and has greatly interested me in the movement." Brainin corrected Shaw. "Zangwill is not a Zionist, but a Territorialist," he explained—"that is, one who doesn't look upon Palestine as the only possible home for the Jews, but will be content with any land in any part of the world."

One of Zangwill's bitterest opponents in his effort to win the Zionist Congress for the acceptance of the British offer in East Africa was Dr. Gaster, the Haham of the Sephardic Community in Great Britain. While Zangwill spoke at the Congress Dr. Gaster kept objecting that Zangwill had no right to speak there because he was no longer a Zionist. "Get out, Zangwill!" he shouted. During the Uganda crisis Gaster was one of the leaders of the Zion-Zionists in the English-speaking countries. "We can understand the repugnance which Zionists like Dr. Gaster must feel at the apparent abandonment of a Jewish State in the ancestral home for the sake of a settlement among half-savage tribes. Is this what is to become of the Zionist dream?" the *Jewish Chronicle* wrote at the time. More than thirty years later Dr. Gaster became the Honorary President of the Freeland Territorial movement, founded to renew the quest of Zangwill's Jewish Territorial Organisation for a land of Jewish settlement outside Palestine. "I am to-day as enthusiastic a Zionist as ever I was," he said. "But you must look at the practical side. How big is Palestine? What shall we do about the millions of homeless Jews all over the world?"

So Reuben Brainin too, who had carefully explained to Shaw that Zangwill was not a Zionist, but a Territorialist, fell into strong disfavour with the Zionists, and was attacked by them, even having to defend himself against a charge of "treason to Zionism" made by the poet Bialik, because he became an active propagandist for the scheme of Jewish settlement in Russia. When Brainin went to South Africa in 1929 to raise funds for Jewish settlement in Russia, the South African Zionist Federation denounced him in an official statement. It "felt in duty bound," it said, "to oppose a movement whose primary aim is to paralyse world Jewry's effort for Palestine."

The Soviet attitude to the idea of Jewish mass colonisation in the

Ukraine, Crimea and Biro-Bidjan has changed since this movement was started about 1924; it seems to have been abandoned. But when Reuben Brainin propagated it, the Soviet Government was holding out hopes of a large autonomous Jewish settlement in those areas. There was even talk of bringing in Jews from outside Russia, from Poland and Lithuania.

Zangwill had believed in the possibilities of this Russian Jewish settlement. His last public meeting, less than six months before he died, with his old friend and Ito colleague, Dr. Jochelman in the chair, was held in support of the Jewish Colonisation movement in Russia. He was not altogether sure of the position under the Bolshevik Government. "The only trouble," he said, "is the relation of the Jews to the Soviet régime. But the Jews have nothing to do with Bolshevism. It is a question of bread and homes for hungry millions. I had conversations with high representatives of the Soviet. I urged them not to distribute the Jews in different remote parts of the country. Concentration is a vital necessity. We should demand of the Russian Government one particular territory where the Jews could settle." Lord Wedgwood, who was a Zionist, was also a supporter of Jewish colonisation in Biro-Bidjan. He visited the area, and found it "constructive work well done."

Zangwill spoke about the Russian Jewish Colonisation movement in his 1923 address to the American Jewish Congress; he thought if it "really brings my own Organisation's ideal of an autonomous Jewish territory into being in the region where Jews are already aggregated" it might "largely modify" the Jewish situation. It was in fact, he said, "one of the many potentialities" he had considered. The idea was in Zangwill's mind before the Russian Revolution, when Russia was still Czarist. "In Siberia" (where Biro-Bidjan is situated) "only ten millions of people eke out a livelihood," he wrote, "and a Continent half as large again as the United States has been left almost in primeval forest. Is there any reason why the Jews instead of being cooped up in stinking poverty in the towns of the Pale should not be invited to carve out a province with the ploughshare from these vast neglected territories?"

Zangwill commented in one of his speeches that Dr. Bernstein-Kogan, one of the "Nine" who with Ussischkin drafted the ultimatum to Herzl against East Africa, because it was not Palestine, had after settling in Palestine in the first years of the Balfour Declaration, returned to Russia because he could not adjust himself to Palestine. He died in 1929, in Dnepropetrovsk, formerly Ekaterinoslav, his own and Ussischkin's native town. He was an old associate of Dr. Weizmann's. Jacob de Haas, in his Herzl biography, remarks of the new Democratic fraction at the Fifth Zionist Congress in 1901, that it was "led by two old Zionists, Leo Motzkin, and

Bernstein-Kogan, aided by one newcomer, Dr. Chaim Weizmann."

Another old Zionist, a pre-Herzlian Zionist, Dr. Nathan Birnbaum, who is credited with the actual coining of the word "Zionism," became a Territorialist. "Nathan Birnbaum could legitimately claim to have been the first serious exponent of that form of Jewish Nationalism known as political Zionism," de Haas wrote in his Herzl biography. Beginning as an unbeliever, preaching modern materialist philosophy, Birnbaum became a strictly observant orthodox Jew, associated with the Agudas Yisroel. He was one of the founders of the organised Yiddishist movement, and convened its first Conference in 1908 at Czernowitz. During the pogroms in the Ukraine at the end of the First War he urged planned emigration to regulate what was becoming an unorganised panic mass flight. After the Hitler régime he started in Holland an organisation for "establishing extensive Jewish settlements having religious-national autonomy on sparsely populated or unpopulated territories."

Zangwill died before this happened, and his Ito had been wound up in 1925, less than a year before he died. I have a copy dictated by Zangwill, with notes in his handwriting, of the report of the meeting of the Headquarters Council of the Ito at which the decision "to close its activities" was adopted. Zangwill told the meeting that his physicians had warned him to reduce his activities. He was too ill to lead the movement. Sir Meyer Spielman, the Vice-President of the Ito, said that "the Ito without a figurehead like Mr. Zangwill, who carried so much weight, was now hopeless. It might revive later."

Zangwill had raised this question of the figurehead at one of the first Conferences of the Ito. He pointed out that the Ito Constitution contained no provision for a change of President, and "it was all the more incumbent upon him, therefore, to honour the democratic principle by tendering his resignation." He advised its acceptance on other grounds, the necessity of dissociating so great a movement from a single personality, whose withdrawal from Jewish politics was demanded by so many enemies." The Conference demanded that Zangwill remain President, and "the Conference broke up with enthusiastic cries of 'Hedad' to Mr. Zangwill." Yet Zangwill did not dislike the idea of a one-man leadership of "a great movement." He had approved and supported Herzl's personal leadership of the Zionist movement. When Herzl died, he went to the next Congress with instructions from a group of English Zionist societies who elected him as their delegate "to support the election of three leaders, Dr. Nordau, Herr Wolffsohn and Professor Warburg. Dr. Nordau had retired," he reported back. "As a result the triple leadership was abandoned, and Herr Wolffsohn, already Chairman of the Jewish Colonial Trust, silently became sole leader. As I personally am a believer in one-man leadership," he said, "I am not displeased."

That was the Seventh Zionist Congress in 1905, the last Zangwill attended, and from which he came away as leader of the Jewish Territorial Organisation. Zangwill said he had not intended to form a new organisation. Mrs. Zangwill told me (and this period was within her personal knowledge and personal participation, for she became a member of the first International Committee of the Ito) that Dr. Jochelman had organised the Territorialist group, and Zangwill had then been pressed as the man with an international reputation to become the leader. "He had only joined the Territorialist group on condition that it was not a talking group," Zangwill told the Maccabeans when he addressed them soon after his return to London. "He was tired of congresses and talking," he said. "He was tired of paper parliaments. What they had to do was not to talk but to colonise a country." He pointed out that most of the leaders of the Ito were in Russia, "which was only natural, seeing that the bulk of the Jews and the Jewish problem was in Russia."

The first thing Zangwill did as President of the Ito was to write to Mr. Lyttleton, who had succeeded Joseph Chamberlain as Colonial Secretary, to ask him "in view of the formation of an international body to go on with the scheme" (Jewish autonomous settlement in East Africa), that the site proposed for the Zionist East African Colony should not be otherwise disposed of before he had an opportunity of discussing the matter with him. The Colonial Secretary replied on 16th September 1905: "Dear Mr. Zangwill, I have your letter of the 8th of this month, in which you ask that the territory which was originally suggested for a Zionist settlement in East Africa should not be otherwise disposed of before you have had an opportunity of discussing the question with me, in view of the formation of an international body to go on with the scheme. I was, of course, aware that you had protested against the decision of the Zionist Congress at Basle not to proceed further in the matter, and that you have announced the decision of your party to secede and to hold separate meetings for the prosecution of your views. But I had understood that a portion of the minority which you represented had subsequently rallied to the majority, and that it was not likely that the secession movement would assume important dimensions. On receiving, therefore, through Mr. Greenberg, an official notification of the decision of the Basle Congress, I informed the Commissioner for the East Africa Protectorate that the land which had been proposed for the settlement need not be reserved any longer. In view of these circumstances and further observing from your letter in *The Times*, that you are yourself not by any means assured that the land which you propose should be withheld from disposition elsewhere is suitable for your requirements, I feel that it is impossible for me to grant the request contained in your letter. I need hardly add that this will be no obstacle to the consideration by His Majesty's Government of any well-considered proposals which you may hereafter feel yourself in a position to make."

Zangwill's next step was to tell Mr. Lyttleton in a letter dated 20th September 1905, that "as soon as the Council and Honorary Officers have had time to consider fully the questions involved in their programme, I hope, on their behalf, to be able to avail myself of your kind permission to lay before you a Territorial scheme which may be found acceptable by His Majesty's Government."

But before anything could be done the Conservative Government headed by Balfour, in which Mr. Lyttleton was Colonial Secretary, had to resign, and the general election of 1906 resulted in the overwhelming defeat of the Conservative Party, and the return of a Liberal Government headed by Campbell-Bannerman and Asquith. "The resignation of the Government naturally made Mr. Zangwill's interview with Mr. Lyttleton a mere exchange of views," said a statement issued by the Ito at the time, "but his detailed suggestion for a Jewish land of refuge has been formally deposited at the Colonial Office, and as the project of the Ito has enlisted sympathisers on both sides of the House, it is expected that the negotiations, though they will naturally be considerably delayed while the new Ministry is settling into the saddle will, in due course, be resumed."

In the half-century since the East African offer was made by Joseph Chamberlain, East Africa, including the Guas Ngishu plateau which was the area proposed for the Jewish colony, has developed tremendously. But it is now the centre of the Mau Mau terrorist movement. Zangwill was not sure even then that the land was suitable for white settlement, the whites doing the work themselves—not employing black labour. "In our privately published Blue Book will be found the history of this transaction and of the gradual abandonment of the project," Zangwill said afterwards, "partly from the fear that our neo-Jewish civilisation would be based on black labour." His plan included Jewish productive labour: Jews to do everything, from sweeper to President. During the height of the Uganda controversy he wrote: "East Africa has its natives, who though clad only in loin-cloths may soon be catching up the cry against alien immigration." "Is East Africa that soil?" he asked. "I do not know. I await the report of the Commission."

Zangwill was not committed to acceptance of the East Africa offer. His objection was to the Chovevei Zionists who, "even if the report of the Commissioners is favourable, will still say 'no.' They seem to think," he suggested, "that if you shut the East African door, this by some mysterious spring opens the Palestine door.

But you may simply see all doors closed; not only East Africa and Palestine, but London and New York. And then—not only will remain the terrible tragedy of our wandering populations, but Zionism itself, the one gleam in the Russian darkness, may be extinguished in Russia by the iron hand of Plehve. For Plehve's policy is quite open. Zionism he will tolerate so long as it is an emigrating movement, but a speechifying Zionism, that merely unsettles the Russian Jew, this he will utterly destroy. And with all doors closed in your face, where are you going to emigrate your Zionists to?"

After Britain's Uganda offer, which led Zangwill to form the Ito, the Ito in 1905 considered a Dutch offer of Surinam, where in the eighteenth century there had been a flourishing Jewish settlement. Surinam came up again for consideration in 1938, when the stream of Jewish emigration was desperately seeking an outlet; but nothing happened. Together with Surinam or Dutch Guiana, as it is now known, British Guiana, which adjoins it, was mentioned by the British Government as a possible area of Jewish settlement.

But Zangwill's reason for founding the Ito was the rejection by the Zionist Congress of the British offer in East Africa, and this followed the presentation of an unfavourable report by the Expedition that had been sent to the area by the previous Congress, when Herzl, still alive, had presided. There were differences of opinion between the three members of the Expedition. Major Gibbons, the English expert, presented a favourable minority report, attacking the views of his two colleagues, Professor Kaiser and Mr. Wilbusch. I have seen the reports, but they are now of only historic interest. It is more relevant that as Mr. Lyttleton had reminded him, Zangwill was not himself "by any means assured that the land is suitable for your requirements." He realised it was wild country, and that "some pioneers must perish. There are wild beasts in East Africa," he said, "but in Jerusalem there are wilder creatures. Wherever we go we shall find no absolutely safe proposition. Territories are not got by making speeches on Zionist platforms." As for the objection that East Africa was not Zion, Zangwill argued that "a flourishing community of Jews on a fertile territory of eighteen thousand square miles would be nearer to Palestine than all the Zionist societies in the world talking all day long. Not that I mean," he said, "that the Jewish East Africans themselves must necessarily migrate to Palestine, only their territory would be the centre of Jewish political force."

Zangwill also saw it as a British force. "Had the conception been carried out," he wrote ten years after, in the first year of the Great War, "England would to-day have had a Maccabean force to defend that zone of war against the Germans." There were Jews from East

Africa in the British forces. "When Joseph Chamberlain offered the Zionists a plateau in East Africa, the half-dozen local Britons held a 'mass-meeting' of protest," Zangwill wrote. "Yet to-day, though the offer was rejected of the Zionists, fifty Jewish volunteers are serving in the Defence Force enlisted at Nairobi."

"The Jewish Settlement in British East Africa dates from 1903, when the British Government offered the Zionist Organisation a territory in the present Kenya for an autonomous Jewish settlement," says the Jewish Year Book. There are about 1,000 Jews there. They have active Zionist societies, but they do not seem to want to leave for Israel. Major Edward Ruben came there as a boy from Palestine, where his father was an early settler, to join an uncle who was farming coffee. He fought with the British in 1914 in East Africa and again in 1939-46. During a visit to Johannesburg, he said "one of my major activities is organising Zionist endeavour in the colony. My wife and I divide our holidays between Israel and the United Kingdom. We both have strong family links with Israel, but think only of Kenya as the country where we have roots." I met in Israel Mr. Somen, the "unquestioned leader of Kenya Jewry." He is a keen Zionist, and Honorary Consul for Israel in East Africa, but his home is Nairobi.

In Zangwill's day the territory was spoken of in Zionist controversy as Uganda, on which it borders. Zangwill also called it Jewish East Africa or British Judea, which he suggested should be its official name; he discussed the possible appointment of an English Jew with Colonial administrative experience as Governor. The man he had in mind was Sir Matthew Nathan, a member of the Council of the Ito, who held then and later a number of British Colonial Governorships, the Gold Coast, Natal and Queensland. He claimed that the Colonial Secretary, "Mr. Lyttleton agreed that under such a scheme Sir Matthew Nathan would provide an ideal figure for the post." At that time Sir Andrew Cohen, who became Governor of Uganda, was not yet born. He is the son of another member of the Council of the Ito, Mr. Walter S. Cohen, later Honorary Secretary of the Economic Board for Palestine.

There were not only Zionist objections to "Uganda." There were in 1904 and 1905 also objections from the European settlers, though these numbered but a few hundred. "I seem to hear dogs barking in the manger at Mombasa," said Zangwill.

Though Chamberlain was no longer a member of the British Government he continued to support the East African scheme. At the end of 1905 he wrote to Mr. Langerman, one of Zangwill's supporters: "I understand that you and your friends have determined to renew the effort on the lines suggested by Dr. Herzl, and although the delay has certainly increased the difficulties in the way, all that has since occurred, and particularly the recent terrible persecution of the Jews in the East of Europe, has intensified the necessity for finding some immediate remedy for the existing state of things, and has added to the responsibility of Christian nations in regard to it. I should therefore most gladly give any aid and influence that I can command in support of any application that may now be made by a responsible organisation to the British Government to consider favourably the scheme prepared by Dr. Herzl, or any amendment of it which experience has shown to be desirable."

There seems ground for the belief that Joseph Chamberlain and Arthur Balfour, who was Prime Minister at the time of the East Africa offer, were moved to suggest this outlet for the Jewish refugees from Russian oppression to keep them out of England. Their Government set up the Aliens Commission before which Herzl gave evidence, and introduced the Aliens Act, to restrict the immigration of alien Jews. I have just re-read an editorial in the *Jewish Chronicle* in December 1904, on Mr. Chamberlain's anti-alien speech delivered that week in the East End, where feeling was high against the alien invaders. "The usual bogeys were raised," it said, "and the usual mis-statements indulged in. But these things seem to be of the essence of anti-alienism. Mr. Chamberlain suggests that the best solution of the question is Zionism. He even mentions the East African Colony in this sense. We do not know whether this specific will completely solve the immigration question; but it ought certainly to mitigate it very materially in time."

"We quite accept Mr. Balfour's repudiation of antisemitism," the *Jewish Chronicle* wrote, "but we cannot admit that disclaimer in the case of some supporters of the Bill." Zangwill was not so sure about Mr. Balfour. His speech which was the subject of the *Jewish Chronicle* editorial contained some very near-antisemitic expressions. One was aimed, for instance, at a very large section of the Jewish immigrants from Russia, which included Zangwill's father, those who refused to do military service for a country which denied them equal rights and persecuted them as Jews. "Reference was made," said Mr. Balfour, "to certain Russian reservists who left their country because they in one sense did not approve of the war, and in another because they did not get a pension. Are we to offer them unlimited shelter simply because they come over here? These foreign immigrants drive the British workman from Whitechapel." When the Balfour Declaration came Zangwill thought he could see "the cloven hoof of the antisemite," who wanted the Jews to go to Palestine or to some other place, instead of England. "Zionism," he said, "received his support as 'a serious endeavour to mitigate the age-long miseries created for Western civilisation by the presence in its midst of a Body which it too long regarded as alien and even hostile, but which it was equally unable to expel or absorb.' If Mr. Balfour's Zionism is an attempt," he wrote, "to assist 'Western civilisation' to rid itself of its unwelcome Body . . ."

In 1923, Zangwill reversed his view of the Balfour Declaration as inspired by the antisemitic desire to rid England and "Western civilisation" of the "unwelcome" Jews, or by the desire to use Jewish idealism and Jewish need to grab Palestine for the British Empire. "I do not agree," said Zangwill, "with the slanderers of Britain. No, though the Balfour Declaration has been reduced to a scrap of White Paper, Balfour was unquestionably sincere."

In 1905, Zangwill was not so sure about Balfour. Above all, he repudiated Balfour's charge that the Jews had brought "age-long miseries" for Western civilisation. "The Jews have brought 'Western civilisation' not miseries," he said, "but untold blessings." The Liberal Government headed by Campbell-Bannerman and Asquith, which succeeded Balfour's Conservative Government, may not have been as much concerned with Zionism or with a Jewish colony in East Africa because the Liberals did not consider the immigrant aliens a menace to be kept out of the British Isles by the offer of a territory elsewhere. Campbell-Bannerman, Asquith and other Liberal Ministers, including Lloyd George and Winston Churchill, had fought the Aliens Act when it was before Parliament. Asquith related in his speech on the Aliens Act in the House of Commons in 1905, that he had been to the Jews' Temporary Shelter in Whitechapel, and had seen "about 300 to 400 of these refugees who have been pouring in from Russia. If one might judge from their appearance they were not undesirables," he said. He opposed the idea of excluding the emigrants "on the ground of poverty. Some of the best strains in our population were founded in days gone by," he reminded the House, "by persons who could not have stood such a test." And "he wanted to preserve the principle of asylum in this country for the victims of political and religious persecution."

When the Liberal Government was formed, the Home Office, in charge of Lord (then Mr. Herbert) Gladstone, with Herbert Samuel as his Under-Secretary, issued orders for certain easements in the operation of the Act. "The regulations were somewhat relaxed," the *Jewish World* noted. The Board of Jewish Deputies said in its 1906 Annual Report: "No fault can reasonably be found with the attitude of the Government, and it is only fair to say that they have throughout exhibited an anxious and praiseworthy desire to interpret the Act in a generous and merciful sense." But the Act was maintained. It may have been kept to check any antisemitic agitation that its removal might have caused. The feeling of a great many Liberals and Radicals and their Labour allies in the 1906 general election was much like that of Bernard Shaw who, in his interview with Reuben Brainin, after all the Zionist and Territorialist persuasion tried on him by "my friend Zangwill," said: "I don't know why the Jews should be looking for a land of their own. They get on wherever they settle, like Irishmen, who languish in their own country, but flourish in every other."

Asquith refused, even in the days of the Balfour Declaration and Britain's acceptance of the Palestine Mandate, to be carried away by the idea of a Jewish national restoration in Palestine. When Lord (then Herbert) Samuel as a member of the Cabinet submitted a pro-Zionist memorandum to the Cabinet of which Asquith was Prime Minister, he dismissed it as "dithyrambic." He was more in agreement with the anti-Zionist attitude of Lord Samuel's cousin, Edwin Montagu, who was also a member of his Liberal Government.

Yet that Cabinet contained also men like Winston Churchill, who had in the early days of the Liberal Government "endorsed" Chamberlain's conception in what Zangwill calls "a letter of noble eloquence." "I agree most heartily with the spirit of Mr. Zangwill's letter," he had written. "I recognise the supreme attraction to a scattered and persecuted people of a safe and settled home. I do not feel that the noble vision you behold ought to be allowed to fade." There was too Lloyd George, who at the time of Chamberlain's East Africa offer in 1903 had drawn up for Herzl the draft charter for Jewish autonomy in East Africa. Zangwill described him as "a Christian to whom the Jews of the world are more indebted than to any other living statesman—a man who has always tried to help them both by word and deed. So far has he gone in championing us that he has been labelled a Jew himself, or at least an instrument of the 'Elders of Zion.' As I myself figure as one of these Elders . . ." Zangwill concluded. In the House of Commons debate on the East Africa offer, Mr. Lloyd George said that "he had not been one of those who sympathised with the opposition to the establishment of a Jewish colony. He did not himself see any objection to a Jewish settlement."

The opposition was not all on the Jewish side. Sir Edward Grey, in that same debate, objected that "over and over again something which had a perfectly innocent and harmless and, perhaps, even a laudable appearance, had led to serious trouble in parts of Africa, the circumstances of which were not understood in the House, but were understood by the people on the spot. In the present case the people on the spot had doubts and apprehensions."

Sir Charles Eliot, who had resigned his post as High Commissioner for the East Africa Protectorate, objected to "a colony of foreign Jews. If this project had any clear and philanthropic value, I should raise no objection to it," he wrote, "but I cannot see that the sufferings of the indigent and persecuted Jews in Eastern Europe would be appreciably alleviated by settling a few hundred of them in the interior of Africa; for even if the experiment succeeded beyond all expectation there is not room in the limits assigned to the colony for the reception of any number which would sensibly reduce the Jewish population of other countries. In establishing this Zionist colony we shall be devoting a fine piece of country, of which the ordinary British agriculturist could make good use, to an experiment whose success is more than doubtful, and which if successful is not likely to prove of any utility to those in whose interest it is made, but rather to provoke racial conflicts."

Therefore, when the Balfour Government fell, and was succeeded by the Liberals under Campbell-Bannerman and Asquith, the *Jewish Chronicle* wrote in an editorial: "The political crisis which has come upon the country has sadly interfered with the plans of Mr. Zangwill and his friends. A question that will concern many members of our community is the attitude likely to be taken up by the new Colonial Secretary towards the scheme for an autonomous Jewish settlement which has just been deposited by the Ito at the Colonial Office. It remains to be seen whether the Earl of Elgin will prove less sensitive to the plea of the Ito than his predecessor, Mr. Lyttleton. We may recall the speech which Sir Edward Grey (later Lord Grey, the Foreign Secretary) delivered last year on the occasion of a debate on the East African project, in which he displayed the best of good feeling towards our people, although he did not view the East African scheme with strong favour. A statesman who can take so sympathetic a view of the Jewish position will, we are sure, not be found wanting when it is a question of helping in the redemption of our downtrodden brethren in other lands."

In the debate on the East African project in Parliament in June 1904, Sir Edward (Lord) Grey had said that "something had turned on the point that it was a Jewish settlement that was contemplated. They all knew what antisemitic feeling was, and what it gave rise to. But there was another view of the Jewish race, that of millions of persecuted people who had been, through generation after generation, scattered without homes and without hope; and he said frankly that if it was the intention to attempt to provide a refuge and a home for people of that description in the British dominions it would have his entire sympathy. Whether it was wise to make the settlement in the part of East Africa at this time was another matter."

The hope that Sir Edward Grey might help in a plan of a Jewish settlement was not justified. Zangwill approached him in 1906, "asking whether there was some other part of the British Empire where a settlement of Jews would help British interests, but this question he diplomatically ignored. History does not repeat itself, you see," said Zangwill.

In 1906, Lord Selborne, who had been a member of the Balfour-Chamberlain Government which made the East Africa offer and was then High Commissioner for South Africa, spoke at an Ito meeting in Johannesburg. "It seems to me," he said, "that this project of a Jewish colony free to all subjects of the King, but reasonably framing its municipal life in accordance with Jewish sentiment and Jewish custom and Jewish religious observances—it seems to me that this idea should become an ideal at once wise, noble and practicable. And I rejoice as a British subject that the prospect exists of such a colony growing in the coming years into a nation—one of the family of nations in the British Empire." The *Jewish Chronicle* reported the same week from South Africa that General Smuts had joined the local branch of the Ito.

Before that, in October 1905, Zangwill explained to the Maccabeans in London that he had a territory in mind, but did not propose to mention any particular territory. "He had already received so many applications from syndicates, railway companies, etc., that he was sure the suggestion they were about to take up any particular territory would open the door to Stock Exchange speculations. The territory must be decided by a geographical commission sitting secretly. A number of suggestions had been made publicly. Mr. Lucien Wolf suggested Manchuria, and after him, as if it were entirely original, the same territory was mentioned by Dr. Isidore Singer and the Rev. Joseph Levy, of Pittsburg, who seemed to have had actual conferences with Japanese officials on the subject. Surinam, Rhodesia, Western Australia, Canada, Cuba, had all been mentioned, so that he had sometimes felt as if he had been taken up by the devil to a high mountain and shown all the kingdoms of the earth. He would reject Queensland under the conditions mentioned by the assistant to the Agent General. The official was asked, 'Do you think it would be feasible for Jewish philanthropic organisations to assist Jews to emigrate to Queensland?' He answered, 'Provided they work quietly and send the right sort of settlers there would be no objection.' Nothing could more clearly bring out the need of self-government. The area was twelve times that of England and had a population in 1901 of half a million, including coloured. The whole British Empire was in the same weak position. There were less people in all Australia than in the London four-mile radius."

Zangwill's contention that there is room for many millions of people in the under-developed, under-populated parts of the world, and notably in the British Dominions, still holds good. But Zangwill came to realise that while his argument was logically sound, it did not open to him the under-populated territories. "I discovered," he confessed in 1923, "that the population of the world was mostly dog-in-the-manger. In so late an age of history, when every place in the sun has its ferocious claimants, and earth-hunger has passed from an appetite into a greed," he wrote, "the prospects of acquiring a territory are not rosy. At the time Mr. Joseph Chamberlain made his offer to Dr. Herzl the future of East Africa was embryonic. The white population settled in its vast area could not have filled a village church. And when the Ito won Mr. Chamberlain's assent to the project of converting the entire territory into a British Judea, with a Jewish Governor, a country to be, when developed, an equal member of the great family of nations which constitute the British Empire, a prospect was opened out of a really great Jewish future. But the Ito's elaborate memorandum on the subject remains in the archives of the British Colonial Office."

"A further possibility investigated by the Ito," Zangwill wrote, "was Canada, where a population smaller than that of London occupies an area nearly as large as Europe. Sir Wilfred Laurier, then at the height of his power, said to me in 1907: 'You are ten years too late. Ten years ago we were begging for immigrants, and would gladly have given you a tract under local autonomy to be developed into one of the States of a federal Canada.' Lord Strathcona said the same. Ten years ago!" Zangwill went on. "But that had been just the date of the first Zionist Congress. Had Jewry really come together to take counsel, had it opened its eyes and looked round the world instead of shutting them and swallowing the formula stuffed into its mouth by the pre-existing Chovevei Zionists, the first thing it would have perceived would have been Canada, and it would have made instant application to the Canadian Government."

Zangwill and the Ito continued to search the world without result. There were several suitable territories, but the Ito could not obtain the charter and autonomy conditions, nor even the right of large mass immigration which it required. Sir Wilfred Laurier told him, he said, "that if we chose to send out our men—each to make individual application for his 160 acres—and if we so planned their holdings as to produce a Jewish Commonwealth, the Canadian Government would not try to thwart a scheme executed under its constitution. But to carry out such a scheme without the glamour and protection of public policy," he said, "without a charter and a flag, and in face of the Zionist clamour and the anti-Zionist outcry, did not seem feasible. Nor did the numerous perspectives tentatively explored by the Ito in Australia, Mexico and South America seem more calculated to produce the necessary unity."

So Zangwill had to admit himself beaten, and in his search for a territory feel that he was being twitted again with the moon. Herzl too had been twitted with the moon. His employers, Bacher and Benedikt, the owners of the Vienna *Neue Freie Presse*, laughed at him for his constant approaches to rulers and statesmen, Czar and

Kaiser, Pope and Sultan, Ministers and diplomats, now with his idea of Jewish settlement in Mesopotamia, now in El-Arish, now in Cyprus, now in Mozambique, now in East Africa. He had even been willing to consider Salonica. When he was in Constantinople the Sultan asked him: "How many Jews are there in Salonica?" And Herzl thought (as he recorded in his diary): "Is he perhaps thinking of giving us the Salonica area?" Zangwill had the idea that "a city like Salonica, where the Jewish Sabbath came to prevail of itself, might have been made the nucleus of a commonwealth like Venice."

On the third birthday of the Ito, in 1908, Zangwill said he had found that if Mount Zion was forbidden, and the Sultan had set bounds round it, and a large notice-board, "Trespassers will be prosecuted" most of the other mountains in the world "are as forbidden as Mount Zion." "Why should I deceive you?" he said. "We can only try our hardest. The shame lies not in falling, but in not having tried to climb." That was the year of the Commission which the Ito sent out to Cyrenaica. The report was not favourable. "Tragic and unexpected was the report of the Expedition," wrote Zangwill, "with its demonstration that Cyrenaica, by its lack of water, could neither hold nor ever have held a really large population. The unfortunate porosity of the soil made the water largely unconservable and irrecoverable. In the most painfully literal sense of that much-abused metaphor the project did not hold water. The improvement of the water-supply in Cyrenaica is a very costly business, and one that may even baffle the modern engineer. Zionists will note," Zangwill added, "Professor Gregory's remark on the geological superiority of Palestine in this regard."

As it happens, Israel too has its water problem, and much of its agriculture and general reclamation depends on irrigation. And Zangwill proved to have been over-pessimistic about Cyrenaica's ability to hold water. The Italians when they annexed Cyrenaica got over that difficulty. Dr. Eder, Zangwill's cousin and colleague in the Ito, who had been a member of the Cyrenaica Expedition under Professor Gregory, and afterwards became a member of the Zionist Executive, working in Palestine, wrote in 1932: "A fate other than that of being an Itoland has been the lot of Cyrenaica. It never seemed impossible that by the expenditure of several millions some system of water conservation might be carried out. We Ito Jews had no millions."

The Ito turned to another part of Africa, Angola, in the South-West, which belonged to Portugal. Herzl had thought of another African Portuguese colony. In 1903 while he was dealing with Chamberlain over British East Africa he recorded in his diary: "From Chamberlain's Uganda offer I came to Mozambique. I shall try to obtain this land from the Portuguese Government for a Chartered

Company." In 1912 the Portuguese Government passed a Bill authorising the Government to "grant concessions of land on the high plateaus of the Province of Angola to Jewish immigrants who shall become naturalised Portuguese." The Ito sent out an Expedition, again headed by Professor Gregory, who submitted his Report in 1913. It was to be submitted to the Ito Congress in Zurich in August 1914; it never met because the Great War broke out that month. "If I were asked by an ordinary Scotch farmer whether I would advise him to go to Angola or to such countries as Canada, Australia or British East Africa, I would certainly not advise him to go to Angola," Professor Gregory wrote in his Report. "I have considered the suitability of Angola rather for refugees who wish to escape poverty and ill-treatment in their own countries and wish to remain in a Jewish Community. I thought this country more hopeful for refugee immigrants than for any other class. I see no reason why such settlers should not in time build up a colony themselves."

Zangwill's comment was that it was "never the Ito's view that our colonists are to enjoy either a featherbed or a fireproof existence. The Jew, if he wishes to obtain a land of his own, cannot be wholly guaranteed from those risks which were cheerfully run by the founders of every one of those United States to which the Jew now hies himself with such a sense of security." But there were also other difficulties. "The negotiations for Angola," Zangwill confessed, "were handicapped by the fiscal narrowness of Portuguese Colonial policy." In addition, and perhaps more important, it was on the eve of the Great War. Germany and Britain were powerful rivals, also in Africa, where Angola bordered on German West Africa."

Zangwill went to Portugal with Dr. Jochelman. They were received by the President of the Portuguese Government, who told them he supported the Angola Jewish settlement project. The *Jewish Chronicle* reported that he said: "We, the representatives of Young Portugal, must correct the great mistake committed by our ancestors in exiling the Jews. Both nations suffered much from the expulsion act, and I feel convinced that the union of the Portuguese and the Jews will bring happiness to both." The 1914 war killed the Angola project.

During the first years of the Ito's existence the question of Jewish settlement in Australia was put forward by Dr. Richard Arthur, President of the Immigration League of Australia. The Hon. J. W. Taverner, the Agent-General for Victoria, proposed Jewish settlement in Victoria. The Northern Territory of Australia was suggested to the Ito by Mr. Deakin, the Australian Prime Minister. Zangwill did not like it. "The land," he wrote, "would have to be one desirable for other white races—not a derelict tropical desert like the Northern Territory of Australia, once suggested to the Ito by the Premier,

Mr. Deakin. And to be commensurate with the need the territory must, besides being fertile and healthy, be large enough to sustain a real Jewish commonwealth. A toy republic would be no compensation for all the sweat and travail—still less a territory that was not even autonomous." It was Herzl's attitude—an area large enough, and autonomous conditions. It must be on a large scale, or not at all, Herzl insisted. "What is impracticable or unattainable on a small scale need not be so on a large scale." And there must be self-government. "This territory must be on an autonomous basis," Zangwill insisted. "Whoever heard of people colonising except to have liberty to live after their own fashion?"

He was not intimidated by the possibility of "the impossible happening, if through the rise of a Jewish State all the Jews were in the course of centuries banished to it—what a horrible fate!" he exclaimed. "The most cohesive people in history doomed to live together, as the French in France or the Italians in Italy. Children doomed to be born citizens of their own free land, forced to grow up without persecution, compelled to create a Jewish social order, a Jewish art and literature! Pray, do not shudder, it will not happen in your day." He saw the objection of "the comfortable English Jew," but it was not to be expected that the Jewish State "should regulate its policy by those who stay outside."

Even in his leadership of the Ito, Zangwill could not confine himself exclusively to Jewish needs and interests. He was not guilty of the charge that H. G. Wells made against him, that he "cared not a rap for the troubles and dangers of English, French, Germans, Russians, Americans or any other people but his own." When the Ito was founded, Holman Hunt, the painter, wrote to ask "whether in the Jewish colony, which the Ito would wish to set up under British protection, welcome would be given to the aliens of other races." "I will only inform him," Zangwill replied, "that in the recent sudden inrush of Russian refugees into London, a London committee, exclusively of Jews, sent at enormous expense the whole mass of fugitives, Jews and Christians, to Canada and found them excellent situations; so that one of the Christians exclaimed, 'In our country we persecute them and here they help us!' At the same time, I would draw Mr. Holman Hunt's attention to the fact that for the other people he mentions—Russians, Armenians, Poles, Finns, and Moslems—no such tragic necessity exists for a specific land of refuge. Not only have they real fatherlands of their own, but the countries to which they are flying do not hold in advance any prejudice towards them, analogous to antisemitism. Should, however, as Mr. Holman Hunt suggests, a supplementary colony be formed, the two colonies could certainly work in harmonious co-operation in developing that region of the British Empire."

Although the Australian Prime Minister, Mr. Deakin, favoured Zangwill's scheme, his local Premiers would not agree. "Lord Strathcona saw it for Canada, but not Sir Wilfred Laurier," said Zangwill. "Mr. Deakin saw it for Australia, but not his local Premiers. Your Colonial Briton is ever a dog-in-the-manger." "For years," said Zangwill, "I have been treating with Australian statesmen and particularly in regard to West Australia, with its ludicrous population of 200,000 in a million square miles. Australia, which is in such pressing need of population, shows neither magnanimity nor political wisdom. One Australian Government succeeds another, the Press is busy discussing or denouncing the Ito's proposals, but every proposal shatters itself against Australia's passive resistance. With the Labour Party in power even English immigration is difficult. So blind to realities is Australia that it even treats its tropical and arid Northern territory as though to settle there were the white emigrant's dearest dream."

By 1913, when the Ito published the Angola Report, Zangwill was beginning to doubt not only the possibility but also the need of an Itoland. In March 1913 he said: "Nor can I any longer claim that Itoland is an immediate practical necessity—to receive our emigrating masses against whom America is about to close her doors. This was my original ground of appeal: to prepare against the evil day when our brothers would have no outlet of escape from the Pale of persecution. When the Ito was founded this panic fear pervaded all Jewry and was voiced by the late Chief Rabbi in his historic question: 'Wohin? Whither?' To which I replied: To Itoland. But this fear I now believe to be a mere bogey. And if there is no danger of America shutting her doors, there is no need of an immediate land of refuge. And if there were such a need, no new settlement could possibly cope with even a tenth of the emigrants who pour out of Russia into America. With America remaining open, not five per cent. of the emigration would turn to Itoland. It is precisely because I soon discovered that Itoland could not be an immediate practical refuge, if only because of the years necessary to find it," Zangwill went on, "that the Ito, while making the quest for such a land its central line of activity, established also a branch line to America in the shape of the Galveston work. This too had behind it the fear that America, provoked by the congestion of Jews in New York and the Eastern cities, would close her ports to them, and it was thought that if the flow could be diverted inland, west of the Mississippi, the arguments of the Restrictionists would be silenced. But quite apart from its dubious tactical reasons, it was a good move economically. A new and vast region was thus opened up for Jewish emigration. America has ample room for all the six millions of the Pale: any one of her fifty States could absorb them. And next to being in a country of their own, there could be no better fate for them than to be all together in a land of civil and religious freedom, of whose constitution Christianity forms no part, and where their collective votes would practically guarantee them against future persecution."

It was ten years since the British offer of East Africa to Herzl in 1903, and for eight years the Ito had pursued its quest for an Itoland without result. The Galveston work was not a new thing that the Ito had started in 1913, when Zangwill was beginning to have doubts about an Itoland. It was one of the first things he had done, a year after its foundation, in 1906. Zangwill urged on his supporters that "the immediate regulation of immigration cannot await the foundation of a State." "I went to the Rothschilds, who at once financed the European end of it," Zangwill said. He went to Jacob Schiff, in America, who financed the American end. When the Ito was wound up in 1925 Zangwill, while conscious of the failure of the quest for an Itoland, took credit for the "successful Galveston emigration." Lucien Wolf, when Zangwill died, said in his tribute: "It was characteristic of the practical genius of Zangwill that even in the moment of failure he availed himself of a proposal to deal with some of the pressing exigencies of his problem within the practicable limits of conventional emigration. With the support of Lord Rothschild and Mr. Jacob Schiff he carried out the famous Galveston scheme, of which it was truly said in an address presented to him last year, that it 'not only rescued many thousands of our Eastern European brethren from bondage and squalor, but did so on a methodical plan of selection and distribution which, if more largely adopted to-day would render immigration restrictions unnecessary and would recognise in the Jewish emigrants a new and valuable source of economic and social fertilisation."

Professor Max Apt, who devoted himself largely to the study of the refugee problem, commenting on the award of the 1954 Nobel Prize to the United Nations High Commissioner for Refugees, wrote: "If we consider historically his achievements and those of his predecessors, I am sure that Zangwill deserved the Nobel Prize much more for his Refugee work."

The Galveston work stopped in 1914, a few weeks before the outbreak of the war, though not for that reason. Mr. Jacob Schiff explained that there had been several reasons. "The fact that only one line of transportation from Europe to Galveston was available —the North German Lloyd steamers from Bremen—placed the emigrant who wished to come to Galveston more or less at the mercy of this single steamship company, and while on the whole the accommodation furnished was reasonably satisfactory, a journey of twenty-three days in steerage quarters brought in itself discomforts, which frequently led to not always unjustified complaints on the part of the emigrants.

"But what has proved the greatest handicap was the attitude of the Federal Government, which, having an immigration station at Galveston, did not always show itself as sympathetic as the Committee believed it was justified in expecting. The Committee had assumed that its efforts to deflect immigration from the congested centres of the North Atlantic Coast and open a new route leading directly into the American Hinterland, where the labourer is still much in demand, would meet with every encouragement on the part of the Federal authorities, who, however, to the contrary in recent times, since immigration has been transferred from the Department of Commerce and Labour to the newly created Labour Department, have shown what must be called a repressive policy, which has become most marked at Galveston."

"The abandonment of the experiment seems to have been brought about in the main by the unfriendly attitude of the immigration officials at Galveston," the *Jewish Chronicle* commented.

Zangwill had by 1913 lost confidence in an Itoland. Everywhere he found dogs-in-the-manger and antisemites. He returned to his being twitted with the moon. Sir Francis Montefiore had declared that "a politically virgin territory can be found only in the moon." "Not even there, I fear," Zangwill said. "For there is a man in the moon, and he is probably an antisemite." He wrote a letter to one of his Ito colleagues in 1913 suggesting that he should resign from the Presidency of the Ito. "I have not lost faith in the necessity of the Ito," he wrote. "My 'faith' in the Ito is faith in our own human power to do the work, and in the duty to try. Such a faith cannot survive the refusal of all possible territories, some by Jews, the rest by the owners. Nevertheless, I have never spoken of resigning from the Ito, and only from the Presidency in the event of the work descending to a non-political plane. But the fact that you wish to close the Ito merely because of the danger of my resigning shows more than ever I ought to have vacated the chair long ago. To pin an institution to a single life is unheard of."

"In these days of earth hunger, when Great Powers are ready to go to war for any tract, however tropical or derelict . . . where is Itoland to be?" he asked. "There is literally no land on earth which has not been brought to our attention during our long quest." He came back in 1914 to Palestine. By that time his hatred of the Turks had become intensified by the fact that Turkey was at war with Britain, by the side of Germany, and that the Turks were persecuting the Jews in Palestine. "Even if Turkey, under German shrewdness made an offer to the Jews, I for one would hold no truck with the assassins of the Armenians," he said. "The acceptance of Palestine from such a Power would be an anti-climax to Jewish history." But "if Britain took Palestine, she could make no greater stroke of policy than to call in the Jews to regenerate it for her."

Side by side with his hopes for Palestine ran his belief in America as the true centre of Jewish life. "If it turned out that there was no such land in existence that could become an Ito land," he said, "the Ito would acknowledge it frankly. If there remained any such possibility in Palestine, which was also a territory, he would work for Palestine, and recommend to his friends and followers to do likewise. Were it to turn out, however, that there were no chances for an Itoland whether in or outside Palestine, his own inclinations would then tend towards America." "That was the path of salvation which the instinct of the masses found for itself when the pogroms of the early 'eighties began to break up Russo-Jewish life," he said, speaking after "the dispossession of the Turk, the assassin of the Armenians and the despoilers of Palestine," had opened the way to "the return of the Jews to Palestine." He was already disheartened by "the pogrom in Palestine which Jabotinsky accused the British military authorities of having incited." He turned with a sad heart from the "whittled down Balfour Declaration" to "the road of safety and opportunity in America." Even with the Jewish National Home in Palestine, which he described as "the tiny British-Arab territory in Palestine," he believed that "America whose immigration laws will inevitably be relaxed under the dearth of white labour and the need of production, will as inevitably—by whatever port of entry—resume her old place as the Jewish land of refuge."

Whatever the judgment of history will be on the Jewish Territorialist movement, its effect in Jewish life cannot be disregarded. It came into existence when the cry of millions of Jews in the old Russia was "Wohin, Whither?" It investigated a number of territories "with the scrupulous responsibility and thoroughness of a Government," as Dr. Levenberg, the Jewish Agency representative in London admits. No one in those days foresaw the Great War, which came a decade later, and opened the way to the British conquest of Palestine and the beginnings of the Jewish National Home. People were at that time not so wise as we are, who look back on the liberation of Palestine. In 1904 it did not seem likely. The *Jewish Chronicle* published in 1904, a full-page forecast of Jewry in 1950. To the forecaster it appeared that "the Zionist movement has made no progress at all," while "the East African colony, or 'Israelia,' is one of the brightest spots in the world." So short-sighted are people who have not the advantage of looking back at history. The *Jewish Chronicle* forecaster in 1904 was perhaps an Itoist, but Mr. Paul Goodman, who was a Zionist, wrote in his history of Zionism in England that "it seemed in August 1914 as if Zionism were to be relegated to the limbo of lost causes beyond the reach of all possible propaganda." It was the Balfour Declaration and the British Mandate for Palestine that made Zionism a force.

I have a letter Zangwill wrote on 8th January 1915. He says: "I hear Lloyd George and Herbert Samuel have become Palestinians." That was the result of Turkey's entry into the war against Britain, which made the conquest of Palestine a practical British project. Zangwill made an interesting speculation in this connection. If East Africa had been established in those ten years, from 1905 to 1915, as a Jewish State, or a Zionist colony, he suggested, it might have been "in a position to claim and take over the Mandate for Palestine."

He pointed out that the Ito had been searching for a suitable territory for "only eight years, a very brief period." Sir Meyer Spielman, speaking two years after Zangwill's death, in 1928, when he had become a staunch Zionist, like Dr. Eder and other former Ito leaders, said: "I do not think it was generally realised how near we (the Ito) were to success." Even Dr. Max Raisin who, in his supplement to Graetz's *History of the Jews*, bringing it up to date, calls Territorialism a "complete failure," does not overlook the work the Ito did in "regulating immigration to the United States, by way of Galveston in Texas."

When Zangwill wound up the Ito in 1925 he said he was "convinced that the pressure of tragic forces would perpetually bring to the surface this solution of the question." Spontaneously, without knowledge at first of each other, groups of Territorialists came into existence in Germany, Poland, Austria, France, England and America. In July 1935 a Conference of the groups was held in London and the Freeland League for Jewish Territorial Colonisation was formed with Dr. Gaster, Zangwill's old opponent over the Uganda issue, as Honorary President, Mr. Leopold Kessler, a former President of the English Zionist Federation, Chairman, and Dr. Myer S. Nathan, who had been Treasurer of Zangwill's Ito holding the same position. Mrs. Israel Zangwill and her sister Mrs. Ayrton-Gould, who was afterwards active in Parliament in support of Zionism, took part in the early work, and there were several old Itoists in it, including Dr. Jochelman, Mr. Herwald, who had been a member of the Ito Council and, like Dr. Jochelman, a delegate at the Seventh Zionist Congress where the Ito was formed, Dr. Lvovitch and Dr. Syngalovsky, of the World ORT Union, Dr. Kruk, Professor Dr. Max Apt, Dr. Doeblin, the German novelist, and Dr. I. N. Steinberg, who afterwards visited Australia with a plan for a Jewish settlement in East Kimberley, in Western Australia.

Someone wrote to the *Jewish Chronicle* suggesting a revival of the East African project. "Would Great Britain repeat her offer?" he asked. "My suggestion, of course," he said, "does not detract in

the slightest from the Palestine movement." There was an impression
that the Ito had left funds which could be used for the new organisation. Dr. Nathan wrote to me: "I was Honorary Treasurer of the
Ito. You correctly quote the resolution that was come to. No existing
Branch could be found to take over the funds and there was some
proposal of founding a Zangwill Colony in Russia. This fell through,
and in December 1928 the whole balance of £465 was transferred to
the Zangwill Memorial Fund. This was done after consultation with
Mrs. Zangwill, Lucien Wolf, Sir Meyer Spielman, Dr. Jochelman
and everybody else interested in the matter. The papers and archives
of the Ito were sent to the Hebrew University in Jerusalem."

This is not the place to trace the story of the Freeland movement,
which tried to revive Zangwill's Ito, only to encounter everywhere
the same dog-in-the-manger attitude that he and his colleagues in
the Ito found. The trouble was not that there were no places for
settlement, but that they were kept closed. "The world is divided,"
said a Zionist leader, Berl Locker, "into countries where Jews cannot
live and countries which they may not enter."

Dr. Steinberg and others, mostly in the U.S.A., are still running
the Freeland League, "to acquaint Americans with the possibilities
for Jewish settlements in sparsely populated areas of the world."
"It is surprising to learn that the Freeland League is still in existence,"
the *Zionist Review* commented. "One would have thought that since
the creation of the Jewish State Dr. Steinberg would have felt
satisfied that his objective had been attained, even though in
Palestine." Oddly, the *Freeland Magazine* in New York about
the same time quoted an article in an Israeli paper, by Dr. von
Weisl, a former Zionist-Revisionist, urging the need of more land
for Jewish settlement, and taking the view that as expansion beyond
the borders of Israel would mean conflict with the Arab countries,
such land should be sought in territories belonging to European
Governments which cannot exploit them. He suggested the Portuguese colonies, which means Mozambique and Angola, which
Herzl and Zangwill tried, and the French colonies, which sounds like
Madagascar and New Caledonia.

Zangwill's contention is justified that "the globe, though politically
occupied, still contains undeveloped healthy territories. The word
'Utopia' is too loosely flung about," he said. "I happened to write
the word 'nowhere,' and my typist put it 'now here'—exactly the
same letters."

Many people are urging now quite in Zangwill's spirit that an
authoritative inquiry into the problem of peopling the British
Dominions is overdue. Not long before he died, the Australian
Premier, Mr. Chifley, said that Australia "can absorb and support a
population of 20 million, at a conservative estimate." Even at the

present rate of immigration, 850,000 new immigrants entered Australia since the end of the war, including over 25,000 Jews. Chief Rabbi Brodie, who was for many years Rabbi in Melbourne, said on his return from a pastoral tour in Australia that he had seen a tremendous development in Australia's Jewish Community since he left Australia fifteen years before. Jewish life had become intensified with the arrival of Anglo-Jewish settlers and Jewish refugees from Europe. He urged the Board of Deputies of British Jews and the Anglo-Jewish Association to encourage Jewish men and women to emigrate to Australia.

Zangwill was convinced that "America's immigration laws will inevitably be relaxed," and "America will resume her old place as the Jewish land of refuge." After he considered the possibilities of Zionism and Territorialism, he came to the conclusion that neither will solve the Jewish question—that there is no one solution. "I freely admit," he said, "that after Territorialism (which includes Zionism) America is the best solution of the Jewish question." That this should be his conclusion after a lifetime of work in the Zionist and Territorialist movements, started under what was to him primarily Herzl's Zionist influence, would not have disconcerted Zangwill, for he knew that "movements started to produce a certain result may produce the exact contrary. Herzl's attempt to destroy the Diaspora has ended in arresting its natural dissolution."

America was to Zangwill always "the great country of Jefferson, Lincoln and Theodore Roosevelt." He saw its dangers, the tendencies which led to such grotesqueries as the Ku Klux Klan, but he was sure that the spirit of Washington and Lincoln would assert itself. He was a Jew who knew that "the Pilgrim Fathers came straight out of the Old Testament, and that our Jew-immigrants are a greater factor in the glory of the American Commonwealth than the freak-fashionable who are undoing the work of Washington and Lincoln." "Is America forsaking the ideals of her founders?" he asked. "Alas, ideals can be forsaken swiftly or easily enough, and every day sees America receding further from them. Her recent legislation restricting immigration," he said, "is a repudiation of the ideal symbolised by her Statue of Liberty." He did not suggest that the American Jews were different from other Americans. "Though American Jewry has proved itself boundlessly generous in relieving the misery of the East European Jews, I cannot help suspecting," he said, "that its older elements are themselves relieved by the stemming of the immigration."

"The exclusion of healthy and willing immigrants" was a crime to Zangwill. "America professes to have the right," he said, "to exclude and re-ship the poverty-stricken European immigrant after he has sold off his all in the quest for a better labour-market."

One of Herzl's friends, Dr. Katznelson, of the Jewish Colonial Trust, said when he visited America in 1914, a few weeks before the outbreak of the war, that Ellis Island, where the immigrants who were to be sent back were detained, "floats on the tears of the immigrants. The policy of exclusion or restriction of immigrants, however mercifully carried out, is inevitably cruel." The tragedy was to be shut out of America. Inside there was hope and opportunity. "The Jews demand the freedom of the lands," Zangwill said. Not the Jews only. For "Moses told the Jews 'Thou shalt love thy neighbour as thyself.' "

When Zangwill set out the causes for which he had "been personally a fighter," they were, in this order, "the movements for the emancipation of women, for the rights and re-integration of the Jews, for the amelioration of our drama, for the freedom of emigration and the maintenance of the American ideal, for the clarification of creeds, for human brotherhood and peace." Always, in spite of and outweighing her lapses and her aberrations and, among some Americans, "the hardening to a sort of Nordic nationalist nonsense," Zangwill looked towards "the maintenance of the American ideal"; he saw "the genius of America" like "a lamp cheering all humanity with the radiance of a nobler world." "I saw," he said, "that America's contribution in good work of every sort far outweighed that of all the rest of the world put together." "The great American ideals," he proclaimed, "are Jewish ideals, and their destruction would be more tragic for the world than even the destruction of the Jews." Therefore he called to American Jewry to stand by those ideals. "If Europe has taken the wrong turning," he said, "your mission is to help America to take the right one, to help America to keep American."

The Jewish Territorial Organisation brought Zangwill to America. His great ode to America, his play *The Melting Pot*, "sprang directly," he said, "from the author's concrete experience as President of the Emigration Regulation Department of the Jewish Territorial Organisation," and its purpose, he explained, was "to bring home to America both its comparative rawness and emptiness, and its true significance and potentiality for history and civilisation." "Here shall they all unite to build the Republic of Man and the Kingdom of God. What is the glory of Rome and Jerusalem where all nations come to worship and look back, compared with the glory of America, where all races and nations come to labour and look forward!"

Chapter VIII

THE PLAYWRIGHT

"CRITICS have argued whether the *Melting Pot* is a good play or a bad play from the point of view of dramatic art," Holbrook Jackson wrote, "but such considerations in the light of the uplifting tragedy of a race could only occur to whippersnapper minds. *The Melting Pot* succeeds by power of impression and not by approximation to canons of art. It is not a problem play even, it is a message play, a modern Gospel of race-fusion. Not since Walt Whitman wrote *Leaves of Grass* have we had so inspiring a picture of America." One might argue that a play that "succeeds," by whatever "power," has achieved what it set out to achieve. St. John Ervine, who speaks as a dramatist, thought *The Melting Pot* was "written with all the stage skill which Mr. Zangwill possesses," and that it "could hardly fail to be successful," because it appealed "to a people of noble sentiments, and the theme fitted in with the policy of the American Government in the matter of immigration until the end of the First World War."

Though Zangwill wrote a number of plays, and had been writing plays almost from the beginning of his literary career—his first play was produced in the West End of London the same year his book *Children of the Ghetto* appeared—the dramatists would not accept him as a playwright. They insisted that he was a novelist. Sutro, who was a fellow-playwright, and a friend and admirer of both Shaw and Zangwill, found Zangwill's plays, as he wrote in his note on Zangwill in the *Dictionary of National Biography*, "nearly all works of merit, but a certain formlessness that was apparent in his novels bulked more largely in his plays and detracted from their value." Yet he held that they "revealed high dramatic gift and penetrating insight." The writer of the note on Zangwill in the *Encyclopedia Britannica* thought "he was greater as a playwright than as a novelist."

Wells, who unlike Zangwill and Bennett did not attempt to write plays, thought the "tremendous work of human reconciliation and elucidation" could be done much better in the novel—"Regarded as a medium for startling and thought-provoking things, the Stage seems to me an extremely clumsy and costly affair." But Zangwill, who discovered to his cost, that the stage was indeed a "costly affair," was convinced that he could write plays. A year before he died, he wrote of his plays that "theatrical justice has not yet been done them. The judgment of my greatest contemporaries emboldens me to think so."

As a young man Zangwill had written a paper on "The Drama as a Fine Art." "Everything begins as something else," he said there. "And every form of Art has grown out of Religion. The first drama was a religious Dance. When David danced before the Ark or— better—when Miriam sang her Song of Deliverance and the women went out after her with timbrel and dances, we have in germ the three great arts—Poetry, Music and the Ballet." He thought "the Drama which began as a branch of religion may with advancing civilisation return to its old role as a potent factor in the life of the peoples."

"What we need from our stage is a drama that helps us to move on the high plane," he wrote many years later. He wanted it to "feed its spiritual fires," "a drama raised to the atmosphere of *Hamlet*, *Oedipus* or *Antigone*." "Mr. Zangwill, regarding literature as before all things a spiritual force, writes a powerful and interesting play," Shaw said of Zangwill's *The Next Religion*.

Zangwill fought battles for his plays. His last venture in the theatre, which ruined and killed him, was one continuous battle, in which he was defeated. Of his play, *The War God*, he complained that it was "mysteriously assassinated in the heart of London in broad daylight. It was followed—soon after the outburst of war—by the Foreign Office prohibition of my play *The Melting Pot*, at the request of Russia. A third play of mine, *The Next Religion*, had already been prohibited by the Lord Chamberlain." The fight against the censor was one in which all his fellow-playwrights were engaged. Shaw's play *Mrs. Warren's Profession* had been prohibited. When the Censorship Inquiry was held, Zangwill appeared as a witness, and in what Mr. A. E. Wilson, in his book *Edwardian Theatre* calls "his very forthright evidence," spoke of "a play now running in London with a character who follows Mrs. Warren's profession as the central figure, and that is the most popular play in London. The difference between that play and Shaw's is that its central figure appears in a life of gaiety, while Shaw's pictures not the pleasures but the perils of vice." "If we were to abolish the censorship," Zangwill was asked, "do you think we should be approximating to French ideas?" "Then so much for the hypocrisy of the British people," he answered, "if it is only by the censorship that they are prevented from being as bad as the French." He quoted from his book, *Without Prejudice*, a passage where he had written: "If I were State Censor of the English Stage I should suppress half our plays for indecency. The other half I should suppress for their fatuity." "I would, if I were Censor," he said. "That shows the absurdity of having any individual as Censor." His idea was to leave it to the police to prosecute for indecency. Not by police suppression, but by trial in a police court. Trial in a police court has the advantage of publicity, he said, whereas censorship means a secret trial.

"Mr. Zangwill is an ambitious dramatist; why is he not a more successful one? He chooses great and serious themes," *The Nation* wrote in 1918. "Style is not wanting to him. He can be serious and eloquent; he not only possesses wit, but displays it with prodigality. Did a mischievous fairy provoke him to the dramatic career and deny him the gift for it? No; he has written more than one fine play, and he can arrange the business of the stage with dexterity and brilliancy. All that one feels is that he has not completely arrived. Something of concentration is wanting; something of proportion. Mr. Zangwill is a little too copious; jokes and fine writing come rather too easily to him. When he speaks out and thinks out, when he has got a subject that exactly suits him, when he can write a scene in which nothing comes amiss, and purpose, colouring and characterisation work together, he should produce the stuff that endures."

Zangwill knew what was the secret of play-writing. "Confined to a few feet of space and a few hours of time a play must achieve a concentration and a tenseness undemanded of the novelist," he wrote. But he could not resist overwriting. He could not check what Mrs. Zangwill called "his delightful but sometimes obstreperous wit." He himself said of his play *We Moderns*: "My young friend Thomas Moult writes me that the first two movements" (he meant the first two acts—Zangwill had in the programme called them movements —the three acts being Allegro, Andante and Adagio) "were 'not too long but too rich.'" St. John Ervine wrote of another of his plays: "One has the sensation that if Mr. Zangwill only gets going, nothing in the heavens above or the earth beneath, or the waters under the earth will stop him. The intention is good, and the purpose sound, but the play leaves me longing for the Zangwill who wrote *The Children of the Ghetto* and *The King of Schnorrers*."

It is of a piece with Matheson Lang's description of Zangwill coming to his dressing room after one of his performances of *The Merchant of Venice*—"Israel Zangwill in his happily impulsive way sat down and nearly talked my head off." His views, expressed "with great vehemence." "were so arresting and convincing that they entirely won me over," he admits, but "he nearly talked my head off."

"He could have been a great dramatist," M. J. Landa concluded his chapter on Zangwill in his book *The Jew in Drama*. "He had every accomplishment for the role, and a far more complete equipment than others who hold the boards that he could not conquer. He had a flair for the theatre. He had qualities that stamped him as unique. That uniqueness was his undoing. He laid down his own rules and was impatient because of the reluctance of the Press and public to accept them as standards of measurement."

Zangwill was not content with staging his plays. "I always say to dramatists, 'publish your play,' " he wrote. "Henry James observed to me once, 'Publish your play if you are not ashamed of it. Let us see what your success looks like in cold print.' "

Zangwill admired Shaw. "Such a lord of the European stage as the author of *Pygmalion*," he called him. *The Showing up of Blanco Posnet* was to him a play "that would hallow Good Friday," as against other plays "that would profane Bank Holiday." Shaw called *The Showing up of Blanco Posnet* "a religious tract," which explains its attraction for Zangwill. It had the added attraction of being forbidden by the Censor. Zangwill found *Joseph and his Brethren*, which Louis N. Parker made out of the Bible story, "a purely pagan play," while Shaw's *Androcles and the Lion* was "a Christian mystery-play," and *The Doctor's Dilemma* "came as a special delight." "In an era of pyjama plays" Shaw's plays to him were sanctified. It was not a matter only of the theme—it was the spirit. That was his feeling too about "Jewish plays." They could be, he said, "plays expressing the Jewish spirit, in which there need not be any Jewish characters at all, but the thing itself must be of a Jewish character." He claimed that his play *We Moderns* "belongs to this class."

Arnold Bennett, who found that Zangwill talked too much, made that same complaint about Shaw. "Shaw talked practically the whole time, which is the same thing as saying he talked a damned sight too much," he wrote. He didn't think much of some of Shaw's plays. His verdict on *Pygmalion* was· "on the whole poor. Most of the characterisation is quite rotten. The last act is foozled." "I had to go to Shaw's *Heartbreak House*," Bennett wrote. "Three hours fifty minutes of the most intense tedium. I went to sleep twice, fortunately." Bennett went to see Zangwill's *Melting Pot* when it was produced in London in 1914. "A dreadfully bad piece," he decided. "We left after the third act. Hollow, reverberating with clumsy echoes of old-style eloquence. No human nature in it, except a bit regarding home life of Jews." Zangwill returned the compliment. In his contribution to the series "My Religion," to which Bennett also contributed, he wrote, as his closing sentence: "I have always regretted that Arnold Bennett annexed the title *The Great Adventure* to an insignificant play."

When Shaw was expelled during the First World War from the Dramatists' Club, because of the views he expressed about the war, "Zangwill would have resigned," Shaw wrote in a letter to Mr. Hesketh Pearson, "but I persuaded him to stay and carry on his campaign for the admission of women to the club." Zangwill did not agree that a literary society could expel a member because of his political opinions. But he disagreed very strongly with Shaw's opinions about the war, and said so at that time. When Shaw suggested there was nothing to choose between German and British militarism, Zangwill wrote: "Mr. Shaw's pretext for beclouding a distinction which is as clear to his uncommon as to my common sense, is that in practice British militarism and Prussian work out much the same. But then, they are not always *in* practice, and it is not for a writer to put together what a merciful heaven has put asunder."

"If this war, with all its world-tragedy and epical happenings does not suggest to us a modern handling of the drama," Zangwill wrote, "we may well agree that upon the high tragedian the curtain has been rung down. Tragedy, interpreted as the clash of forces, and with the symbolisation of these forces by individuals, or by masses seen through individuals, is our modern form of the higher drama." He found its exemplification in Galsworthy's *Strife*, in Hardy's *Dynasts*, whose "atmosphere of Fate," he found a "far more serious contribution to the modern drama"—"The *Armageddon* of Mr. Stephen Phillips, though its matter is burningly topical, is not a modern drama at all," he said—in Maeterlinck's *Hour of Destiny*, the Maeterlinck who in "The Hour of Destiny," taught by the German occupation of Belgium, by "nameless tortures and numberless dead" "enjoined to destroy 'root and branch' as ruthlessly as Samuel hewed Agag in pieces before the Lord, an enemy who is in secret alliance with the evil influences of the earth." Shaw had not yet written *St. Joan*. "Think," cried Zangwill, "what a contemporary English poet would have made of Joan of Arc! Think what even the author of *Henry VI* made of her."

Then strangely, because his own plays were mostly topical and concerned with causes, Zangwill pointed out the risks of topical drama and the drama of causes. "Like the political pamphlet, it is apt to become obsolete," he said, "by its own success or failure, and to turn into a platitude or an absurdity. The poet is safest in limiting himself to the clash of forces. These abide eternally, and appeal afresh and under constantly changing aspects to every fresh generation. To the apostle of causes the lack of the didactic will appear as a grave defect, but if the poet has written greatly he cannot avoid teaching." And unlike Wells, he held that "the drama, whose life is clash, is the truest of all literary forms."

Zangwill was very early attracted to the theatre. Not only as a boy spectator, watching the performance at the "Brit" in Shoreditch or the Pavilion in Whitechapel, when he hadn't enough coppers after he had climbed the gallery stairs, to buy himself "a ginger-beer and Banbury," on sale during the entr'actes, but as an aspiring playwright. When he was sixteen he "had written a three-act farcical comedy at the request of an amateur dramatic club. I had written out all the parts," he recalled, "and I think there were rehearsals. But the play was never produced." He entered at the same time a competition in a paper called *Society*, which wanted a short novel and a comedietta. His story, called "Professor Grimmer," won the prize and was published; "my comedietta was lost in the post." He had two playlets produced in the West End of London in 1892, the same year that *Children of the Ghetto*, was published; and the same year, too, that Shaw's first play *Widowers' Houses* was produced. They are both slight, amusing farcical comedies, one of them *The Great Demonstration*, being very near burlesque. This kind of thing was popular at the time, and Zangwill's early efforts appeared in the same series of published plays for performance by amateur and touring companies with Brandon Thomas, whose *Charley's Aunt*, first produced at the same West End Theatre the same year as Zangwill's first play, is "still running," and with Sydney Grundy and Louis N. Parker. Zangwill was sure he could do as well. *The Great Demonstration* was written in collaboration with Louis Cowen, his collaborator in *The Premier and the Painter*, and was announced as such. But the play was advertised as "The only dramatic work by Mr. Zangwill," and the Press spoke of it as though Zangwill alone had written it. *The Theatre* wrote: "Mr. Zangwill is a wit of the first water"; another paper found it "packed full of clever things in the vein that has made the *Bachelors' Club* and the *Old Maids' Club*."

He dramatised *Children of the Ghetto*, which was produced with considerable success in America in 1899, and less successfully the same year at the Adelphi Theatre in London. He thought highly of it. In 1925 he wrote that "although there are a number of Jewish dramatists and Jewish plays in existence, there cannot be said to be any complete school of Jewish drama. I had hoped that my play *Children of the Ghetto* might have formed the basis for such a school." The same year he drew attention to a note in the *New York Times* referring to "my *Children of the Ghetto* as 'that masterpiece of our national drama.' " Mr. George Tyler, who produced *Children of the Ghetto*, said "the play was a triumph. But the triumph lasted only from Monday to Thursday. The news came that the Boers had licked the tar out of the British at Spion Kop. With that news the London theatre went out like a light. Everything closed down. Absolutely nothing but to swallow our defeat. But affairs in South Africa had nothing to do with the intrinsic merits of *Children of the Ghetto*. I was more certain than ever that it was as grand as it really was. And Zangwill did more than make up our losses to us. He wrote *Merely Mary Ann*, which did the job, and later, for good measure, presented us with *The Melting Pot*."

Zangwill had turned his book into a play; and as nearly always happens with books turned into plays, it "was overburdened with details, and the drama was well-nigh lost in the medley." One critic suggested of one of Zangwill's plays that "if anyone but the author had adapted his book it might have been more worth the trouble of production. He only seems to have lifted chunks out of his book."

For a man who said (in 1898) that "I don't believe in distorting one's own books to make plays," Zangwill did a lot of turning his books into plays. In *Children of the Ghetto*, and his other dramatised books, like *The King of Schnorrers*, he was anxious to get as much of his book as he could on the stage, with the result that too much got in the way of the acting. There was too much concentration too on the strangeness and the oddities of the "Peculiar People of the Ghetto." There was the actor who dogged the poet Imber, who had been Zangwill's model for Melchitzedek Pinchas, to study his mannerisms and eccentricities, and accentuated them into caricature. Clement Scott in his notice of the play called Pinchas a "most vulgar stage Hebrew." I haven't seen *The Children of the Ghetto*. But I remember how in *The King of Schnorrers*, the actor who played Yankele thought it was his job to indulge in a lot of exaggerated "Jewish gesture," and mock "Jewish speech." I know that in the book Yankele, who is an immigrant from Poland, has a foreign pronunciation. Yankele was "a clumsy, stooping schnorrer, with a cajoling grin on his mud-coloured, hairy face, short, even dingier than da Costa, and with none of his dignity," but he was not "a low comedian." Zangwill didn't want the play produced as low comedy. He wrote a letter in 1905, complaining of the way Jacob Adler, who was a fine dramatic Yiddish actor, was interpreting his characters in a New York production of *The King of Schnorrers*. "I am particularly annoyed at Mr. Adler's misconduct," he wrote to Bernard Richards. "We meant him to make a dignified character-creation in comedy. The third act, for example, is almost tragic, and could not possibly resemble 'musical farce.'" The New York correspondent of the *Jewish Chronicle* reported that "Jacob Adler, the great Jewish actor, is playing a dramatised form in Yiddish of Zangwill's *King of Schnorrers*, which has been turned into real opera-bouffe. The Zangwillian sallies are lost in the midst of much buffoonery."

Merely Mary Ann, one of Zangwill's most "pleasing" and success-ful plays, was another dramatisation from his own stories. It seems to have been successful, when it was performed at the Duke of York's Theatre in 1908, with Henry Ainley, Gerald du Maurier and Eleanor Robson in the chief parts. Mr. George Tyler, who produced it, regarded the play as one of his successes. "It did the job," he says. "It was in *Merely Mary Ann*," he said, "that Eleanor Robson was first recognised. We had been trying to bring her along. But it took *Merely Mary Ann* to demonstrate to the public at large what she could be like. You don't have to take my word for what Eleanor Robson was like in *Merely Mary Ann* days," he writes. "The effect she had on George Bernard Shaw should prove my point. I've never seen anything like the way Eleanor Robson conquered the English stage in a single night in that role. After the play Mr. Shaw wanted to see me. He remarked that as I'd put on some plays of his he thought he might come round and get acquainted. He wouldn't have dinner. He said he could get the proper vegetarian dinner only at home. All during the meal he directed everything he said at Miss Robson. This gave me an idea. I suggested that perhaps he might like to write something for Miss Robson. Maybe he would, he said. When Miss Robson was in San Francisco, half-way through a highly prosperous tour with *Merely Mary Ann*, there arrived a cable from Shaw. It said that he had finished a play for Miss Robson—*Major Barbara*—and would I please see that Miss Robson was in England in time for rehearsals. I answered that I couldn't chuck a highly profitable tour. Shaw answered that I'd be sorry. It was years before he got through sending me direct and indirect messages telling me just how much damage I'd done Miss Robson in particular and the theatre in general by being unreasonable."

It sounds like a success, but reading the play, and his story from which Zangwill dramatised it, one would not expect it. It was a typical Frohman piece, and Zangwill, who said "Frohman never produced an 'unhappy ending,' never allowed his dramatists to suggest that a beloved and blameless person might be crushed mercilessly between two giant forces at clash," provided a happy ending to the play, which is not in the book, Mary Ann become Marian, almost Lady Marian, and gaily surrounded by Lady Chalmers and Lady Foxwell and Lady Rowena and Lord Valentine. Zangwill once referred to a musical comedy writer as "a confectioner." He ran the danger of becoming one himself in *Merely Mary Ann*. It is true Sinclair Lewis thought Lancelot, the handsome young composer in *Merely Mary Ann*, an interesting figure, reminding him of the "charming" Floppington in Zangwill's *Premier and the Painter*. But here too Zangwill had laid himself open to the danger of his Jewish music publisher, Brahmstein, the forerunner of Pappelmeister in *The Melting Pot* being played as a burlesque comic Jew. When Zangwill heard this was how Brahmstein was being played in the American production, he resented it and wrote to New York to have it stopped. Yet there was something in Brahmstein, as Zangwill created him, that invited such an interpretation. Landa, in *The Jew in Drama*, accuses Zangwill of having deliberately drawn conventionally unpleasant stage Jews like Karl Blum in *The War God*, and the vulgarised Karl Blum, Baron Gripstein in *The Cockpit* and in *The Forcing House*.

Merely Mary Ann was popular in its day as a light comedy, and achieved a successful production in 1906 at the home of light comedy, the Burg Theatre in Vienna, where his friend Dr. Herzl, a Viennese, had several of his own light comedies produced. It was filmed several times. *Children of the Ghetto* too was filmed. Zangwill could, but for the agony of his divided mind, which in the very act of turning out quips and puns and jokes, drove him to teach and preach and protest, have become a popular "confectioner" of light comedy. One of his actresses, Jane Bacon, said after his death that he "could have been a popular playwright. When I played for him I was astonished at the world-wide popularity of *Merely Mary Ann*." His political plays and his religious plays, she said, had "that discursiveness which makes Zangwill's later work so difficult to present." He would not be content with his popular successes. "Personally I was saved by my daily business of plucking Jews out of the pale of Christian massacre," he said, "from regarding modern life as altogether 'a huge good-natured comedy.' " His political plays and his religious plays were forced out of him by his inability to escape the realisation that there was "so much mass-tragedy."

In 1904, Frohman commissioned Zangwill to write a play for him, which was an elaboration of one of his short stories, *The Serio-Comic Governess*. "Zangwill has written so little for the stage," Mr. Frohman said when he made the announcement, "that he is almost unknown as a dramatist, but I am sure he is the coming man." *The Serio-Comic Governess* is an Irish convent girl who comes to London as a governess, shows a talent for dancing and singing and finds her way to the music-hall stage. "It was one of those early Victorian halls of the people, with fixed stars and only a few meteors." "How delicious," she says, "to have an emotion which you feel will last forever, and which you know won't." While he was writing it Zangwill made a study of the music-hall. There was a note in the gossip-columns of the time, that Zangwill was busy in the wings of the Alhambra Music Hall, during the performance, "in the interests of the comedy he is writing for Cissie Loftus and Charles Frohman. One of the scenes takes place in a music-hall, and Mr. Zangwill wanted to get the right local colour." This note was linked to another in the same paragraph, that "Mr. Zangwill is to be married tomorrow, and will complete the play in the South of Spain." The play was produced in New York at the end of 1904, but it was "a complete failure," the New York Press reported, "despite Cecilia Loftus (the star in the title role) and her talent, for whose quality and range great opportunity is given. Without her the play would soon be off the boards." A later report indicates that the play did better in the provinces than in New York. "*The Serio-Comic Governess* is quite a success on the road, touring the provinces," it said. Zangwill had "made some changes" in it between the New York production and the provincial tour, "which helped to give it vogue," but according to Mr. Liebler, his agent, this was not done without a good deal of "Zangwill's insistence that the weaknesses complained of were not important, and the Zangwill 'stubbornness' which was to embitter his relations with other producers (he managed to get himself thoroughly disliked by everybody who had anything to do with the production of *The Serio-Comic Governess*)."

At the time of the luckless production of *Children of the Ghetto* in London, Beerbohm Tree announced that he had engaged Zangwill to dramatise for him *Uriel Acosta*. Owing to the British reverses in the Boer War, which cast a gloom over the theatre, the idea was dropped. It was not to have been a dramatisation of Zangwill's own *Uriel Acosta* in *Dreamers of the Ghetto*, but Zangwill's version of the play of that name by the German novelist and dramatist, Karl Ferdinand Gutzkow, which was first produced in 1847. It was not intended however to be a straight translation. It was (with a fore-shadowing of the later *War God* which Tree produced), to have been "in blank verse throughout."

Zangwill's *Great Demonstration* was "a mere trifle, a light trifle, but nevertheless a dramatic trifle." The characters are a young man with idealistic Socialist views, a rich heiress who must by the terms of the will marry this young man, and has taken a post as parlour-maid in the house where he lives, to see what he is like; they fall in love—so much that he doesn't want to see the heiress he is required to marry—and a working man named Bill Boggles, who sponges on the Socialist idealist and steals from him. There is a sneer at the working man's Socialism, on the lines of "What's yours is mine." The parlour-maid, Mary, also referred to as Mary Ann, says: "He practises what you preach." To which the retort comes: "But I don't preach what he practises. What I preach is division, what he practises is sub-traction."

Six Persons is more amusing. It has only two characters, a young girl, played at the first performance by Irene Vanburgh, and a young man; they meet at a dance and become engaged. The next morning both want to back out. She is sure she could marry much better. He can't understand what made him propose. "It isn't easy to tell a girl you've made a mistake and have come to back out." Both act as though they were unpleasant people, but can't keep up the pretence and finally discover that they love each other.

Zangwill continued for a time to turn out these dramatic trifles. He did a short burlesque pantomime called *Alladin at Sea*, a one-act play *At the Moment of Death*, also called *The Moment Before*, which "starts with the first hour and ends on the stroke of the twelfth," and *The Revolted Daughter*, a three-act comedy. He collaborated with Karl Marx's daughter, Eleanor Marx Aveling, in an Ibsenite skit called *The Doll's House Repaired*. His mind kept running to skits

and burlesques and farces. Even afterwards, when he was President
of the Ito, in 1906, he announced that he "lightened his serious
labours in connection with the Ito by writing a comedy called
Nurse Marjorie, which will begin its career in New York in the
autumn, with Miss Eleanor Robson in the title role."

But his mind was busy too with more serious drama. He wrote
an article discussing the Beilis blood libel trial in Russia as a theme
for drama. Wilson Barrett, the actor-manager, who had made a
popular success of *The Sign of the Cross* said in 1894 that he wanted
Zangwill to collaborate with him on a modern drama, but Zangwill
was too busy, "and this story is one that cannot afford to wait."
Reversing his usual method, Zangwill wrote *Jinny the Carrier*
first as a play, which was produced in Boston in March 1905, and
was followed by an English run. He wrote the novel of that name in
1919.

Soon after he had completed his dramatisation of *The Children
of the Ghetto* Zangwill set to work on a dramatisation of his novel
The Mantle of Elijah. "I can recall," wrote Mr. Liebler, "reading the
proof sheets of the magazine serialisation of the novel, which my
father had brought home at the time when the possibility of its
dramatisation first came up for discussion. I can recall disappointment with Zangwill's scenario or outline of his proposed dramatisation. The proposal came to nought."

The King of Schnorrers, which was first printed as a serial in
Jerome K. Jerome's magazine *The Idler*, in 1893, was written, so
Zangwill confessed, in his light-hearted burlesque mood, "merely
to amuse myself and to amuse idlers by incarnating the floating
tradition of the Jewish Schnorrer." He was so light-hearted about it
that Bensusan told me Zangwill had meant to kill it half-way, "had
condemned him to death, and had reprieved him on the intercession
of Jerome who was greatly impressed by it." But his interest in "The
King" grew with the years. By 1926, the year of his death, he was
writing in a note for the London *Jewish Graphic*, which was serialis-
ing the story: "*The King of Schnorrers* has wandered far and wide
since he first appeared in *The Idler*. There is hardly any country in
which he has not made his appearance, nor any language in the
world in which he has not schnorred and I have been much amused to
see how artists of different countries have created him pictorially.
He has added the word Schnorr to the vocabulary of many languages
as a verb, and Schnorr is now conjugated even in French. Now here
he is again in the *Jewish Graphic*, bringing him to the knowledge of a
young generation that has grown up and knows not Manasseh."

A West End production of *The King of Schnorrers* in London in
1950 had a disappointing Press; I felt the production was at fault.
Ernest Milton, who played the King as though he were acting

Benedick, missed the big, impudent, swaggering robust bravado of the part. And Yankele, played by the Yiddish actor, Tzelniker, was a Jewish "low comedian." The spirit of the play was wrong. The production was slow. It dragged, and became tedious. Everyone struck attitudes and poses, almost as if it were a ballet or a mime. Mr. Trewin said in the *Observer* that Mr. Milton played "The King in the wrong key. This master-beggar of eighteenth-century London should have broader, quicker treatment." "The actors," said the *Daily Telegraph*, "seemed not to have caught the riotous spirit of the piece. The funeral pace was calculated to break the back of the most accomplished farce."

Zangwill wrote *The Melting Pot*, which was produced in America in 1908, and in London not till January 1914, as a play, not a dramatisation of one of his novels or short stories. It exists only as a play. Zangwill did not turn it afterwards into a novel based on the play. Nevertheless, Mr. St. John Ervine did not find it convincing as a play. There were complaints in the Press that the play had not been sufficiently "refined in the melting pot of art, which refines bulk to intensify quality." "Reduced by three fourths," a critic wrote, "David" (Zangwill's hero) "might have been sterling stuff."

It is generally assumed that Zangwill coined the term "melting pot" in the sense in which it is used in America, and that it gained its vogue through his play. Its popularity certainly derives from Zangwill's play. But the term was used before him. When I was in New York I read in *The New York Times* that the late Rabbi Samuel Schulman, of Temple Emanu-El, New York, had "in the early years of this century coined the phrase 'The Melting Pot' to describe the process of Americans 'becoming one and equal as the American ideals of brotherhood are increasingly realised.'" Looking it up, I found a report in 1908, while Zangwill's play was being produced in America, that Rabbi Schulman had "anticipated the title of Zangwill's new play in a sermon delivered on 30th May 1907." I imagine Zangwill must have been at work already by that time on his play. But the phrase is 125 years older than Rabbi Schulman's sermon. It was used in 1782, by the French-American, Michel St. Jean de Crevecœur, also known as Hector St. John, one of America's first back to Nature writers, in his book *Letters from An American Farmer*. "Here in America," he wrote, "individuals of all nations are melted into the race of men." *The Literary History of the United States* says "the melting pot theory was assumed since the time of Crevecœur, and translated into a crusade by such men as Israel Zangwill and Theodore Roosevelt." Zangwill's play certainly gave the term its vogue, and it was with Zangwill's play in their minds that New Yorkers in 1914 celebrated "the Dutch tercentenary of New York with a street historic pageant, emblematic of the progress from the

Dutch Settlement to the present day. Of some sixty or seventy floats in the procession, far and away the best was 'The Melting Pot.' "

"The melting pot theory was translated into a crusade by such men as Israel Zangwill and Theodore Roosevelt" says *The Literary History of the United States*. Roosevelt liked Zangwill's play. He attended the first performance in Washington, and "applauding it very heartily leaned over his box and shouted to Mr. Zangwill, 'It's a great play.' " Zangwill's version is that "Roosevelt shouted boyishly at the end, 'That's a great play, Mr. Zangwill, that's a great play.' "

Zangwill, displeased with the dramatic critics, who told him that the play "as a work of art for art's sake simply does not exist," consoled himself with the thought that "Mr. Roosevelt, with his multifarious American experiences as soldier and cowboy, hunter and historian, police-captain and President, comes far nearer the ideal spectator, for this play at least,than Mr. Walkley," who was the critic of the London *Times*, and had called the *Melting Pot* "romantic claptrap." "To Theodore Roosevelt, in respectful recognition of his strenuous struggle against the forces that threaten to shipwreck the Great Republic which carries mankind and its fortunes, this play is, by his kind permission, cordially dedicated," reads the inscription on the fly-leaf of the printed *Melting Pot*.

The Melting Pot, Zangwill confessed in his book *The War For the World*, which he wrote eight years after the play, and two years after it was printed with this dedication to Roosevelt, "was but a dramatic expansion of these ideas—'A fig for your feuds and vendettas! Germans and Frenchmen, Irishmen and Englishmen, Jews and Russians—into the crucible with you all. God is making the American!' "

That crucible idea brought Zangwill a lot of trouble. The idea must have been in his mind a great deal, because he had originally intended naming the play "The Crucible." Jewish newspapers and periodicals, Rabbis and others persisted in interpreting what he meant as a melting of the Jew in the crucible, and his disappearance. "The Jewish pulpits of America have resounded with denunciation of its supposed solution of the Jewish problem by dissolution," Zangwill admitted in his Afterword to the play. People seemed to overlook that the intermarriage in *The Melting Pot*, was on both sides. "After all," Vera reminds David, "I was brought up in the Greek Church. And we oughtn't to cause all this suffering, unless——" The butcher of Kishineff is her "Dear little father." "You, a Revendal, would mate with an unbaptised dog!" he cries. "Love a Jew? Impossible!"

Incidentally, in the Yiddish translation of the play, which was produced by Jacob Adler in New York, and by Esther Rachel

Kaminsky in Warsaw, the name Quixano appears as Kechana, which could be a form of Kahan or Cohen. But Zangwill meant David to be of Spanish descent. He made Vera explain: "In Spain his ancestors preferred exile in Poland to baptism."

"David Quixano is not offering a panacea for the Jewish problem, universally applicable," Zangwill argued in his Afterword to *The Melting Pot*. He returned to his own panacea, Territorialism. "David Quixano asks his uncle," he pointed out, "why, if he objects to the dissolving process, he did not work for a separate Jewish land." "I will just say this," Zangwill wrote, "and it can be taken as a general observation on the discussions going on in Jewish papers on the *Melting Pot*. There are two ways of being melted up. You can be melted up in something inferior or in something superior. Ordinarily it is in something inferior as with the rich snobs who get baptised for the sake of social position. Quite a different sort of being melted up is that which takes place in a human brotherhood without any surrender of one's beliefs or ideals. In the eyes of David Quixano the American constitution as it was laid down and built up by the Puritan fathers, by Washington or Lincoln, was a mere modern attempt to set up the Mosaic ideal of a perfect State. And in David's conception the Jew in America should not seek a separate future from the rest of the human brotherhood. After all, Palestine was also a 'Melting Pot,' in which many native races were melted up with Jews, not to mention the mixed multitude who went up with the Jews out of Egypt, all of whom were to be governed on the basis of equality. 'There shall be one law for the stranger as for the indweller'; that is practically expressed in Roosevelt's 'Square Deal.' No doubt, American life caricatures the idea of David, but none the less is it the same ideal that was preached by the Hebrew prophets. Nor does David's ideal demand the dissolution of the Jews in other countries or under less noble conditions. But whether David is right or wrong, I hope your readers will not infer that the *Melting Pot* is purely a preachment. They will find, if the experience of hundreds of thousands who have already seen it is any guide, an entertainment blending humour and pathos, and with a number of character studies all of which are extraordinarily well played." Zangwill, speaking to the Race Congress in 1911, explained: "In one of my plays I compared America to a melting pot. America does not attempt to fuse the various peoples that seek her shores by force. By the sheer pressure of not pressing them she turned them into one." He went on to argue that by becoming part of the American nation the Jews did not cease to be Jews. "The Jewish nationality has been preserved not as a nationality but as a religion," he said. He reminded the Jews of America that "The·Jew is here citizen of a republic without a State religion." He saw no reason why they should not as

Americans observe Judaism. It is the Christian servant maid Kathleen in *The Melting Pot* who "mutters contemptuously: 'Call yourself a Jew and you forgettin' to keep Purim!'"

In the Purim scene in *The Melting Pot* Zangwill showed he could write theatre. As always with Zangwill the memory of the pogroms underlies his theme. The Carnival is kept because, as the Book of Esther records, "the Jews of Persia escaped massacre." Kathleen knows it. "That's what the misthress is so miserable about. Ye don't keep the Carnival. There's noses for both of ye—but ye don't be axing for 'em. And to see your noses layin' around neglected, faith, it nearly makes me chry meself." She goes about wearing her "grotesque false nose." After the scene with his uncle, who tells David to leave the house—"marry your Gentile and be happy, but don't stay here and break my mother's heart"—they both stay to make merry when the old lady comes in. "A merry Purim!" says Mendel Quixano "bitterly." It is Kathleen who tells Mendel Quixano that "to-night being yer Sabbath you'll be blowing out your bed-room candle, though ye won't light it; Mr. David'll light his and blow it out too; and the mistress won't even touch the candlestick." Mendel regrets "that in this great grinding America, David and I must go out to earn our bread on Sabbath as on weekdays. She never says a word to us but her heart is full of tears." "My object is not to depict the Sabbath peace, but its profanation," Zangwill said, ex-plaining why he had turned down the suggestions from "many artistic minds" who had been "led to instruct me that the first act of *The Melting Pot* would end more beautifully if the curtain came down on the Sabbath blessings and the picture of Sabbath peace." In the play, David is writing while the old lady lights the Sabbath candles and says the Hebrew blessing. Throughout the scene the old lady is sobbing. "Will you allow me to explain," Zangwill wrote, "that the reason why Frau Quixano merely lights the Sabbath candles and does not put the bread and salt on the table is that no Sabbath meal is eaten in that house. The men go out to their work that evening. The old lady therefore takes her Sabbath meal in the kitchen with the faithful Kathleen, and the lighting of the candles remains the only bit of ritual left to the poor old lady in the New York 'melting pot.' So many Jews are ashamed of anything Jewish," he went on. "I was told of a lady in the dress circle who expressed apprehension lest the Christian spectators should imagine that she carried on like Frau Quixano—reading a prayer-book and doing strange ritual things. Really, the Bayswater Jews seem utterly ignorant that their neighbours have also their ritual, and even Princesses of the Roman Catholic faith read out of prayer-books and indulge in ritual."

In his letters to friends Zangwill passionately denied that his

Melting Pot was meant to preach intermarriage and Jewish dissolution. He also realised that the dissolution of the Jew would not be welcomed by all non-Jews, that they might feel contempt for the spineless Jews who were ready to be melted away, or would resent the half-melted matter. Zangwill referred in his Afterword to the play to Dr. Charles Eliot, the President of Harvard, who had expressed a dislike of "the still unmelted heaps of racial matter."

The fact is that Zangwill himself doubted the full efficacy of the Melting Pot. "There will be neither Jew nor Greek," he said of his *Melting Pot* in 1914. But in 1916 he was writing: "It was vain for Paul to declare that there should be neither Jew nor Greek. Nature will return even if driven out with a pitchfork. Still more if driven out with a dogma." He did not like Bergson's lament that the Jews are unwilling "to melt entirely while we are in the pot." He could not see the Jew disappearing except "by way of a long-drawn comedy of hypocrisy and unmanliness. The other decision," he said, "calls upon all that is strong and noble in the race."

The story of *The Melting Pot* was presented in *The Readers' Digest of Books* by Helen Keller (MacMillan, 1929) as a melting of "all race differences and feuds." Zangwill's story has been retold by many commentators, by some approvingly or indignantly as a call to intermarriage and assimilation, by others as a warning against intermarriage and assimilation. The *Jewish Chronicle* was among those who interpreted its lesson as "Beware of the deadly forces of assimilation."

Zangwill insisted that the play is not concerned with Russia, "except as a place to escape from. Its theme is America." It did not save *The Melting Pot* from being banned in England early in the war, because it was held to be insulting to England's ally, Russia. The question was raised in Parliament; it fell to Lord Robert Cecil, later Viscount Cecil of Chelwood, to answer for the Foreign Office. "The performance of the play was not prohibited," he quibbled, "but at the request of the Foreign Office it was suggested informally to the producers of the play that, in present circumstances, they should replace it by another play. This they were good enough to do." "The play so fatuously suppressed by the Foreign Office," was Zangwill's comment. "The Foreign Office prohibition of my play *The Melting Pot* at the request of Russia."

"So far as it deals with Russia," Zangwill went on, "*The Melting Pot* is on historic ground. The pogrom at Kishineff in 1903 has already a whole literature devoted to it, and the notion that foreign history can be hushed up in any particular country when the political conditions demand opens up a geographical conception of history which transcends even Pascal's *Truth Ends at the Pyrenees*." The pogrom at Kishineff in 1903 has indeed a whole literature devoted to it. When its memory was fresh, the utterance of the one word Kishineff was enough to electrify an audience. It shook the Zionist Congress. "The whole Congress, delegates and audience arose, as Herzl uttered the word 'Kishineff' and remained standing silently as he read that part of his address and then as silently sat down." Not only Jews; the whole civilised world was horror-struck. Public opinion in Europe and America was aroused to such a pitch that the Russian Government was forced to institute legal inquiries."

Vera, Zangwill's heroine, had been in Siberia, one of the many children of Russian aristocrats who flung themselves into the revolutionary movement, like Prince Kropotkin, whom Zangwill knew. She detested the Czarist regime, with its oppression and brutality, of which the pogroms against the Jews were one manifestation. "In Russia I fought against the autocracy," Vera tells her father. David was one of the countless pogrom victims, a survivor, who had the murder of his parents and others of his family fixed in his memory. He was obsessed by it and overwrought, like the survivors of the later Hitler extermination who went through Belsen and Oswiecem and Terezin and Transnistria. They were neither of them normal, calm people. What David went through was enough to have unhinged him. Zangwill recalls that the survivors who found their murdered kin after the pogrom "were crazed and hysterical." For a young girl like Vera to have been caught plotting against the Czar and his rule, sent to Siberia, and to have escaped from there was an experience she could not forget even in free America. The relief of being in a country where there were neither pogroms nor Siberia made them regard this natural condition as though it were a miracle, something to shout about, to rejoice in, to sing thanksgiving to, and to be jealous of anything and anyone seeming to threaten a return to the evil they had escaped. "This story is told," Zangwill quoted one who had been through Kishineff, "in the hope that Americans will appreciate the safety and freedom in which they live and that they will help others to gain that freedom." That is why David ranted at Quincy Davenport, "You who are undoing the work of Washington and Lincoln." When Davenport tells Baron Revendal that Americans "don't take much stock in the Kishineff massacres," the Russian Baron retorts: "Don't you lynch and roast your niggers?" Zangwill had not forgotten in his obsession with the Jewish problem "that black problem which is America's nemesis for her ancient slave-raiding."

The word Kishineff was fresh in the minds of the audiences who saw Zangwill's *Melting Pot* when it was produced five years after the pogrom, in America, and even eleven years after in England. I was a Whitechapel schoolboy of eleven at the time of the Kishineff pogrom. I remember its impact. But when I sat in New York in

1952 listening to a reading of *The Melting Pot,* I looked at the rest of the audience and wondered to how many of them the word Kishineff created the effect Zangwill intended by its repeated iteration in the play. To-day, after the Hitlerist extermination of six million Jews in Europe, after the death camps of Belsen and Oswiecem and the crematoriums, does the word Kishineff still hold the same horror? If it does not, will the conflict that David and Vera resolve through their love, still be intelligible? It is Shakespeare's theme: "My only love sprung from my only hate." Has Zangwill in *The Melting Pot* fixed Kishineff timelessly, so that its horror conveys itself even to those who never heard the word before? "The mangled breasts of women and the spattered brains of babes and sucklings," are just as terrible whether they were at Kishineff or at Belsen or in the Armenian massacres. The Warsaw pogrom of 1940 and the slaughter in the Warsaw Ghetto in 1943 stand as symbolic of that whole period, as the Kishineff pogrom of 1903 is the symbol of the entire wave of pogroms which swept through Russia in that period, or of the Ukrainian pogroms of 1919, which stirred Zangwill to write his poem "Our Own,"

> "By devastated dwellings,
> By desecrated fanes,
> By hearth-stones, cold and crimsoned,
> And slaughter-reeking lanes,
> Again is the Hebrew quarter
> Through half of Europe known,
> And crouching in the shambles,
> Rachel, the ancient crone,
> Weeps again for her children."

That is the theme of the scene in *The Melting Pot* between David Quixano and Baron Revendal, the butcher of Kishineff, with Vera, David's love who is Revendal's daughter as the tragic chorus. "The voice of the blood of my brothers crying out against you from the ground," David raves. And Vera, bewildered, uncomprehending, says: "But this is my father." "You could have stopped it!" Vera appeals to her father. "I had no orders to defend the foes of Christ and the Czar," he answers. "It is only Jewish history," David's uncle, Mendel Quixano explains to Vera. "David belongs to the species of pogrom orphan—they arrive by almost every ship. Every few months the newspapers tell us of another pogrom, and then he screams out against that butcher's face, so that I tremble for his reason." There is the scene between Mendel Quixano and David when David tells him he will marry Vera. "But you are a Jew!" cries Mendel. "Vera loves me," answers David. When Mendel

R

reminds him of all the fires in which the Jew had been tried, David replies: "Fires of hate, not fires of love. That is what melts." He wants to "forget all that nightmare of religions and races," to "hold out my hands with prayer and music toward the Republic of Man and the Kingdom of God. The past," he says, "I cannot mend. Take away the hope that I can mend the future, and you make me mad."

It is an echo of Zangwill's own conflict, his turning towards and from and back towards Jewish separateness and Judaism and the Synagogue—even if he tries to explain through Mendel Quixano that "it is not so much the Synagogue, it is the call of our blood through immemorial generations." When Kathleen, the Irish Catholic maid in the Quixano household, says: "Begorra, we Jews never know our way," it is Zangwill's personal cry.

His personal cry is everywhere in the play. There is a duologue with himself where David and Mendel Quixano clash over David's intention to marry Vera. "Spare me that rigmarole," says the sober Mendel side of Zangwill to his ideal-intoxicated other self projected into David: "Spare me that rigmarole. Go out and marry your Gentile and be happy." And at once David, who has been spouting Zangwill's own ideas about breaking free from "the nightmare of religions and races," and his determination to "go away," is struck with dismay by his victory. "You turn me out?" he cries. Zangwill was always torn in two by the conflict and, like David, a little "meshugga," a little mad. Every time he turned back—he could not help turning back—to his Jewish roots and his specific Jewish concerns, he felt like David that he was false to his mission. "That is what I mean by failure. I preached of God's Crucible, that could melt up all race-differences and vendettas, that could purge and re-create. God tried me with his supremest test. He said 'Cast it all into my Crucible.' And I said, 'Even thy Crucible cannot melt this hate, cannot drink up this blood.' "

Zangwill was told his plays were melodramatic. David's "ravings about the massacre at Kishineff and his harangues on the United States, but for good manners we would clap hands to one's ears. Hyde Park is the place for this, not the Court Theatre," said the *Observer*. But it admitted that "David would very likely behave so." Zangwill found in the war a "vindication of melodrama." Melodrama was the way people acted when something terrible happened to them, he said. "Violated virgins and imprisoned citizens" had been to Maeterlinck, he went on, "the outworn motifs of the obsolescent theatre of 'blood, external tears and death.' " But when Belgium was invaded by the Germans Maeterlinck turned to melodrama.

I have heard Zangwill's plays also dismissed as unactable, lacking the stuff of dramatic action, full of lines that the actors cannot speak.

I have been told that Zangwill hadn't the instinct of the writer for the stage, that he broke all the rules, that his characters don't lead up to their big scenes, but enter and dash straight into them, and so destroy the tension; that his dialogue is that of the novel, of narrative, and not of the play. I have heard *The Melting Pot* condemned on all these grounds. Yet Zangwill is treated seriously as a playwright in the standard works. The *Oxford Companion of the Theatre*, published in 1951, calls *The Melting Pot* "the most important," of his plays, "a great success, and several times revived."

Zangwill was not so successful with his later plays. He envied the success of Noel Coward's *The Vortex*, which was playing to full houses when his own plays were failing and ruining him in 1925, and was praised by the critics who found fault with his own plays. He did not conceal his jealousy of the success of what he considered a false play, by someone he called a "whippersnapper." Of a recent revival the critics said: "It would be easy to write off *The Vortex* as a dated and spurious psychological melodrama—Sardou plus some psychology." Zangwill, who was not ashamed to admit that he was jealous of the "whippersnapper's" success would have felt himself vindicated.

When Zangwill went into West End management he announced that "Box-office draws will play no part in the casting." "During my season at the Fortune I hope to give most of my plays by making the popular pay for the 'high-brow.'" He believed he had them all, the popular, the comedies and farces, the melodramas and the romantic sweet-endings, and the "high-brow" plays, the problem plays, the plays of purpose and mission. He announced that *We Moderns*, would be followed by *Merely Mary Ann*, *The War God*, *The Next Religion*, *Plaster Saints*, *The Melting Pot*, *The Cockpit*, *The Forcing House* and *Too Much Money*. In another announcement he added *The King of Schnorrers*. "I shall be my own producer," he said, and he signed, "Yours fortunately Israel Zangwill."

He did not consider himself so fortunate when he got caught up in the technical and business affairs involved in being a producer. "After a feverish week of wrestling with theatrical folk and businessmen, I am alone," he wrote in 1926, shortly before the nervous breakdown from which he never recovered. That feverish wrestling with people who knew their job, in which he was a self-confessed "greenhorn," unhinged his mind and undermined his body.

The *Encyclopedia Britannica* speaks of *Merely Mary Ann* and *Too Much Money* representing "his lighter gift." *Too Much Money* was a farce, which in parts become slap-stick. He had "just missed," Mr. H. W. Massingham, the Editor of *The Nation*, wrote, "making his Mrs. Broadley a great contemporary portrait in the comic vein. As it is, neither she nor the attendant Scottish ruffian possesses the distinction, the verisimilitude of great comic portraiture." Zangwill explained that he had written a farce because there was nothing else left for him to add to the series of plays he had already written, and he referred to a story in the Talmud in which a Rabbi declared that "the man who made others laugh had the greatest likelihood of attaining Paradise." He also explained that "when Lord Byron heard that his mother was dead, he is said to have sought relief in boxing: during the tragic tension of the Great War I sought similar relief in writing a farce." The war took revenge. Zangwill said: "The defeat of the Fifth Army killed off almost everything on the London stage and in spite of Miss Lillah McCarthy's brilliant performance it did not get much beyond its fiftieth performance."

I saw the play with Zangwill at my side, but he was talking to me all the time, and I missed much of the fun. There was the scene when Lillah McCarthy at the wash-tub was put into hand-cuffs by the police, and the soapsuds descended on a passing head below. "That is better," said Mr. Massingham, "than to see an innocent girl drunk on a cocktail, as one of Mr. Zangwill's dramatic rivals exhibits her." William Archer described the play as a burlesque, satire and "irresistible horse-play" in one. A lot of distinguished people came to the play, Bernard Shaw, Mr. and Mrs. Asquith, Lord Samuel, Solomon J. Solomon, Bishop Garbett, then of Southwark, afterwards Archbishop of York. Zangwill was delighted when the Bishop wrote to him that he had enjoyed the play, and he sent me the letter.

I said We Moderns had a good Press. There were exceptions. Mr. Hubert Griffith in the Observer wrote an open letter: "Dear Mr. Zangwill—if I may say so—how could you! The parents were all right. Any comedy would have been proud to possess them. But their offspring! Where did they, or Mr. Zangwill, acquire them? I enjoyed Mr. Zangwill's wit. And the actors came through with flying colours. Would that it had been in a better cause." The Spectator coupled Galsworthy, whose play The Show was produced at the same time, with Zangwill, and said both plays were "unreal Realism." "It is always fatal to Mr. Galsworthy's purpose that his incidents and characters should seem unreal; for then we are not stirred by the thesis. But the edge of Mr. Galsworthy's observation seems by contrast unerringly sharp and biting when you go from his play to listen to Mr. Zangwill as (once more) he contrasts pre-war and post-war generations in We Moderns. Mr. Zangwill, one dares to say, has not met the younger generation."

Zangwill resented the suggestion that he had not understood the younger generation. He had met them, he said, and he had been struck by the "laxity of modern discipline" and "the dangers springing from the adventurous irresponsibility of the young generation." He quoted the Fifth Commandment, and a text from Malachi, as its theme: "And he shall turn the heart of the fathers to the children, and the heart of the children to their fathers." He explained that he had wanted to demonstrate through his play that civilisation is a very complex affair, and the idea that immature and inexperienced youths and maidens can airily override the experience of the race is a fallacy that has been foisted on the young by sundry eminent authors." He was in revolt against modern thought. What he tried to bring out was that in reality the moderns under their words and poses are the same as the old. "You moderns are always monkeying with words—but you can't monkey with facts," he declares. He concludes his play with Mary, the advanced modern, wanting her mother. "I want my mother! Oh, I want my mother!" The curtain falls to those words.

Zangwill said about this play that his conclusion, so far as there can be a conclusion to a dramatic study, is contained in two speeches of the last act. The daughter in self-defence says to her father, "But how could I know that? That happened before I was born." The father replies, "But so many things happened before you were born. So many happened before I was born, before the human race was born."

"Can I forget my oath to war on War?" cries Lady Norna in Zangwill's *War God*. Zangwill described this play, which Beerbohm Tree produced in London in 1911, as a play "of war and peace." It was considered a pacifist play, and was attacked and defended as if it were a piece of pacifist propaganda. Zangwill seemed to want it to be treated as such, by ending the play with the glorification of the slain apostle of peace, the Tolstoy-like Count Frithiof, and the triumphant singing of the Frithian hymn:

> "Frithiof is risen,
> The Prophet of Love;
> Earth laughs beneath us,
> And Heaven above.
>
> Green lie the valleys,
> No more to be red.
> Love shall be living,
> And War shall be dead."

But Zangwill was not quite so sure that "War shall be dead." "Perpetual Peace, in its literal sense, is as much a fallacy," he wrote, "as perpetual motion, nay, a greater fallacy, for perpetual motion, though we cannot create it, at least exists in Nature, whereas Perpetual Peace does not exist at all. If it did, it would mean a universe not of life but of death, and it is as barren an ideal for humanity as for Nature. What is meant however is not stagnation, but movement without murder. Even this cannot be found in Nature, nor can humanity create it except within the narrow human sphere." Even this, he thought difficult, and for our time impossible. "So long as our conceptions remain unchanged," he went on, "so long as no new world-religion flames into being with a new passionate sense of brotherhood and a new scale of human values, so long we shall cry Peace, Peace, where there is no Peace." Did he mean that Frithianism, or Tolstoyism would be that new world-religion? Hardly. For facing this passage, on the opposite page, he insists that "the Angel of Peace is Hebrew, and Hebrew only. It is Isaiah with his great vision of a brotherhood of toilers, it is Jesus, with his quite scientific doctrine that whoso takes the sword shall perish by it. 'And they shall beat their swords into ploughshares.' This is the only scrapping that will be effective in the end." Zangwill wrote this during the First World War, five years after the production of *The War God*. But the dream of world peace based on Isaiah's great vision was always with him. When the production of *The War God* was announced, the *Jewish Chronicle* asked him if the play "contained any Jewish interest." He answered: "Mr. Israel Abrahams lately said that all my work was Jewish. In this spiritual sense I think that this particular work will be found more Jewish than anything I have written."

"Are there any Jewish characters?" he was asked. "There are some ten principal characters, all of some importance in the world. Now could you ever find a Minyan of prominent Europeans without at least one Jew among them?" he answered. "What role does your one Jew play?" "He is the Secretary to the Chancellor." "Then I suppose Gothia is a tolerant country, if he has such a high post." "Oh no!" said Zangwill. "He has had to be converted to the dominant faith. Towards the end of the play he makes some remarks on this subject, touching the grievances under which the Jews of Gothia labour." Landa, in *The Jew in Drama*, was annoyed with Zangwill "that he should deliberately select a Jew for the one objectionable character in the play. Blum might have been drawn," he said, "by some writer with malice aforethought." Zangwill spoke of Blum making some remarks about the grievances under which the Jews of Gothia labour. When Blum turned Frithian, refuses to drink to war, the Bismarckian Chancellor calls him "a dirty Jew." "Ha," says Blum, "dirty Jew— although you had me washed in Graaf's cathedral font. But it is true. I never turned a Christian." He confesses that he "mocked you, your Church, and most of all, myself. Had Christians handled us with Christliness," he goes on, expounding Zangwill's favourite belief, "there would not be a single Jew in Europe. We should have melted in your love as I have melted in Count Frithiof's. Since, however, you Gothians shut us out from every post, dishonour is our only door to honour. I knew your weakness for converting Jews, so played upon it." Hypocrite, Landa calls Blum, renegade Jew, a contemptible figure. "Zangwill has but followed stage tradition." As it happened, Zangwill objected in his essay on "Stage Jews" to that tradition. "In Sheridan," he said, "the Jew was still the money-lender. Shaw, with more verisimilitude makes him a doctor. In Jerome the Jew is a bookmaker. No, it cannot be said that the stage-Jew has yet shaken off his past."

Arthur Bourchier, whom I saw play the Chancellor, made up as Bismarck, as Sir Herbert Beerbohm Tree as Frithiof made up as Tolstoy. (Wolmark in his frontispiece to *The War God* for the collected edition of Zangwill's works published the year before Zangwill died, made the Chancellor, with Zangwill's knowledge, a portrait of Bismarck. Zangwill had at first intended calling his play "The Man of Iron," the term used for Bismarck. He had also thought of calling it "The War Lord," and "The God of War," before he settled on *The War God*).

His "Iron Chancellor," who is so much Bismarck, but also has the ambitions that Zangwill sensed in the German Kaiser when he saw him in 1896, wants "to strike at Alba." Gothia is very much like Germany. There is an echo of Bismarck's dismissal by the Kaiser. "I left an Empire, where I found a jungle. He sacks me as one sacks a thieving valet." And when the dismissed Chancellor with his own son dead, thinks of "the hundred thousand sons of others" whom his wars killed, it is reminiscent of the real Bismarck musing: "There is no doubt that I have caused unhappiness to great numbers. But for me, three great wars would not have taken place; 80,000 men would not have been killed and would not now be mourned by parents, brothers, sisters, widows and sweethearts." Zangwill knew, when he presented the Tolstoyian ideal in Count Frithiof that the ideal would not translate into real life. "Despite Tolstoy and his tracts," he said, "the people who stop will not think, and the people who think will not stop. To convert the world is the one miracle that the saints have never compassed. Tolstoy to be of effect would have to move all mankind at once to renounce its ways. And he would have to keep on moving it, or back it would roll."

Landa called the peace propaganda of *The War God* "New Testament." But even after he has become a Frithian, Osric thinking of Norna, at the mercy of enemies, cries: "Then how could I not fight! My God! Were foul hands laid on you!" That is not the passive resistance of the early Christians. Zangwill knew that the wars of liberation, from the rising of the Maccabeans to the regeneration of Italy under Garibaldi meant hard fighting and bloodshed; he was wholly with the warriors of liberation. He spoke with pride of the Jews who put their faith "to the test of the sword." He rejoiced at the thought of Judea's fight with Rome. "Was not the Lord a man of war? Pharaoh's chariots and his host he had cast into the sea. The Psalmist shouted for joy in the time of victory, and in the name of God set up our standards. When David returned from the slaughter of the Philistine, did not the women come out of all the cities of Israel, singing and dancing—'Saul hath slain his thousands, and David his ten thousands.' " Zangwill's heart quickened to the thought of that joy and that singing. He spoke during the war at a meeting in support of a resolution moved by Rudyard Kipling. "For quickening the pace of the march of victory there is no fresh power that we can call to our aid so potent as the power of music," he said. "Like the sound of the trumpet is that heroic uplift of the civilian's soul as he offers himself for his country. Music helps us to remember that war with all its inevitable evil and ugliness has also nobleness and beauty, and that this war in particular is the war of the spirit against the spirit of war." Zangwill was no starry-eyed pacifist, though pacifists and others interpreted his *War God* as a tract against war. It betrayed, like everything he wrote and said and did, his dualism, his seeing at the same time both sides of every question, and giving them both full force. Worse than war was to him "the peace of the devil," the acceptance of evil. The man who fought against evil stirred his blood.

Zangwill who, lamenting his dead friend and leader Herzl, invoked Napoleon with whom to compare him for greatness, and who was stirred by the Jewish self-defence in the Russian pogroms, by Jabotinsky's self-defence in the Jerusalem pogrom and by Trumpeldor's heroic death in the battle at Tel Hai, was not blind to the value of the warrior, any more than he was deaf to the heartening sound of martial music, "the call of the trumpet and the beat of the drum."

"*The War God*, which should have been Zangwill's greatest success, is just the reverse," Landa wrote. "It excited a certain amount of curiosity, but after its few performances it passed, keenly regretted however by those who regarded it as a tract, which it is. The cast was a remarkable one. The staging was worthy of the best traditions of the theatre, and the production was on a high artistic scale which would have gained success for the play had it been merited." The *Observer* said "Sir Herbert Tree never showed sounder judgment than in limiting to three matinees his production of Mr. Zangwill's devout but dull didactic drama. *The War God* acts far less effectively than it may probably read," it continued, "though its literary style is that of the leading article put into blank verse. Its argument is flat, and the play melodramatic and the sentiments rhetorical. If there had been less talk about some of the action it might have hit home better." It found the play had "too much sermonising," and "Blum's confession is not in keeping." But H. W. Massingham, the Editor of *The Nation*, called *The War God* "a powerful play, by far the most important event of the dramatic season of 1911." John Masefield, himself a dramatist as well as a poet, thought "it is splendid, altogether a fine and noble thing, with all the beauty and depth which one has wanted for so long. It is much the biggest thing done here for many years." And William Archer, the dramatic critic, called it "a very fine piece of symbolic drama."

Zangwill meant *The War God* to be a drama on the theme of war and peace, as he said. But it went very far in the direction of becoming the drama of the conflict in a man's soul, Chancellor Torgrin's, who plans and schemes and builds mightily, who dreams of his succession by his son Osric and by Lady Norna, and their children and grand-children, who would be "well-nigh royal," and instead sees his son dead. "They told me he had died an hour ago. But when I saw his face I felt he had been dead a million years." The Iron Chancellor had "thought to play at Providence." And he discovered that "Life's too big and tangled for our meddling." "You've come to kill me?" he says to Lady Norna. "What is left to kill? A little naked scuttling spider . . ." He suddenly remembers—"who called me that? Ah, yes, it was Frithiof." "You think to bind the future? Poor grey spinner!" Frithiof had said to him. "Fate, the blind housewife, with her busy broom shall shrivel at one sweep your giant web, and leave a little naked spider." It is the opposite, at the diminishing end, of the expanding image he used in *We Moderns*—"there's one shrivelled mummy of a Professor of Astronomy whose skull embraces the stars."

Zangwill devoted the Foreword to the printed play to a defence of his use of blank verse for *The War God*. He quoted what William Archer had said about it, "rather than multiply words of my own." Archer had said: "All the great scenes of the play are, and ought to be, and cannot help being, rhetorical; why should the author deny himself the swing and resonance of verse? 'But,' it may be said, 'all the scenes are not great scenes. In many of them the dialogue is quite commonplace and unrhetorical. Why should not they, at any rate have been in prose?' Here again, I unhesitatingly defend Mr. Zangwill. In spite of Elizabethan precedent, there is nothing more irritating on the modern stage than the drama which is couched in two mediums. Mr. Zangwill did entirely right in adopting his medium and sticking to it; but he did right because he happened to have a peculiar art of writing smooth, easy, flowing blank verse. He makes the most ordinary talk (not even excluding slang) fall naturally and without incongruity into the iambic movement. I will go further and say that he uses the verse wittily." "While fully sensible to this praise," Zangwill commented, "the reverence for blank verse as for a medium debased by anything but the finest poetry is the mere superstition of the semi-literate."

Reading *The War God*, as I have read it several times, I keep turning to a notice of a book of his poems, which says that "Mr. Zangwill has succeeded very frequently in giving us English poetry." He was not a great poet. There is some poetry in his blank verse, and there is fine rhythmic speech. But there are passages which jar because they are in blank verse and would have sounded better in prose. There are sudden drops, as when he has caught the mood of the ambitious father in the Iron Chancellor speaking to his dead wife's picture:

> "Ah, sweetheart, why could you not stay and watch
> Our little rogue climb up, as swiftly as
> He climbed the pear-tree in our cottage garden."
> (Wipes his eyes. Then gruffly)
> "What's in my letters?"

There are many lines and passages that in blank verse sound stilted. The diction is twisted. "We are the brains behind!" says Konrad.

Yet Lady Norna, breaking away from her lover Osric, can cry:

> "Tempt me no more with dreams of happiness.
> I was not born for pasture in the valley.
> A trumpet calls me to the mountain-top,
> And I must battle where a whirling snow
> Blinds every track and gap. My only light
> A great red sun that, monstrous through a mist,
> Looms like a giant gout of blood: I walk
> Alone, unguided, chartless, footsore, frozen.
> Then comes a mocking mountain-fiend who cries:
> Rest, weary wanderer, your journey's over.
> This glacier is a cosy, glowing hearth,
> This precipice a couch from which to peer
> Into the ruddy fire and see sweet pictures,
> This mound of snow a stool to prop your feet.
> Oh go! Do you not see you make still bleaker
> The mountain waste, the snow, the sun of blood,
> And that lone path which I must tread alone!"

When Norna tells the bereaved and deposed Iron Chancellor who feels that he is now useless, fit only for death, that she has come to kill him, he welcomes it:

"How often have I longed to cast off life
Like this soiled dressing-gown and creep to bed!
But I have never been so tired as now."

When she reprieves him, to live, he protests:

"To wait and wait. . . . Such empty, endless years!"

Zangwill believed he was doing something towards restoring the poetic drama. I heard Beerbohm Tree when he spoke to the audience in 1911 after the curtain fell on *The War God* say "More will be heard of this noble play." But it has not been heard again.

Zangwill had a lot of trouble with Beerbohm Tree and with the other members of the cast during the rehearsals. There were thirty rehearsals. Zangwill grumbled that "Bourchier found the blank verse difficult and wanted to throw up the part." "Lillah McCarthy" he reported, "again said: 'You'd like somebody else for the part.'" Tree was "lackadaisical," and "tetchy." Once Tree told Zangwill he had played greater dramatists, even Shakespeare. When Zangwill retorted that Shakespeare couldn't say how he wanted his work played—he was dead, Mrs. Zangwill called out: "You soon will be." Zangwill was worried and angry and sleepless. He kept taking bromides for his insomnia. But between rehearsals he attended to Ito business—"We discussed Paraguay." At the twenty-sixth rehearsal Zangwill found Tree in a better mood. He told him the play "will make money." At the first performance, "Tree sent for me after Act I and seemed very pleased. After the performance he promised I should be put on for a run." But two days later, "Tree was rehearsing *Orpheus* as if Frithiof were buried. He said he would try and attempt another performance. But he said Box Office didn't like it." Then "I got letter from Tree—'Not financially keen about *War God*.' I went to see Tree, but I saw there was nothing to discuss. He still applauded me 'out of respect for you.'"

I have a feeling that if *The War God* like *The Melting Pot* could be stripped of some things that have been outdated (they were both pre-First World War) and of some superfluities and banalities, it might in the hands of a stage-craftsman be successfully revived.

I am not so sure of either *The Cockpit* or *The Forcing House*. Zangwill carried over too much in them from his other plays, echoes of *The War God*, and aspirations from *The Melting Pot*. In fact he called *The Cockpit* "a pendant to *The Melting Pot*." "If the politicians would only leave it alone, *The Cockpit* would become *The Melting Pot*," he said. It is his old theme, which he has stated sufficiently elsewhere—"The fires of hate harden. The fires of love melt." He knew that the politicians would not leave it alone. He gave the answer in his own ending to *The War God*—"Life's too big and tangled for our meddlings." The "tragic maze" could not be whisked away by telling politicians or other people to stop being and doing. He had discovered that "the politicians, bad as much they do is, are not free agents, that they work with the tools and the materials they have, and that there are no others—that even war is a necessity and an indispensable factor, like wind and fire and water in shaping the world and its distribution among the peoples. As the rain-gauge records rain, so history records blood," he said. "Human nature is in conflict with the merely abstract virtues."

That was the theme of his play *Plaster Saints*, and of *The Next Religion*. *Plaster Saints* is the story of a clergyman whom his wife loves and reveres as a saint, and then discovers to be a sinner. He had committed adultery, in her own home, and has an illegitimate child, whose mother since married a man who agreed to accept the child as his own. He has been offered an important office in his Church, to carry on a work in which he and his wife both believe. He has confessed his sin to her, and swore it is ended, a closed chapter in his life. He claims that through sinning he has learned to understand better the people who come to him for guidance and help. "How can beardless boys who have not experienced life preach to life-battered men and women!" he cries. "It is because I have known sin at first-hand that I was able to comfort that poor woman. Now I know the difference between good and evil. This fantastic hypothesis of perfection! A sea captain who has never made a voyage —and you trust him with the ship. The seaman does not seek the storm, but he puts out to sea. A hurricane whirled me from my moorings—but haven't I fought back in the teeth of the gale?" His wife, a stern puritan, refuses to forgive him. She insists she will leave him, will divorce him, will expose him to his Church and to the world.

He accepts the exposure as inevitable—the publicity of divorce, and the end of his calling and his living. He begins to glory in the idea. "If they cast stones at me, I will take those stones and of them I will build a new church, the church of reality." "Sweep away this cant of the plaster priest! All the saints and prophets of the world were sown in sin—as lilies were reared in peat. St. Augustine, St. Francis, Tolstoy, there isn't a church in the world to-day would have given any of 'em a post!"

Then the wife proves she is the plaster saint, when she discovers that her husband's degradation would mean the disappointment of her hopes for her daughter's marriage to the son of the rich lay head of her husband's Church, a stern and narrow Puritan. She forgives her husband. She makes him promise to hush it all up. "You are beginning to be acquainted with yourself," she says to him. "I too will become acquainted with the real you." There is a hint of what a decade later became his theme in *We Moderns*—"The gulf between the generations is too wide to talk across. One can only shout." There are Biblical allusions: The Mayoress's picture hat at the reception "is giant as the gourd that came up over Jonah." "We owe something to ravens for feeding Elijah." The final message of the play is "the sun never goes out of heaven. It is we who turn away from the sun."

The play, whose entire action passes between tea-time and dinner of one day, seemed to have a chance of being successful. But Zangwill was again unlucky. It was May 1914, and the First World War broke out a few weeks later. According to the *Fortnightly Review* it had "excited heated controversies: and in many cases the author's theme and purpose have been misunderstood and misrepresented." A critic wrote: "Mr. Zangwill calls his play a problem play, and perhaps the problem consists in his one question: Is confession, which proverbially is beneficial for the soul, to be regarded as so absolute a duty that it must take precedence of every other consideration—the happiness and the lives of people incidentally concerned which may be blasted by confession? It is a nice point whether a man or woman is weaker or stronger who, having done wrong determines to bury the wrong even though the corpse of sin prove a heavy and lasting burden to the soul, or the man or woman who having sinned determines to become spiritually released, and to face the consequences in confession. Mr. Zangwill does not propound the answer to the problem."

The clergyman in *Plaster Saints* bears considerable resemblance to the clergyman in Zangwill's *Next Religion* which was produced in London two years earlier, in 1912, but was banned by the Censor. Landa in *The Jew in Drama* quotes a critic describing it as "nothing less than an attack on Christianity couched in terms of needless offensiveness." The *Observer* felt like that about it. "Christians may justly complain that his criticism of Christianity was out of date and puerile," it wrote. "We are all for the open discussion of religious questions on the stage. We regard the *Showing up of Blanco Posnet* as a play that must not only interest every unprejudiced person that sees it, but must 'do good' to a great many troubled souls. Those whom Christianity can no longer satisfy will resent Mr. Zangwill's pawing of things they believe and resent his humbugging self-seeker (Stephen) being set up as a model of their kind. The play has gained some notoriety through the Lord Chamberlain's refusal to license it. Had it been submitted to the general public, the public, we believe, would very soon have shrouded it in a merciful obscurity." On the other hand, the *Methodist Times*, a Christian religious paper, praised the play, and thought "the Lord Chamberlain has done wrong to religion by forbidding the play." Zangwill said at the time that "all the religious papers without exception have praised it." One religious paper commented: "Mr. Zangwill's religious views may be liberal—I imagine them to be not far removed from those of Dr. Stanton Coit—but I cannot imagine any reason for suppressing them." William Archer said: "*The Next Religion* is a splendidly vivid epitome of the spiritual struggles of the age. It is noble as thought, it is powerful as drama—and of course it is mown down by the Censorship." Mr. Massingham, the Editor of *The Nation*, declared: "The Censorship grows daily a more palpably wicked institution. In the line of drama Mr. Zangwill is trying to do what Matthew Arnold or Dr. Martineau or Tolstoy have tried to do." In an interview with a Nonconformist paper, Zangwill said: "I have great sympathy with the Nonconformist position because I belong to a Nonconformist sect myself."

Zangwill also said that if he had been concerned with money, he could have had the play produced, by making a few changes that the Censor had required. But he never let anyone dictate changes to him.

The clergyman in his *Next Religion* has a different problem than the clergyman in *Plaster Saints*. The Rev. Stephen Trame, a country vicar, has discovered that he is "not really a Christian." He wants a wider religion, "larger than Christianity, the religion all honest men are coming to—the religion the world is thirsting for—the religion that accepts the Revelation of Science." Though Stephen Trame is a Christian clergyman and Zangwill was a Jew, most of what Stephen Trame feels is what Zangwill felt. He doubted the efficacy of prayer —"Can you save the plague-stricken millions of India by prayer?" —though sometimes he admired the faith of those who believed in prayer. If people did not observe the rules of hygiene, tuberculosis would come to them "even through the Communion chalice." How could he, knowing that the sun is only one of the twenty million stars of the Milky Way, "prate of the creation of Adam and his rib on this pokery little planet"? His college friend, a freethinker, tells him to "chuck it." But Stephen Trame is held back from chucking it by the belief that it would break his wife's heart. She is a religious soul, a devout believer. "She's a saint," says Stephen. "How can I tell her that these chrysanthemums she's dressing up the church with are only a relic of Greek paganism?" "The truth I dare not utter is a fire burning inside me." In the end, he tells her—"Mary, I cannot stand it any longer." He blurts out his doubts to her. "We might have cleaned out our swamp of misery and evil centuries ago if we hadn't looked to some gigantic genie in the clouds to do all our dirty work." "And do you say there is nobody in the skies?" Mary asks, with white set face. "I say there is somebody in ourselves," Stephen answers. He wants to resign from the Church. She threatens to leave him. "My vows cannot bind me to spread atheism," she says. But when he "chucks it," resigns from the Church, Mary goes with him. Zangwill sends them to live in Whitechapel, he in "shabby lay attire," with nothing left to pawn. His book *The Next Religion* has been published. Mary sobs: "Only the success of an anti-Christian book stands between us and starvation." Her father, a Bishop, arrives, to take her away. But she stays with her husband. While he talks of spiritual hunger she talks of their real hunger, and of seeing their little son "growing coarser and coarser. In those moments your striving to alter the world's religion appears to me so puny, so pitiful, so hopeless."

Then the father of Trame's freethinking college friend, Sir Thomas McFadden, a millionaire armaments manufacturer, walks in. He has read the copy of *The Next Religion* Trame sent his son, who has turned Christian, and has been disinherited by Sir Thomas, an anti-Christian, "as free from superstition," he boasts, "as his smelted iron from slag." This "Next Religion," "free from superstition," appeals to Sir Thomas, who offers Trame all the money he wants to establish the "New Church," "a Temple tip-top enough to wipe out that shrine of superstition in Westminster." Stephen is revolted. "The man doesn't understand the next religion," he cries. "His only idea is to build buildings, with paid priests, and a ritual that will run as mechanically as his steam-rollers." But Mary says: "You can't organise the believers without a building, and the building must have ministers."

So St. Thomas's Temple is built as the Church of the Next Religion, with a perpetually lit taper burning before a portrait of Sir Thomas McFadden, with coloured windows in which Mazzini, Emerson and Swinburne appear like saints, with richly dyed cloths and clerical robes, with processions of youths and maidens bearing palms and Madonna lilies, and Stephen, a white-bearded prophetic figure in flowing creamy satin robes. "Ah," says Stephen, "if only Sir Thomas could have seen it!" Sir Thomas's son, Stephen's friend, the freethinker turned Christian, visits the new church, and tells Stephen that the millions spent on it were wasted—"millions that might have served some great purpose. You have a Temple, but not so beautiful as St. Paul's or the Abbey. I see priests and choristers, pomp and pageantry, but your ritual, like your building and your furniture lacks the historic glamour which comes with centuries of tradition. I see a hymn-book, but free as it is from the crudities which unfortunately disfigure our Christian hymn-book, your liturgy cannot compare with the massive majesty of the Bible. The next religion?" he asks. "Before we've worked out the last? What have you found more beautiful or uplifting than the words of

Christ? And this religion has the advantage of being already organised—it carries the inspiration and consecration of the centuries. Vivify it, scour it, bring it back to the Founder. Perhaps Christ's own religion has never had a chance—perhaps that's the next religion." Zangwill's other voice is speaking. For Stephen and his friend echo Zangwill's own conflicting thoughts. Even his doubts instilled in him by scientific teaching vanish. "New? What is there new that is true? Time, Space, Life, Death, Soul, Body—what old, old mysteries, what terrible brand-new realities, as strange under the electric light as they were under the stars of the ancient East. Think what Science shouted when you and I were at Oxford, and how one dogma after another has broken down. How much is left even of Darwin and Herbert Spencer? The revelation of Science! I, a man of science, tell you that we know nothing."

Stephen Trame and Hal McFadden are the two sides of Zangwill's mind debating with each other. Mary Trame is the most human character in the play. She is frightened by her husband's "glacial truths," by his "Arctic religion." She tries to stop him from resigning his position in the Church, because it would mean "our lovely home broken up"; but she goes with him to poverty in Whitechapel. "I took you for better or worse," she says—"for wiser or sillier." She even types his book for him, though it is "full of heresies, even blasphemies." And when her parents come to Whitechapel to take her away, she cries: "How can I leave him? He is my husband." It is too much coincidence that as she is praying in their cold Whitechapel room: "O, Father, which art in heaven, look down upon us Thy suffering children, send us a redeemer——" Sir Thomas McFadden, the millionaire, walks into the room, and offers to finance the new religion. Afterwards she claims "it was in answer to my prayer that Sir Thomas came." When Stephen raves about Sir Thomas tempting him with his money she silences him with her simple common sense: "You are not going to refuse his millions?" She is proud of his success, and reproaches herself that "I stood out against you. I live with a king of men and did not know his greatness." But when their son is dead, it is "Your miserable religion." "I don't want your world of peace and perfection, I want my Wilfy."

Mrs. Burr, one of Trame's villagers in the play, has the word for it. "It's bitter hard the way us women be dragged at the heels of our donkeys. There was I, milking my cows and curing my bacon, when smack! jolt! off goes the donkey-cart to the New Jerusalem!" Farmer Burr is one of Stephen Trame's converts. His unforgiving enemy, the village blacksmith, obsessed with the thought that he is God's instrument to destroy the heretics (he would "go to the gallows for God any day"), tries to smash Burr's head with his hammer, but only stuns him. He breaks into the Church of the new religion, intending to kill Stephen, but meeting Stephen's son, Wilfred, kills him instead. "Every spark that flew up from my anvil cried out: 'Go up—Go up, for this is the day of the Lord God of Hosts, a day of vengeance.' "

The play closes with Stephen and Mary mourning their dead son. There is an elaborate funeral service, a procession of youths and maidens making the choir-circuits for the dead. Mary weeps for her child. "He called out 'Mother' when the blow fell. Didn't you hear it? Just like when he was a little boy and something frightened him. That was his last word—'Mother!' "

Mary's old faith triumphs. She cannot bear Stephen's talk that "our dear son's death will be transmuted to a higher form of life in the generations that his memory will inspire." "Wilfy is dead," she cries. "And you can still talk words! Reason is only words. You are afraid of losing your miserable religion. That is why you won't let your heart speak. Do you think I could bear to hear the earth dropping on the coffin and not go mad? Do you think I would not run out into the streets and cry to the people: 'Let there be no more marrying nor giving in marriage, for Death stalks around with his hammer, waiting to fell your children like bullocks'? Stephen, do you really believe that if you or I die, we shall meet no more for all eternity, and be nothing but decaying dust? I forbid you to make this dark world darker. I tell you that the great live-world will never take your religion, and that even if you deluded all male humanity, the mothers would rise up and tear it to pieces." She seeks the old comfort, her belief in the Resurrection and the Life. "I will tell them," she cries as the curtain is falling, "that this corruptible shall put on incorruption and this mortal immortality, and I will cry, O death, where is thy sting? O grave, where is thy victory?"

Chapter IX

THE NEXT RELIGION

WHAT seems to have worried Zangwill terribly in *The Next Religion* is the problem of death and survival. He was not really such a stoic as he thought he was when he spoke of "the old faith," by which he meant Judaism, having "got cumbered up with alien doctrines about the future state picked up from weaker and less stoical peoples." He complained that "Orthodox Judaism" was "making death a bogey. The Ghetto loves to weep. I say we must bear everything with a stout heart." His heart was not so stout when his mother died; and Dr. Redcliffe Salaman told me that his own dying was full of agony and terror. Louis Zangwill knew that "my brother's practice diverges from his formal thinking." He affected to be scornful as a young man about the chances of survival after death, and argued that seventy years was long enough "to go on dressing and undressing oneself." But he concluded that though "a future life is unthinkable" it is not "therefore impossible and there are not a few people," he said, "I should love to see again or to atone to." He meant, of course, with our human knowledge and memory. For "what does it matter," he asked, "if I am not myself, but somebody else in his fifth plane or nineteenth incarnation? Where is the point of a progression through stages, if there is no continuous consciousness?"

Judaism believes in the future state, in survival after death, in resurrection. Jews praise God in our prayers every day, because "Thou quickenest the dead." We say it in the burial service, as the coffin is carried to the grave. "Blessed be the Lord our God who will restore you to life." "The dust," we say in our memorial prayer for the dead, "returneth to the earth as it was, but the spirit returneth unto God who gave it." As far as Jews have a catechism it is Maimonides's Thirteen Articles, of which the final Article declares: "I believe with perfect faith that there will be a resurrection of the dead." This creed is recited every day, and it has a rhymed form, the Yigdal hymn, sung at every Synagogue service, forming part of each day's prayers, a fourteenth-century versification, which Zangwill himself translated in the Synagogue Prayer Book and reprinted in his *Voice of Jerusalem* as the first of his "Songs of the Synagogue." Verse 13, the final couplet, reads in Zangwill's translation:

> "God will the dead again to life restore
> In His abundance of almighty love."

Before he made his own translation, Zangwill knew it in the Singer Prayer Book translation, which appeared in 1891, while he was writing *Children of the Ghetto*. He quoted that in *Children of the Ghetto*. Hannah in Synagogue heard the choir sing "the final hymn: 'The dead will God quicken in the abundance of His loving-kindness. Blessed for evermore be His glorious name.'"

He was therefore well aware of it. He need have gone no further than the Jewish Prayer Book service in the house of mourning for Mary Trame's exultant affirmation of her belief in the Resurrection and the Life, instead of taking it from the New Testament—"He will destroy death for ever, and the Lord God will wipe away tears from all faces."

All Zangwill's last scene in the play is obsessed by his thoughts and fears about death. He had been jotting down such thoughts for years. "When Abel was slain," he had written, "Adam and Eve did not understand death. It was the first time death came into the world. Alas, the sons of Adam and the daughters of Eve have since grown wiser about death. Yet every death of someone we know and love is just as new and strange and terrible as the first death." In his play, the dead are "loathsome logs. All of us turning into loathsome logs. And so on and so on till this revolving graveyard is shrivelled up by a wandering star. The great procession of death. . . ." The thought revolted him. His innermost thinking repudiated his formal thinking. "Not logs are the dead, but alive. 'The Resurrection and the Life!'" He even invoked the science on which his doubts of his faith were based, to strengthen his belief. "Why do you trust so to appearances? You who say that this solid-seeming matter is only a whirl of wild forces, that the very rocks are alive with radium! Surely in all these mysteries that encompass us there is room for hope, surely we may open one little window to the sun."

Zangwill was born and had his early education in the midst of the great Darwinian discovery and the Evolution controversy, in which all the clever young people were on the side of science against creed. His contemporary Wells spoke of those who were too old and set to accept "the invincible case of the biologists and geologists against the orthodox Christian cosmogony." The younger folk accepted it. Shaw called that period in which, he said, "I had discarded the religion of my forefathers," "the infidel half-century." "The pre-Darwinian age had come to be regarded as a Dark Age in which men still believed that the book of Genesis was a standard scientific revelation." Though for Shaw Darwin and Huxley and Tyndall and Spencer "passed away," his belief that "we Darwinians could do without God, and had made a good riddance of him" remained. He had no use for "the Christian religion, which is the Jewish religion, an Oriental religion—and it does not fit us." Like Zangwill he considered that "a new religion is necessary." He thought he had found it in what he called Life Force. "I say that Life Force is God," he said. The God who created Adam and Eve had no place in his belief.

Zangwill was like Shaw and Wells an explorer in the realms of new religions. They all tried to reconcile science with their need of a religion. It is not always right to identify an author with the words spoken by his characters, but Zangwill said: "I agree with the hero of *The Next Religion*." Science had seduced him from the faith of his pious father. Yet he could say—even "an irreligious man like myself talking about religion"—that "a religion is a series of hopes and beliefs, not of facts, a set of feelings."

Zangwill was not happy with the materialist views to which he sometimes leaned. "On religion, who to-day is open?" he said. "Only those whose minds are closed—be they ultra-pietists or atheists. Both forms of extremist are brainless. But the immemorial instinct of mankind would justify the former rather than the latter." Yet he was the product of his period, his teaching and environment. It is true that their age produced not only Shaw and Wells, but Chesterton and Belloc, who found and adhered to their Faith. The general tendency however was away from Orthodoxy. "I, the least orthodox of all," Zangwill said of himself. It was in the air. Professor Charles Singer was the son of a Rabbi whom Zangwill knew, the compiler of the Singer Prayer Book, the translation of the Jewish liturgy used in our Synagogues. He is a scientist. To him, "the critical year is 1859. The thunders of the evolutionary conflict have in our day become rather distant," he writes. "The air has long been cleared." To-day, he feels that "to the question, 'What does science say about religion?' the strictly true answer is, 'Nothing whatever.'"

But during the critical period, the conflict was very real and very thunderous. In 1876, when Professor Charles Singer was born and Israel Zangwill was a boy of twelve, Felix Adler, the twenty-five-year old son of a New York Rabbi, having gone to Germany to study for the Rabbinate, discovered that he could no longer believe in Judaism or traditional religion; he organised in New York the Ethical Church, "based on the principle of the promotion of right living, independent of religious, dogmatic or sectarian views."

The stirrings of Comtism, of the Positivist Church, were still felt. Comte died in 1857, when Felix Adler was six. But his influence continued into his early manhood and beyond. In 1880, when Zangwill was an impressionable reader of sixteen or seventeen, George Henry Lewes, George Eliot's husband, wrote that "the Positivist religion claims to resume and complete all previous religions." It was "The New Religion, the Religion of Humanity."

Zangwill was inclined to accept the claims of the Positivists, that moral beauty can be achieved without belief in God and without prayer. He had his doubts of it at times, and sometimes he seemed to have become religious, but often he talked like a Positivist or an Ethical Culturist. As a young man of twenty-five, he noted in his diary: "My Positivist attitude has gained in deepness and strength." In the way he had of relating everything to Judaism, he even spoke of "Positivism being only Judaism depolarised."

"Then in the next religion there won't be any prayers?" Hal asks in *The Next Religion*. "Not in the sense of asking favours," Stephen Trame answers. Yet Zangwill could in some moods be very much moved by the idea of prayer. He thought highly of the prayers of Abraham and of Jacob, that great supplication of Abraham's, his controversy with God: "Wilt Thou indeed sweep away the righteous with the wicked?" And Jacob's prayer after he had seen in his dream the angels ascending and descending: "If God will be with me, and will keep me in this way that I go, and will give me bread to eat and raiment to put on, so that I come back to my father's house in peace." A modern psychologist like Dr. William Brown sees nothing impossible in the answering of prayer. "For myself," he writes, "I find it is practically impossible to carry out auto-suggestion with conviction without it being really a form of prayer, since some kind of belief in the spiritual nature of the Universe seems to be implied in the belief that power is there to make the result suggested come true."

Zangwill came to feel a great respect for his pious father, and for such types of "self-abnegation as my dear father." He often envied him his complete, unquestioning faith. "He seems to be praying quite happily there," he wrote of his father in Jerusalem, praying at the Wailing Wall. He was impressed by his fellow-worshippers. "I remembered at the Wailing Wall," he wrote, "countenances as beautiful and tender as the Da Vinci Christ, heads as noble as those of the grey-bearded Senators in the Venetian masterpieces, or the Rabbis that Rembrandt found in the birthplace of Spinoza." Indeed, Zangwill seemed at times to accept the belief in the efficacy of prayer. He quoted with apparent acceptance the thought expressed "in a Synagogue poem of the tenth century, by a Rabbi of Mainz, which is recited on the eve of the Day of Atonement: 'He is a God who softens at our cry.' " Speaking of the Fatherhood of God, he contended that " 'fatherhood' involves the anxiety, as well as the protecting love, of human fatherhood." How else would Zangwill have undertaken the translation in the Festival Prayer Book of the prayer:

"Hear my petition before the Ark of Thy Covenant of old.
Hear me from heaven, Thy dwelling; hear me, O Lord, and behold,

Lo, I am standing in tremour under the weight of my sins.
Suffer, I pray Thee, my pleading; let not my cry go unheard."

In Scribner's new *Treasury of World Poetry* (1952) Zangwill is
represented by two translations of Jewish prayer-book hymns by Ibn
Gabirol: "I have sought Thee daily at dawn and twilight," and "My
tongue hastens to proclaim Thy praise."

Yet marching together with his Judaism was the sceptic, who
needed a lot of salt to swallow Genesis, the Positivist, whose belief
in science kept clashing with his desire to believe as his father
believed, the "liberal" who liked to think that the moral law could
be something apart from religion. "Mr. Zangwill's religious views
may not be far removed from those of Dr. Stanton Coit," a Methodist
paper wrote when Zangwill's play *The Next Religion* was suppressed
by the Censor. Dr. Stanton Coit was in my time the head of the
Ethical Culture Church at South Place. There were effigies of the
great teachers of humanity in the Ethical Culture Church. Zangwill
has them in his Church of the Next Religion, "coloured windows, in
which Mazzini, Emerson and Swinburne appear like saints."

Zangwill must have drawn too on his memories of Mrs. Humphrey
Ward's *Robert Ellesmere*. It was like *The Next Religion* the story of a
Christian clergyman who has lost faith, resigns his position, goes to
live in the East End of London, and founds "The New Brotherhood"
Church. He has a Comtist among his followers. He has the same
procession of famous men, "Jesus of Nazareth taking his turn with
Buddha, Socrates, Moses, Shakespeare and Paul of Tarsus." Mrs.
Ward, describing Ellesmere's new Church, wrote: "We are in the full
stream of religion-making. Our present religion fails us; we must,
we will have another."

"The next religion," cries Zangwill's doubting parson. "The
religion all honest men are coming to—the religion the world is
thirsting for—the religion that accepts the Revelation of Science."
Zangwill might have introduced his parson to his own conclusion that
"it is better to bear the religions we have, than fly to others that we
know not of." Or his quip about the Congress of Religions at the
World's Fair—"I understand that the best religion will be awarded
a gold medal."

Robert Ellesmere tells his wife, like Zangwill's Mary Trame a
devout Christian, that his faith is dead. She wants to leave him. "I
thought of losing my own faith. It was a nightmare." Yet she stays.
"Poor woman's heart!" cries Mrs. Ward. "One moment in rebellion,
the next a suppliant. She, poor soul, is now always with him. She
no more believes in his ideas, I think, than she ever did; but all her
old antagonism is gone."

Zangwill's parson, Stephen Trame, too tells his wife Mary, that he is "no longer a Christian," and she cries: "I will baptise you again with my tears." She thinks of leaving him. "My vows before God's altar cannot bind me to spread atheism," she tells him. But she goes with him to the poor room in Whitechapel, and though she stands out against the new religion, "she joins in our social work." As Ellesmere's wife had done.

Miss Wilhelmina Jacobs, who has written a study of Zangwill's *Next Religion*, sees Mary Trame in the play "patently modelled upon Mrs. Zangwill. Her resemblance to Edith Zangwill is basic." (Mrs. Zangwill seems to have been Zangwill's chief critic in his writing of *The Next Religion*. He has references in his diaries to reading the play to her, and notes: "Revised play, mainly by Edie's criticisms.") Miss Jacobs is not sure about her conversion to Zangwill's religion any more than Mary was converted to Stephen Trame's new religion. "She is the faithful wife, the Ruth who forsakes all others to cling to her husband." She says: "Stephen Trame (the Christian whose doubts turn him from Christianity) and Dr. Hal McFadden (the atheist turned Christian) are both probably different facets of Zangwill's mind. But the truth lies if anything closer to Hal than to Stephen, and Zangwill's views, as he grew older, grew closer to Judaism as Hal's to Christianity, despite his stubborn refusal in 'My Religion' to admit that it was Judaism. In fact, Zangwill explicitly states in his essay *The Voice of Jerusalem* that it is difficult to see how any new religious conception 'can differ fundamentally from one of the two aspects of Judaism. For if it is theistic, it is not likely to be other than monotheistic, and if it is not theistic what remains but sociology and the service of man?' The 'next' religion then was not—nor was it intended to be—a rejection of Judaism."

Zangwill did a great deal in *The Voice of Jerusalem* to vindicate Judaism. "So far from the Gospels of Love and Justice being sharply divided between the two Testaments," he wrote, "it is in Exodus that we find the Jewish God defining Himself as 'The Lord, the Lord God, merciful and gracious, long suffering and abundant in goodness and truth, keeping mercy for thousands, forgiving iniquity and transgression and sin." He might have added that the passage has not been left for Bible reading, but was put into the prayer book, and is sung by the whole congregation at the Reading of the Law in the Synagogues. He is not so sure about Science in this essay, which was written eight years after *The Next Religion*, and after all the revaluation of his thinking that was forced upon him by the Great War that lay between—"Science, for all its practical boons, has wrought but negatively, so far as all deeper values are concerned." "From a purely theological point of view," he continues, "the popular distinction of Judaism from Christianity may be seen in the Synagogue hymn Adon Olam:

"For He is one, no second shares
His nature or his loneliness;
Unending and beginningless,
All strength is His, all sway He bears."

This translation is Zangwill's own, and his use of the word "loneliness" is not warranted by the Hebrew original. The translation is
more correctly in Chief Rabbi Hertz's Prayer Book: "He, the singular
and lone," meaning that "he has no equal nor consort," the One
God. The version in the Singer Synagogue Prayer Book reads:
"And He is One, and there is no second to compare with Him.
Without beginning, without end. To Him belong strength and
dominion." "To sink into this incomprehensible infinitude,"
Zangwill goes on, "is—in the concluding stanzas of the hymn—to
find deeper life.

He is the living God, to save,
My Rock while sorrow's toil endure,
My banner and my stronghold sure,
The cup of life whene'er I crave.

I place my soul within His palm
Before I sleep, as when I wake,
And, though my body I forsake,
Rest in the Lord in fearless calm."

The Synagogue service translation reads:

"He is my God—my Redeemer liveth.
A rock in my travail, in my distress.
He is my banner and my refuge,
The portion of my cup on the day I call.

Into His hand I commend my spirit,
When I sleep and when I wake.
And with my spirit, my body also.
The Lord is with me. I will not fear."

"Thus," Zangwill comments, "the Hebrew required no mediacy by
way of a humanised aspect of a trinitarian whole; indeed, he found
the idea of vicarious atonement opposed to his virile sense of Justice."
But then Zangwill returns to his "new religion" or "next religion"
theme. "In this still unresolved quarrel of Church and Synagogue
both sides forget," he says, "that the future will belong to the religion
that first fits itself to the future." In *The Melting Pot* he saw the

future belonging to the people who make the land of the future, not "the land of our fathers," but "the land of our children." In *The Next Religion*, the future is with "the religion of our children." He hoped in *The Voice of Jerusalem* that there might come "a fusion or federation between the Liberal Synagogue and the Church, or what is more practicable, between ex-Jews and ex-Christians." "Even Mr. Claude Montefiore, whose saintly life-work has supplied an eirenicon between Judaism and Christianity, holds out no near prospect of fusion," he complained. "It scarcely seems worth while for Judaism to go through such tragic travail of soul," he thought, "only to come out almost as tribal as before; even the New Testament, that work of exclusively Jewish authorship, being still excluded from the Jewish curriculum. Mr. Montefiore struggles against himself and his parochial followers, for at heart he obviously aspires to make the Synagogue universal, and he tries to do justice even to the Gospels. But if (as he expressly declares) to the world as a whole the Bible will always continue to include the New Testament as well as the Old, how is this to be reconciled with the hope of Judaising the world? Indeed, his prophecy that the religion of the future 'will be a developed and purified Judaism' and will cherish the New Testament, seems to accept as a fact that Judaism proper will still remain outside the next world religion. Mr. Montefiore seeks to evade this conclusion by pleading that the Jews have to remain a distinct religious community 'for a very long time indeed.' What a waste of work, after destroying the old Judaism, to create merely a new Ghetto! If the Martians were to invade the earth, men of all colours would be found fighting side by side. So in a period when the divine, and even the ethical, are savagely questioned and assailed, one would rather expect theists to stand together than to let themselves be sundered by theological systems equally unintelligible." "If Christians are ready to abandon the doctrines of the Incarnation and the Atonement, in their narrow and episodical sense, there is no reason why Jews should not admit that the heroic tragedy of the great Galilean illumines the cosmic problem of suffering."

Zangwill's ashes were buried in the Liberal Jewish cemetery, and a Liberal Rabbi conducted his cremation service. But Zangwill was not happy with Liberal Judaism. It went too far for him in some ways, and not far enough in others. His Judaism, he kept repeating, was not ethnical, or sometimes he said, not biological, but ethical. He wanted Judaism to be "the next religion." "If there were only a single God, and He a God of justice and the world, how could He be confined to Israel?" he wrote. "Religion, not race, has always been the guiding principle in Jewish history."

"The Next Judaism" was the heading of a two-page review by Zangwill in *The Nation* of Dr. Claude Montefiore's book *Outline of*

Liberal Judaism, which appeared in 1912, the year of Zangwill's
Next Religion. "I make no apology," he began, "for quoting from
my own play" (*The Next Religion*). His quotation is from Stephen
Trame's dialogue with his wife Mary about their small son Wilfred:
"It is his childish questionings about God and man," says Stephen.
"How shall I answer him?" "As your father answered you," replies
Mary. Stephen responds: "Exactly. My father answered me as truly
as he knew. Shall I give answers I know to be false?" "For it is in
precisely such a dialogue," he went on, "that Mr. Claude Montefiore
tells us his *Outlines of Liberal Judaism* took its origin. 'So you would
teach your children many things which you yourself disbelieve?'
he asked a friend. 'Yes,' was the reply. 'I would.' And so Mr. Montefiore was driven to show in a book that his friend's position was
untenable—that there was no necessity to mislead the Jewish child."
He found the trouble with Mr. Montefiore was that he had "that
humility which does not distinguish the founders of religions. These
may have been humble with God; they have never been humble with
man. They have come with peals of thunder and flashes of lightning.
Their message has been as definite as the Decalogue. No doubt,"
Zangwill suggested, "the value of faith is the greater the more it has
been saturated with scepticism, but a prophet should give the world
his conclusions rather than his hesitations, his finalities, not his
fumblings." Then back to his favourite theme: "For what reasons Mr.
Montefiore, having evolved for himself a religion so noble and sustaining, so rational and universal, yet addresses his ministrations to
Jews exclusively, I have never been able to make out."

Zangwill had both the dream of a universalist faith, the next
religion, which would unite all people in the worship of the one God,
and the knowledge that such things are dreams and not reality. He
often invoked the Alenu prayer, but he always came back to proclaim the indestructability of separate Jewish belief, and the continued existence of the Jews as a missionary people. "Has Israel no
contribution to offer?" he asked. "Has Judaism less future than
Buddhism? Has it less inspiration than the vision of Zoroaster?"
It made him indignant with Wells when he seemed to him to appreciate Judaism only when he contrasted it "with Buddhism, or
Hellenism or with the doctrines of Lao Tse or Confucius," but not
"when compared with Mohammedanism or Christianity."

He had played with the idea of a "new religion" as far back as
1891, when he was writing *Children of the Ghetto*. Not only Strelitski's
call for Judaism to "become cosmic, universal." "Let us start a new
religion," he said there. But his mouthpiece for that was the cynic,
Sidney Graham, who wanted the new religion to have only "one
commandment, 'Enjoy thyself.'" "That religion has too many
disciples already," replies his more thoughtful self expressed through

Esther Ansell. He contemplated Judaism merging in a new universal religion, and rejected the idea, even if it were called "Judaising the world." It is, he objected, "the solution of those who would have the Jews abandon their mission." The suggestion had been made that the Jews dissolving in the new solution would sweeten the whole cup. No, replied Zangwill, "the resulting fluid is no *eau sucree*; it is still tea." When someone at a lecture said that Zangwill had "distinguished between Christ who was a Jew, and Christianity, and that his greatest work was his outspoken challenge of Christianity," Zangwill replied that "unless Jews exercised their right to tell Christians what they thought of them, Judaism was absolutely useless."

He was in two minds also about the relationship between religion and science. He was aware of "the astronomer's enlargement of the horizon of space, the transformed perspective of geological time and the doctrines of Darwin" which had "co-operated to displace the Book of Genesis as an interpreter of the universe and its story," yet he believed that "the time had come for a new religious expression, a new language for the old everlasting emotions in terms of the modern cosmos; a religion that should contradict no fact and check no inquiry." And in the same passage he spoke of "the ever-living, darkly-labouring Hebraic spirit of love and righteous aspiration." He returned to God. "Why should we give up God because He is shown to be infinitely larger than the God of our fathers?" He admitted nostalgically that "orthodoxy makes for happiness, and with all my larger opportunities and means, my life has probably been less enviable than that of my penurious father, who in his old age left his home and family 'to die in Jerusalem'." He wanted the new religion, "so that children should grow up again with no distracting divorce from their parents and their past." In *The Next Religion*, when Mary comes back to Stephen, "I said to myself," she explains to him, "if the heart of youth goes towards this religion, then surely this religion is blessed of God to be the next religion, and we that are old and set must cast off our prejudices, we must try to look through the eyes of youth." "Excellently argued," says Stephen. Then comes the tragedy of Wilfred's death, which turns Mary in a frenzy against Stephen's new religion, "your miserable religion," she calls it over the dead body of their son. His religion is to her "Arctic," "glacial," what Louis Zangwill described as his brother's "somewhat inhuman universalistic position." The conflict in his own mind never ceased. It was the pattern of his life, its warp and woof, the criss-cross weaving that formed the pattern. He was not, he explained, an "ite" or an "ist." He could never have subscribed to a belief, much as he spoke of wanting a universally-accepted belief, without making his personal reservations and objections. "The orthodoxy of a religion may be defined as its adjustment to the average mentality," he complained. And he was not of the average mentality, to be bound, as he said, by "homogeneity and rigidity." He was driven to distraction by the division in his own mind by what he wanted to believe and what he could believe. He had got his own life muddled, and he tried to make his ideas clearer to himself by preaching to the Jews what he wanted to preach to himself. Always he found himself faced by another division.

He was divided in his approach to Jesus, whom in the Christian shape of the Incarnation and the Atonement he rejected, but in the Jewish form of teacher and martyr he gladly accepted. Of course, Zangwill saw Jesus as he wished to see him, as he could fit him to his own conceptions. He shared that failing with his contemporaries, Shaw and Wells. He said himself of Shaw that "his Jesus resembles the author of *Man and Superman*." And he found "a suspicious similarity between Mr. Wells's own Gospel and his reading of Christ's." It is true of all three, in the sense in which St. John Ervine remarks that "When Mr. Wells turns a corner of his Utopia, he expects to meet Mr. Wells." "Mr. Wells admires Jesus as a man after his own heart," said Zangwill. Wells insisted that he was no Christian. He could even say Jesus "does not and never has attracted me. The Christian's Christ is too fine for me, not incarnate enough, not flesh enough, not earth enough." Yet Zangwill who was a Jew found Wells prone to exalt Christianity at the expense of Judaism. It was the common failing, he said, of Christians who have dropped Christianity. "Martineau, the Unitarian, still calls his book *The Christian Life*. For Euken, although Jesus is not divine, the 'Absolute Religion' that remains after shedding the Christ story is—'Christianity!'" So with Wells Zangwill complains "it is in the chapter on the rise of Christianity that Mr. Wells shows himself least able to override his unconscious prejudice against Judaism and his unconscious prejudice in favour of Christianity. Like most modern thinkers, he makes up for the denial of divinity to Jesus by divinising his doctrine and his life. Similarly Renan," he proceeds, "dares to predict that no son of man will ever surpass him. Jewish thought," Zangwill protests, "which impartially records the sins of Moses and David, knows no such human perfection." His Jewish mind and upbringing rebel against the "curious arrogance of the translators of the authorised version," who "imported into the Old Testament by way of head-lines their dogmatic interpretation of the text, and thus started its readers with a misleading prepossession. That is why— apart from the mistakes of the translators—not one Christian in a million," he said, "has ever really read the Old Testament. These deceptive interpolations are particularly concerned with dramatising the Old Testament into a continuous prophecy of the coming Saviour. The line of proof is as absurd as the sense is distorted or misrendered."

Yet he could find "the basic idea sound." "For," he said, "the Old Testament contains, though in a jumble of strata, all the traces of the evolution from the crude psychology of primitive civilisation to that form of Jewish psychology popularly known as Christian." He counted the Bible as a complete whole, Old and New Testament together. "The soul of this 'peculiar people," he said in *The Voice of Jerusalem*, "is best seen in the Bible, saturated from the first page of the Old Testament to the last page of the New with the aspiration for a righteous social order, and an ultimate unification of mankind. Of these ideals the race of Abraham originally conceived and still conceives itself to be the medium and missionary."

Wells born a Christian denied that "the fierce unreal torment of the cross comes close to my soul." Zangwill, the Jew, thought that "Naught that man has suffered or man imagined, no Dantesque torture nor Promethean agony, can equal the blackness of that ninth hour when Jesus cried with a loud voice, saying Eli, Eli, lama Sabachtani!"

"It is Sunday morning in the Temple," Zangwill wrote in *My Religion*. "The church bells are ringing, and though I was born a Jew and know that the original Templars on the day they recaptured Jerusalem and the tomb of Christ slew every Jew, man, woman and child—I would willingly quit the work of writing this to sit in the Temple Church." "By a Jew," he wrote under the heading of an essay he contributed to *The Queen's Christmas Carol*, an anthology published in 1905. He reminded his Christian readers that the land where Jesus lived and preached was Jewish Palestine. "That sea of Galilee, down which I sailed, was alive with a fleet of fishing vessels. The Palestine through which the Galilean peasant wandered was a developed kingdom of thriving cities and opulent citizens, of Roman roads and Roman pomp." He reminded them that "the hands of Philistine piety have raised Churches over all the spots of sacred story. Even Jacob's Well is roofed over with ecclesiastical plaster. Churches," he said, "are after all a way of shutting out the heavens, and the great open-air story of the Gospels seems rather to suffer asphyxiation, overlaid by these countless chapels and convents. Is it, perhaps," he asked, "allegorical of the perversion of the Christ-teaching?" He reminded his readers that "holly and mistletoe do not grow in Palestine; the snowy landscapes of our Christmas cards are not known in Nazareth or Bethlehem; mince-pie was not on the menu of the Magian kings, and the Christmas-tree has its roots in Teutonic soil." But he could understand what had been done, as "a true instinct. The message, as well as the man, must be translated into native terms—a psychological fact which missionaries should understand." He spoke of the wide popularity of Christmas, "held to-day in so catholic a spirit that no man has an excuse for not eating his pudding like a Christian, and Jewish circles have adopted it so fanatically that the little Jewish girl could ask compassionately, 'Mother, have the Christians also a Christmas?' " Nevertheless, he felt this wide popularity of Christmas meant that its pagan aspects were uppermost. "Over large stretches of the planet and of history it is Christianity that has been converted to Paganism," he said. "Russia was baptised a thousand years ago, but she seems to have a duck's back for holy water. And even in the rest of Europe, upon what parlous terms the Church still holds its tenure of nominal power. What parson dares speak out in a crisis, what bishop dares flourish the logia of Christ in the face of a heathen world? The old gods still govern," he said. "Thor and Odin, Mars and Venus— their shrines still await them in the forests and glades; every rock still holds an altar. Their statues are still held in adoration. The Christian festival was compelled to take over and transform to higher import the saturnalia of earlier religious and natural celebrations of the winter solstice." But he welcomed Christmas "in that it preserves for us the word 'merry.' " It reconciled him "to the pagan aspects of Christmas, to the monstrous paradox of celebrating the birth of Jesus with pantomimes."

But he liked pantomimes. "The pantomimes of the Pavilion," which he explained was in the Whitechapel Road, "were frolicsome and wondrous," he wrote. The incongruity of pantomimes at Christmas had struck Zangwill before 1905. In *Children of the Ghetto* Sidney Graham said: "Christ ran amuck at human nature, and human nature celebrates his birthday with pantomimes."

Heine, whose story Zangwill told in *Dreamers of the Ghetto*, claimed that he had started the speculation, "in my earliest writings," about the old gods displaced by the rise of Christianity, still living in woods and on mountain-sides, and still worshipped "by weak Christian folk." "Many other writers, following up my hint," he wrote, "have since developed the idea more thoroughly than I did." Zangwill, nearly a century later, followed his hint. "Heine," he said, "prophesied the Germans wakening Thor from his thousand-year sleep." "Idolatry is catching. We have George Moore crawling underground—as if Heine's fantasy about the gods going under- ground were a reality—in quest of old Irish gods."

In his story *They That Walk in Darkness*, Brum explains to his mother: " 'There were Pagan gods that people used to believe in at Rome and in Greece.' 'And what's become of them now,' his mother asked. 'They weren't ever there, not really.' 'Yet people believed in them? Is it possible?' Zillah clucked her tongue with contemptuous surprise. Then she murmured: 'Blessed art Thou, O Lord our God, who openest the eyes of the blind.' "

Zangwill was fiercely opposed to idolatry. When he saw there was danger of the heathen gods returning, he called to both Judaism and Christianity to unite against the danger. He reminded them both of "their common antagonism to atheism, polytheism and pragmatic pluralism." Yet even as he called to them to unite against their common enemy he discarded the idea of their merging, with which he had played. "Judaism needs to live in its own spirit," he proclaimed, "true to its ardent belief in life—full-blooded, manifold life." He even discarded his idea of a new religion which should "accept the Revelation of Science." "For religions," he decided, "are not true in the sense in which scientific facts are true. They live by what is true in the appeal of their ideals, and by the organisation which they provide to link the generations."

In the end, he did what he objected to the Jews doing, halting between two opinions—if the Lord be God, he exhorted them in Elijah's words, "follow him; but if Baal, then follow him"— and he answered the question "what 'The Next Religion' should be in the spirit of Renan, who urged that only drama, giving through its personages even opposite answers, can give the full reply; it became clear that the Next Religion was to him Judaism, the Judaism that Schechter and Israel Abrahams taught, Judaism that has "the mission to bring about God's kingdom on earth and to include in the kingdom all mankind," when "at last the God of Israel will be the God of the whole world," "the day when there will be no religions, but only Religion, when Israel will come together with other communions, or they with Israel." He quoted Lincoln: "When any church will inscribe over its altar, as its sole qualification for membership, 'Thou shalt love the Lord thy God with all thy heart, and with all thy soul, and with all thy might, and thy neighbour as thyself,' that church will I join with all my heart and with all my soul," and he cried out that "what Lincoln sought is here, in Judaism." "Judaism is so modern," he told Wells who was in search of his own new religion.

Did Wells find God? " 'God is God,' he whispered to himself, and the phrase seemed to him the discovery of a sufficient creed," Wells wrote in *The Soul of a Bishop*. "God is his own definition; there is no other definition of God." "It would seem from Mr. Wells's novel about *The Soul of a Bishop* that he has moved on," Zangwill commented—"moved on, that is, towards the acceptance of God, whom he had previously rejected." "Forced to choose between God's omnipotence and his own omniscience, Mr. Wells opts for the latter," Zangwill had remarked of the earlier Wells. He had been guilty himself of that failing. He had once published a poem, he said, "that still seems to me to sum up all that Shaw and Wells have said as to God's omnipotence. Since then I have become less omniscient." They all played at new religions, Shaw, Wells, Zangwill. "They set up a new religion in which there was no Deity," Shaw wrote in *Back to Methuselah*. "Instead of worshipping the greatness and wisdom of the Deity, men gaped foolishly at the million billion miles of space and worshipped the astronomer as infallible and omniscient." Shaw too moved on, from Methuselah, when he took his *Black Girl in Search for God*.

"Wells and Shaw are modern Manichaeans," Zangwill said. "Mr. Wells is really a modern Mani. What he is breaking himself against is the old problem of the nature of evil, and the old antinomy of whether a beneficent God would have created it. Isaiah with sublime boldness utters that 'everlasting Yes' which is the keynote of Judaism.

> 'I am the Lord and there is none else.
> I form the light and create darkness.
> I make peace and create evil.
> I am the Lord.' "

Wells and Shaw were born and brought up as Christians, and turned back in their God-searching to their early Christian teaching. Zangwill, born and brought up a Jew, always turned back to his early teaching.

"Absolute religious truth?" Zangwill asked in *Dreamers of the Ghetto*. "How could there be such a thing? Each religion gave the human soul something great to live by, and to die for." Is there something of his own feeling in his story *The Joyous Comrade*? "Perhaps it was my Jewish training, perhaps it was that none of the Christians I lived with had ever believed in Christ."

It was his constant theme that Jesus was a Jew, and could be understood only in line with Jewish teaching. "As I have often said," he wrote, "the people of Christ has been the Christ of peoples. 'Nathan! Nathan! Ihr seid ein Christ!' cries the friar to the old Jewish sage in Lessing's fine play. 'By God, you are a Christian! There never was a better Christian!' " When Zangwill died, his friend Jerome K. Jerome, said of him: "To you he was a great Jew. To me, he will always seem one of the sweetest Christian gentlemen I ever knew."

Zangwill's quotation from Lincoln of what he looked for in his search for a church to join came from the Jewish "Shema," the proclamation of Jewish faith: "Hear, O Israel, the Lord our God, the Lord is One. And thou shalt love the Lord thy God with all thy heart, and with all thy soul, and with all thy might." "Thou shalt

love thy neighbour as thyself," is Jewish teaching, and is in Leviticus.
Rabbi Akiba said of it: "That is the greatest principle in the Law."
Yet Zangwill knew Judaism is not only ethics, but also the practice
of a very complex code of observance, "these six hundred and
thirteen precepts of the Mosaic code," Zangwill said of it, and called
them "in the main only an attempt at a practical idealism, a sanctified
sociology, an order in human affairs." There are the dietary laws.
"The great majority of Jews continue to abstain from forbidden food
not from personal aversion but because our Father in Heaven has
decreed that we should abstain from it," Chief Rabbi Hertz wrote,
discussing "the ancient gibe, revived in modern days, that 'Not what
goes into the mouth, but what comes out of it, defileth man.'"
"But poison," he pointed out, "does defile, and likewise diseased
meat, adulterated milk, unripe fruit and; many of the Christian
Churches, say alcohol. And out of the mouth comes speech, which
raises man above the brute, prayer that unites man to his Creator,
words of cheer and faith spoken to the sorrow-laden." Zangwill knew
of the abstentions and the observances. He found that even "Mr.
Wells unconsciously accepts in principle the dietary and sexual
regimen of Judaism. For 'the believer owes all his being, and every
movement of his life to God, to keep mind and body as clean and
pure, wholesome, active and completely at God's service, as he
can.'" Zangwill placed that declaration of Wells's at the side of
the practice of Orthodox Judaism, where "the guidance is not left
to individual ignorance." When Schechter went to America as head
of the Jewish Theological Seminary in New York, Zangwill said he
had been asked by an American girl: "Shall we keep everything when
Dr. Schechter comes?" So that he recognised that there is more in
Judaism than the love of God and of one's neighbour.

Indeed, he recognised in the Jewish observances a complete and
valuable system of sociology. "The secret of Jewish longevity, of
Jewish immunity from certain diseases," he said, "is at last being
sought. Science has just awakened to the importance of the Ghetto
as an experiment in sociology. One of the greatest practical authorities on medicine, Sir James Cantlie, is reported as testifying that
we have never upset one of Moses's laws in regard to hygiene, sanitation or medical science, that all the scientists of to-day, with their
microscopes and text-books did was to prove that the ancient
Lawgiver was right, and that we had been trying hitherto to cure
disease instead of preventing it, as Moses did. Now, too, at last the
marriage laws of Leviticus and the Talmudical Tractate that am-
plifies them are being studied—with admiration. Circumcision
seems now a recognised prophylactic. We have no studies yet on the
value of the dietary code, whether for example there is any point in
the prohibition of pork outside a sub-tropical country." He spoke

T

of a comparison made in Leeds between the Jewish children of the poorest quarter and the Gentile children of the same quarter, so that their bad circumstances they all had in common, and the only distinction was parental care, which found that the average Jewish child weighed more than the average Christian child, even including the richest classes. "This superiority of the Ghetto was not obtained," Zangwill argued, "by a cold eugenic system. Captain Peter Wright told us how a Polish Jew was badly mishandled by soldiers rather than let them force a piece of meat that was not kosher through his teeth; while another was cruelly beaten rather than sign his name on a Saturday. One can scarcely imagine such obedience being rendered to a merely legal code. Sociology was transformed into poetry, the professor was disguised as the prophet, and the driving-force found in the love or the fear of God."

There was, Zangwill knew, a House of Israel, bound together by the belief in God and the observance of His Commandments. "With everlasting love hast Thou loved the House of Israel, thy people," he quoted, "a Law and commandments, statutes and judgments hast Thou taught us." "Such is the sentiment translated into impassioned images by Amos in the eighth century B.C.," he commented, "and such is the evening benediction still uttered to-day by millions of Hebrew lips."

Almost in the same breath as he was preaching Jewish universalism he was exhorting the Jews to maintain their separateness. Even on holiday. "It is difficult," he said, "to connect the fostering of Jewish ideals with the admission of Jews into Gentile hotels. If they are orthodox Jews they have no right to be in those hotels." He invoked the dietary laws, the inability of observing Jews to eat of un-Jewish cookery. He even made out a case for Jewish separateness in the movement for women's suffrage. He wanted a Jewish League for Woman Suffrage. He wanted it "most decidedly. I am proud, and Jews ought to be proud," he said, "to be able to do anything to enfranchise another class of the population, after their own arduous struggle for emancipation. As to Jews having a separate society of their own, they can hardly join the Church League Society! There is no reason why Jews should not have a similar body to accentuate their special part in the movement, especially if they regard themselves as a religious body."

But he knew that Jewish ethics are the base of Jewish teaching. In the words of Micah the Prophet: "It hath been told thee, O man, what is good, and what the Lord doth require of thee: Only to do justly, and to love mercy, and to walk humbly with thy God." What "next religion" will better that teaching? None, Zangwill finally confessed. "It is difficult to see," he wrote, "how any new religious conception can differ fundamentally from one of the two aspects of Judaism." "In so far as our age is striving for justice on earth and goodwill to all peoples," he said, "it is returning to essential Judaism."

Searching always for the "next religion," or for "the new Judaism," how far did Zangwill really get away from the old Judaism, of which he said in *Children of the Ghetto*: "All your new Judaisms will never appeal like the old, with all its imperfections. It is beautiful—that old childlike faith in the pillar of cloud by day and the pillar of fire by night"?

In his search for "The Next Religion" which went on all his life, from his earliest writings till his death, Zangwill kept forever turning back to his beginnings, to the Jewish teachings in which his pious father had instructed him, until he came to the conclusion that what he sought is in Judaism. "The heart," said Zangwill, "was the Jewish heart, and the forces of the future are still with it."

AFTERWORD

ISRAEL ZANGWILL was a Jew, inspired by the Jewish spirit, and belonging to the line of the Hebrew Prophets. He thought and wrote about the Prophets. By prophecy he did not mean foretelling the future. "None of the Hebrew words for 'prophet,' " he pointed out, "contains the idea of forespeaking which that Greek word has unfortunately accentuated. The Hebrew nabi means a mouthpiece. The Prophets are not magnified but diminished," he said, "when regarded primarily as Old Moores or political tipsters. Admonition rather than prediction is their true essence."

Jeremiah, whom he called "the greatest of the Old Testament prophets," "has left us," he wrote, "an almost scientific diagnosis of prophecy proper. He is mocked and derided. Nevertheless

'There is in my heart as it were a burning fire
Shut up in my bones,
And I weary myself to hold it in,
But cannot.'

"It is the same fire," he claimed, "with which every reformer or social critic burns, which enkindles the artist to liberate his conception and no other."

Jeremiah too was stricken with the duality that marked Zangwill —war and peace, nationalism and universalism. He could sing: "Make bright the arrows, fill the quivers. Set up a standard against the walls of Babylon." And he could counsel the people not to fight, to "sit ye down low." He exhorted Jews to build houses and dwell in them in the lands of the Diaspora, and to pray for the cities in which they made their homes—"for in the peace thereof shall ye have peace," and he promised them the return: "Behold, the days come when Judah shall be saved, and Jerusalem shall dwell safely." So Zangwill too prophesied war and peace, Jewish nationalism and Jewish universalism. "The Voice," I called him in 1923, when he went to address the American Jewish Congress, "the voice of all Jews, speaking for them all, even when they contradict each other."

Because that is so, there are people who seize on the contradictions, pounce on the things that have been said that they do not like. Zangwill was "mocked and derided." I found a note in the *Jewish Chronicle* in 1919, rebuking Professor Norman Bentwich for things he had been saying about Zangwill: "Mr. Zangwill may be right or wrong in the views he takes upon Jewish problems, but his services to the Jewish cause deserve something more serious than a facetious reference to the 'scintillating speeches from the erratic Ito leader.' " Norman Bentwich has had the satisfaction since Zangwill died of seeing "Fulfilment in Palestine." Zangwill's vision was not clear about that fulfilment. As things looked when Zangwill died, the "fulfilment" did not seem at all sure. Dr. Weizmann said in his autobiography that "the years between 1920 and 1929" (Zangwill died in 1926), "were for the Zionist movement and the National Home years of alternating progress and setback, of slow, laborious achievement sown with recurrent disappointment." I remember Dr. Weizmann telephoning me at the J.T.A. the news of his decision to resign from the Zionist leadership after the Passfield White Paper. He said he could see no purpose in trying to go on. He did not then foresee the "fulfilment," which would make him President of the State of Israel. Many things had to happen first, which no one could have foreseen, any more than Herzl and Nordau and Zangwill and the Zionist movement and the Jews of the world could have foreseen in 1905 the Great War of 1914-18, which liberated Palestine from Turkish rule and made it possible for Britain to lay the foundations of the Jewish National Home. Hitler had to come and the Second World War, the murder of six million Jews in Europe and the pressure of the survivors before the gates of Palestine were forced open. Just before the Second World War started in 1939, speaking at the Zionist Congress in Geneva in August 1939, Dr. Weizmann said in words that Zangwill might have used to explain his own failure and the failure of the Ito: "Our policy has not failed. We have not failed. It is others who have failed us."

He was speaking nearly thirty-five years later, as Zangwill had spoken in "Uganda" days, of what Dr. Weizmann called almost in Zangwill's own words, "the vast and tragic problem 'Whither.' " "Hundreds of thousands of Jews," he said, "are faced with cold pogroms, physical torture, destitution. A comparatively small number have been fortunate in finding a secure home. Hopes were raised when President Roosevelt convened the Evian Conference. But the Evian Conference has so far produced results which are incommensurate with the tragic magnitude of the problem."

The breaking up of Czarist Russia transformed Jewish life. Russian Jewry had been the largest and Jewishly the most important half of world Jewry. It dwindled after the Revolution in numbers and Jewish achievement. Its Jewish potentialities were largely destroyed, especially those based on religion. But before it happened about a million Jews had emigrated to America from Russia. Zangwill included a table of immigration into the United States as an appendix to his published *Melting Pot. Children of the Ghetto* closed with Esther Ansell, who was largely the projection of himself, sailing to America, though as one might expect from Zangwill, who was always looking not only forward but back, with the intention of returning to England. Yet the final words of the book are of "the throbbing vessel that glided with its freight of hopes and dreams across the great waters towards the New World." Whatever else went wrong of Zangwill's prophecies, his prophecy of the rise of America, and with it of American Jewry was marvellously fulfilled.

In the rise of the State of Israel, too, as far as a man can be a Prophet Zangwill has been justified in his prophecy. Before the beginning of our century, at the end of 1899, when few were prepared to prophesy about Zionism, and the Zionists meeting in Congress were still a small band of dreamers, Zangwill was saying: "The object of Zionism is not to ingather Israel or to fulfil the prophecies. Religious and racial emotions are indeed enkindled by Zionism, but they did not enkindle it. Zionism is not spontaneous combustion: it is the flame of the hammered explosive." And in the same speech: "It is impossible to believe that the Jewish commercial genius should fail, even in Palestine." At the Zionist Congress in Basle in 1903, the last Congress which Herzl attended, Zangwill declared: "Zionism would not hold so much of our hopes if it did not include the hope that the Jewish State would find for the world the solution of these social problems, and that the race whose first law-giver was so immeasurably ahead of all other legislators, would again produce a steersman to guide it as brilliantly through the new era."

But Zangwill was a prophet not only for the Jews. He was born in England in a generation that was brought up to listen to prophets, and produced prophets. He was seventeen or eighteen when Carlyle, Darwin and Disraeli died. Ruskin, who died in 1900, when Zangwill had already made his name, was a living influence all through Zangwill's young manhood and that of his contemporaries. Shaw spoke of Ruskin as a prophet. And called Dickens a prophet. He regarded himself too as a prophet. "You must not imagine that prophets are a dead race, who died with Habakkuk and Joel," he said. "The prophets are always with us." They all tried to found religions. "Shaw's is a vast and universal religion," Chesterton remarked, "and it is not his fault that he is the only member of it." Wells, in *God the Invisible King*, expounded his idea of "the new religion." "Those who may be counted as belonging definitely to the new religion are few and scattered and unconfessed," said Wells. But "there is a stirring and a movement." Zangwill found "the sole difference between Mr. Wells's God and the Hebrew's, that Mr. Wells's God is finite. In His Unity, invisibility or incorporeality, righteousness, jealousy and unreserved and exclusive claim for service, He is identical with Jehovah. And it is extremely interesting to witness," he said, "the re-formation of ancient conceptions in an ultra-modern mind." Even Thomas Hardy, the rationalist, played with the idea of what he called "the religion of the future." Chesterton found his new religion in the Catholic Church. Zangwill found his new religion in Judaism.

They all sought, each in his own way, to build Jerusalem in England's green and pleasant land. Zangwill's message as much as that of the rest of the group was addressed to the English people, the people of the land where he was born, where he lived all his life, and whose speech was the instrument with which he did all his work. They would have understood him when he said that "not upon the playing fields of Eton are our victories won, but in the factories of Manchester, and the mines of Newcastle, and the shipyards of the Clyde. I admire the soldier who plods uncomplainingly the dusty road of duty and death, but I cannot see that the humble factory hand does less for England and the Empire. He too may be mutilated by machinery. Is duty heroic only when it is clad in khaki? Why have the fighting classes the monopoly of the motto that 'England expects every man to do his duty'? Why is it not hung up in workshops to counteract the teaching of the trade unions that it is wrong to do an honest day's work? And developing this thought in my ignorant literary way, I ask why under the guise of strikes and lock-outs are our commercial battalions allowed to fire at one another, for the destruction of England and the Empire? Let us educate our schoolboys in true Imperialism—to feel that whichever army they enter they are equally serving their country. As every line drawn from the centre of a circle to the circumference is equal, so within the circle of the community is every faithful service alike honourable."

Zangwill considered himself, he said, "the child of two great civilisations"—the Jewish and the English. He had a guilt complex about the Jews, that he was not enough with them, was not doing enough for them. But when he went deeply into the Jewish question, though he often had doubts about his Jewish religious orthodoxy, he always emerged with the certainty that he was a Jew religiously, and otherwise an Englishman. What linked him to other Jews, he kept repeating, was "Judaism qua religion." Zionist and Jewish nationalist though he was, he was forever turning back to the distinction between Jews and Christians, not Jews and English. It was a religious difference that divided him from other Englishmen. Even that, he argued, was no great division. For Christ was a Jew, and Christianity was Jewish. "The divinity of Christ is practically all," he said, "that Judaism denies." His literature was of course both Jewish and English—the Hebrew Scriptures and all the other Jewish writings, but because his language was English and his readers

English, "our own literature" to him was English literature, in which he has taken his place. "Our own literature" to him was "Chaucer, Shakespeare, Milton, Browning, Swinburne, Tennyson, Matthew Arnold, William Morris, George Meredith, George Eliot, Carlyle, Emerson, Hawthorne, Whitman, Lowell, Holmes, Rudyard Kipling, Stevenson, Hardy, Howells, Henry James, Mill, Spencer, Darwin and," he added, "a score of others who do the modern man's thinking."

In his end was his beginning. In the nursing home at Midhurst, near his home at East Preston, on the Sussex coast, where he died, Israel Zangwill who was born in Ebenezer Square, off Stoney Lane, in Whitechapel, completed the journey on which he had set out as a schoolboy attending the Jews' Free School. His wife said of him that "it might almost be said that Israel Zangwill was born with a pen in his hand. He could never remember a time when he had not been certain that he was going to be a writer." He made young Benjamin Ansell in *Children of the Ghetto* speak for him of his boyish ambition "to write books—like Dickens." It was English literature that attracted him, and the desire to be an English writer. He didn't "reckon Hebrew or Yiddish." Everybody knew those, everybody like his father and his father's friends and neighbours. What he wanted was to write something that would get him on in the big world. There were moods in which Zangwill would parade the notice printed at the back of some of his books, from the *Leeds Mercury*, that his non-Jewish book about the general life, "*The Master* in our judgment, is vastly superior to *Children of the Ghetto*."

Zangwill was sixty-two when he died, a weary man, thin and frail. He was worn out physically and mentally. Shaw said in his Preface to *Methuselah* when he was sixty-three that his sands were running out. He went on for another thirty years. Towards the end "he was very tired." Zangwill had been very tired long before he died at sixty-two. "He was worn out, and could find no rest." It was not just abstract talk when he wrote in the last year of his life, "But agonised incurables must be relieved of their agony."

That chirpy Cockney, Wells, said of himself that "he droops at times like most of us, but for the greater part he bears himself as valiantly as a sparrow." It was the earlier Wells he was describing, the "plump little man with an unattractive tenor voice" (which I remember was squeaky) "that argues and argues and becomes at times aggressive." At the end Wells was less cocky, less sparrow-like. He had lost his Kipps-ness. He was ill and depressed, filled with a sense of futility. Zangwill would not have chosen the sparrow for his picture of himself, though he too came from the London streets. Louis Golding speaks of him being hawk-like, "a little infirm of limb but hawk-like in spirit, though I must claim for this antithesis," he added, "a hawk that shall be half a dove." Sparrow or hawk or dove, Zangwill remained valiant, as long as his pain let him be sane. "He still made puns and gleams of his old self would show through his weariness."

I have been emphasising the autobiographical character of Zangwill's writings. They are autobiographical because they are drawn from the scenes and people that he knew. He wrote with his own early life in mind. He pictured himself repeatedly in his characters. He wove his own thoughts into theirs. Till the end of his life he kept coming back to the ideas and emotions and the hopes and ideals which had seized his imagination as a child, as a small boy at the Jews' Free School, in his pious father's poor home, and in the little Whitechapel Synagogue to which he had accompanied him every day, whose poetry remained with him always, colouring all his later experiences and thoughts, so that however far he went away from that life, its sights and its sounds were forever in his eyes and ears. All his thinking and writing was founded on it, in affirmation or in denial, which usually ended in reaffirmation. It was the essence of everything he said and did. It was his vision of life.

Zangwill brought his father Moses Zangwill into *Children of the Ghetto* as Disraeli brought his father into *Vivian Grey*, as Wells said that in all his books he was writing his autobiography, as Hardy was always drawing on his memories of his Wessex boyhood. "You are Joseph the dreamer of dreams," Hardy says of Jude. Zangwill was a Joseph the dreamer. And being a dreamer his people are more than real; they are symbolic, a type and a symbol. That is why Zangwill's London Jews of the 1890s did not die when their originals were lowered into their graves, but still live.

Of course, Zangwill as a writer has faults. Those who complain of his faults are not wrong. It is not difficult to pick any writer to pieces. "A frightful minus," Henley said of Dickens. "His faults were many and grave. He wrote some nonsense; he sinned repeatedly against taste; he was often mawkish and often extravagant. Yes, he had many and grave faults." I have no wish to make Zangwill out to be a greater writer than he is. I am certainly not going to claim for him a faultlessness from which greater writers are not free. But his work is such that we can keep coming back to it with interest, with curiosity, with admiration, with a feeling that we are meeting in his pages living people, a rich company of characters who remain in the memory, some of them great comic creations like Melchitzedek Pinchas in *Children of the Ghetto* and Manasseh da Costa, the King of Schnorrers. His people overflow with life. They are Jews, Jews living in England; they are credible living human beings. Zangwill has more than anyone else working in this field painted a true and convincing picture from the inside of a group of people, with their

struggles and hopes, their beliefs, their toil, their suffering, their
humour, their separateness and their universal human oneness.

The life he painted was his own life, the life of the people he knew,
whose experiences had so moved and shaken him that they were
emotionally his own experiences. He had such rich and inexhaustible
stores of childhood memories that he could forever draw on them,
and transmute them through his imagination, through his vision. "A
musician can take a few simple notes," he wrote, "and out of this
theme evoke endless intricacies, enlargements, repetitions, echoes,
duplications, parallelisms and permutations, and then transform the
whole into another key and give it to you all over again." Zangwill
had another quality—his childhood memories, though harsh and full
of the experiences of bitter poverty, had not made him bitter. His
work was not drab and pessimistic, twisted and tormented. He had
learned that the life of the poor is not necessarily drab or tortured
life. It had humour and contentment and cheeriness. Bread could be
made "ambrosial by treacle." Small wind-falls were "Godsends,"
and there were many things that "brightened and warmed" poor
folk and made certain days "memorable."

Yet the memory of his childhood poverty had impressed itself
on him unforgettably. *Children of the Ghetto* begins with young
Esther Ansell speeding through the freezing mist of the London
December evening, her little plaid shawl drawn tightly around her,
her chilled feet absorbing the damp of the murky pavement through
the worn soles of her cumbrous masculine boots, which had been
kicked off by some tramp and picked up by Esther's father. Towards
the end of the book, when Esther flees back to the Ghetto from her
West End home and rich friends, she sees, as she mounts the staircase of her childhood home "a childish figure break from the gloom
ahead, satchel in hand, wearing her cumbrous, slatternly boots."
He could not forget having worn those boots. He never forgot his
early poverty and struggle. "I was then poor and obscure," he said,
recalling in later years his first meeting with Joseph Jacobs. As he
told us of Esther Ansell, he was always seeing his childhood walk
ahead of him. Its memories were inescapable. When his brother
Louis said Israel Zangwill went back to the Ghetto note-book in
hand he added it was to refresh his memory. He was not just a chiel'
taking notes. He was a chiel' back in the streets and among the
people of his chielhood, comparing his memories with the later
scene. As he walked up the staircase of his boyhood home the boy
he had been walked ahead of him. He made reunions. They were old
friends, or others like them that he met and spoke to. "I've come
back" was his cry, even as it was Esther Ansell's. "Are the same
people living here?" he asked, as she did. And when he went visiting
the old friends he found them still with their old foibles, like Mrs.

Belcovitch, with one leg, "a thick one, and one a thin one. And so one goes about."

He remembered the little Synagogue where his father took him as a child, its furniture bare benches, a raised platform with a reading desk in the centre and a wooden curtained Ark at the end, containing two parchment Scrolls of the Law. The back window gave on a yard where there were cow-sheds, and "moos" mingled with the impassioned supplications of the worshippers, in their workaday garments and grime. There was never lack of a congregation. "It was their home, as well as the Almighty's."

It was London mist through which Esther sped, and it was London's wet pavements along which Hannah, the daughter of Reb Shemuel stepped, thinking in a fever of impatience of her coming flight with her lover from her father's house. How Zangwill fixes the attention on "the little Dutch clock on the mantlepiece." "The hands of the clock crept on. It was half-past nine. If it were only ten o'clock, it would be too late. The danger would be over. The clock ticked out loudly, fiercely, like a summoning drum. The rain beat on the window-panes. The wind rattled the doors and casements."

The little Dutch clock found its way later into his Essex countryside story, *Jinny the Carrier*. Jinny sits on a squat wooden arm-chair "till the Dutch clock startled her with its emphatic declaration of the hour."

Zangwill could write handsomely of his later acquired taste for English public-house food eaten at the bar, "a cut of the joint, strong mustard pickles, a hunch of good bread, a pint of porter and the freedom of the cheese to follow." But he had travelled a long way to get it, from the Ghetto's "chunks of cold fried fish," from the motzos of the Seder table, and the Passover meal, with the quaffing of the four cups of wine. He had got there by way of the Jewish Christmas dinner, such as he described in the home of the wealthy Goldsmiths, who had taken up Esther, and adopted her. "Daintily-embroidered napery, beautiful porcelain, Queen Anne silver, exotic flowers, glittering glass, creamy expanses of shirt front and elegant low-necked dresses"—a Christmas dinner in a wealthy Jewish home, with "none of those external indications of Christmas; no plum-pudding, snapdragon, mistletoe, not even a Christmas tree." "I have had many happy moments," said Esther Ansell-Israel Zangwill at the Christmas dinner, "realised many childish ambitions, but happiness is as far away as ever. My old school colleagues envy me; yet I do not know whether I would not go back without regret." He remained to the end the Child of the Ghetto.

When he felt deeply about anything, it became immediately connected with an early memory of his Ghetto childhood and youth.

His early life had filled him with richer human material than he ever obtained in the rest of his life.

I will not say that a writer is less able or less truthful who seeks to escape, as some do, from the memories of childhood. Not only Jewish-born writers try to. There are writers who spend their lives trying to escape from disagreeable childhood memories, of poverty, cruelty, humiliation. There are Jewish-born writers who admit that their Jewish birth and upbringing was a source of humiliation to them, and who try deliberately to escape from their Jewish memories. Freud speaks of a more unconscious repression, what he calls "concealing memories, the forgetting of childhood." It has its origin in resistance. It makes a writer blind and deaf to something in the life he has lived, part of which he deliberately shuts out from his field of vision, so that the work he produces, whatever its other qualities, misses something, is deprived of something. Zangwill had his share of such resistance, and of the desire to escape from his Jewish childhood memories. Was there not something of his own shame in that of Isaac Levinsky, who ran away from home to call himself Ethelred Wyndhurst, in Zangwill's story *To Die in Jerusalem*? "The older Isaac Levinsky grew, the more ashamed he grew of the Russian Rabbi whom heaven had curiously chosen for his father. Early in his school-life he discovered that other fathers did not make themselves ridiculously noticeable; nay, a few—O, enviable sons!—could scarcely be distinguished from the teachers themselves." But Ethelred Wyndhurst discovered "in high heathendom a vast secret contempt mingled with the admiration for him. He had, it is true, a certain vogue, but behind his back he was called a Jew." Zangwill went back from "high heathendom" to the Jews.

Children of the Ghetto contains Zangwill's imaginative reconstruction of his life and background, his experiences and emotions, the life in which he grew and which shaped him. It is a story, or rather several stories, spun by a true yarn-spinner; but it is also an authentic social study of a part and a period of London life. His stories reveal, as Professor Henry Morley says in his book on English literature, "aspects of London." He clothed with flesh and blood the statistics and factual details about these people contained in Booth's Survey of London Life. The 1932 Survey of London Life and Labour says: "The appalling squalor in Charles Booth's time of the Spitalfields area" (where the Jews' Free School was and much of the East End Jewish settlement) "has since been well-nigh swept away by wholesale demolitions and rebuilding, and (it is fair to add), by the displacement of Gentiles by Jews" (the Gentiles being of "the unsavoury class, a local aggregation of poverty and degradation"). The 1932 Survey also pointed out that "according to the 1921 Census 74 per cent. of the population of Stepney were born in London, and 17 per cent. abroad. In Whitechapel, especially, a large proportion of the inhabitants are Jews." Since 1921 the proportion of native-born Jewish population has increased, and the problem of "the foreign Jew" of the time Zangwill wrote and Charles Booth compiled his Survey, no longer exists. My friend A. K. Chesterton would object, and no doubt others would uphold his objection that this part of London life is not English, and therefore no theme for English literature. Its people, he would say, are not my people, my own English people, living in the land of our fathers; and their ways are not our ways. What's Esther Ansell to him or he to her? Zangwill answered that when he spoke of the same human nature running underneath and through us all. He answered it more convincingly when he showed it to us in the experiences and emotions of his people. What is there alien to the English non-Jewish reader in the scene that closes the First Book of *Children of the Ghetto*, when Hannah, with her lover with whom she is to elope, standing outside the door behind which her family is celebrating the Passover, decides that she cannot leave them? "She threw open the street-door. The face of David loomed upon her in the darkness. Great drops of rain fell from his hat and ran down his cheek like tears. His clothes seemed soaked with rain. 'Quick, Hannah,' whispered David. 'We can't wait a moment more. Put on your things. We shall miss the train.' For answer she drew his ring out of her pocket, and slipped it into his hand. 'Good-bye,' she murmured in a hollow voice; and slammed the street-door in his face. 'Hannah!' His startled cry of agony and despair penetrated the woodwork, muffled to an inarticulate shriek. He rattled the door violently in unreasoning frenzy. 'Who's that? What's the noise?' asked her mother. 'Only some rough shouting in the street,' answered Hannah."

The darkness through which David loomed upon Hannah as she opened the door was London darkness, and the rain that ran down David's cheeks was London rain. That London rain which fell faster, that London wind growing shriller, are the accompaniment of Hannah's tragedy and David's agony, as the London hansom cab is the accompaniment to the tragedy of Hannah's father and brother. The English language is part of their life, of their tragedy and their ·comedy and their everyday life. In the Synagogue "Hannah scanned the English version of the Hebrew in her Machzor," her prayer book. In the same way, Mrs. Cohn, in "Anglicisation," felt the beauty of the old Hebrew blessing, "The Lord bless you and keep you. The Lord make his face to shine upon you" only "when she read the English words in the gilt-edged Prayer-Book." "In business, in civic affairs, in politics, the Jew has mixed freely with his fellow-citizens," Zangwill says, explaining the Jewish-Christian relationship. "The English Jew keeps his Judaism in the background. He never obtrudes his creed. Why expect Jews to be martyrs more than other Englishmen? Isn't life hard enough?" But he also shows where this keeping Judaism in the background leads: "A Christian friend of mine fell in love with a girl. He proposed; she told him to ask her father, and he then learned for the first time that the family were Jewish, and his suit could not therefore be entertained. Could a satirist," he comments, "have invented anything funnier? This family is not an exception; it is a type."

The world cannot be kept out. Zangwill knew it was so everywhere. In his story *A Child of the Ghetto*, where the Ghetto is Italian, in old Venice, it was "forced upon the child's understanding that the world was not all Jews." And though the child knew his prayers in Hebrew he could also translate them into Italian, into the Venetian dialect, which found its way into the Ghetto. Not only human speech. The sounds of common life penetrated. As the child sat in the Synagogue listening to the chanting from the Pentateuch, "the interminable incantation," he thought of sprinkling it with bird's song, and made the Scroll of the Law warble." Even Reb Shemuel, that unbending pillar of orthodoxy—"a witty old fellow," says Zangwill, "and everybody loved him"—"spoke English" though "with a strong foreign accent, he and his wife." The language of the home, with their children, except for some admixture of Yiddish, was English. As Zangwill saw the process in the ancient Venice Ghetto, he saw it in an older generation of Anglo-Jewry. "In the days when Lord George Gordon became a Jew, and was suspected of insanity," "there had been a special service of prayer and thanksgiving for the happy restoration of His Majesty's health, Royal George and 'our most amiable Queen, Charlotte.' The congregation was large and fashionable—far more so than when only a heavenly sovereign was concerned." The Anglo-Jewish Community, he says, "was Anglicised. The conventional Anglican tradition was established."

Zangwill painted the lives of the people in the Ghetto, Rabbi and school-teacher, tailor, shoe-maker, carpenter, poet, labour-leader, scholar, demagogue, humbug and saint. Those sweated workers in the Ghetto's tailoring shops were working for "Government contractors, making great coats for London policemen." "Their shoulders stooped" from the work. Shosshi Shmendrik, the young carpenter, takes a proper pride in his handicraft, and when he goes to interview his future parents-in-law and his intended bride, he arrives "with his arms laden with choice morsels of carpentry," evidence of his skill and his ability to earn a living. "He laid them on the table for her admiration." When his courtship struck a difficult corner—they ultimately married—Shosshi, like any other young man "went about broken-hearted."

These people were Jews; their feelings were like those of other people. "Human nature undergoes little change," Sir Arthur Quiller Couch remarked. "The story of Ruth is as intelligible to an Englishman as though Ruth had gleaned in the stubble behind Tess Durbeyfield." Zangwill had a clear understanding of Hardy's English mind, as he showed in his appraisals of "Tess" and of "Jude." So much so, that when Hardy wrote to Zangwill setting out his feeling about the Jewish Territorial idea that Zangwill proposed, Zangwill commented: "Mr. Hardy has expressed in a nutshell my own views on every point of a complex question." "This sentiment among Jews is precisely the one I can best enter into," Hardy wrote to Zangwill, "so that if I were a Jew I should be a rabid Zionist, no doubt. A Jewish colony in, say East Africa, could make a bid for Palestine. I think you know," Hardy added, "nobody outside Jewry can take much deeper interest than I do in a people of such extraordinary history and character."

"I am a man of letters, and regard literature as the greatest of all weapons in the enrichment of mankind," Mr. T. P. O'Connor said in a lecture he delivered in November 1919, on "The Jew and Christian after the War." "It is to be regretted," he went on, "that there are not more writers like Zangwill to give to the outer world the picture of Jewry from the inside." Mr. W. L. Courtney found the psychological interest of Zangwill's London Jews "very real and very understandable." His Jews in England, even those who came as immigrants from other countries, felt that something of England had entered into them. It made them different. His Palestine Pilgrim, asked on landing in the Holy Land, "Where are you going?" said: "To live in Palestine." "Where do you come from?" the Turkish official asked. " 'England,' he replied triumphantly, feeling that this was a mighty password throughout the world." When A. K. Chesterton suggested that something in my culture and my way of expressing myself in my English speech was remote from his own Englishry I was puzzled, and asked St. John Ervine if he felt that too. "I do not think you need bother yourself about Mr. A. K. Chesterton's attitude," he replied. "I found nothing remote from my mind in your writing, and I am pretty certain that Chesterton found only what he wanted to find." Even Chesterton does not deny that there are Jews in England, who form part of his scene, and are met with by himself and by others, and who in some way play a part in the life of English people and the life of the country. "I went to school," he writes, "with scores of Jews, and had some among my friends. My best friend and most efficient brother-officer in the Abyssinian campaign was a Jew. I knew a number of Jews, liked some of them, disliked none so much as I disliked some Gentiles." The contact is there, even if it becomes one of dislike. George Orwell reported hearing a man say: "I don't care about using the Underground from Golders Green nowadays. There's too many of the Chosen Race travelling on that line." They are in evidence, and writers write about things which are in evidence, kindly or unkindly, with sympathy or hatred. If Jewish authors don't write about them as Zangwill did, from the inside, showing them as understandable human beings, it does not mean that they will not be written about. They exist, they impinge upon the life of others, they create an impression and a reaction. There are Jews, savage, noble, condemnatory and apologetic, Fagins and Riahs, in the work of English non-Jewish writers, from Shakespeare to Smollet, to Dickens and Reade and George Eliot, Trollope and Shaw and Wells, Somerset Maugham and T. S. Eliot, Aldous Huxley and Graham Greene. They cannot be ignored. Zangwill's achievement was that he showed the Jews in the English scene as credible, living human beings.

Esther Ansell and her like, she and her male counterpart in our thousands, have become a part of the life of England. I do not say this apologetically, but as a fact which may have drawbacks and faults on both sides, but remains a fact nevertheless. They were and are some of the school-teachers in our English schools, not only of Jewish children, they are artists and scientists, musicians and writers and journalists, actors and playwrights and politicians, active like their fellow citizens in every Party in the State. They are shaped for good and ill by this English soil and speech and life, as much as all others who share the English heritage. We belong to this land, and if we bring to it something that is inherent in our origin and in our Jewish creed and way of life, we are also moulded and changed by it into something that is Jewish, indeed, but is also definitely, unmistakably English. A young Anglo-Jewish writer sent me recently a novel of Anglo-Jewish life, and added this note about it "Curious to see the effect, I removed all the Jewish material from the book. The story stands on its own, without any Jewish interest. The clashes of personality are as intense. I do not mean that I wish to remove the Jewish interest, but though the Jewish interest seemed to me essential in my conception of the story and the life of my characters, it is not indispensable. The same conflict expresses itself, the same passions, the same incompatibilities, the same atmosphere. David is as much a misfit not being Jewish as he was as a Jew."

I don't think it is possible to take the Jewish life out of *Children of the Ghetto* without destroying the book. That is perhaps the greatest thing about it, that it is so completely of one piece. But the other possibility indicates that there is much of the distinctive Jewishness of Anglo-Jewish life that can be, and unfortunately is only too easily dropped and forgotten. So easy it is in one's land and among the people of whom one is part, to drop, without a constant awareness and continual self-assertion and the cultivation of one's differences and one's nonconformity, all that makes us different and distinctive, and to merge and be swallowed up, as so many have been, are being merged and swallowed up. I can imagine Zangwill's *They That Walk in Darkness* being made equally the story of Protestant parents with a beloved only child gone blind, after every hope of restoring his sight had failed, yielding despairingly to the possibility suggested by a Catholic friend that the Pope had the power to be the great healer, could open the eyes of the blind.

There are conflicting influences at work in the English Jew which are not only Jewish but English, as Zangwill saw when he put down his friend Joseph Jacob's aim "to reform the study of English Literature . . . rescue it from the clutches of those vapouring Oxonians, Matthew Arnold and the rest" to "his Cambridge heart." Sir Arthur Quiller Couch, who was an Oxonian, confessed that "Cambridge men appeal to me less at one time than another." There was something besides Jewish grotesquerie in Zangwill's Pinchas and Manasseh. He had learned from the creators of Falstaff and Uncle Toby and Mr. Micawber.

I think if Zangwill had not been tempted back to the Ghetto by the commission to write *Children of the Ghetto* he would still have written a book or several books introducing London Jews, as other English writers, Jews and non-Jews did. The Jews who live in this city and this country form a part of our life; they meet and establish relationships with other people, and affect their lives and are affected by them. They do not live in self-contained compartments. Writers, not only Jewish, encounter them and find them crossing the paths of their other characters. Joyce's Bloom is not a practising Jew; he is a Catholic, and the son of a Catholic mother, only a half-Jew. His sub-conscious Jewish memories are a hotch-potch. But the Jewish part of him struck Joyce so powerfully that he wove him into his story as the ever-present accompaniment to his own thoughts and movements. He saw Bloom as a part of the Dublin scene. George Eliot wrote *Daniel Deronda* because she had Jewish friends and had observed their life here. Dickens came into contact with Jews. A Jewish family bought his London house when he retired to Gad's Hill, and it is said to have been on their account that he afterwards drew the figure of Riah in *Our Mutual Friend*.

Recently I sat with several writers in a public discussion on certain aspects of literature, and Zangwill's name came up. One of my colleagues said that Zangwill is no Shakespeare nor Dostoevsky nor James Joyce. Nor is he, I agree, Milton or Goethe, Tolstoy or Cervantes, Homer or the writer of the Book of Job. I have never understood this passion for having the world peopled only by giants. It is as though no mountain could command respect unless it towers to the height of Everest or at least of Mont Blanc. I have a very healthy respect for the much smaller mountains of the Derby Peak, and I see no reason to despise the Surrey Downs. The world would be poorer without these lesser hills. If Zangwill is no Everest and no Mont Blanc, he reaches nevertheless a very impressive height, and is worth an ascent. There is wonderful country to be viewed. We meet people in his country who are worth knowing.

The important thing about Zangwill is that in his own field he conveys a sense of reality, of genuineness, of truth. He has it all, the life of it, the sunshine and the shadow, the comedy and the tragedy, the humour and the grimness. He paints the life of the humble with its joy; he does not overlook its suffering and its pity. His people are not onesided, neither all sweetness, nor all acid. They are human, compounded of all the human qualities. Poverty does not degrade them, and nobility does not cloy. Not all Zangwill's work is of equal merit. Every author produces books that do not last. Only the student of literature makes it his business to read the entire body of work of an author. But I can name a dozen of Zangwill's books that should and I believe will live. They have truth enough and genius enough to justify his continuing place in English literature. If people will only read him, they will, I am sure go on reading him.